Health and The Social Environment

Health and the Social Environment

Edited by
Paul M. Insel
Rudolf H. Moos
Stanford University

D.C. Heath and Company
Lexington, Massachusetts
Toronto   London

Library of Congress Cataloging in Publication Data

Insel, Paul M.   comp.
Health and the social environment.

1. Medicine, Psychosomatic. 2. Environmental health. I. Moos, Rudolf
H. 1934-   joint comp. II. Title.
RC49.155   616.08   73-21110
ISBN 0-669-92858-5
ISBN 0-669-92866-6 (pbk.)

Copyright © 1974 by D.C. Heath and Company.

Published simultaneously in Canada.

Printed in the United States of America.

International Standard Book Number: 0-669-92858-5

Library of Congress Catalog Card Number: 73-21110

To Marcia Insel, who contributes enormously
to a healthy social environment,
and to
Hilde and Teddy Salinger
for sharing their environment

Contents

Preface

This book attempts to integrate a diverse health literature and place it into a social environment perspective. It presents an overview of basic theories, research strategies, intuitions, issues, and conclusions about the impact that the psychosocial environment has on health and illness.

We have organized this material with two basic assumptions in mind. Human behavior cannot be understood apart from the environmental framework in which it occurs. Physical and social environments are inextricably tied to each other; one cannot be understood without the other.

The material in this book provides a social ecological approach to the study of health processes, in that it is multidisciplinary and is concerned with the assessment and development of optimum human milieus. For a more extensive introduction to the area of social ecology the reader may refer to *Issues in Social Ecology: Human Milieus*, referred to in Chapter 1.

Health and the Social Environment has been conceived to meet the needs of a broad audience. It brings together material from both a theoretical and an empirical perspective to illustrate the interactive effects of man, environment, and health. We feel that this book might be appropriate for courses dealing with medical sociology, community health, environmental health, social work, and epidemiology. It might be used as reading for courses concerned with the environment and its effects on human functioning. In addition, it should provide excellent source material for researchers investigating health and environment issues.

The book has ten parts, presented in a sequence that attempts to provide a coherent, integrated survey of the field. Part I sets the stage for the rest of the book by introducing conceptualizations of the social environment and providing an overview of the relationship between health variables and the social environment. Part II, "Psychosomatic Disorders and Environmental Stimuli," examines the social stimuli or contributors to such problems as ulcers, hypertension, diabetes, and acne. This section also reviews the "sick role," seeking of medical care and the situational variables that influence the process and outcome of illness. The chapters in part III, "Social Correlates of Heart Disease," relate the social environment to the development of heart disease. This section explores the effects of both stressful and supportive social environments in their roles as contributors and mediators with respect to risk factors in heart disease. Part IV, "Social Processes and Immunity," presents material that either directly or indirectly suggests that the social environment affects the subsequent biological immunity of an organism. This section examines the social dimensions that link susceptibility to and recovery from infectious disease, and raises questions about environmental influences on the presence and progression of cancer. Part V, "Social Dimensions in Obesity," describes some of the antecedents, in both children and adults, to the development of obesity, and emphasizes the vital role of the social environment in the treatment of obesity. Part VI, "The Social Environment and Mental Health," focuses on the assumptions made about abnormal behavior and its treatment, and the impact the social environment may have on shaping our views of mental illness. Part VII, "Drugs and Social Consequences," discusses how the social environment might reinforce drug taking and encourage smoking behavior. This section focuses on drug addiction as a way of adapting and coping with a stressful social environment. Part VIII, "Urban Stress and Contemporary Life," explores the impact of the city, advanced technology, and industrialization on the health of the urban dweller. Such phenomena as noise, input overload, and commuter travel are discussed in this section. Part IX, "Theory and Research," examines some of the methodological issues in conducting environmental health research. This section reviews the ecological perspective in psychosomatic medicine and the effects of stressful life events and their relationship to organic disease and psychological disorders. Part X, "Toward a Healthy Environment," emphasizes the importance of creating a social climate that considers the long-range health consequences of technological research. In addition, this final section of the book raises questions about man's optimum environment in relation to his evolutionary past.

We wish to acknowledge and express our gratitude for the help of the members of the Social Ecology Laboratory at Stanford University. In particular we would like to thank Rick Bliss, Louise Doherty, Susanne Flynn, and Marcia

Insel. We would also like to acknowledge the support of grants MH 16026 and MH 8304 from the National Institute of Mental Health, grant AA00498 from the National Institute of Alcohol and Alcohol Abuse, and Veterans Administration Research Project MRIS 5817-01.

March 1974
Palo Alto, California

I

The Psychosocial Environment: Introduction and Overview

Commentary. Part 1 sets the stage for the rest of the book by introducing the concept of the social environment, its general impact on health, and some of the physiological effects that are related to social environmental variables.

In the first chapter Paul Insel and Rudolf Moos examine stressful social environments and some of the physiological mechanisms involved. The authors review the general adaptation theory developed by Hans Selye, the life events and illness susceptibility schedule developed by Holmes and Rahe, person-environment fit, the social climate of cities and the effects of a supportive social environment.

In Chapter 2, Stewart Kiritz and Rudolf Moos link three properties of social environments to various physiological effects. They summarize studies involving support, a relationship variable, and physiological outcomes. One study, for example, reported the mortality rates of widowers during the first six months of bereavement to be 40 percent higher than the expected death rate for married men of the same ages.

The authors review relationships between the environmental press of responsibility (a personal development dimension) and physiological changes. One interesting study indicated that pilots in charge of manning aircraft had higher pulse rates than the more passive copilots sitting next to them. When the men changed places and the copilot took charge of the aircraft the pulse rates were reversed.

Kiritz and Moos examine clarity (a system maintenance dimension) and its relationship to physiological processes. Uncertainty, for example, along with the possibility of physical or psychological harm and the inability to escape until the situation was clarified, was related to increased blood pressure.

The authors suggest that the best predictor of an individual's physiological behavior in a particular environment may be that person's perception of that environment. This point of view has specific relevance for the issue of person-environment congruence. Social environmental data could provide physicians and other relevant professionals with information to help their clients in making prudent decisions about their social milieus. Thus, as Kiritz and Moos indicate, measuring social climates systematically could become a significant part of the diagnostician's work.

Both chapters in this section suggest that the social environment has important effects on physiological and health processes. While this is not a new idea, its full impact has only recently been realized as new research efforts have extended the area of psychosomatic medicine to include a more comprehensive view of the health of man and his social milieu.

1

The Social Environment

Paul M. Insel
Stanford University School of Medicine
Rudolf H. Moos
Stanford University School of Medicine

The social or psychosocial environment is made up of people and their interactions with each other. These people create a "climate" or "atmosphere" that may be unique to the environment. In a sense the social climate represents the personality of the environment. Like people, environments have different personalities. Some people are supportive; some environments are supportive. Some people need to dominate or control others, likewise some environments are extremely controlling. Some individuals require order in their lives and some environments emphasize order and organization.

The study of the social environment and its effects on health is a relatively new field of inquiry. Much of the evidence in this area, while suggestive, remains inconclusive and theoretical and should be considered tentative until more research has been done.

What are the ingredients or factors in the social environment that affect the health state of an individual? Emotional factors related to a stressful environment have been implicated in many illnesses including hypertension, peptic ulcers, migraine headaches, dermatitis, obesity, asthma, rheumatoid arthritis, and heart disease (Alexander & Szasz, 1952; Wolff, 1953; Selye, 1971).

One interesting example of how body chemistry and emotion are related can be found in a study showing that tears secreted during an emotional experience contain more albumin than tears induced by an onion (Brunish, 1957).

3

Studies with animals have shown that prolonged stress can result in tissue damage. For example, peptic ulcers have been experimentally produced in rats subjected to a stress-provoking situation. In this study nine rats were kept in a large rectangular box for thirty days. Food was placed at one end of the box and water at the other. The floor near the food and water was charged with electricity so that if a rat left the central area of the box to eat or drink he received a shock. Only during every forty-eighth hour was the current turned off. Thus the rats experienced a chronic conflict between a desire to eat and drink and a desire to avoid shock. A control group of five rats were given food and water at forty-eight hour intervals, but were not put into a conflict situation. Six of the nine experimental rats developed peptic ulcers, whereas none of the control group did (Sawrey & Weisz, 1965).

One interesting approach relating stress to disease originates with Dr. Hans Selye. According to Selye's theory the body's reaction under stress takes place in three major phases: (1) the alarm reaction; (2) the stage of resistance; and (3) the stage of exhaustion (Selye, 1953, 1956). The alarm reaction is the organism's first response to a stress-provoking agent, or stressor. The alarm reaction consists of various complex bodily and biochemical changes associated with emotion. These physiological changes usually have the same general characteristics regardless of the exact nature of the stress-provoking stimulus. Thus, people suffering from various specific illnesses may have similar symptoms such as headache, fever, fatigue, aching muscles and joints, loss of appetite, and general feelings of malaise.

In order to test this theory Selye exposed a large number of animals to a wide variety of stressful conditions including starvation, poisoning, infections, extreme cold, extreme heat, surgical hemorrhage, and others. He found that the physiological reactions which resulted were not confined to the stress-provoking condition but rather consisted of a general pattern of change which was much the same for all stimulus situations (Selye, 1950).

If the exposure to the stress producing situation continues, the alarm reaction is followed by the second phase of the general adaptation syndrome called the stage of resistance. According to Selye the organism appears to develop a resistance to the particular stressor which provoked the alarm reaction. The symptoms that occur during the first stage of stress disappear in spite of the fact that the disturbing stimulation continues. Resistance to the stressor seems to be accomplished mainly through increased activity of the anterior pituitary and adrenal cortex, whose secretions (ACTH and Cortin) help the organism adjust to stress. The physiological processes disturbed during the alarm reaction now appear to resume normal functioning.

If exposure to the harmful stressor continues for too long, a point is reached where the organism can no longer maintain its stage of resistance. It thus enters the final phase of changes related to stress, the stage of exhaustion. The anterior pituitary and adrenal cortex are unable to continue secreting their hormones at the increased rate, with the result that the organism can no longer adapt to the continuing stress. Many of the physiological malfunctions that originally appeared during the alarm reaction begin to reappear. Selye indicates that if the stressor continues to act upon the organism after this time, death is likely to occur.

The physiological response to a stressful environment varies from person to person. The action of the adrenal glands, for example, is different in different people subjected to similar kinds and amounts of stress. It has been shown experimentally that early experiences are related to how an organism's immune system is affected by stressful situations (King and Henry, 1955). Experiments with rats handled during infancy, for example, have shown that they were more resistant to infection than rats that were not handled (Levine, 1957).

Another and perhaps more recently acknowledged stress-related problem is coronary heart disease. Dr. Meyer Friedman, a widely quoted cardiologist, has suggested that "the milieu of Western society" may be implicated in heart disease. The distinguished historian Arnold Toynbee captured some of the flavor of man's pressures when he wrote: "At the earliest moment at which we catch our first glimpse of Man on Earth we find him not only on the move but already moving at an accelerated pace. This crescendo of acceleration is continuing today. In our generation it is perhaps the most difficult and dangerous of all current problems of the human race."

While the relationship between coronary heart disease and a stressful social environment has not been conclusively proven, there is inferential evidence that makes the relationship a likely probability. For example, *triglycerides* and *cholesterol*, which have been implicated in coronary heart disease, have been shown to increase under stressful conditions. Autopsies performed on soldiers killed in combat in Korea showed that a high percentage had advanced atherosclerotic disease with fatty deposits on the walls of their coronary arteries (Enos et al., 1955). The authors suggest that the coronary disease could be attributed in part to stress.

Several studies have indicated a relationship between heart attacks and stressful work environments. In one study stress was defined in terms of the percentage of men working more than forty-eight hours a week. The investigators found that a significant relationship exists between men in non-farm occupations in the age range of twenty-five to forty-four who work more than forty-eight hours a week and death from heart attacks (Buell and Breslow, 1960).

Work pressure is likely to be an important element in the development of heart disease. Numerous studies have shown that the average serum cholesterol level will rise significantly in subjects who are confronted with a situation in which they are required to strive or struggle against a background of a sense of time urgency (Dreyfuss and Czazckes, 1959; Grundy and Griffin, 1959; Peterson et al., 1962; and Wertlake et al., 1958).

Life Events and Susceptibility to Illness

Holmes and Rahe (1967) suggest that events leading to significant change, pleasant or unpleasant, can lower an individual's resistance to disease. They studied several populations and found a significant relationship between the magnitude of life changes and the time of disease onset. In addition they found a strong positive correlation between magnitude of life change and the seriousness of the illness experienced.

They constructed the Social Readjustment Rating Scale (SRRS) which consists of life event items (Table 1-1) weighted according to the adaptive requirement of the life event. Eighty percent of the people exceeding a SRRS

Table 1-1
Life Events and Weighted Values

Life Event	Value	Life Event	Value
1. Death of spouse	100	20. Foreclosure of mortgage	30
2. Divorce	73	21. Change of responsibility at work	29
3. Marital separation	65	22. Son or daughter leaving home	29
4. Jail term	63	23. Trouble with in-laws	29
5. Death of close family member	63	24. Outstanding personal achievement	28
6. Personal injury or illness	53	25. Wife beginning or stopping work	26
7. Marriage	50	26. Beginning or ending school	26
8. Fired at work	47	27. Revision of habits	24
9. Marital reconciliation	45	28. Trouble with boss	23
10. Retirement	45	29. Change in work hours	20
11. Change in health of family	44	30. Change in residence	20
12. Pregnancy	40	31. Change in schools	20
13. Sex difficulties	39	32. Change in recreation	19
14. Gain of new family member	39	33. Change in social activity	18
15. Change in financial state	38	34. Mortgage less than $10,000	17
16. Death of close friend	37	35. Change in sleeping habits	16
17. Change of work	36	36. Change in number of family get-togethers	15
18. Change in number of arguments with spouse	35	37. Change in eating habits	15
19. Mortgage over $10,000	31	38. Vacation	13
		39. Minor violations of law	11

Source: Adapted from Holmes, T.H. and Rahe, R.H. The Social readjustment rating scale. *Journal of Psychosomatic Research*, 11:213, 1967.

score of 300 in one year for example became depressed, had heart attacks or developed other serious illnesses.

Person-Environment Fit

A source of distress and ill health is the situation in which a person attempts to function within an environment with which he is basically incompatible. Let us illustrate this idea with a hypothetical example. Robert Jones was a creative person, who required a great deal of freedom and independence. He was used to making his own decisions and felt hampered whenever his parents tried to impose structure upon his life. In addition he was somewhat self-absorbed and usually unaware of details, which often gave him an appearance of being forgetful. After graduation from high school Robert Jones volunteered for the draft in order to put his military obligation behind him. Unfortunately he was totally unprepared for military life, and found himself in an environment with which he was chronically in conflict. He had to rise at a specific time and go to bed at a specific time. He was required to follow orders and pay attention to details. One morning he awoke with a painful headache, nausea, and palpitations. By the time he reported to sick call he was vomiting and required hospitalization. His blood pressure turned out to be abnormally high, as was his pulse. The diagnosis was nonspecific gastrointestinal infection. After three days he was released from the hospital and returned to duty as completely well. However, after two days at the barracks he appeared at sick call with precisely the same symptoms and was hospitalized again for another three days. He was released from the hospital again and returned several times before a medical examining board finally decided that Robert Jones did not belong in the army.

Allan Smith, to use another hypothetical example, had a somewhat different kind of experience with army life. Like Robert Jones, he was a creative person, but required deadlines and clear instructions in his life in order to get anything done. After high school Allan Smith volunteered for the draft and found himself in an environment in which he flourished. His frequent indigestion disappeared. He had a regular schedule. He didn't have to cope with the ambiguities of civilian life. Essentially he had found an environment with which he was perfectly compatible.

These examples are, of course, the exception rather than the rule. Most of us will tolerate incompatible environments for longer periods of time, and rarely will we find an environment that will meet our every need.

The Social Climate of Cities

The "climate" found in the "big city" is dramatically different from the small town and rural areas. Even among the great cities of the world one finds marked differences in social atmosphere. In comparing London with Paris the pacing, the tone, and the texture of each have different qualities. For example, the atmosphere of Paris has been described as "alive and vibrant," with its sidewalk cafes and parks "contributing to the sense that Paris is a city of amenities." London has been characterized as a city whose climate emphasizes "courtesy and tolerance."

It has been suggested that the city differs from rural areas in three ways: large numbers of people, a high population density, and many different kinds of people interacting with one another. One also finds many more health problems in the city. The rates of heart disease and cancer is higher in cities. Psychiatric disorders occur at a significantly higher rate in cities compared with rural areas. How can we account for such a difference in health problems between city and country? It is not an easy task. Moreover the reasons are confounded by many variables such as: people have more opportunity to infect one another because of the density of population; some people with particular problems may be attracted to the city; health hazards would be less conspicuous in the city, and so on. Some researchers have suggested that the heart of the problem lies in the quality of the social environment, input overload in particular (Milgram, 1970; Galle et al., 1972; Keyfitz, 1966). Input overload refers to an individual's inability to process inputs or received stimuli from the environment because there are too many inputs for him to cope with at one time. Overload also occurs when input B is presented for processing before input A has been properly dealt with. City life involves social interactions that are characterized by continual overload properties. In order to survive, the city dweller must have priorities and adapt to all these excessive stimuli as best he can. How does one adapt to input overload in the city? The city dweller comes into contact with vast numbers of people each day as compared to his rural counterpart. The small town inhabitant has the resources and energy to develop more intense relationships with the people he meets whereas in the city time alone would prevent the development of deep relationships with everyone encountered. Thus one might find the climate in the city characterized by superficial relationships, anonymity and transitory affiliations; the results of allocating less time to each input.

Another way of handling too many inputs is to disregard those with low priority. Have you ever noticed that many people in cities appear to have unfriendly expressions on their faces? Discouraging other people from making social overtures is one way to establish a barrier to inputs. The full impact of inputs is diminished by filtering devices, so that only weak and superficial forms of involvement with others are permitted.

In large cities one finds many institutions between the individual and society. One could not just drop in for a chat with the mayor for example. Just to see his immediate subordinate requires overcoming an extraordinary number of obstacles. Just visiting the library to check out a book might involve the stress of input overload. This lack of direct contact and spontaneous integration with the environment can cause one to become what Erich Fromm calls "the alienated man." The individual is both protected and estranged from his social environment. It has been suggested that this alien situation underlies many internal conflicts related to physical and mental illness.

Milgram suggests:

> ... the ultimate adaptation to an overloaded social environment is to totally disregard the needs, interests, and demands of those whom one does not define as relevant to the satisfactions of personal needs, and to develop highly efficient perceptual means of determining whether an individual falls into the category of friend or stranger. The disparity in the treatment of friends and strangers ought to be greater in cities than in towns; the time allotment and willingness to become involved with those who have no personal claim on one's time is likely to be less in cities than in towns. (1970, p. 1462)

The social environment of the city emphasizes noninvolvement with others and diminished social responsibility. This aspect of city life becomes most apparent in crisis situations, when bystanders may refuse to aid someone who is desperately in need of help. For example, in New York City one might see people stepping around somebody lying in the street.

Less critical issues of involvement are underemphasized in the city. People bump into each other or knock over another person's packages without apologizing or offering assistance. In smaller communities traditional courtesies are more likely to be observed.

Another aspect of the social climate of cities is the feeling of anonymity. Dr. Philip Zimbardo at Stanford University studied the relationship between social anonymity and vandalism, comparing the big city with the town. He arranged for automobiles to be left for sixty-four hours near the campus of New York University and near Stanford University in Palo Alto, California for the same amount of time. Neither car had license plates and the hoods were open to provide "releaser cues" for potential vandals. In New York the car was stripped within twenty-four hours, and by the end of three days it was nearly unrecognizable. Most of this destruction took place during the day under the scrutiny of others. In Palo Alto the car remained untouched. Zimbardo suggests that the difference in treatment of the two cars is related to the acquired feelings of social anonymity found in a city like New York.

Why does one find such vastly different behaviors between urban and rural areas? Are there different kinds of people living in cities? Probably not. The city has an environment to which people respond adaptively. It is likely that the contrasts one finds between city and small-town behavior reflect the reactions of similar people to very different situations.

Adapting to the Social Environment

One way for one to adapt to his social environment is to become ill. Prolonged and recurrent maladaptation to the social environment is related to various illnesses.

In a study conducted in the Eastern Health District of Baltimore, sixty-three families were selected for study on the basis of an index child who had had more than three illnesses during the preceding year. These families were compared with another fifteen families whose index child had either no illnesses or fewer than three during the same period. The two groups of families were comparable with respect to such variables as size, degree of crowding, income, and level of education.

The primary aim of the research was to find out if the two groups of families revealed proportional differences in frequency of illness among the children over time. Such illnesses as acute communicable diseases, infectious skin conditions, tonsillectomies, and chronic illnesses were excluded from the analysis of the data.

Nevertheless dramatic differences were noted.

Siblings of the families selected on the basis of a child who had three or more illnesses had an annual rate three times as great as the rate among siblings of the index cases in the other families. . . . Further study indicated that there was a tendency for children to remain at about the same sickness level over a period of five years; that is sickly children remained sickly. (Downes, 1949, p. 146)

The investigators concluded that no differences in heredity could account for such contrasts in frequency of illness. But something in the family environments of the two groups produced health among one set of children and recurrent physical illness among the other set.

The Effects of a Supportive Environment

There is some evidence that a supportive environment can counteract such effects of predisposing factors to disease as stress, lack of exercise, a large consumption of animal fat, cigarette smoking, etc. In a series of studies in an Italian-American community in Roseto, Pennsylvania, it was found that the death rate from heart disease was remarkably low despite the prevalence of predisposing factors to heart disease. A twelve-year study of this community of seventeen hundred people found that death from heart disease occurred at a rate of less than half that of neighboring communities or in the United States at large. A subsequent study of relatives of people residing in Roseto who were living in urban and suburban areas around New York and Philadelphia revealed many deaths from heart disease under the age of fifty. In Roseto during the same period there had been only one death from heart disease under the age of forty-seven; most of the deaths had occurred in men and women in their seventies and eighties.

Evidence of heart disease was found in some persons in their forties and fifties in all neighboring communities, but no evidence in Roseto for subjects under fifty-five years of age. There was a greater incidence of obesity in Roseto compared with other neighborhoods, but diabetes was less prevalent. The serum cholesterol levels did not differ significantly among all the communities, although there appeared to be a higher incidence of high blood pressure among Roseto men. In spite of this there was little difference in documented hypertensive disease. The diet of Roseto inhabitants was relatively high in calories, including animal fat. Cigarette smoking was found to be as prevalent among men in Roseto as in other communities. Treated mental illness was less in Roseto than in other communities.

The most dramatic differences between Roseto and its surrounding communities was found in its social environment. The study indicated that Roseto is cohesive and mutually supportive, with strong family and community ties. The social environment emphasized an overriding concern of the inhabitants for their neighbors, mutual support, understanding and unfailing sustenance in time of trouble. The investigators concluded that "emotional support from the environment somehow provides protection." (Bruhn et al., 1966)

Summary

We have suggested that the social environment can play an important part in the health state of individuals. While this is not a new idea its full impact has been unrealized until very recently as more research information has focused on the relevant issues.

One of the new disciplines that have helped to define and clarify the relevant issues in social environments is Social Ecology. Social Ecology is the multi-disciplinary study of the impact that physical and social environments have on human beings (Moos & Insel, 1974). Although it arises mainly from the behavioral sciences it is linked to the main currents of scientific thought in psychiatry, medicine, and epidemiology in its special emphasis on the identification of dysfunctional reactions and their relationship to environmental variables.

References

Alexander, F. and Szasz, T. The psychosomatic approach in medicine, in *Dynamic Psychiatry* (F. Alexander and H. Ross, eds.). Chicago: University of Chicago Press, 1952.
Bruhn, J.G., Chandler, B.C., Miller, M., Wolf, S., and Lynn, T. (1966) Social aspects of coronary heart disease in two adjacent, ethnically different communities, *American Journal of Public Health*, 56:1943.

Brunish, R. Cited in *Saturday Review of Literature*, 40:41, 1957.

Buell, P. and Breslow, L. Mortality from coronary heart disease in California men who work long hours. *Journal of Chronic Disorders*, 11:615-626, 1960.

Downes, J. Social environmental factors in illness. Milbank Memorial Fund Backgrounds of Social Medicine, 1949.

Dreyfuss, F. and Czazckes, J. Blood cholesterol and uric acid of healthy medical students under the stress of an examination. *Archives of Internal Medicine*, 103:708-711, 1959.

Enos, W., Beyer, J. and Homes, R. Pathogenesis of coronary disease in American soldiers killed in Korea. *Journal of American Medical Association*, 158:912-914, July 1955.

Galle, O.R., Gove, W.R. and McPherson, J.M. Population density and pathology: What are the relations for man? *Science*, 176:23-30, 1972.

Grundy, S. and Griffin, A. Effects of periodic mental stress on serum cholesterol levels. *Circulation*, 19:496-498, 1959.

Holmes, T.H. and Rahe, R.H. The social readjustment rating scale. *Journal of Psychosomatic Research*, 11:213, 1967.

Keyfitz, N. Population density and the style of social life. *Bioscience*, 16:868-873, 1966.

King, S. and Henry, A. Aggression and cardiovascular reactions related to parental control over behavior. *Journal of Abnormal Social Psychology*, 50:206-210, 1955.

Levine, S. Infantile experience and resistance to physiological stress. *Science*, 126:405, 1957.

Milgram, S. The experience of living in cities. *Science*, 157:1461-1468, 1970.

Moos, R. and Insel, P. *Issues in Social Ecology: Human Milieus.* Palo Alto: National Press Books, 1974.

Peterson, J., Keith, R. and Wilcox, A. Hourly changes in serum cholesterol concentration: Effects on the anticipation of stress. *Circulation*, 25:798-803, 1962.

Sawrey, W.L. and Weisz, J.D. An experimental method of producing gastric ulcers. *Journal of Comparative Physiological Psychology*, 1956, 49:269-270.

Selye, H. *The physiology and pathology of exposure to stress*, Acta Inc. 1950.

Selye, H. The general adaptation syndrome, in *Contributions toward Medical Psychology*, Vol. 1 (A. Weider, ed.). New York: Ronald Press, 1953.

Selye, H. *The stress of life.* New York: McGraw-Hill, 1956.

Selye, H. The evolution of the stress concept, in *Society, stress, and disease*, (L. Levi, ed.). New York: Oxford University Press, 1971.

Wertlake, P.T., Wilcox, A.A., Haley, M., and Peterson, J. Relationship of mental and emotional stress to serum cholesterol levels. *Proceedings in Social Experimental Biological Medicine*, 97:163-165, 1958.

Wolff, H.G. Life stress and bodily disease in *Contributions towards medical psychology*, Vol. 1 (A. Weider, ed.). New York: Ronald Press, 1953.

2

Physiological Effects of the Social Environment

Stewart Kiritz
Monterey Community Hospital
Rudolf H. Moos
Stanford University School of Medicine

Introduction

A physician advises a harried executive with high blood pressure to spend a week in the country. A pediatrician recommends that an underdeveloped, neglected child be sent to a foster home. A social worker encourages an asthmatic client to seek a job with more human contact. A cardiologist urges an administrator to delegate some of his responsibilities to others in his office. Each of these workers is, in part, responding to the belief that the social environment has important effects on physiological processes. In addition, their recommendations reflect the assumption that one can distinguish different types or dimensions of social environmental stimuli; that these dimensions can have distinctive influences on physiological processes; and that the effects may differ from one individual to another. We believe that these assumptions are valid. In this paper, we summarize some of the evidence supporting these assumptions, present a model for conceptualizing social environments, and discuss implications for person-environment interaction.

The measurement of the environment is a relatively recent development in psychology. Dissatisfaction with trait conceptualizations of personality is, in part, responsible for recent interest in environmental variables. This dissatis-

Reprinted with permission of *Psychosomatic Medicine*, Vol. 36, (March-April, 1974), pp. 96-114.

13

faction stems from the low correlations obtained between measures of personality traits and validity criteria, and from growing evidence that substantial portions of the variance in response to questionnaires and in behavior may be accounted for by situational variables [1]. Recent studies indicate that the variance accounted for by consistent differences among settings and by the interaction between setting characteristics and personal characteristics is generally as great or greater than the variance accounted for by consistent differences among persons [2,3]. In addition a number of studies have demonstrated that substantial differences may occur in the behavior of the same persons, when they are in different settings or milieus [4].

There are six major methods by which human environments have been assessed and characterized [5]. (1) Ecological analyses, including geographical, meteorological, and architectural variables; (2) behavior settings, which are characterized as having both ecological and behavioral properties; (3) organizational structure, such as size/staffing ratios and average salary levels; (4) personal and behavioral characteristics of the individual members of a particular environment, e.g., average age, socioeconomic status; (5) functional analyses of environments in terms of social reinforcement contingencies; and (6) psychosocial characteristics and organizational climate, including, in particular, perceived social climate.

Measurement of the perceived social climate is a recent and particularly promising field of study for the systematic investigation of the general norms, values, and other psychosocial characteristics of diverse environments. Moos and his associates have studied nine types of environments extensively and have developed perceived climate scales for each of these environments: treatment environments such as (1) psychiatric wards [6] and (2) community-oriented treatment programs [7]; "total environments including (3) correctional institutions [8] and (4) military basic training companies [9]; educational environments including (5) college dormitories [10] and (6) junior and senior high school classrooms [11]; (7) primary work group environments [12]; (8) therapeutic and task-oriented groups [13]; and (9) families [14].

Each of the scales (which contain approximately ten dimensions) discriminates among environmental units, shows good profile stability, and has been or is in the process of being standardized on extensive normative samples.

The construction of the scales was inspired by the premise that environments, like people, have unique personalities. Just as some individuals are usually experienced by their associates as warm and supportive, some environments are felt to be supportive by their members. Some individuals are bossy and controlling; similarly, some environments are extremely controlling. Order and structure are important to many people; correspondingly, many environments emphasize regularity, system, and order.

An important aspect of this work is that similar dimensions are relevant to each of the nine types of environments and that these dimensions resemble those which have been found by other investigators. Moos conceptualizes three basic types of dimensions which characterize and discriminate among different subunits in each of the nine types of environments. (1) *Relationship* dimensions assess the extent to which individuals are involved in the environment and the extent to which they help and support each other. Examples are *involvement, affiliation, peer cohesion, staff support*, and *expressiveness*. (2) *Personal development* dimensions assess the basic directions along which personal development and self-enhancement tend to occur in the particular environment. Although an *autonomy* or *independence* dimension appears in all the environments, the exact nature of other personal development dimensions vary somewhat among the nine environments studied, depending on their functions. For example, on psychiatric wards and community-oriented treatment programs a dimension of *practical orientation* occurs which does not appear in military companies. *Responsibility* is also conceptualized as a personal development dimension. Finally, (3) *system maintenance* and *system change* dimensions are relatively similar across the nine environments. The basic dimensions are *order and organization, clarity* and *control*. An additional dimension in work environments is *work pressure*, and a dimension of *innovation* or *change* is identified in educational, work, and small group environments.

There is some initial evidence that these dimensions are related to important criteria such as morale and treatment outcome and that they may be applicable crossculturally.

Finally, many of the dimensions found by Moos are strikingly similar to those found by other workers, [15-19], indicating that they may be salient characteristics in a wide variety of different social milieus.

In this review we shall survey some evidence concerning the physiological effects of selected dimensions of the social environment from each of the three categories as conceptualized above. Although the dimensions were derived from questionnaires concerning the perception of an environment by participants in the system, there is no inherent reason why information relevant to the identified dimensions could not be obtained by outside observers. The fact that the dimensions discriminate among environment subunits, and their apparent generality across environments and investigators make them promising candidates for the study of the relationship between environment and physiological responses. Their derivation from individuals' perceptions of environmental influences, rather than from "objective" stimulus factors is also important, especially in light of the evidence that individual differences in defenses and coping strategies can affect physiological responses to the same situation [20-22].

After summarizing evidence for the relationship of physiological changes and perceived social environmental dimensions, we discuss the interaction of environmental and individual variables and conclude with a discussion of the utility of measuring perceived social climate for the diagnosis and treatment of person and environment. In this paper we hope to offer and illustrate what we believe to be a useful framework by which social environments can be conceptualized and assessed.

Relationship Dimensions

Support

There is abundant evidence that *support* is a crucial dimension of the psychosocial environment, especially with regard to maturing organisms. Spitz' classic study of Foundling Homes vs. Nursery [23,24] related maternal and social deprivation to increased infant mortality, susceptibility to disease, retardation in growth, and failure to achieve developmental milestones. Spitz studied 130 infants in two institutions with comparable quality of food and levels of hygiene. In Foundling Home, the infants were cared for by nurses whereas in Nursery, the infants were cared for by their mothers. In contrast to Nursery children, Foundling Home children showed extreme susceptibility to disease. Almost all the children had histories of intestinal infection despite the fact that the Foundling Home maintained excellent conditions of hygiene, including bottle sterilization. Contrary to what would be expected, older children—those who had been in Foundling Home longer—were more likely to die during a measles epidemic than younger children. In addition, growth levels, talking, and walking were severely retarded in the Foundling Home children.

McCarthy and Booth [25] describe a syndrome which, in some respects, resembles Spitz' "hospitalism" but occurs in children living at home with their parents. The most prominent abnormalities are dwarfism and subnormal weight/height ratio, with evidence of little if any malnutrition. Other symptoms are skin changes suggestive of hypothyroidism, and such behavioral features as inability to play, bodily neglect, apathy, and subnormal intelligence levels. In a study of ten mothers of these children, seven were judged by a child psychiatrist to have rejecting attitudes towards their children. Two of the remaining mothers were judged "inadequate" by the authors, one because of subnormal intelligence and the other because of neurotic depression. In most cases the symptoms, including the dwarfism, reversed themselves when the child was removed from home and placed in the hospital, where, presumably, the staff had at least a minimally supportive attitude.

Powell et al. [26,27] studied 13 children initially believed to have idiopathic hypopituitarism. Interviews with parents revealed histories of emotional deprivation. About half the parents were divorced or separated and almost all the fathers spent little time at home. The children were all short for their ages and manifested polydipsia, polyphagia, and retardation of speech. Deficiencies in ACTH and growth hormone were found in a majority of cases. The physical symptoms and the hormonal deficiencies reversed themselves when the children were removed from home and placed in a convalescent hospital.

Reinhart and Drash [28] give a detailed account of a female fraternal twin who stopped growing normally between the ages of 6 and 12 months. During this time her mother was suffering from clinical depression and the child was forced to spend numerous weekends with relatives while her brother remained at home. Psychiatric interviews revealed that initial differences in activity levels had led to differential treatment of the twins and eventually hostility and deprivation directed toward the female. At age 7½ the girl was placed in special classes where she was given a great deal of attention by the teacher and a nurse. She began to grow rapidly during this period, both physically and intellectually, and by age 13½ she had reached approximately the same developmental level as her normal brother.

Some authors [29] criticize the assertion that it is deprivation of maternal love or support which is responsible for the physical, emotional and intellectual abnormalities in children such as those described above. Instead, they argue that a deficiency in the amount of stimulation, (visual, tactile, vestibular, or social) required for normal development is chiefly to blame. There is evidence from the animal literature that handling can increase developmental and growth rates [30], and much of the evidence cited above is amenable to the hypothesis of insufficient stimulation. However, we believe that the most reasonable interpretation of the available data is that both certain kinds and certain quantities of stimuli are required for normal development. Some of these kinds of stimuli, occurring predictably from the same persons and in sufficient quantity, are what is meant by a supportive psychosocial environment, particularly for infants and young children.

We have provided evidence that insufficient support is associated with retarded growth and other physical and behavioral abnormalities in the infant and young child. Lack of support also has varied physiological concomitants in maturity. Malmo et al. [31], for example, found that psychiatric patients experienced decreased muscular tension following praise, whereas sustained muscular tension followed criticism by an experimenter. Van Heijningen [32] observed that rejection by a loved one frequently preceded the clinical emergence of coronary disease.

The loss of a mate can represent a sudden severe loss of support. Parkes et al. [33] followed the death rates of 4,486 widowers of 55 years of age and older for nine years following the death of their wives in 1957. Of these, 213 died during the first six months of bereavement, 40% over the expected death rate for married men of the same ages. Death rate from degenerative heart disease was 67% above expected. The mortality rate dropped to that of married men after the first year. Since only 22.5% of the husbands' deaths were from the same cause as their wives' deaths, it is unlikely that a jointly unfavorable environment was the chief cause of the phenomenon. The authors argue that "the emotional effects of bereavement with the concomitant changes in psychoendocrine functions" accounted for the increased death rate.

An interesting study by Robertson and Suinn [34] demonstrated that mutual understanding, or empathy, on the part of stroke patients and their families is related to the patients' rates of rehabilitation. Both the patient and his family were administered 30-item Q-sorts including statements reflecting various positive and negative attitudes toward the illness. The family's ability to predict how the patient would sort the items correlated 0.43 with the patient's rate of progress, as judged by his physical therapist.

In a related investigation, Throughman et al. [35] studied two groups of patients with intractable duodenal ulcer and other intractable diseases—those who had good results in surgery and those who had poor results. The latter group scored higher on a scale of environmental deprivation which included such factors as emotional impoverishment within the family and in other social relations, providing further evidence that support is beneficial in recovery from serious illness.

Cohesion

Social environments may be distinguished on the basis of how close their members feel toward each other. Such a dimension can be called *cohesion* or *affiliation*. There is some evidence that cohesion or affiliation results in (a) physiological covariation between the members of an environment; (b) reduction of stress responses.

Physiological Covariation

A number of studies of individuals working closely together show a clustering on certain physiological indices. Mason and Brady [36] cite a study [37] in which three closely working crewmen on a long B-52 flight reached similar elevated 17 OHCS levels of 13 mg per day. They report another study in which clustering of 17 OHCS levels occurred in two all-girl groups in a volunteer ward of college age adults. A mixed-sex ward had no clustering, even after five weeks. This suggests that something more than simple exposure to a common physical environment was responsible for the clustering in the all-girl groups. In a third study [38] covariation of menstrual cycles occurred in best friends and roommates in a college dormitory. Randomly selected pairs of girls in the dorm did not show covariation.

Other findings support the conclusion that affiliation and not simply exposure to common environmental stimuli is responsible for physiological covariation. Kaplan, Burch, and Bloom [39] found that pairs of individuals who like each other were more likely to experience physiological involvement (GSR) when talking to each other in a group than were pairs of individuals with neutral attitudes towards each other. This was also true for pairs of individuals who disliked each other, however, suggesting that positive *or* negative involvement with others in one's psychosocial environment promotes physiological covariation (see below).

Several studies of the physiological responses of patient and therapist found significant covariation in their physiological responses, e.g., DiMascio et al. [40] found a positive correlation between patient and therapist heart rate responses. Coleman, Greenblatt, and Solomon [41] over a period of 44 interviews found that the patient's heart rate was highest during anxiety, lowest during depression and intermediate during hostility; the therapist manifested the same heart rate responses as the patient. DiMascio, Boyd, and Greenblatt [42] found that both patient and therapist manifested higher heart rates during interviews characterized by tension and lower rates during interviews characterized by tension release. Kaplan et al. [39] suggest that physiological covariation could provide an index of rapport in psychotherapy.

Reduction of Stress Responses

There is experimental evidence suggesting that *cohesion* or *affiliation* reduces susceptibility to physiological stress responses. Back and Bogdonoff [43] report a group experiment in which free fatty acid (FFA) levels were higher in subjects who were recruited individually than in subjects who were prior acquaintances. In another experiment, group agreement led to a decline in FFA level, when the groups were performing more difficult tasks. Costell and Leiderman [44] monitored GSR during a Crutchfield type conformity experiment. There was some evidence that deviation from the group led to a rise in skin potential, and that when a previously deviant member conformed, his skin potential dropped. These experiments suggest that a cohesive group is less susceptible to stress, and also that a member may experience stress responses if he deviates from the norms of an otherwise cohesive group.

Involvement

Closely related to *affiliation* and *cohesion* is the notion of *involvement* in one's social environment. Involvement implies a strong affective relationship towards the members and goals of the environment in which one is participating. Clearly some environments are more involving for most of their members than other environments. Moos and his associates have shown that it is possible to distinguish among college dormitories [11] and psychiatric wards [8] in terms of the members' perceived levels of involvement. Involvement as conceived of in this manner has yet to be related to physiological variables. There is interesting data, however, concerning the physiological correlates of one individual's involvement with another person, or his involvement in a task or situation.

We have already cited the study by Kaplan, Burch, and Bloom [39] in which medical students who liked *or* disliked each other exhibited significantly more GSR response when interacting than those who had neutral attitudes, i.e., were uninvolved with each other. A study by Nowlin, Eisdorfer, Bogdonoff, and Nichols [45] found covariation in elevation of free fatty acid and heart rate in pairs of subjects, one of whom was listening passively while the other was answering personal questions. Postexperimental questionnaires and interviews revealed that the passive subjects felt involved in the responses of their partners. In this study, involvement in the emotion-arousing task of another person is associated with covariation of physiological responses.

Williams, Kimball, and Williard [46] had hypertensives and normals answer five personal questions displayed on cards by an interviewer. The questions were displayed two times and the interviewer was either warm and interactive or neutral and noninteractive. The subjects exhibited higher diastolic blood pressure in the high interaction than the low interaction interview, even though the content of the two interviews was found to be about the same. The authors concur with Singer [47] that it is the "transactional involvement with other people, rather than the sheer content of what people talk about in interviews ... " that is the relevant variable for correlation with "concomitant physiologic behavior."

Mason and Brady believe that pituitary-adrenal cortical activity can be seen, in part, "as a general index of interaction or involvement of the animal with the physical and social environment" [36, p. 9]. They present evidence that the mere presence of others with whom to interact leads to increases in 17 OHCS excretion. In one experiment, rhesus monkeys were housed in individual cages in the same room. When the cages were removed to separate rooms, 17 OHCS excretion dropped. In another study, a hospitalized patient experienced a drop in 17 OHCS excretion every weekend, when he was transferred from a bustling surgical ward to a quiet hospital across the street.

In an extensive review of psychoendocrine research Mason [20] concluded, in part, that elevation of 17 OHCS level is not related to a highly specific affective state, such as stress or anxiety, but "appears to reflect a relatively undifferentiated state of emotional arousal or involvement, perhaps in anticipation of activity or coping" [p. 596].

Back and Bogdonoff [43] manipulated the "importance" of an aircraft identification task by varying instructions. In the "important" condition, Naval ROTC cadets were told that the task was very relevant to their training and that the results would be given to their commanding officer. There was a significantly greater rise in free fatty acid during the important than the unimportant condition.

It is particularly necessary, in the case of the dimension of involvement, to consider the interaction of personal and environmental variables, to be discussed more fully below [pp. 21ff]. This is exemplified in a study by Friedman et al. [48]. They studied the 17 OHCS excretion of parents of children hospitalized with leukemia and found that the steroid levels of the 43 subjects tended to remain within a relatively restricted range, even when the parents were exposed to severe acute stresses associated with the illnesses of their children. However, the subjects' rankings of mean daily 17 OHCS excretion were related to how emotionally vulnerable they were to their children's plight, as judged by the experimenters. The most vulnerable parents exhibited the most extreme elevations of 17 OHCS. Those parents who were judged to use denial defenses had the lowest 17 OHCS levels. These parents were, in a sense, insulated by their psychological defenses from involvement in the social environment which included their fatally ill children. Thus even extreme environmental press for involvement can be countermanded, at least temporarily, by the individual's defenses and other stable personality mechanisms.

To summarize, we believe that these findings support the general hypothesis that environments characterized by higher levels of involvement will be associated with increased hormonal activity in their members. It will be necessary to study more enduring environments, however, in order to determine the physiological effects of sustained participation in a highly involving environment, where physiological and psychological adaptation effects might be crucial. We suspect that the most extremely involving environments have a relatively short duration; little is known about the physiological effects of differences lower on the involvement continuum. Finally, individual personality differences must be taken into account, because of the evidence that some individuals can avoid becoming involved even in environments with extreme pressure for involvement.

Personal Development Dimensions:
Responsibility

Within a given social environment, roles and duties may exert differential pressures on the members. Some individuals may have greater *responsibility* than others. Some environments may have greater press towards responsibility for all members than others, e.g., a disarmament conference vs. a cookout. There is evidence that responsibility is a dimension of the social environment which is associated with physiological changes in its members. Miller [49] indicated that responsibility was one of the factors leading to increased blood or urine 17 OHCS in military aviators. Miller et al. [50] studied 17 OHCS secretion and self-reported anxiety in the 2-man crews of jet aircraft during practice carrier landings. The pilots who had exclusive control of the aircraft had greater corticosteriod responses than the passive radiomen. This was so even though the radiomen reported greater anxiety on the self-report measures than the pilots.

Another study found 17-20% higher heart rates in active pilots manning aircraft than in the passive copilots at their sides; the difference reversed itself when pilot A became passenger and pilot B took charge of the aircraft [51]. French and Caplan found that responsibility for other individuals was positively correlated with diastolic blood pressure in employees of the Goddard Space Flight Center [52]. Morris [53] reports a greater incidence of coronary atherosclerosis in drivers than in fare collectors in London buses. Here differences in responsibility and differences in physical activity are confounded, however.

There is a considerable experimental literature supporting the claim that the active, responsible member of a pair of individuals subjected to the same threat experiences greater physiological stress. Brady showed that if a pair of monkeys is subjected to a noxious stimulus in an avoidance situation, the *executive* monkey (the one permitted to press a lever to avoid the noxious stimulus to both monkeys) develops gastrointestinal lesions, whereas the other animal does not [54]. Davis and Berry [55] applied this experimental method to pairs of human subjects, one of whom was able to press a button to avoid a strong auditory stimulus to both, while the other was a passive control. The executive members of the pairs had significantly greater amplitude of gastric contractions than the control subjects.

On the other hand, Weiss found that being the "executive" rat that learns an avoidance task to avert a shock to itself and to a passive "yoked" animal reduces the amount of stomach lesions when the task is simple and clear-cut. When the task is difficult and produces conflict, however, "responsibility" greatly increases the amount of lesions [56].

Returning to observational studies, a number of workers find greater stress responses in those in positions of greater responsibility. Marchbanks [57] studying B-52 aircraft, found the highest level of 17 OHCS excretion in aircraft commanders. Bourne et al. [58] found that mean urine 17 OHCS excretion was considerably higher for two officers than for ten enlisted men in a team of soldiers during a time of anticipated attack by Viet Cong. They also found that on the day of the expected attack an officer and a radio operator showed a rise in 17 OHCS whereas the other men showed a drop. Bourne et al. suggest that leadership, responsibility, and response to the demands of the group are all involved in elevation of urinary 17 OHCS.

When key NASA personnel were suddenly given additional responsibility, for example, put in charge of a project or called upon to deliver a report at a high-level meeting, sharp increases in heart rate resulted. The medical director of the project concluded "something we simply call responsibility often results in extremely high cardiac rates and is probably a much larger factor in rate changes than was formerly thought" [51]. Even top executives, men with long experience in the handling of responsibility, almost invariably had marked ECG increases when given additional responsibility.

Responsibility is a complex social environmental dimension. The evidence demonstrates that responsibility for the avoidance of threat to oneself or others, as in the Brady paradigm, can produce physiological stress responses. The evidence further suggests that assuming responsibility for more symbolic outcomes, as in the NASA study, can also cause physiological changes. Thus, even that sort of responsibility which might be seen as ego-enhancing and positive by the individual may elicit increased activation of some physiological mechanisms. Such activation is not invariably aversive for the organism, however. More work is necessary to determine when, for example, heart rate or corticosteriod elevation becomes detrimental, and what aspects of responsibility are most conducive to aversive levels of activation.

System Maintenance and System Change Dimensions

Work Pressure

Rosenman and Friedman have identified a behavior pattern which they believe is associated with high risk of coronary artery disease [59]. The coronary-prone behavior pattern, designated Type-A as distinguished from the low risk Type-B, is characterized by extreme aggressiveness, competitiveness, and ambition, along with feelings of restlessness and, in particular, a profound sense of time urgency. In one prospective study over 3,400 men free from coronary disease at intake were rated Type-A or Type-B without knowledge of any biological data. Two and one half years later, Type-A men aged 39 to 49 years had 6.5 times the incidence of coronary disease as Type-B men in the same age group [60]. Although their early work has been criticized on methodological grounds [61], Rosenman and Friedman's findings have, in general, received support in the critical literature [62].

Type-A persons are engaged in "a relatively chronic struggle to obtain an unlimited number of relatively poorly defined things from the environment in the shortest period of time" [59]. Rosenman and Friedman believe that the contemporary Western environment encourages development of this pattern. They also believe that the pattern represents the interaction of environmental influences and individual susceptibilities and argue that it may not occur if a Type-A individual is removed to a Type-B setting.

Caffrey [63,64] has shown that it is possible to rank environments according to the degree to which their "atmospheres" encourage Type-A behavior. He had three physicians rate 14 Benedictine and 11 Trappist monasteries using paired comparison methods. The individual monks were also rated by their Abbots and peers. Caffrey then showed that groups of monks having a higher proportion of Type-A's living in Type-A environments and taking a high fat diet had the highest prevalence rates of coronary disease.

Caffrey's work, in connection with that of Rosenman and Friedman, points to the existence of a dimension of the social environment associated with coronary artery disease, at least in predisposed individuals. We propose the term *work pressure* to include the sorts of environmental infuences which encourage the sense of time urgency experienced by the Type-A personality.

The association of work pressure and coronary disease gains support from elsewhere in the literature. Kritsikis [65] studied 150 men with angina pectoris in a population of over 4,000 industrial workers in Berlin. He found that work in the pressured environment of the conveyorline system was associated with the disease. Sales [66] has reviewed the evidence and holds that work overload is implicated as a precursor of cardiovascular disease. French and Caplan studied 22 white collar males at NASA over a three day period. They telemetered heart rate, measured serum cholesterol and had observers rate behavior. "Quantitative work overload," as indexed by the observers' ratings, was positively correlated with serum cholesterol. Subjective indices of work overload were correlated with both physiological measures [52].

Other studies demonstrate relationships between work pressure and physiological changes. Mjasnikov [67] referred to the high prevalence of essential hypertension among telephone operators working in a large exchange, under pressure to complete a large number of transactions per unit time, with few rest periods. Froberg and his associates [68] studied twelve young female invoicing clerks during four consecutive days when performing their usual work in their usual environment. On the first experimental days, piece-wages were added to the subjects' salaries. Urine samples taken three times a day were assayed for adrenaline and noradrenaline. During the salaried control days, the work output was very close to normal. On the piece-work days, which the girls described as hurried and tiring, the mean adrenaline and noradrenaline excretion rose by 40% and 27%, respectively.

There is evidence that the dimension of work pressure can be distinguished in practice as well as in principle from the responsibility dimension discussed above. Type-A pattern and Responsibility emerged as distinct factors in a principle competents factor analysis conducted on the monastery data [63]. In addition, Rosenman reports that no correlation has been found between Type-A pattern and occupational position [59]. It would seem reasonable, however, that when both responsibility and work pressure are high, coronary risk would be maximal. And in fact the monks with the highest incidence of coronary disease, the Benedictine priests, achieved the highest ratings of Type-A pattern and of responsibility.

Another finding supports the hypothesis that responsibility and work pressure have a cumulative, noxious effect. Air traffic controllers, who work under extreme time pressure and with the responsibility for hundreds of lives, have higher risk and earlier onset of hypertension and peptic ulcer than a control group of second class airmen [69].

The question of the relative contribution of work pressure and responsibility in the etiology of cardiovascular disease and peptic ulcers remains to be answered. But it is the possibility of conceptualizing distinct social environmental dimensions which allows us to frame this sort of question, with its implications for the differential diagnosis and treatment of persons and environments.

Clarity

Environments which are low in *clarity* seem to promote physiological changes. Ostfeld and Shekelle [70], in a review of the literature on pressor responses, found that uncertainty, along with the possibility of physical or psychological harm and the inability to flee until the situation was clarified, was associated with increased blood pressure.

Reiser et al. [71] manipulated the relative uncertainty as to the exact nature of an interview situation in an army subject population. Half of the subjects were immediately reassured as to the benign nature of the procedure and half were not given this information. The uninformed subjects experienced a greater rise in either blood pressure or cardiac output during the interview (depending on another experimental manipulation) than the informed subjects. In a number of experiments, differential GSR and heart rate responses occurred when temporal uncertainty concerning the receipt of a painful shock was manipulated. The data are complex, and reflect the subjects' extreme sensitivity to variations in experimental procedure [72].

French [73] uncovered a number of interesting relationships between "role ambiguity," physiological measures, and other social environmental factors in a study at Kennedy Space Center. For example, role ambiguity was positively correlated with serum cortisol, but only in those subjects reporting poor relationships with their work group subordinates. Those with good relations did not have elevated cortisol.

Mason and Brady distinguish between two stress response patterns. Elevated 17 OHCS and norepinephrine characterized rhesus monkeys' physiological behavior in a conditioned avoidance situation with a known noxious stimulus. In contrast, elevated epinephrine occurred in the ten minute intervals preceding experimental sessions characterized as "varied and unpredictable" [36].

Ruben et al. [74] in a study of naval underwater demolition training found that introduction of new equipment and procedures about the use of which the men were uncertain, produced elevations in serum cortisol. "The determination of transient increases in adrenal cortical activities . . . seemed to be the anticipation of an unknown situation more than the inherent difficulty or stress of the situation itself."

Change

Closely related to clarity is the dimension of *change*. There is considerable evidence that individuals experiencing change in their environment undergo physiological changes and are more susceptible to disease.

In his review paper, Mason [20] implicates change and novelty as influences leading to 17 OHCS elevation. Men being laid off their jobs experience elevated blood pressure until they are settled in their new jobs for a period of time [75]. Syme et al. [76] found that independent of diet, cigarette smoking, parental longevity, etc., geographically and occupationally mobile men had incidences of coronary artery disease respectively two and three times that of stable men. Bruhn et al. [77] found that educational and occupational mobility distinguished coronary men and control subjects even when age, I.Q., and social class were equated.

Marlowe discovered a large increase in death rate among old people being relocated after the closing of Modesto State Hospital (California) in 1969. Of the 349 survivors, 45.6% had physically deteriorated, 24.9% had improved and 29.5% had remained unchanged [78]. Other geriatric workers report similar findings [79].

Numerous studies by Holmes, Rahe, and others [80] relate increased incidence of disease to increases in frequency of life changes as measured by the Schedule of Recent Experiences (SRE). In one study, for example, (cited in Rahe, 1971) tubercular patients were found to have experienced the greatest number of life changes in the final two years prior to onset of their illnesses. Another study [81] found a 0.648 correlation between number of life changes and seriouness of illness in a group of 232 patients.

Certainly some changes must reduce stress rather than increase it. An example might be the replacement of a hated boss by a well-liked one, or a reduction of working hours in an overworked staff. Examination of the Holmes data leaves some questions concerning the relative contribution of "positive" changes and negative changes or "stressors" to the correlations between change and illness in studies utilizing the SRE. It is Holmes' contention, however, that it is change *per se*, "by evoking adaptive efforts by the human organism that are faulty in kind and duration," that lowers 'bodily resistance' and enhances the probability of disease occurrence [82].

The Interaction of Personality and Social Environmental Variables

We believe that the social environment can be seen as a system of interpersonal stimuli exerting influences on the individuals within that environment. These influences or *presses* can be categorized (see above) as relationship dimensions, personal development dimensions, and system maintenance and system change dimensions. Although individuals are sufficiently similar and environmental stimuli sufficiently potent that the individuals within a given environment can make reliable and consistent judgments about the magnitude of a given dimension, the social stimuli do not act directly on the individual. Rather, it is his *perception* of the social environment, as mediated by personality variables, role and status relationships, and his behavior within the environment, which affects him directly, and in turn affects his personality and behavior (see Figure 2-1).

There are two main ways in which individual and social environmental variables can interact, leading to differential physiological responses.

(1) Given the same social environmental presses, two individuals may perceive different levels of the same dimension. For example, a paranoid person might, because of his suspicious cognitive style, perceive little support in an office seen as very supportive by his less suspicious coworkers. In time, of course, this individual might very well come to receive less support than his peers, thus confirming his perceptions.

(2) Given similar perceptions two individuals may still differ in their affective and adaptational responses to these perceptions. Person A and person B, for example, work in an office which both perceive as offering little support. Person A has a loving wife and children, many friends, and a history of interpersonal successes. Person B is recently divorced and has long regarded himself as an interpersonal failure. It is likely that A and B would differ in their emotional responses to the office environment, and in their resources for coping with or defending against the emotions aroused.

In practice it is often difficult or impossible to distinguish the operation of an individual's perceptions of a situation from his defenses or coping strategies. However, without attempting to differentiate perceptual from coping factors, it is possible to point to a number of studies which illustrate the interaction of personality and environmental variables.

Several studies demonstrate that certain psychological defenses, especially

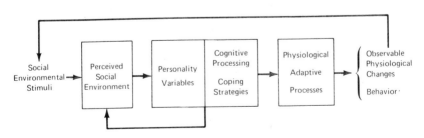

Figure 2-1. Conceptual Model for the Relationship Between Social Environmental Stimuli and Observable Physiological Changes.

denial, are associated with reduced 17 OHCS secretion in what one would expect to be extremely stressful situations.

Katz et al. [83] assayed 17 OHCS in 30 women in hospitals with breast tumors, several days before biopsy was to be performed to determine if the patients had breast cancer. The subjects showed a broad range of values of 17 OHCS secretion, none of them remarkably high. In addition, the subjects were extensively interviewed to determine their patterns of coping and "adequacy of ego defenses." The three measures of adequacy of defenses were significantly correlated with 17 OHCS; those with the least effective defenses showed the greatest 17 OHCS elevations. Patients who used one of the three defensive patterns labeled "stoicism-fatalism," "prayer and faith," and "denial with rationalization" experienced considerably less disruption, as judged by the steroid hormone secretion rates and the psychiatric rating scores. These findings recall the study of leukemic children by Friedman et al. [49], in which those parents who utilized denial had low levels of 17 OHCS secretion. Summarizing much of this literature, Mason [20] points out that too much reliance has been placed "upon situational criteria of 'stress' and upon mean group values, with a relative lack of systematic evaluation of the important and often marked individual differences between subjects in their emotional and defensive reactions to a given situation" [p. 676].

Other studies underline the importance of the interaction of personality and social environmental variables. Kasl and Cobb's [75] study showed that men being laid off work experienced elevated blood pressure until they were settled in their new jobs. Men with higher ego resilience, lower irritation and higher self-esteem experienced a quicker drop in blood pressure after going on a new job. There is a small body of literature linking *status incongruence* with disease. Cobb [84], for example, showed that individuals who were equal on the two status dimensions of education (personality variable) and income (environmental variable) have a much lower incidence of rheumatoid arthritis than those whose education was higher than their income.

Several studies from Lazarus' laboratory [85,86] suggest that a person's style of ego defenses can affect his response to an unpleasant film. Subjects with high scores on MMPI-derived scales of denial and repression experienced greater GSR elevations when shown a silent version of the film "subincision," which displays painful native puberty rites. In addition, it seems that denial/reaction formation film commentary and introduction conditions were effective in reducing arousal with the high denial but ineffective with the low denial subjects.

Measurement of the perceived social climate could, we believe, provide an important bridge between "objective" environmental stimulus configurations and individual physiological responses, which are mediated by differences in perception, coping, and defense. The most efficient predictor of a person's physiological behavior in a given environment may consist of how he perceives that environment.

Conclusions

In conclusion, the evidence cited above supports the view that social environmental factors have pronounced effects on human physiological processes. It is difficult at this point to make conclusions about the specific kinds of effects associated with different psychosocial stimuli, given the diversity of the populations, variables, and settings considered. It does appear, however, that the social stimuli associated with the relationship dimensions of *support, cohesion,* and *affiliation* generally have positive effects—enhancing normal development and reducing recovery time from illness, for example. Personal Development and System Maintenance and System Change dimensions such as *responsibility, work pressure* and *change* can increase the likelihood of stress and disease.

One might argue that most of these physiological changes could be subsumed under the rubric of "stress" and that the evidence merely indicates that too little support and clarity or too much responsibility and change lead to stress responses. Individuals perform best within restricted ranges of levels of the social environmental variables. The physiological changes could represent the concomitants of adaptive efforts taking place when a perceived social environmental dimension is not of optimal magnitude. Rather than labeling the process by means of the global term *stress,* however, we feel that it is more fruitful to investigate the specific physiological effects of distinct social environmental dimensions.

For example, different dimensions may give rise to different affects. In a study of eight military basic training programs, Moos (unpublished data) found that low *office support* is correlated with hostility, whereas low *peer cohesion* is correlated with depression. There is evidence that different affective states are associated with distinguishable psychophysiological responses [87,88]. Thus social milieu dimensions might relate differentially to different physiological effects. This would be in accord with the notion of stimulus specificity—that distinct stimuli (or situations) tend to evoke characteristic psychophysiological responses [89].

For these reasons we feel it would be more useful to study the complex relationships between environmental dimensions, personality characteristics, and physiological indices without imposing *a priori* conceptual closure. Social environmental measurement might enable us to predict which environments would be aversive or beneficial for particular groups of individuals, or to suggest specific and limited changes in environments in which a disproportionate number of individuals suffer from particular symptoms.

There is another important motivation for studying social environmental variables in connection with physiological processes. The social milieu may *moderate* or *mediate* the physiological effects of other ecological characteristics of an environment. Kellam et al. [90] found that schizophrenics treated with phenothiazines exhibited differential improvement rates depending on the environmental characteristics of their wards. Thus the milieu may moderate the effects of drugs. Moos [91] found that changes in size and staffing had differential effects on a number of perceived climate dimensions in hospital wards. Perhaps the physiological effects of such ecological variables as population density are mediated by changes in the social milieu. If this is the case, then it might be possible to effect important changes in an environment by manipulating the social milieu directly, when population density, size, or staffing ratios are fixed at aversive levels.

Finally, the measurement of perceived social climate has specific relevance for the issue of person-environment congruence. Social environmental profiles could enable the clinician, physician, or social worker familiar with the probable physiological effects of various configurations of dimensions to aid their clients in making prudent choices or in effecting beneficial changes in their social milieus. The systematic measurement of social climates could become an important aspect of the work of the diagnostician.

Summary

Recent studies indicate the importance of settings or environmental variables in accounting for individual behavior. Measurement of the perceived social climate is a particularly promising way of investigating the psychosocial characteristics of diverse environments. Three types of dimensions characterize and discriminate among environmental subunits: relationship dimensions, personal development dimensions, and system maintenance and system change dimensions. There is evidence that dimensions within each of these three categories have important effects on psychological processes. Individual and social environmental variables can interact, leading to differential physiological responses. Measurement of perceived social climate could provide a bridge between "objective" environmental stimuli and individual physiological responses, which are mediated by differences in perception, coping, and defense. Measurement might enable us to make environments healthier in general, or improve person-environment fit for specific groups of individuals.

References

1. Mischel, W.: Personality and Assessment, New York, Wiley 1968
2. Endler, NS, Hunt, JMcV: S-R inventories of hostility and comparisons of the proportions of variance from persons, responses and situations for hostility and anxiousness. J Pers Soc Psychol 9:309-315, 1968
3. Moos, RH: Sources of variance in responses to questionnaires and in behavior. J Abnorm Psychol 74:405-412, 1969

4. Barker, RG, Gump, PV: Big School Small School. Stanford, Stanford Univ. Press, 1964

5. Moos, RH: Systems for the assessment and classification of human environments: An overview, in Issues in Social Ecology: Human Milieus. Palo Alto, National Press Books, 1974 (Edited by RH Moos, and PM Insel)

6. Moos, RH: Ward Atmosphere Scale Manual. Palo Alto, Consulting Psychologists Press, 1974

7. Moos, RH: Community-Oriented Programs Environment Scale Manual. Palo Alto, Consulting Psychologists Press, 1974

8. Moos, RH: Correctional Institutions Environment Scale Manual. Palo Alto, Consulting Psychologists Press, 1974

9. Moos, RH: Military Company Environment Inventory Manual. Palo Alto, Consulting Psychologists Press, 1974

10. Moos, RH, Gerst, M: University Residence Environment Scale Manual. Palo Alto, Consulting Psychologists Press, 1974

11. Moos, RH, Trickett, E: Classroom Environment Scale Manual. Palo Alto, Consulting Psychologists Press, 1974

12. Insel, PM, Moos, RH: Work Environment Scale. Palo Alto. Social Ecology Laboratory, Department of Psychiatry, Stanford University, Stanford, California, 1972

13. Moos, RH, Humphrey, B: Group environment scale technical report. Palo Alto, Social Ecology Laboratory, Department of Psychiatry, Stanford University, Stanford, California, 1973

14. Moos, RH: Family environment scale. Palo Alto, Social Ecology Laboratory, Department of Psychiatry, Stanford University, Stanford, California, 1973

15. Stern, GG: People in Context: Measuring Person Environment Congruence in Education and Industry. New York, Wiley 1970

16. Pace, CR: College and University Environment Scales, Technical Manual, Second ed. Princeton, Educational Testing Service, 1969

17. Peterson, R, Centra, J, Hartnett, R, Linn, R: Institutional Functioning Inventory: Preliminary Technical Manual. Princeton, Educational Testing Service, 1970

18. Halpin, AW, Croft, DB: The organizational climate of schools. Chicago, University of Chicago Midwest Administration Center, 1963

19. Walberg, HJ: Social environment as a mediator of classroom learning. J Educ Psychol 60:443-448, 1969

20. Mason, J: A review of psychoendocrine research on the pituitary-adrenal cortical system. Psychosom Med 30:576-607, 1968

21. Mason, J: A review of psychoendocrine research on the sympathetic-adrenal medullary system. Psychosom Med 30:631-653, 1968

22. Mason, J: A review of psychoendocrine research on the pituitary-thyroid system. Psychosom Med 30:661-681, 1968

23. Spitz, RA: Hospitalism, Psychoanalytic Study of the Child, Volume 1. New York, International Universities Press, 1945

24. Spitz, RA: Hospitalism: a follow-up report, Psychoanalytic Study of the Child, New York, International Universities Press, 1947 (Volume 2)

25. MacCarthy, D, Booth, EM: Parental rejection and stunting of growth. J Psychosom Res 14:259-265, 1970

26. Powell, GF, Brasel, JA, Blizzard, RM: Emotional deprivation and growth retardation simulating idiopathic hypopituitarism. I. Clinical evaluation of the syndrome. New Eng J Med 276:1271-1278, 1967

27. Powell, GF, Brasel, JA, Raiti, S, Blizzard, RM: Emotional deprivation and growth retardation simulating idiopathic hypopituitarism. II. Endocrinologic evaluation of the syndrome. New Eng J Med 276:1279-1283, 1967

28. Reinhart, J, Drash, A: Psychosocial dwarfism: environmental induced recovery. Psychosom Med 31:165-172, 1969

29. Casler, L: Maternal deprivation: a critical review of the literature. Mon Soc Res Child Devel 26:1-64, 1961

30. Levine, S.: Stimulation in Infancy, Frontiers of Psychological Research. San Francisco, WH Freeman 1966 (Edited by S Coopersmith)

31. Malmo, RB, Boag, T, Smith, A: Physiological study of personal interaction. Psychosom Med 19:105-119, 1957

32. Van Heijningen, K: Psychodynamic factors in acute myocardial infarction. Int J Psychoanal 47:370-374, 1966

33. Parkes, CM, Benjamin, B, Fitzgerald, RG: Broken heart: a statistical study of increased mortality among widowers. Brit Med J 1:740-743, 1969

34. Robertson, EK, Suinn, RM: The determination of rate of progress of stroke patients through empathy measures of patient and family. J Psychosom Res 12:189-191, 1968

35. Thoroughman, JC, Pascal, GR, Jarvis, JR, Crutcher, JR: A study of psychological factors in patients with surgically intractable duodenal ulcer and those with other intractable disorders. Psychosom Med 29:273-278, 1967

36. Mason, J, Brady, J: The sensitivity of psychoendocrine systems to social and physical environment, in Psychobiological Approaches to Social Behavior. Stanford, Stanford University Press, 1964 (Edited by PH Leiderman, D Shapiro)

37. Mason, J: Psychological influences on the pituitary adrenal-cortical system. Rec Prog Horm Res 15:345-389, 1959

38. McClintock, M: Menstrual synchrony and suppression. Nature 229:244-245, 1971

39. Kaplan, HB, Burch, NR, Bloom, SW: Physiological covariation and sociometric relationships in small peer groups, in Psychobiological Approaches to Social Behavior. Stanford, Stanford University Press 1964 (Edited by PH Leiderman, D Shapiro)

40. Dimascio, A, Boyd, R, Greenblatt, M, Solomon, HC: The psychiatric interview: a sociophysiologic study. Dis Nerv Sys 16:2-7, 1955

41. Coleman, R, Greenblatt, M, Solomon, HC: Physiological evidence of rapport during psychotherapeutic interviews. Dis Nerv Sys 17:2-8, 1956

42. Dimascio, A, Boyd, R, Greenblatt, M: Physiological correlates of tension and antagonism during psychotherapy: a study of "interpersonal physiology." Psychosom Med 19:99-104, 1957

43. Back, KW, Bogdonoff, M: Plasma lipid responses to leadership, conformity, and deviation, in Psychobiological Approaches to Social Behavior. Stanford, Stanford University Press 1964 (Edited by PH Leiderman, D Shapiro)

44. Costell, RM, Leiderman, PH: Physiological concomitants of social stress: the effects of conformity pressure. Psychosom Med 30:298-310, 1968

45. Nowlin, JB, Eisdorfer, C, Bogdonoff, MD, Nichols, CR: Physiological response to active and passive participation in a two person interaction. Psychosom Med 30:87-94, 1968

46. Williams, R, Kimball, C, Williard, H: The influence of interpersonal interaction on diastolic blood pressure. Psychosom Med 34:194-198, 1972

47. Singer, MT: Enduring personality styles and responses to stress. Trans Assn Life Ins Med Dir of Amer 51:150-173, 1967

48. Friedman, S, Mason, J, Hamburg, D: Urinary 17-hydroxycortico-steroid levels in parents of children with neoplastic disease. Psychosom Med 25:364-376, 1963

49. Miller, R: Secretion of 17-hydroxycorticosteroids (17-OHCS) in military aviators as an index of response to stress: A review. Aerospace Med 39:498-501, 1968

50. Miller, R, Ruben, R, Clark, B, Crawford, W, Arthur, R: The stress of aircraft carrier landings. Part 1: cortical steroid responses in naval aviators. Psychosom Med 32:581-588, 1970

51. Responsibility brings jump in pulse. JAMA 201:23, 1967

52. French, J, Caplan, R: Organizational stress and individual strain, in The Failure of Success. New York, AMACOM, 1973 (Edited by A Marrow), pp. 30-66

53. Morris, J: Occupation and coronary heart disease. AMA Arch Int Med 104:903-907, 1959

54. Brady, J, Porter, R, Conrad, D, Mason, J: Avoidance behavior and the development of gastroduodenal ulcers. J Exp Anal Behav 1:69-72, 1958

55. Davis, R, Berry, F: Gastrointestinal reaction during a noise avoidance task. Psychol Rep 12:135-137, 1963

56. Weiss, J: Effects of punishing the coping response (conflict) on stress pathology in rats. J Comp Physiol Psychol 77:14-22, 1971

57. Marchbanks, V: Flying stress and urinary 17-hydroxycorticosteroid levels during twenty-four hour missions. Aerospace Med 31:639-643, 1960

58. Bourne, P, Rose, R, Mason, J: 17-OHCS levels in combat: Special forces "A" team under threat of attack. Arch Gen Psychia 19:135-140, 1968

59. Friedman, M: Pathogenesis of Coronary Artery Disease. New York, McGraw-Hill 1969

60. Rosenman, R, Friedman, M, Straus, R, Wurm, Jenkins, D, Messinger, H: Coronary heart disease in the Western Collaborative Group Study: A follow-up experience of two years. JAMA 195:86-92, 1966

61. Keith, R: Personality and coronary heart disease: A review. J Chron Dis 19:1231-1243, 1966

62. Jenkins, CD: Psychologic and social precursors of coronary disease. New Eng J Med 284:244-255, 307-317, 1971

63. Caffrey, B: Reliability and validity of personality and behavioral measures in a study of coronary heart disease. J Chron Dis 21:191-204, 1968

64. Caffrey, B: Behavior patterns and personality characteristics related to prevalence rates of coronary heart disease in American monks. J Chron Dis 22:93-103, 1969

65. Kritsikis, S, Heinemann, A, Eitner, S: Die Angina pectoris im Aspekt ihrer Korrelation mit biologischer Disposition, psychologischen und soziologischen Einflussfaktoren. Deutsch Gesundh 23:1878-1885, 1968

66. Sales, S: Organizational role as a risk factor in coronary disease. Admin Sci Quarter 14:325-336, 1969

67. Mjasnikov, A: Discussion, in Proc Joint WHO-Czech Cardio Soc Symp Pathogen Essential Hypertension, Prague, 1961

68. Froberg, J, Karlsson, C, Levi, L, Lidberg, L: Physiological and biochemical stress reactions induced by psychosocial stimuli, in Society, Stress and Disease. London, Oxford University Press, 1971 (Volume 1, edited by L Levi)

69. Cobb, S, Rose, R: Hypertension, peptic ulcer and diabetes in air traffic controllers. JAMA 224:489-492, 1973

70. Ostfeld, M, Shekelle, R: Psychological variables and blood pressure, The Epidemiology of Hypertension, Proceedings of an International Symposium. New York, Grune & Stratton, 1967 (Edited by J Stamler, R Stamler, T Pullman)

71. Reiser, M, Reeves, R, Armington, J: Effects of variations in laboratory procedure and experiments upon the ballistocardiogram, blood pressure, and heart rate in healthy young men. Psychosom Med 17:185-199, 1955

72. Bowers, K: The effects of UCS temporal uncertainty on heart rate and pain. Psychophys 8:382-389, 1971

73. French, J: Person role fit. Occupat Ment Health 3:13-20, 1973

74. Ruben, R, Rahe, R, Ransom, A, Clark, B: Adrenal cortical activity changes during underwater demolition team training. Psychosom Med 31:553-564, 1969

75. Kasl, S, Cobb, S: Blood pressure changes in men undergoing job loss: A preliminary report. Psychosom Med 32:19-38, 1970

76. Syme, S, Borhani, N, Buechley, R: Cultural mobility and coronary heart disease in an urban area. Am J Epidem 82:334-346, 1965

77. Bruhn, J, Chandler, B, Miller, M, Wolf, S, Lynn, T: Social aspects of

coronary heart disease in two adjacent, ethnically different communities. Am J Pub Health 56:1493-1506, 1966

78. Marlowe, D: Personal communication with Stewart Kiritz, 1972
79. Blanker, M: Environmental change and the aging individual. Gerontologist 7:101-105, 1967
80. Rahe, R, Mahan, J, Arthur, R: Prediction of near future health changes from subjects' preceding life changes. J Psychosom Res 114:401-406, 1970
81. Wyler, A, Masuda, M, Holmes, J: Magnitude of life events and seriousness of illness. Psychosom Med 33:115-122, 1971
82. Holmes, T, Masuda, M: Life changes and illness susceptibility. Unpublished manuscript, 1970
83. Katz, J, Weiner, H, Gallagher, T, Hellman, L: Stress, distress and ego defenses. Arch Gen Psych 23:131-142, 1970
84. Cobb, S, Kasl, S, Chen, E, Christenfeld, R: Some psychological and sociological characteristics of patients hospitalized for rheumatoid arthritis, hypertension and duodenal ulcer. J Chron Dis 18:1259-1278, 1965
85. Speisman, J, Lazarus, R, Mordkoff, A, Davison, L: Experimental reduction of stress based on ego-defense theory. J Abnorm Soc Psychol 68:367-380, 1964
86. Lazarus, R, Alfert, E: Short-circuiting of threat by experimentally altering cognitive appraisal. J Abnorm Soc Psychol 69:195-205, 1964
87. Ax, A: The physiological differentiation between fear and anger in humans. Psychosom Med 15:433-422, 1953
88. Ekman, P, Malmstrom, E, Friesen, W: Heart rate changes with facial displays of surprise and disgust. Unpublished manuscript, 1972
89. Engel, B, Moos, R: The generality of specificity. Arch Gen Psych 16:574-581, 1967
90. Kellam, S, Goldberg, S, Schooler, N, Berman, A, Schmelzer, J: Ward atmosphere and outcome of treatment of acute schizophrenia. J Psych Res 5:145-163, 1967
91. Moos, RH: Evaluating Treatment Environments: A social ecological approach. New York, Wiley, 1974

Psychosomatic
Disorders and
Environmental
Stimuli

Commentary. An early investigator in psychosomatic research suggested that "it is often more important to know what kind of patient has the disease than what kind of disease the patient has" (Dunbar, 1943). This point of view underlies the traditional approaches to psychosomatic medicine and is prominent in the psychoanalytic school, where it is thought that particular personality constellations are associated with specific diseases (Alexander, 1950). This point of view has been challenged by more current researchers in the field, who suggest that all psychological and social experience can affect a person's physiology, even to the extent that stressful environments can result in illness responses (Grinker, 1961; Wolff, 1953). Schwab (1970) has suggested that "the concurrence of mental and physical symptomatology should be regarded as natural when we view man as a biosocial organism whose nervous system functions as the central integrating medium (p. 594)." Wolff and his associates have collected considerable data that have indicated that socially threatening life situations can result in symptom formation and tissue damage. They have demonstrated that events such as loss of status, loss of security, or unsatisfactory interpersonal relations are significantly related to illness. Similarly, Holmes (1962) found that life crises tend to increase in the two years preceding the onset or relapse of tuberculosis. In their study of illness in relatively healthy populations, Hinkle and Wolff (1957) found that persons who had the greatest number of physical illnesses, regardless of kind, also experienced the greatest number of disturbances in mood, thought, and behavior. Similarly, Matarazzo, Matarazzo, and Saslow (1961) concluded that the incidence of physical illness in a population is a good predictor of mental illness, and vice versa.

In the first chapter in this section, C. David Jenkins reviews the psychosomatic research literature along four dimensions:

1. Studies of the etiology of disease;

2. Studies of psychological and behavioral concomitants of physiological change;

3. Studies of the "sick role" and seeking medical care; and

4. Studies of the course of disease: recovery, chronicity, and outcome.

In Chapter 4 David Mechanic examines situational and background variables that affect the process and outcome of illness. He suggests that self-esteem may be an intervening variable between situation and response. Individuals with high self-esteem, for example, view themselves as better able to deal with threatening situations and thus are less vulnerable.

The social environment appears to strongly influence the outcome of illness. In an interesting study cited by Mechanic, children admitted to the hospital to have their tonsils removed were randomly assigned to experimental and control groups. In the experimental group, patients and their mothers were admitted to the hospital by a specially trained nurse who attempted to create a social climate that was supportive and facilitated communication about details of the operation. The results indicated that support reduced the mothers' stress by shifting their view of the hospital situation from cold and antiseptic to warm and helpful. This in turn had a positive effect on their children. Children in the experimental group had fewer changes in blood pressure, temperature, and other physiological measures. They also adapted better to the hospital and recovered more rapidly than children in the control group.

While a supportive social environment may alleviate the effects of a stressful situation, a stressful social environment can provoke pathological organic changes (Selye, 1969). In Chapter 5, Sidney Cobb and Robert Rose examine the hypothesis that the work environment of air-traffic controllers is stressful, and that they consequently have a high incidence of certain diseases related to the stress of the job. When comparing this group with a control group of second-class airmen, the authors found a significantly higher prevalence of hypertension, peptic ulcers, and diabetes. They compared the prevalence rates of these diseases among air-traffic controllers by stress level as measured by traffic density, and concluded that the controllers are at higher risk for hypertension and peptic ulcer when working at high-traffic-density towers and centers.

Psychosomatic disorders are often expressed through the skin. The skin is a highly sensitive indicator of emotional states because it is well supplied with small blood vessels. When a person is embarrassed, for example, his skin tends to flush; when frightened his face may blanch, because the blood is drawn away from the capillaries in the skin. People who are stressed sometimes develop a rash or other psychosomatic skin reactions. In the last chapter in this section Stephen Kraus studied medical students with a prior history of acne in a stressful situation to test the commonly held clinical impression that emotional stress can exacerbate acne vulgaris. His results indicate that not only did the subjects have a significant increase in number of acne lesions, but the stressful experience and acne exacerbation were associated with an increase in skin surface free fatty acid production which may underlie the pathogenesis of this type of psychosomatic reaction.

References

Alexander, F. *Psychosomatic Medicine.* New York: Norton, 1950.

Dunbar, F. *Psychosomatic Diagnosis.* New York: Harper, 1943.

Grinker, R.R. *Psychosomatic Research.* New York: Norton, 1961.

Hinkle, L. and Wolff, H. Health and the social environment: Experimental investigations, in A.H. Leighton, et al. (eds.) *Explorations in Social Psychiatry*, 105-132. New York: Basic Books, 1957.

Holmes, T. Psychosocial and psychophysiological studies of tuberculosis, in R. Roessler and N. Greenfield (eds.), *Physiological Correlates of Psychological Disorders.* Madison: University of Wisconsin Press, 1962.

Matarazzo, R., Matarazzo, J., and Saslow, G. The relationship between medical and psychiatric symptoms. *J. Abnormal and Social Psychol., 62*:55, 1961.

Schwab, J.J. Comprehensive medicine and the concurrence of physical and mental illness. *Psychosomatics, 11*:591-595, 1970.

Selye, H. Stress. *Psychology Today, 3*: (4), 24-26, 1969.

Wolff, H. *Stress and Disease.* Springfield, Ill., Thomas, 1953.

3

Social and Epidemiologic Factors in Psychosomatic Disease

C. David Jenkins
Boston University
School of Medicine

Attention to human behavior has been intertwined with the epidemiologic method in the study of health and disease at least since the days of Hippocrates. For the Hippocratean writers, the study of human behavior was an important component of all medical investigation. "One should consider the mode in which the inhabitants live and what are their pursuits, whether they are fond of drinking and eating to excess and given to indolence or are fond of exercise and labor."[17] A much later talent in the history of medicine, John Snow, revealed a sensitivity to human behavioral psychology in the anecdotal evidence he cited to support his explanation of the London cholera epidemics. We recall the arrogant landlord who drank his tenant's water to prove that it was not contaminated, and forthwith contracted cholera and died; and the sick woman who lived far from the Broad Street well but had sent her son to fetch that water because it tasted best to her.[46]

The rapid development and amazing success of the germ theory in the early 20th century turned the view of medical scientists towards the infectious agent and away from the host. One cannot question the great scientific progress and improvement in health brought about by the efflorescence of laboratory medicine, but in turning from *in vivo* to *in vitro* concerns the science of medicine sustained a serious loss in perspective.

Reprinted with permission of *Psychiatric Annals*, Vol. 2 (August, 1972), pp. 8-21.

A reawakening of interest in human behavior is now taking place within medicine for two reasons. The first is scientists' increasing social consciousness and active concern for the human problems of 20th century society, and the second is the growing ability to study human behavior with precise and quantified methods. Techniques for measuring attitudes, beliefs, feelings, traits, group interaction and interpersonal and social conditions make it possible to include behavioral variables in medical research and practice without sacrificing the rigor of scientific method. This is a fitting accompaniment to the noteworthy advances in laboratory techniques and clinical medicine.

The behavioral sciences (I am referring here primarily to psychology, sociology and anthropology) can make great potential contributions to the scientific study of health and disease in human communities. The ability of a community to function is intimately related to the personal reaction of individuals to their social environment. Psychosomatic medicine can illuminate many layers of this interactive fabric of social environment, personal reaction, health and disease. Additional progress probably depends on the degree to which psychosomatics is able to move towards the *socio-psychosomatic* approach. In so doing, it would need to move from the consulting room and the hospital into the community. If psychosomatic medicine is to move from studying small samples of people in clinical settings to studying populations within communities, it will need to obtain from the behavioral sciences the basis for reliable measures which can be applied validly and economically in large-scale community studies.

What kinds of contributions can the behavioral sciences make to psychosomatic research? Three levels of contribution immediately come to mind: theories, concepts and techniques. Over the years psychologists and sociologists have developed a variety of theories in an attempt to explain and predict human behavior, and certain of these are useful frames of reference for study of the interrelations between behavior and health.[6] The relevance of a particular behavioral theory, of course, depends on the issue under study; different theories would apply if the issue involved psychophysiology or habit formation of health-relevant group behavior. Although behavioral science theories have provided many significant concepts, others equally important were derived from pragmatic generalizations by astute observers. These concepts provide health scientists with an established symbol system which supplements and extends psychiatric theories and thus aids in describing and interpreting human behavior. The third contribution is the methodologies for gathering, measuring and analyzing information about knowledge, attitudes, feelings, personality structure, overt behavior, social interaction, cultural norms and other important variables. A wide variety of psychological tests and sociological indices are now available, and the methodologies themselves can be used to construct new rating scales, questionnaires or tests for any kind of overt behavior or attitude system which the clinician can describe clearly and identify constantly.

The behavioral sciences can make important contributions in a number of health areas, but I should like to confine my discussion to four frontiers of psychosomatic research:

1. studies of the etiology of disease;
2. studies of psychological and behavioral concomitants of physiological change;
3. studies of the "sick role" and seeking of medical care; and
4. studies of the course of disease: recovery, chronicity and fatal outcome.

Studies of the Etiology of Disease

When epidemiologic study is pursued in a programatic fashion, investigators are soon confronted with the necessity to consider psychic factors. These can affect health adversely either through covert physiologic mechanisms or through overt behaviors, and psychosomatic medicine needs to discover the psychodynamics in the latter situation as well as the former.

Epidemiologists studying lung cancer have considered many possible causal variables including heredity and the physical environment (particularly atmospheric pollution), but the strongest risk factor proved to be a behavioral one, cigarette smoking. Studies of the epidemiology of lung cancer repeatedly lead back to the behavior cigarette smoking. We should not stop at this point, however, but should try to push back the veil of the unknown one step further and study the determinants of smoking.

Two groups of variables have been found associated with this behavior: host factors and environmental factors. A recent study of a large group of employed men from a variety of industries revealed that heavy cigarette smokers differed from others (those who had quit smoking or who had never smoked) in serum lipids, hematocrit, type of occupation, level of income and amount of schooling.[27] Studies of the smoking habits among adolescents have revealed the importance of the social environment; young people who smoke are more likely to associate with a peer group where smoking is the norm and to have parents who smoke, in clear contrast to nonsmoking adolescents in the same schools.[2]

We now turn to a very different disease, paralytic poliomyelitis. Epidemiologic studies of polio have shown that the individuals most at risk of a paralytic polio attack are those who failed to obtain a natural immunity through very early childhood exposure to the polio virus and who have further failed to obtain an artificial immunity through receiving an effective vaccine. (Thus the epidemiology of paralytic polio is reduced to the epidemiology of the absence of appropriate antibodies.) Serological surveys conducted in various parts of the world before the mass distribution of polio vaccines revealed the association between environment and antibody levels. It was first thought that tropical environments favored the dispersion of the polio virus with consequent early acquisition of natural immunity and reduced risk of paralytic polio later in life.

Later studies showed that the key factor was not the geographic latitude of the community but its social class, a sociological concept.[39] Backett subsequently pursued this association to more specific levels of cause, and these were found to be behavioral such as the play habits and personal hygiene of children.[1]

The development and distribution of safe, live-virus vaccines means that in an environment where sanitation is good and infant mortality low, the epidemiology of susceptibility to polio (i.e. lack of antibodies) can be reduced to the epidemiology of nonacceptance of polio vaccine. Such nonacceptance has been studied intensively, and while standard epidemiologic variables of age, race and sex have been associated with the rate of vaccine acceptance, sociological and psychological variables emerged as even more potent predictors. The perception that most of one's friends had taken vaccine or a personal orientation towards planning ahead, trust in medical experts, ability to postpone gratification and a generally "productive" orientation were strongly associated with the acceptance of polio vaccine, and these traits can be studied in communities.[29] Would it not also be appropriate to turn to psychiatry, psychology and psychosomatics to clarify the psychodynamics behind the nonacceptance of proven measures for disease prevention?

Psychological and social factors have also been found to relate quite directly to the dynamics of respiratory infections. Holmes' studies argue for the complicity of life change and life crisis in timing the clinical appearance of tuberculosis,[20] and Hinkle and colleagues have demonstrated the temporal clustering of life stress and illness over a long time span.[16] A series of studies of military recruits showed that particular human environments generate different levels of nonspecific susceptibility to illness. The social environment was a more accurate predictor of differences in sickness rates than were such specific causes as spread of an infectious organism or exposure to a common hazard,[47] and incongruity in social status (that is, simultaneous possession of attributes derived from contrasting social levels) was associated with higher risk of respiratory infection.[49]

The Risk Factors of Coronary Heart Disease

Coronary heart disease, the pandemic of the modern world, is a disease of complex etiology, but epidemiologists have traditionally been reluctant to consider systematically the role of behavior in both predisposition to and precipitation of coronary disease. CHD has both behavioral and biological risk factors, and many of its biological factors are demonstrably influenced by psychological ones.

Most investigators agree that the best-established risk factors for CHD are cigarette smoking, elevated serum cholesterol, elevations of other lighter-density serum lipids and elevated blood pressure.[8] Excess weight has been implicated by some but not by others. Diets rich in fats have been associated with coronary disease when whole nations are compared, but diet has not usually been found associated with CHD rates[9] (nor even with serum cholesterol levels) when free-living persons within a nation are studied.[30,37] Let us consider the role of behavior in each of these risk factors.

Cigarette smoking is obviously a learned behavior; the habit is initiated by imitation of desired role models and maintained through both pharmacologic and psychologic reinforcement. The most effective procedures for discontinuing the habit are behavioral: the learning of incompatible responses, substitution of other oral gratifications and deconditioning through aversive reinforcement. Considerable experimental and clinical literature exists on the influence of psychological factors on serum lipid levels, and it is common knowledge that excitement raises the blood pressure. Both these issues are discussed in the next section of this paper.

Three additional CHD risk factors are diet, obesity and exercise. Dietary practices are influenced by an individual's social and cultural background as well as by his current economic state. Psychoanalytic theory holds that early experiences, particularly the relationship with the mother and the act of feeding, make a lifelong imprint on character structure, and even those who do not accept many derivations from psychoanalysis find it hard to deny that childhood eating experiences influence dietary habits and the role of food in the psychic economy.[7,15] Obesity is an area of traditional concern to psychosomatic researchers, taking on added social importance because of its association with several of our major killing and debilitating diseases.

The amount of physical exercise performed is related to both CHD incidence and mortality.[10] Much of the average person's daily physical exertion occurs in his occupation, but now that even blue-collar occupations are becoming largely sedentary, voluntary (nonoccupational) physical activity emerges as the major exercise opportunity for most people. Sheldon has asserted that the propensity for active sports is in part constitutionally determined.[45] It is also likely that habits of physical activity can be learned and, if socially reinforced, will be maintained. Psychologically oriented studies could isolate and specify the personality characteristics of persons most and least likely to engage in physical exercise, and could delineate the social circumstances that best promote such healthful activity.

In addition to these traditional risk factors with their psychosocial dimension, research studies implicate some purely psychological and social variables as additional, independent risk factors for CHD.[24] They are observed and measured at the psychosocial level, but their roles in the pathogenesis of coronary disease are no doubt mediated by neurophysiological or biochemical mechanisms.

The hypothesis that stress promotes CHD had led to including indices of anxiety and neuroticism in heart research. High scores on some scales of the Minnesota Multiphasic Personality Inventory (MMPI), especially Hypochondriasis and Hysteria, have been repeatedly associated with coronary disease, particularly when it manifests itself as angina pectoris. Other psychometrically-derived scales of anxiety or stress have registered higher scores among coronary disease patients, but in general these scales have not been used in subsequent studies so the generality of the findings remains untested. It should be noted, however, that in studies where the stress-anxiety issue was approached both by obvious interview questions and by use of a psychometrically validated scale, only the latter showed a significant association with coronary disease.[24]

One of the more intensively studied psychosocial variables is the coronary-prone behavior pattern, a style of living characterized by competitiveness, striving for achievement, aggressiveness (though this is sometimes stringently repressed), haste, impatience, restlessness, hyperalertness, explosive speech, tense facial muscles and persistent feelings of being under the pressure of time and the challenge of responsibility. This concept has developed historically at least from the time of Osler.[11] A broad array of studies all over the world converges in finding that one or more aspects of these symptoms are indeed correlated with the presence of CHD.[40] The work of Rosenman, Friedman and their colleagues has shown that the coronary-prone behavior pattern (Type A) is associated both with CHD prevalence and with CHD incidence in a prospective study of a large industrial population,[44] and their findings have been confirmed in the prevalence survey among monks reported by Caffrey.[5]

The cardiologists who developed the concept of the coronary-prone behavior pattern and directed the research of the Harold Brunn Institute and the Western Collaborative Group Study have called upon psychologists and psychometricians for a wide variety of scientific contributions. The interview procedure for determining the coronary-prone behavior pattern was subjected to content analysis, and clusters of items having similar content were studied in terms of their relationship to "silent" myocardial infarctions and blood lipid levels.[23] A psychologist conducted reliability studies of the interview procedure to determine the degree of interjudge agreement and the stability of the behavior type over time. Other psychologists learned the procedures for behavior typing and applied them in independent studies of coronary disease.[5,32] Bortner has developed new methods for ascertaining behavior type, a battery of performance tests and a short self-administered rating scale.[3] A cardiologist and an electrical engineer, using advanced electronics, developed a method for analyzing the patterns in changes of voice amplitude which are associated with the behavior type and with existing CHD.[12]

An intensive research program for more precise measurement of the coronary-prone behavior pattern was initiated in 1964 by the Harold Brunn Institute and the University of North Carolina's Department of Epidemiology. Thus far it has been shown that higher Type A scores (i.e. higher scores on the A-B scale of the

Jenkins Activity Survey) are found in patients having coronary disease as compared to nondiseased individuals in the same population.[28] Patients with CHD who subsequently have a recurrent episode of disease, such as another myocardial infarction, have higher scores on the A-B scale than do those patients who continue without further infarctions. Preliminary study of a limited sample of men who developed their initial coronary attack after taking the JAS does not show them to have scored significantly higher than their fellows who remained healthy. This raises the possibility that the test in its present form may not be able to predict the CHD candidate even though it has modest success in distinguishing between the behavior traits of men already having coronary disease and those without the disease.[26] Further study and refinement of this test are needed.

Studies of Psychological and Behavioral
Concomitants of Physiological Changes

Alterations in physiological function commonly accompany changes in the individual's life situation or his interpretation of the situation. Such alterations may be adaptive or maladaptive. Sustained deviations of certain biochemical and physiological parameters have been implicated as risk factors for a number of diseases.

The serum lipids, particularly serum cholesterol, have been identified for several decades as risk factors in coronary heart disease and cerebrovascular accident. Researchers of a variety of backgrounds, but sharing a psychosomatic bent, have searched out the behavioral and emotional correlates of deviations in serum lipid levels. One of the earliest of these studies, by Friedman, Rosenman and Carroll,[13] observed cyclical changes in the serum cholesterol of a group of accountants who were studied for a year. Many of the accountants showed a sharp rise in serum cholesterol late in March and during most of April, which led to the hypothesis that stress of income tax preparation increased as the April 15th deadline approached and was accompanied by an elevation of serum cholesterol. This hypothesis was strengthened when the researchers discovered that many of the men who did not show this cholesterol rise during April were corporate accountants whose deadline period coincided with the closing of the fiscal year, December 31. A wide variety of subsequent studies have corroborated this association between work pressure and elevated cholesterol.

The literature suggests that somewhat different emotional parameters may be involved in altering the levels of lighter-density lipids—serum triglycerides and beta and pre-beta lipoprotein fractions. These levels seem to rise when the individual is either in a state of excitation or is actively suppressing his impulses. It is not known whether these behavioral factors operate through alteration of diet or exercise, or act directly through the central nervous system or endocrine system to affect the mobilization or degradation of these substances in the blood. The general thrust of these findings is that more active, aggressive, outgoing, stimulated people have higher cholesterols as do those who are conscientious, suppress their impulses, show high levels of self-control and propriety, and are self-critical.[25]

Psychosomatic research has concerned itself for some time with the hypertensive patient and has demonstrated the role of anxiety and hostility in raising blood pressure levels.[41] Recently, Hokanson has shown that experimental manipulation of hostility also influences blood pressure. His experiment placed college students in a game situation where they could give or receive electric shocks to the finger. Blood pressures rose in subjects receiving many shocks. If these subjects were then allowed to retaliate by shocking the experimenter, their blood pressures promptly declined to baseline levels; when the opportunity for revenge was withheld, blood pressure remained elevated for a longer time.[18,19]

Adults have been trained through operant conditioning to alter blood pressure by changing their heart rate, increasing or decreasing it independent of respiration rate or overt body movement.[36] Various other laboratory experiments and observations of natural situations have also shown the connection between psychological factors and blood pressure.[38] It must be pointed out that most of this experimental work deals with transient alterations in blood pressure level rather than with sustained hypertension, but epidemiologic studies have shown that a single casual reading of elevated blood pressure has predictive value concerning CHD risk.

Serum uric acid has occasionally been suggested as a risk factor in coronary disease, but most large-scale studies have not found it a valuable predictor. It is invariably present in high concentrations, however, in persons with gout. Folklore has long held that gout is the result of extravagant living, particularly over-consumption of rich food and drink; and studies have shown that indeed serum uric acid levels average higher in upper and middle social classes than in lower social classes. High levels have also been noted in geniuses and high-achieving individuals. Psychologists sought to distinguish among these three related concomitants by use of intelligence tests, scales measuring drive for achievement and a social class index for each of these three variables could be measured on a continuous scale and its relation to serum uric acid studied simultaneously with other controlled variables. The work of Brooks and Mueller[4] and of Kasl and his colleagues[31] suggests that drive for achievement is the most important correlate of serum uric acid levels among these three factors. The contribution of behavioral scientists was to introduce the methods of measurement on continuous scales of intelligence and drive for achievement.

Studies of "Sick Role" and Seeking of Medical Care

As we place greater emphasis on studying the utilization of health services, psychosomatic researchers will be called upon to delineate the various factors that influence people to seek help from health professionals. Certainly the presence of disease or physiological changes brings a person to the doctor, but not all people with these same conditions will seek medical care. However, many persons present themselves at clinics and doctors' offices without detectable disease and without apparent physiological abnormality. The use of professional time and facilities by these people is substantial.

Medical sociologists have defined as the "sick role" that set of attitudes towards the self which lead a person to claim the privileges afforded to the "sick" and to initiate corrective actions.[34] If we are to better understand the utilization of medical services, we must understand how the sick role is learned and used. Identifying the reasons behind unwarranted use of the sick role could make possible reduction of the load on medical care facilities, and learning how this role is denied inappropriately could make it possible to bring into earlier care those people whose denial and delay make subsequent curative medicine more difficult. While sick role is a concept developed by sociologists, understanding its dynamics is a psychiatric problem and effective measurement of its properties is a psychometric one.

Closely related to the sick role is the way in which culture and learning alter the modes of experiencing and expressing physical symptoms. Zola,[50] in a study of outpatients at an ear, nose and throat clinic in Boston, found that patients of Italian descent described their symptoms in expansive terms with vivid and dramatic language, implying the involvement of the whole body. In contrast, patients of Irish descent reported localized symptoms in rather laconic terms and did not seem to be suffering unduly. Analysis of the medical charts revealed that the two groups had essentially the same distribution of diagnoses. The interrelation of culture, personality and health is obvious in this example.

Studies of the Course of Disease: Recovery, Chronicity and Fatal Outcome

Different processes seem to be involved in primary resistance to disease than are involved in recovery after a disease or injury has occurred. A rather broad variety of precursors has been reported as being associated with specific disease risks, but rapid recovery from disease and disability appears to coalesce around two major psychological factors: high ego strength and lack of depression.

Delayed recovery from mononucleosis was found to be associated with low scores on the ego-strength of the MMPI and similar scales,[14] and delayed recovery from chronic brucellosis was associated with depression and morale loss as measured on the MMPI scales.[21] Both of these studies, however, were retrospective, and one might properly ask whether the delayed recovery might encourage patients to report complaints and inadequacies consistent with lowered ego strength and greater depression. To answer this question of which came first, Imboden and his colleagues did a prospective study of recovery from Asian influenza.[22] The MMPI scores did not correlate with who became ill with the flu and who remained free of disease, but the depression and morale-loss scores obtained before illness were again significantly lower in those who recovered from the flu in less tham median time.

The Bender-Gestalt test was administered to persons with gastric ulcer, and the results evaluated by a technique which gives scores indicative of high ego strength and impulse control. Persons with intractable ulcer scored much more poorly on these variables.[42] In a replication study similar findings were observed.

Physicians and nurses working on hospital wards containing numbers of terminal cancer patients have commented that the friendly, cooperative patients seemed to die more quickly while the complaining, resistive, cantankerous patients survived longer. It would be easy to assert that the difficult patients just *seem* to survive longer and dismiss the whole hypothesis. Klopfer decided to test this issue empirically and found that the clinical personnel's observation was indeed true. Certain indices on the Rorschach test discriminated between patients with fast-growing tumors. He also discusses previous studies, one of which used the MMPI, that show similar findings.[35]

Survivors and Nonsurvivors among Aging

Tests measuring personality attributes and flexibility of thought processes have been found to discriminate between survivors and nonsurvivors in an aging population. Riegel and his colleagues found seven test scores in their lengthy battery that predicted which persons between ages 55 and 64 would die in the ensuing five-year period. His predictions were significantly better than chance though of course far from perfect.[43] Rigidity and dogmatism were among the significant variables.

Two prospective studies of open-heart surgery, performed at about the same time in different medical centers, agreed in showing that fatal outcome of surgery is far more frequent in patients who are depressed or hopeless before the operation. Anxiety did not correlate nearly so strongly with risk of fatal outcome. Both Kimball at Yale University and Tufo and Ostfeld in Chicago found that over 80 percent of patients who showed severe preoperative depression and inability to discuss postoperative plans died during or after surgery. This is in contrast to approximately 20 percent average mortality for the total patient groups.[33,48]

These examples show the importance of psychiatric concepts in studying recovery from disease, treating situations of delayed recovery and assessing more adequately the risks of adverse response to surgery. Psychosomatic medicine's contribution to such practical matters of patient care is still in its infancy, and rapid advance is possible.

Summary

The field of psychosomatic medicine has traditionally been concerned with the question, "What facets of personality or behavior raise chances of various disease manifestations?" This will continue to be its key concern in the years immediately ahead. What I have presented are some ideas concerning theories, concepts, methodologies and research settings that will play an increased role as psychosomatics renews its attack on the traditional questions.

Theories developed by the behavioral sciences about the interaction of culture, social structures, personality, styles of behavior and common habits will generate new hypotheses for psychosomatic research. The concepts and language of the behavioral sciences, when used selectively and with an understanding of their limitations, can provide basic building blocks for the "behavior" side of the "behavior-disease equation." The methodologies of epidemiology, survey research and psychological measurement can strengthen the research designs, data-gathering systems and data-analysis techniques of psychosomatic research. The opportunities for developing reliable quantitative measures of clinical concepts are particularly challenging. Social and epidemiologic perspectives beckon the psychosomatic researcher to use the community—the natural habitat of health and disease—as his laboratory. Finally, psychosomatics may profitably broaden its areas of concern to include not only the pathogenesis of disease but also alterations in physiological functioning, the psychodynamics of inappropriately claiming or rejecting the sick role and the processes altering rate of recovery and rehabilitation. I offer these intimations about anticipated developments not as original ideas, but rather as emerging changes in emphasis within a field which has traditionally been characterized by continual evolution and growth.

References

1. Backett, E.M. Social patterns of antibody to virus. *The Lancet II* (1957), 778.
2. Bajda, L. A survey of smoking habits of students of Newton High School—a cooperative project. *Amer. J. Pub. Health 54* (1964), 441.
3. Bortner, R.W. and Rosenman, R.H. The measurement of pattern A behavior. *J. Chronic Dis. 20* (1967), 525-533.
4. Brooks, G.W. and Mueller, E. Serum urate concentrations among university professors. *JAMA 195* (1966), 415.
5. Caffrey, B. A multivariate analysis of socio-psychological factors in monks with myocardial infarctions. *Amer. J. Pub. Health 60* (1970), 452.
6. Cassel, J.C. Social science theory as a source of hypotheses in epidemiologic research. *Amer. J. Pub. Health 54* (1964), 1482-1488.

7. Dwyer, J.T., Feldman, J.J. and Mayer, J. The Social psychology of dieting. *J. Health and Soc. Behav. II* (1970), 269.

8. Epstein, F.H. The epidemiology of coronary heart disease: a review. *J. Chronic Dis. 18* (1965), 735.

9. Epstein, F.H. Coronary heart disease epidemiology. In *Trends in Epidemiology*, ed. G.T. Stewart. Springfield: C.C. Thomas, 1971.

10. Frank, C.W., Weinblatt, E., Shapiro et al. Myocardial infarction in men—role of physical activity and smoking in incidence and mortality. *JAMA 198* (1966), 1241.

11. Friedman, M. *Pathogenesis of Coronary Artery Disease.* New York: McGraw-Hill, 1969.

12. Friedman, M., Brown, A.E. and Rosenman, R.H. Voice analysis test for detection of behavior pattern; responses of normal men and coronary patients. *JAMA 208* (1969), 828.

13. Friedman, M., Rosenman, R.H. and Carroll, V. Changes in serum cholesterol and blood clotting time in men subjected to cyclic variation of occupational stress. *Circulation 17* (1958), 852.

14. Greenfield, N.S., Roessler, R. and Crosley, A.P. Ego strength and length of recovery from infectious mononucleosis. *J. Nerv. Ment. Dis. 128* (1959), 125.

15. Hamburger, W.W. Psychological aspects of obesity. *Bull. N.Y. Acad. Med. 33* (1957), 771.

16. Hinkle, L. et al. Ecologic investigations of the relationship between illness, life experience and social environment. *Ann. Int. Med. 49* (1957), 1373.

17. Hippocrates. On air, water and places. Cited in *Epidemiologic Methods*, Preface, B. McMahon et al. Boston: Little, Brown, 1969.

18. Hokanson, J.E. and Edelman, R. Effects of three social responses on vascular processes. *J. Abn. Soc. Psychol. 3* (1966), 442.

19. Hokanson, J.E., Willers, K.R. and Koropsak, E. The modification of autonomic responses during aggressive interchange. *J. Personality 36* (1968), 386.

20. Holmes, T.H. Multidiscipline studies in tuberculosis. In *Personality, Stress and Tuberculosis,* ed. P.J. Sparer, New York: Internat'l Universities Press, 1956.

21. Imboden, J., Canter, A., Cluff, L. et al. Brucellosis: Ill psychologic aspects of delayed convalescence. *Arch. Int. Med. 103* (1959), 406.

22. Imboden, J.B., Canter, A. and Cluff, L.E. Convalescence from influenza. *Arch. Int. Med. 108* (1961), 393.

23. Jenkins, C.D. Components of the coronary-prone behavior pattern: their relation to silent myocardial infarction and blood lipids. *J. Chronic Dis. 19* (1966), 599.

24. Jenkins, C.D. Psychologic and social precursors of coronary disease. *N. Eng. J. Med. 284* (1971), 244, 307. (In two parts.)

25. Jenkins, C.D., Hames, C.G., Zyzanski, S.J. et al. Psychological traits and serum lipids. I. Findings from the California Psychological Inventory. *Psychosom. Med. 31* (1969), 115.

26. Jenkins, C.D., Zyzanski, S.J., Rosenman, R.H. et al. Association of coronary-prone behavior scores with recurrence of coronary heart disease. *J. Chronic Dis. 24* (1971), 601.

27. Jenkins, C.D., Rosenman, R.H. and Zyzanski, S.J. Epidemiologic study of cigarette smokers and nonsmokers. Submitted for publication (1971).

28. Jenkins, C.D., Zyzanski, S.J. and Rosenman, R.H. Progress toward validation of a computer-scored test for the type A coronary-prone behavior pattern. *Psychosom. Med. 33* (1971), 193.

29. Johnson, A.L., Jenkins, C.D., Patrick, R.C. et al. *Epidemiology of Polio Vaccine Acceptance: A Social and Psychological Analysis.* Florida State Board of Health, Monograph #3 (1962).

30. Kahn, H.A., Medalie, J.H., Neufeld, H.N. et al. Serum cholesterol: its distribution and association with dieting and other variables in a survey of 10,000 men. *Israel J. Med. Sci. 5* (1969), 1117.

31. Kasl, S.V., Brooks, G.W. and Rodgers, W.L. Serum uric acid and cholesterol in achievement behavior and motivation. I. The relationship to ability, grades, test performance and motivation. *JAMA 213* (1970), 1158.

32. Keith, R.A., Lown, B. and Stare, F.J. Coronary heart disease and behavior patterns: an examination of method. *Psychosom. Med. 27* (1965), 424-434.

33. Kimball, C.P. The experience of open-heart surgery: psychological responses to surgery. *Psychosom. Med. 30* (1968), 552.

34. King, S.H. Chapter 4 in *Handbook of Medical Sociology*, ed. M.E. Freeman, S. Levine and L.G. Reeder. Englewood Cliffs, New Jersey: Prentice-Hall, 1963. See especially pages 111-116.

35. Klopfer, B. Psychological factors in human cancer. *Jour. Proj. Tech. 21* (1957), 331.

36. Levene, H.I., Engel, B.T. and Pearson, J.A. Differential operant conditioning of heart rate. *Psychosom. Med. 30* (1968), 837.

37. McDonough, J.R., Hames, C.G., Stulb, S.C. et al. Coronary heart disease among Negroes and Whites in Evans County, Georgia. *J. Chronic Dis. 18* (1965), 443.

38. McGinn, E.F., Harburg, E., Julius, S. et al. Psychological correlates of blood pressure. *Psychol. Bull. 61* (1964), 209.

39. Melnick, J.L., Walton, M., Isaacson, P. et al. Environmental studies of endemic enteric virus infections. I. Community sero-immune patterns and polio virus infection rates. *Amer. J. Hyg. 65* (1957), 1.

40. Myocardial infarction and other psychosomatic disturbances. Special Issue. *Psychother. Psychosom. 166* (1968), 189-292.

41. Oken, D. An experimental study of suppressed anger and blood pressure. *Arch. Gen. Psychiat. 2* (1960), 441.

42. Pascal, G.R. and Thoroughman, J.C. Relationship between Bender-Gestalt test scores and the response of patients with intractable duodenal ulcer to surgery. *Psychosom. Med. 20* (1964), 625.

43. Riegel, K.F., Riegel, R.M. and Mayer, G. A study of the dropout rates in longitudinal research on aging and the prediction of death. *Jour. Pers. and Soc. Psych. 3* (1967), 342.

44. Rosenman, R.H., Friedman, M., Straus, R. et al. Coronary heart disease in the Western Collaborative Group Study. A follow-up experience of 4½ years. *J. Chronic Dis. 23* (1970), 173.

45. Sheldon, W.H. *The Varieties of Temperament: A Psychology of Constitutional Differences.* New York: Harper, 1944.

46. Snow, John. On the mode of communication in cholera. In *Snow on Cholera: A Reprint of Two Papers.* New York: Commonwealth Fund, 1936.

47. Stewart, G.T., Voors, A.W., Jenkins, C.D. et al. Determinants of sickness in Marine recruits. *Amer. J. Epidem. 89* (1969), 254.

48. Tufo, H.M. and Ostfeld, A.M. A prospective study of open-heart surgery. *Psychosom. Med. 30* (1968), 552.

49. Voors, A.W., Stewart, G.T., Gutekunst, C.F. et al. Respiratory infection in Marine recruits: influence of personal characteristics. *Amer. Rev. Resp. Dis. 98* (1968), 800.

50. Zola, I.K. Culture and symptoms—an analysis of patient's presenting complaints. *Amer. Sociol. Rev. 31* (1966), 615.

4

Social Psychologic Factors Affecting the Presentation of Bodily Complaints

David Mechanic
University of Wisconsin

Patients often recognize symptoms for which they seek medical assistance, but, on the basis of a history and physical and laboratory examination, the physician cannot obtain evidence to account for or justify the patients' complaints.[1] Such patients conform in part to Gillespie's concept of hypochondria, which he viewed as "a persistent preoccupation with the bodily health, out of proportion to any existing justification and with a conviction of disease."[2] There is considerable disagreement, however, on the appropriate formal definition of hypochondria,[3] and it may be incorrect to apply the same designation to profound and persistent hypochondrical syndromes associated with psychiatric illness and the type of hypochondriasis commonly seen in general practice.

Perceptions of Symptoms

Estimates derived from British and American morbidity surveys indicate that three of four persons have symptoms in any given month for which they take some definable action such as use of medication, bed rest, consulting a physician and limiting activity.[4] In addition, persons experience many other symptoms,

Reprinted with permission of *New England Journal of Medicine*, Vol. 286 (May, 1972), pp. 1132-1139.

which they regard as trivial and which they ignore. Investigators believe that it is pointless to attempt to measure symptoms that do not receive some type of treatment or special attention since they occur commonly and have too little impact to be reported accurately in household surveys.[5,6] Yet such symptoms overlap appreciably with typical presenting complaints among patients seeking medical care.[7]

The major task of this paper is to suggest how normal attribution processes develop in the definition of symptoms. As an initial formulation, it appears that persons tend to notice bodily sensations when they depart from more ordinary feelings. Each person tends to appraise new bodily perceptions against prior experience and his anticipations based on the experiences of others and on general knowledge. Many symptoms occur so commonly throughout life that they become part of ordinary expectations and are experienced as normal variations. Other experiences, such as a young girl's first menstruation, might be extremely frightening if prior social learning has not occurred, but would ordinarily be accepted as normal if it had. In analyzing responses to more unusual symptoms it is instructive to examine situations in which normal attribution processes become disrupted as a consequence of special kinds of learning, and in this regard hypochondriasis among medical students is an interesting example.

The Case of the Medical Student

It has frequently been observed that medical students experience symptom complexes that they ascribe to some pathologic process. This syndrome appears to have high prevalence—approximately 70 percent.[8,9] Factors contributing to the development of this syndrome usually include social stress and anxiety, bodily symptoms and detailed but incomplete information on a disease involving symptoms similar to the bodily indications perceived by the student. Hunter, Lohrenz and Schwartzman describe the process as follows:

The following constellation of factors occur regularly. The student is under internal or external stress, such as guilt, fear of examinations and the like. He notices in himself some innocuous physiological or psychological dysfunction, e.g., extrasystoles, forgetfulness. He attaches to this an undeserved importance of a fearful kind usually modeled after some patient he has seen, clinical anecdote he has heard, or a member of his family who has been ill.[9]

It is not clear from such descriptions to what extent each of the components—stress, bodily symptoms and external cues—is necessary to the process and what specific role each plays. Since both stress and bodily symptoms are extremely common among students in general—and the phenomenon in question does not appear to occur so dramatically or with equal prevalence among them—it seems reasonable to suspect that the medical student's access to more detailed medical information contributes greatly to the attribution process.

An experiment by Schachter and Singer[10] helps explain how information affects emotional response. Subjects were told that the experimenters were interested in the effects of a vitamin compound called Suproxin (a nonexistent substance) on their vision, and these subjects were given an injection. Each subject was then asked to wait, while the drug took effect, in a room with another student who appeared to be a subject who had received the same injection, but who was really a confederate of the experimenter.

The injection received was epinephrine bitartrate (adrenaline), whereas subjects in control groups received a saline solution (the placebo). Some of the subjects who received epinephrine were told to anticipate heart pounding, hand tremor and a warm and flushed face; this group was correctly informed. A second group receiving epinephrine was given no information about what to expect; this group was called the ignorant group. A third group receiving epinephrine was incorrectly informed that their feet would feel numb, that they would have itching sensations, and that they would get a slight headache; this group was called the misinformed group. While the subject was waiting for the "experiment" to begin, the confederate of the experimenter went into a scheduled act in which he slowly worked himself into a "euphoric" state playing imaginary basketball, flying paper airplanes, hula-hooping, and so on. During this period the subject was observed behind a one-way window, and his behavior was rated in terms of relevant categories. Later, he was asked to report as well his subjective feelings. Three additional groups were studied in a variation of the same situation: another epinephrine informed group; an epinephrine ignorant group; and a placebo group. In this second situation the confederate simulated anger instead of euphoria. Thus, it is possible to assess the influences of epinephrine, the various expectations subjects are given for their bodily experiences, and the different enviornmental cues (i.e., an angry or euphoric confederate).

Subjects who received an injection of epinephrine and who had no correct or appropriate explanation of the side effects that they experienced (particularly the epinephrine misinformed group) were most affected in their behavior and feeling states by the cues provided by the student confederate. The nature of the emotion—whether anger or euphora—was influenced by the behavior of the confederate. Schachter and Singer believe that emotion involves a two-stage process requiring physiologic arousal and a definition of it. They maintain that the same internal state can be labeled in a variety of ways, resulting in different emotional reactions. External influences on definitions of internal states are particularly important when persons lack an appropriate explanation of what they are experiencing.

With the use of the Schachter-Singer formulation, "medical students' disease" can be characterized as follows. Medical school exposes students to continuing stress resulting from the rapid pace, examinations, anxieties in dealing with new clinical experiences and the like. Students, thus, are emotionally aroused with some frequency, and like others in the population, they experience a high prevalence of transient symptoms. The exposure to specific knowledge about disease provides the student with a new framework for identifying and giving meaning to previously neglected bodily feelings. Diffuse and ambiguous symptoms regarded as normal in the past may be reconceptualized within the context of newly acquired knowledge of disease. Existing social stress may heighten bodily sensations through autonomic activation, making the student more aware of his bodily state, and motivating him to account for what he is experiencing. The new information that the student may have about possible disease and the similarity between the symptoms of a particular condition and his own symptoms establishes a link that he would have more difficulty making if he were less informed. Moreover, the student—in the process of acquiring new medical information—may begin to pay greater attention to his own bodily experiences and may also attempt to imagine how certain symptoms feel. This tendency to give attention to bodily feelings may assist the development of the syndrome.

Woods, Natterson and Silverman[8] found that contrary to usual belief, "medical students' disease" was not an isolated experience linked to a particular aspect of medical training, but occurred with relatively equal frequency throughout the four years of medical school. Thus, the syndrome's occurrence may depend on the coincidental existence of student arousal, the presence of particular bodily feelings, and cues acquired from new information about disease that seems relevant to existing symptoms.

Hunter, Lohrenz and Schwartzman,[9] on the basis of their study, conclude that symptom choice is influenced by "a variety of accidental, historical and learning factors, in which the mechanism of identification plays a major role." Yet there appears to be a variety of factors that may increase the probability of the occurrence of the syndrome, and it is important to inquire under what conditions concern about illness in contrast to alternative definitions will become manifest. The normal person may have a variety of symptoms without experiencing a fear of illness. Many investigators of hypochondriacal patients note that reported symptoms tend to be diffuse and may change from one occasion to another. Such patients often report numerous complaints referring to a variety of organ systems, or they report nonlocalized symptoms: insomnia, itching, dizziness, weakness, lack of energy, pain all over, nausea, and the like.[11-13] Kenyon,[14] in reviewing 512 patient case records at the Bethlem Royal and Maudsley hospitals, found that the head and neck, abdomen and chest were the regions of the body most frequently affected, and that the most typical complaints were headache and gastrointestinal and musculoskeletal symptoms. Striking features of almost all descriptions of hypochondriacal patients, particularly in early stages, are the lack of specificity of complaint and similarity to frequently occurring symptoms in normal populations. Moreover, many of the complaints tend to be of symptoms that commonly occur under stress and that epidemiologic studies show to have very high prevalence in ordinary community populations.[15,16] The common occurrence of such symptoms and their diffuseness establish conditions under which widely varying attributions may reasonably occur. Incorrect attributions may occur as well in existing organic disease because of the diffuseness of symptoms, referred pain, particular characteristics of the patient or some combination of these factors.

It is noteworthy that "medical students' disease" terminates readily and within a relatively short time. Woods and his colleagues report that the syndrome sometimes disappears spontaneously, but more often through further study of the illness or by direct or covert consultation with an instructor or physician. They suggest that it is "reassurance" that limits the condition, but the term is exceedingly vague and has a variety of meanings. Most reports in the literature concerning more persistent hypochondria suggest that such patients are not easily reassured, and thus it would be useful to have more specific understanding of the mechanism by which "medical students' disease" is short-circuited.

One way in which the medical student discovers errors in attribution is through further understanding of diagnostics. As he learns more about the disease, he may discover that the attribution he made does not really fit or that a great variety of symptoms that commonly occur may be characteristic of the clinical picture. Another possibility is that the stress in the student's life that is fluctuating subsides with some relief in his anxiety, and his awareness of his symptoms may decline. How the incorrect attribution comes to be corrected has never been studied, but possibly the student's growing knowledge of symptomatology sharpens his judgment about his own complaints. If clear knowledge is indeed, necessary to disconfirm the attribution adequately, the syndrome should be more persistent when knowledge is disputed and uncertain. In this light it is of interest that "medical students' disease" of a psychiatric character appears to be less transient and more chronic than such syndromes that develop around fears of physical illness.[8] In the psychiatric area it is more difficult to separate the attribution from the entity to which the attribution is made.

Another issue concerns the origins of the initial attribution of illness. The conclusion reached by Hunter, Lohrenz and Schwartzman[9] that identification plays a major part has already been noted, and this appears to be the most generally accepted psychiatric point of view. The concept of identification as used by the authors in this respect is more descriptive than explanatory, and it encompasses the observation often made that the patient will frequently focus on a disease that affected a loved one. An examination of cases described in the literature suggests that the localization and definition of the complaint may depend on idiosyncrasies or may be fortuitous. Ladee[3] reports the observation of Orbán concerning a veterinary surgeon who felt a pain in the right lower part of his abdomen. Apparently, he feared an incipient bowel obstruction rather than appendicitis, and Ladee explains that appendicitis is rare among cattle whereas ileus is frequent. Felix Brown,[17] in a thoughtful review of 41 cases of hypochondria, notes the important influence of topical suggestions. Many commentators have also observed how frequently symptoms of a particular kind follow publicity given to the illness or death of a well known personality or a dramatic mass-media demonstration concerning some disease.

It appears that the concept of identification may be too diffuse and imprecise in encompassing such varied phenomena as the association between mother and child, audience and public figure, and the occurrence of a stomach pain and seeing a movie concerning a person with stomach cancer. An alternative perspective from which to analyze such influences would involve consideration of factors affecting the perception of personal vulnerability.

Perceptions of Personal Vulnerability

Although persons may vary widely in their sense of invulnerability—which appears to be linked with their levels of self-esteem—psychologic survival generally depends on the ability of people to protect themselves from anxieties and fears involving low-risk occurrences to which all persons are exposed or dangers that they are powerless to prevent.[18,19] Feelings of invulnerability are threatened under circumstances of greatly increased risk such as combat and new and difficult experiences, but even under these conditions, persons generally manage to maintain a relatively strong sense of invulnerability through various psychologic defense processes and coping actions. However, a "near-miss" can dramatically undermine one's sense of invulnerability and may lead to extreme anxiety and fear reactions. The death of a close friend or coworker in combat,[20] being involved in an automobile accident in which others are killed or suffer bodily injury, and learning that someone who is defined as having comparable ability to oneself has failed an important examination that one is intending to take[21] serve to threaten the sense of security.

Basic to the undermining of a sense of invulnerability are social comparison processes. It is much less difficult to explain injury to people of unlike characteristics without threat to oneself in that one can attribute the injury to aspects of the person that are different from one's own. When such persons are more like oneself—in terms of age, sex, life style or routine—it is much more difficult not to perceive oneself at risk, and personal intimacy or physical proximity similarly increases feelings of vulnerability.

Various studies suggest that self-esteem is an intervening variable between situation and response. Although the role of self-esteem is not fully clear, one possibility is that persons with high self-esteem see themselves as more capable of dealing with threatening situations and, thus, are less vulnerable.[22] The awareness that one is able to cope and that one has had success in the past in dealing with adversity insulates the person from anxiety.[23] This concept of the self-esteem effect appears most reasonable in cases in which coping ability can affect the situation and realistically reduce threat; it is not so obvious that self-esteem reduces a sense of threat of impending illness, although many writers on hypochondria note specifically that low self-esteem is associated with this syndrome. A sense of confidence may generalize to situations even when it is not particularly realistic, or may lead persons to focus less on bodily indications. This is clearly an area for more focused inquiry.

Some symptoms present in a fashion that makes them difficult to ignore, and many symptoms are sufficiently impressive in their occurrence or sufficiently disruptive of normal functioning so that variation in response is relatively limited. Moreover, many symptoms occur so as not to allow alternative attributions readily. Hypochondria developing around a fear that one has a fractured leg or an extremely high fever is not found ordinarily; indeed, the response to such symptoms is not mediated in any influential way by social and cultural variables. But when symptoms are more diffuse, variation in response is more likely to occur.

In sum, it has been maintained that most ordinarily occurring symptoms are considered normal or explained in conventional frameworks, as when muscle aches are attributed to unaccustomed physical activity or indigestion to overeating. When such ordinary symptoms occur concomitantly with emotional arousal, and when they are not easily explained within conventional and commonly available understandings, external cues become important in defining the character and importance of such bodily feelings. Such cues may be fortuitous, or they may be the consequence of prior experience, cultural learning or personal need for secondary gain. The manner in which sociocultural and psychologic contexts condition attributional responses requires further examination.

Social and Cultural Influences
on Response to Symptoms

From very young ages children more or less learn to respond to various symptoms and feelings in terms of reactions of others to their behavior and social expectations in general. As children begin to mature, clear age and sex patterns become apparent, and the children become clearly differentiated in the manner in which they respond to pain, their risk-taking activities, and their readiness to express their apprehensions and hurts.[24] Learning influences the tendency of males as compared with females to take more risks, to seek medical care less readily, and to be less expressive about illness and appear more stoical.

The role of cultural differences in identification and response to illness has been described nicely by Zborowski[25] and has been amplified in a variety of other studies.[26] Zborowski, in studying reactions to pain in a New York City hospital among various ethnic groups, noted that whereas Jewish and Italian patients responded to pain in an emotional fashion, "Old Americans" were more stoical and "objective," and Irish more frequently denied pain. He also noted a difference in the attitude underlying Italian and Jewish concern about pain; although the Italian patients primarily sought relief from pain and were relatively satisfied when such relief was obtained, the Jewish patients appeared to be concerned mainly with the meaning of their pain and the consequences of pain for their future health and welfare. Thus, different attributional processes appeared to form the basis of these manifest similarities. Zborowski reported that Italian patients seemed relieved when they were given medication for pain, and their complaining ceased. In contrast, Jewish patients were reluctant to accept medication and appeared to have greater concern with the implications of their pain experience for their future health.

Other studies have similarly found that ethnic groups differentially report symptoms and seek medical assistance for them, and vary in the extent to which they are willing to accept psychologic interpretations of their complaints.[27,28] It is unclear whether the ethnic differences, noted in the literature, are a result of the fact that children with particular prior experiences and upbringing come to have more objective symptoms, interpret the same symptoms differently, express their concerns and seek help with greater willingness, or use a different vocabulary for expressing distress. Such distinctions are important.

Responses to Perceived Illness and Vocabularies of Distress

It is apparent that social learning will affect the vocabularies persons use to define their complaints and their orientations to seeking various kinds of care. It is reasonable to expect that persons from origins where the expression of symptoms and seeking help is permissible and encouraged will be more likely to do so, particularly under stressful circumstances. In contrast, in cultural contexts where complaining is discouraged, persons experiencing distress may seek a variety of alternative means for dealing with their difficulties. Zborowski, in describing the "Old American" family, stressed the tendency of the mother to teach the child to take pain "like a man," not to be a sissy and not to cry. Such training, according to Zborowski, does not discourage use of the doctor, but it implies that such use will be based on physical needs rather than on emotional concerns. One might, therefore, anticipate that persons with such backgrounds might be reluctant to express psychologic distress directly, but might express such distress through the presentation of physical complaints. Kerckhoff and Back,[29] in a study of the diffusion of a hysterical illness among female employees of a Southern mill alleged to be caused by an unknown insect, found that the prevalence of the condition was high among women under strain who could not admit they had a problem and who did not know how to cope with it.

Pauline Bart,[30] in comparing women who entered a neurology service, but who were discharged with psychiatric diagnoses, with women entering a psychiatric service of the same hospital, found them to be less educated, more rural, of lower socioeconomic status, and less likely to be Jewish than those who came directly to a psychiatric service. Bart suggests that these two groups of women were differentiated by their vocabularies of discomfort, which affected the manner in which they presented themselves. She also observed that 52 percent of the psychiatric patients on the neurology service had had a hysterectomy as compared with only 21 percent on the psychiatric service. The findings suggest that such patients may be expressing psychologic distress through physical attributions and, thus, expose themselves to a variety of unnecessary medical procedures.

Most of the understanding of the patient's complaint comes from observation of that part of the process that brings the patient into contact with the physician. It should be clear that this tends to focus on only a segment of the entire sample and excludes patients with comparable problems who do not seek assistance. Various analysts of the medical consultation, such as Balint,[31] note that the symptoms that the patient presents are frequently of no special consequence, but serve to establish a legitimate relation between patient and doctor. He maintains that the presentation of somatic complaints often masks an underlying emotional problem that is frequently the major reason the patient has sought help. Certainly, a complaint of illness may be one way of seeking reassurance and support through a recognized and socially acceptable relation when it is difficult for the patient to present the underlying problem in an undisguised form without displaying weaknesses and vulnerabilities contrary to expected and learned behavior patterns. The emphasis that Balint places on the symptom as a front for underlying emotional distress, although characteristic of some patients, neglects the fact that many patients who are more receptive to psychologic vocabularies may also be viewed as hypochondriacal.

The response to bodily indications may also depend on the social acceptability of certain types of complaints, and even the nature and site of the complaint, according to Balint, is a matter frequently negotiated between patient and physician. Harold Wolff[32] has also noted that minor pains from certain parts of the body may be more frequent because they are culturally more acceptable and because they bring greater sympathetic response. Hes,[33] in a study of hypochondriac patients referred to a psychiatric outpatient clinic, noted the inhibition of emotional expression as a result of culturally determined taboos on complaining about one's fate and a culturally determined excessive use of bodily language. He found these conditions particularly characteristic of Oriental Jewish women, who made up a major proportion of his patients with hypochondria.

Mechanic and Volkart[34] examined the influence of stress and inclination to use medical facilities among 600 male students at a major university. Stress (as measured by indexes of loneliness and nervousness) and inclination to use medical facilities (as measured by anticipated behavior given hypothetical illness situations) were clearly related to the use of a college health service during a one-year period. Among students with high stress and a high inclination to use medical facilities 73 percent were frequent users of medical facilities (three or more times during the year), but among the low-inclination-low-stress group, only 30 percent were frequent users of such services. Among those of high inclination, "stress" was an important influence in bringing people to the physician. Seventy-three percent of persons experiencing high stress used facilities frequently, although only 46 percent did so among those with low stress.[35] A similar trend was observed among those who were less inclined to seek advice from a doctor, but the relation between stress and actually seeking advice was substantially smaller and not statistically significant. These data support the interpretation that stress leads to an attempt to cope; those who are receptive to the patient role tend to adopt this particular mode of coping more frequently than those who are not so receptive. The previous discussion also suggests that when stress helps initiate a medical contact, the contact may be presented through a vocabulary of physical symptoms that frequently impress the physician as trivial or unimportant. A very similar study was carried out with comparable results among British women using two general-practice panels within the English National Health Service.[36]

The impression emerging from these studies is that there are at least two major patterns of behavior that physicians tend to regard as hypochondriacal. The first consists of patients who have a high inclination to use medical facilities and a willingness to use a vocabulary of psychologic distress, openly complaining of unhappiness, frustration and dissatisfaction.[37] The more common and difficult patient to deal with is one who has a high receptivity to medical care but who lacks a vocabulary of psychologic distress. Such patients tend to present the doctor with a variety of diffuse physical complaints for which he can find no clear-cut explanation, but he cannot be sure that they do not indeed suffer from some physical disorder that he has failed to diagnose.

Patients who express psychologic distress through a physical language tend to be uneducated or to come from cultural groups where the expression of emotional distress is inhibited. Such patients frequently face serious life difficulties and social stress, but the subculture within which they function does not allow legitimate expression of their suffering nor are others attentive to their pleas for support when they are made. Because of their experiences these patients frequently feel, sometimes consciously but more frequently on a level of less than full awareness, that expression of their difficulties is a sign of weakness and will be deprecated. They thus dwell on bodily complaints, some that are ever present, and others that are concomitant with their experience of emotional distress. These patients are often elderly, lonely and insecure, and they may be inactive enough to have time to dwell on their difficulties. When such patients seek out physicians they may use their physical symptoms and complaints as a plea for help.

Effects of Emotional Distress on Symptoms

It has been suggested at various points that emotional arousal appears to heighten the experience of symptoms, and in this regard the literature on reactions to pain is noteworthy. Beecher[38] has reported the failure of 15 different research groups to establish any dependable effects of even large doses of morphine on pain of experimental origin in man. He has found it necessary to distinguish between pain as an original sensation and pain as a psychic reaction. As Beecher notes, one of the difficulties with most forms of laboratory pain is that they minimize the psychic reaction, which has an essential role in pain associated with illness. For example, in a comparative study he found that civilian patients undergoing surgery reported strikingly more frequent and severe pain than wounded soldiers with greater tissue trauma. He observed that such variations resulted from varying subjective definitions, and concluded that there is no simple, direct relation between the wound per se and the pain experienced.

A variety of reports both of an anthropologic nature and in the experimental literature indicate how a person's definition of a painful experience conditions how much pain he is willing to tolerate and what he will endure without protest. In experimental situations persons can be given instructions and incentives to endure severe pain stimulation.[39,40,41] Here it is difficult to separate what people may feel from their willingness to control expression patterns, but many such reports suggest that when there is strong positive motivation, people will undergo extraordinary pain without complaint. Also, if intensely involved in some pattern of behavior, they may not become immediately aware of severe body trauma.[42]

The reactive component in illness has long been recognized as an important aspect not only in defining the condition but also in the patient's response to treatment and in the course of the illness. Imboden and his colleagues have studied prolonged convalescence in chronic brucellosis and influenza, in which they argue that emotional stress concomitant with the course of the illness may become intermingled with symptoms of the illness in such a way that the end point of the illness becomes confused with continuing emotional distress.[43,44] They note that symptoms of emotional distress may be attributed to the physical illness well beyond the normal course of the infection, which may serve to maintain the patient's self-concept.

The studies on prolonged convalescence suggest some of the conditions under which misattribution may occur. For example, the course of influenza and brucellosis is likely to leave the patient fatigued, with a lack of energy and interest, weakness and a variety of other somatic symptoms. These symptoms may also accompany depression and other emotional distress. The similarity in the symptoms makes it reasonable for the patient to attribute these symptoms after the illness to the persistence of the illness. The similarity that makes the errors of attribution more likely also makes it difficult for the physician to determine when the symptoms are a product of an emotional problem and when they are complications of the physical illness. Thus, the physician may unwittingly reinforce the patient's confusion.

The manner in which physicians may come to reinforce particular patient tendencies is suggested by a variety of reports.[45,46] Zola,[45] for example, on the basis of a study of patients for whom no medical disease was found, suggests that the patient's cultural background influenced how he presented his symptoms and, thus, how the doctor evaluated them. Although the ethnic groups studied did not differ in the extent of their life difficulties, Italians, who are more emotional in the presentation of symptoms and give more attention and expression to pain and distress, were more likely to be evaluated as suffering from a psychogenic condition.

Treating the Chronic Complainer—
Correcting Errors in Attribution

In a classic paper, Felix Brown[17] defined bodily complaints in five ways: partly on a physiologic or somatic level, associated with anxiety; symbolic of something else; consistent with mood disturbance, usually depression; by substitution or conversion of an affect, usually anxiety, with more or less elimination of the affect; and with more or less conscious purpose for the patient—purposive hypochondriasis.

The first three groups are most typical of the chronic complainer seen in ordinary medical practice. Ordinarily, it is believed that doctors must provide general reassurance, which relieves the patient's level of distress, but if the implications of some of the theoretical statements made earlier are followed, it should become clear why reassurance alone may not be the most effective approach. Frequently, the interpretation that the patient has made of his symptoms is a provisional and vague definition, and, as Balint indicates, this attribution is readily changed by the physician's suggestions. The physician may be able to alleviate the patient's distress to the extent that he can provide the patient with benign interpretations of his distress that are credible and to the extent to which he can reassure him and bolster his esteem and sense of mastery. To provide general reassurance alone may have no effect on the patient's perspective relevant to the meaning of his symptoms, although it may contribute to the alleviation of anxiety. Providing alternative attributions is difficult because they not only must relieve anxiety but also must be culturally and psychologically acceptable to the patient as well. For example, if the patient has learned that a psychologic expression of distress is unacceptable, such an interpretation by the physician may be of little use to the patient, may exacerbate his anxiety, and may disrupt the relation between doctor and patient.

The suggestion that the attribution the doctor provides must be credible means that it must be consistent with what the patient is experiencing and likely to experience in the future. If not, it may serve to arouse the patient's anxiety further and will not be taken seriously. Some evidence on this matter comes from a study by Rickels and his colleagues[47,48] on the effects of placebos. Suggestibility is an important factor in the medical situation, and placebos have been found to alleviate distress in a wide range of medical disorders.[26] Rickels and his colleagues, however, found that patients with prolonged experience with anxiety and the use of tranquilizing drugs do poorly when treated by placebos, and many suffer a worsening of their anxiety state. Patients who are attuned to their inner feelings and have had experiences with psychoactive drugs do not experience placebos as credible. The impact of the suggestion effect is hardly equal to the patients' past experiences of true relief of their symptoms with tranquilizers, and the failure of the placebo to reduce their anxieties to the level they expect may alarm them and make them think that they are more upset than usual.

Such an interpretation is offered by Storms and Nisbett[49] in a study of insomniac subjects. These subjects were given placebos to take before going to bed; some were told that the pill would increase their arousal, and others that it would decrease it. The former reported that they got to sleep more quickly than previously, whereas the latter reported that they took longer to get to sleep than before. Storms and Nisbett believe that the subjects who thought that their arousal was due to the pill felt less upset and could fall asleep more easily, but those who continued to feel arousal despite the fact that the pill was to reduce their arousal defined themselves as particularly upset. Although caution is required in generalizing to clinical situations, such studies illustrate how the efficacy of the doctor's interpretations of his patient's problems will depend on the extent to which they are credible in terms of the patient's experiences and the extent to which he anticipates the patient's reactions to symptoms and treatment.

The adequacy of the doctor's management of the patient is also likely to depend on the kinds of expectations and instructions he provides the patient in preparation for what lies ahead. Whether doctors say anything or not, patients will anticipate and acquire expectations of the course of their condition, how they expect to feel, what is likely to happen and the like. To the extent that the patient is not instructed, his expectations may be highly contrary to what is likely to occur, and this discrepancy may alarm the patient and disrupt his management. Various experimental studies suggest that very modest instruction and information have an important effect on patient outcomes,[50],[51] and on facilitating preventive health actions.[22]

Egbert and his colleagues,[50] for example, selected a random group of patients undergoing surgery and gave them simple information, encouragement and instruction concerning the impending operation and means of alleviating postoperative pain. The researchers, however, were not involved in the medical care of the patients studied, and they did not participate in decisions concerning them. An independent evaluation of the postoperative period and the length of stay of patients in the experimental and control groups showed that communication and instruction had an important beneficial effect.

In a similar experimental study by Skipper and Leonard,[51] children admitted to a hospital for tonsillectomy were randomized into experimental and control groups. In the experimental group patients and their mothers were admitted to the hospital by a specially trained nurse, who attempted to create an atmosphere that would facilitate the communication of information to the mother and increase her freedom to verbalize her anxieties. Mothers were told what routine events to expect and when they were likely to occur, including the actual time schedule for the operation. The investigators found that the emotional support reduced the mothers' stress and changed their definition of the hospital situation, which in turn had a beneficial effect on their children. Children in the experimental group experienced smaller changes in blood pressure, temperature and other physiologic measures; they were less likely to suffer from postoperative emesis and made a better adaptation to the hospital, and they made a more rapid recovery after hospitalization, displaying fewer fears, less crying, and less disturbed sleep than children in the control group.

In sum, credible instructions provided in a sympathetic and supportive way that help people avoid attributional errors and that avoid new reasons for anxiety might be more helpful to the complaining patient than blanket reassurances that provide no alternative framework for understanding his symptoms. Reassurance that does not take into account the patient's assessment of the threat that he faces might serve only to mystify him and to undermine his confidence in his physician. The literature contains frequent reports not only of patients with hypochondria who went from one doctor to another but also of repeated cases in which the patient appeared to get gratification in disconfirming the doctor's appraisal. Therapeutic approaches that facilitate the patient's coping efforts may be particularly useful with these difficult patients.

References

1. Gardner EA: Emotional disorders in medical practice. Ann Intern Med 73:651-653,1970

2. Gillespie RD: Hypochondria: its definition, nosology and psychopathology. Guys Hosp Rep 8:408-460, 1928
3. Ladee GA: Hypochondriacal Syndromes. Amsterdam, Elsevier Publishing Company, 1966
4. White KL, Williams TF, Greenberg BG: The ecology of medical care. N Engl J Med 265:885-892, 1961
5. United States National Center for Health Statistics. Health Survey Procedure: Concepts, questionnaire development, and definitions in the health interview survey (PHS Publication No 1000, Series 1, No 2). Washington, DC, Government Printing Office, May, 1964, p 4
6. Mooney HW: Methodology in Two California Health Surveys, San Jose (1952) and statewide (1954-55). (PHS Monograph No 70) Washington, DC, Government Printing Office, 1963
7. Mechanic D. Newton M: Some problems in the analysis of morbidity data. J Chronic Dis 18:569-580, 1965
8. Woods SM, Natterson J, Silverman J: Medical students' disease: hypochondriasis in medical education. J Med Educ 41:785-790, 1966
9. Hunter RCA, Lohrenz JG, Schwartzman AE: Nosophobia and hypochondriasis in medical students. J Nerv Ment Dis 139:147-152, 1964
10. Schachter S, Singer JE: Cognitive, social, and physiological determinants of emotional state. Psychol Rev 69:379-399, 1962
11. Katzenelbogen S: Hypochondriacal complaints with special reference to personality and environment. Am J Psychiatry 98:815-822, 1942
12. Greenberg HP: Hypochondriasis. Med J Aust 1 (18):673-677, 1960
13. Robins E, Purtell JJ, Cohen ME: "Hysteria" in men: a study of 38 patients so diagnosed and 194 control subjects. N Engl J Med 246:677-685, 1952
14. Kenyon FE: Hypochondriasis: a clinical study, Br J Psychiatry 110:478-488, 1964
15. Srole L. Langner TS, Michael ST, et al.: Mental Health in the Metropolis: The Midtown Manhattan study. New York, McGraw-Hill Book Company, 1962
16. Leighton DC, Harding JS, Macklin DB, et al.: The Character of Danger: Psychiatric symptoms in selected communities. New York, Basic Books, 1963
17. Brown F: The bodily complaint: a study of hypochondriasis. J Ment Sci 82:295-359, 1936
18. Janis IL: Air War and Emotional Stress: Psychological studies of bombing and civilian defense. New York, McGraw-Hill Book Company, 1951
19. Wolfenstein M: Disaster: A psychological essay. New York, Free Press, 1957
20. Grinker RR, Spiegel JP: Men Under Stress, Philadelphia, Blakiston Publishing Company, 1945
21. Mechanic D: Students Under Stress: A study in the social psychology of adaptation. New York, Free Press, 1962

22. Leventhal H: Findings and theory in the study of fear communications. Adv Exp Soc Psychol 5:119-186, 1970
23. Lazarus RS: Psychological Stress and the Coping Process. New York, McGraw-Hill Book Company, 1966
24. Mechanic D: The influence of mothers on their children's health attitudes and behavior. Pediatrics 33:444-453, 1964
25. Zborowski M: Cultural components in responses to pain. J Soc Issues 8 (4):16-30, 1952
26. Mechanic D: Medical Sociology: A selective view. New York, Free Press, 1968
27. Idem: Religion, religiosity, and illness behavior: the special case of the Jews. Hum Organ 22:202-208, 1963
28. Fink R, Shapiro S, Goldensohn SS, et al.: The "filter-down" process to psychotherapy in a group practice medical care program. Am J Public Health 59:245-260, 1969
29. Kerckhoff AC, Back KW: The June Bug: A study of hysterical contagion. New York, Appleton-Century-Crofts, 1968
30. Bart PB: Social structure and vocabularies of discomfort: what happened to female hysteria? J Health Soc Behav 9:188-193, 1968
31. Balint M: The Doctor, his Patient and the Illness. New York, International Universities Press, 1957
32. Wolff HG: Headache and Other Head Pain. Second edition. New York, Oxford University Press, 1963
33. Hes JP: Hypochondriacal complaints in Jewish psychiatric patients. Isr Ann Psychiatry 6:134-142, 1968
34. Mechanic D, Volkart EH: Stress, illness behavior, and the sick role. Am Sociol Rev 26:51-58, 1961
35. Mechanic D: Some implications of illness behavior for medical sampling. N Engl J Med 269:244-247, 1963
36. Mechanic D, Jackson D: Stress, Illness Behavior, and the Use of General Practitioner Services: A study of British women (mimeographed). Madison, Department of Sociology, University of Wisconsin
37. Kadushin C: Individual decisions to undertake psychotherapy. Adm Sci Q 3:379-411, 1958
38. Beecher HK: Measurement of Subjective Responses: quantitative effects of drugs. New York, Oxford University Press, 1959
39. Lambert WE, Libman E, Poser EG: The effect of increased salience of a membership group on pain tolerance, J Pers 28:350-357, 1960
40. Ross L, Rodin J, Zimbardo PG: Toward an attribution therapy: the reduction of fear through induced cognitive-emotional misattribution. J Pers Soc Psychol 12:279-288, 1969
41. Blitz B, Dinnerstein AJ: Role of attentional focus in pain perception: manipulation of response to noxious stimulation by instructions. J Abnorm Psychol 77:42-45, 1971

42. Walters A: Psychogenic regional pain alias hysterical pain. Brain 84:1-18, 1961
43. Imboden JB, Canter A, Cluff LE, et al.: Brucellosis. III. Psychologic aspects of delayed convalescence. Arch Intern Med 103:406-414, 1959
44. Imboden JB, Canter A, Cluff L: Symptomatic recovery from medical disorders: influence of psychological factors. JAMA 178: 1182-1184, 1961
45. Zola IK: Problems of communication, diagnosis, and patient care: the interplay of patient, physician and clinic organization. J Med Educ 38:829-838, 1963
46. Brodman K, Mittelmann B, Wechsler D, et al.: The relation of personality disturbances to duration of convalescence from acute respiratory infections. Psychosom Med 9:37-44, 1947
47. Rickels K, Downing RW: Drug- and placebo-treated neurotic out-patients: pretreatment levels of manifest anxiety, clinical improvement, and side reactions. Arch Gen Psychiatry 16:369-372, 1967
48. Rickels K, Lipman R, Raab E: Previous medication, duration of illness and placebo response. J Nerv Ment Dis 142:548-554, 1966
49. Storms MD, Nisbett RE: Insomnia and the attribution process. J Pers Soc Psychol 16:319-328, 1970
50. Egbert LD, Battit GE, Welch CE, et al.: Reduction of postoperative pain by encouragement and instruction of patients: a study of doctor-patient rapport. N Engl J Med 270:825-827, 1964
51. Skipper JK Jr, Leonard RC: Children, stress, and hospitalization: a field experiment. J Health Soc Behav 9:275-287, 1968

5

Hypertension, Peptic Ulcer, and Diabetes in Air Traffic Controllers

Sidney Cobb
Brown University
Robert M. Rose
Boston University Medical School

It is alleged that the work of air traffic controllers is stressful and leads to excess illness, but there has been very little in the way of data to substantiate this claim. Therefore, an analysis of available periodic examination data was undertaken to test the hypothesis that certain diseases are unduly frequent in air traffic controllers, and that this undue frequency is related to the stress of the job. The study focused on a comparison between air traffic controllers and second class airmen, both of whom are required to have an annual physical examination in connection with renewal of their respective licenses. As far as could be determined for the period under study, the two groups were examined by the same set of physicians.

Nature of the Data

The Medical Statistical Section of the Civil Aeromedical Institute provided the necessary examination data on a set of magnetic tapes. From these tapes were extracted the medical data on air traffic controllers and second class airmen who met the following criteria: (1) they were men, (2) they had an examination in

Reprinted with permission of *Journal of American Medical Association*, Vol. 224, No. 4 (April, 1973), pp. 489-492.

1969 to 1970, and (3) they had at least two examinations with an apparent interval not greater than two calendar years. This made it possible to estimate point prevalence at the 1969 to 1970 examination and to estimate incidence of new cases for the interval from the preceding examination to the 1969 to 1970 examination.

The office of the air surgeon in Washington provided a tape listing 12,332 currently active journeyman air traffic controllers. From these, 5,199 individuals working in towers and centers were extracted. In matching these 5,199 to the medical record file, 874 were identified as having no matching record in the medical file as defined. Of these, 168 had no examination in the 1969 to 1970 period. Most of the others were presumably women or newly hired. This left 4,325 male journeyman air traffic controllers currently working in towers and centers with an examination in 1969 to 1970 and at least one previous examination within the preceding two years. Using the same selection rules, we ended with 8,435 second class airmen for comparison.

Problems with the Data Set

The analysis is of a group of men who had an examination at a specified time. It is not a study of a cohort of men who entered the specified occupation at a given time and were then followed up. The result is that we are dealing with unknown biases due to withdrawal from the occupation of air traffic controller or second class airman by death, failure to meet licensing standards, promotion, and transfer to other occupations.

It is possible that both diagnostic practices and licensing practices might be different for the two groups. These differences are likely to be disease-specific. Therefore, they will be discussed with respect to the individual diseases.

The distribution by age for air traffic controllers is appreciably different from that for second class airmen so all comparisons have to be made on an age-specific or age-adjusted basis. The air traffic controllers average 35.1 years and the second class airmen average 39.1 years.

As in all such data sets, there were certain inconsistencies. The inconsistent findings were by no means excessively frequent, so no attempt was made to deal with them.

Since these examinations were performed for licensing purposes, it is probable that some illness went unreported because the examinees can hardly be expected to volunteer information on the basis of which they might be disqualified for their current employment. This will have a dampening effect on the results, i.e., it will give apparent differences that are smaller than the true differences.

Plan of the Analysis

It was possible to make a serious investigation of hypertension, diabetes, and peptic ulcer. Coronary heart disease was subject to too much licensing bias and so could not be studied. Migraine, hyperthyroidism, and each of the psychiatric diagnoses occurred too infrequently to be studied; other diagnoses of interest, such as rheumatoid arthritis and ulcerative colitis, could not be separated from related diseases in the coding system used by the Federal Aviation Administration.

In order to assess the possible effects of job stress with respect to these diagnostic rubrics, it was decided to ask the following four questions:

1. Is there evidence that air traffic controllers have a greater point prevalence of disease than second class airmen? If so, is the difference likely to be due to the differences in diagnostic and licensing procedures between the two groups?

2. Is the annual incidence of new cases greater for the air traffic controllers than for the second class airmen? If so, could this be explained by a difference in diagnostic standards for the two groups, or by an unwillingness to return for examination if the diagnosis was known to the individual?

3. Is there evidence that onsets of disease occur at a younger age for air traffic controllers than for second class airmen?

4. Among air traffic controllers, is there evidence that the stress level, measured by the traffic density at the assigned station, is associated with differential prevalence of disease?

Results

Hypertension

This has long been thought of as a psychosomatic disease.[1] Elevated blood pressure has been specifically associated with emergency situations,[2] with prolonged combat duty,[3] and with job termination.[4] It is, therefore, reasonable to entertain the hypothesis that the stress of working as an air traffic controller might contribute to elevation of blood pressure and the development of hypertension.

1. The prevalence of diagnosed hypertension in air traffic controllers is about four times higher than in second class airmen. However, this difference is suspect because only 3% of hypertensive air traffic controllers are denied their licenses as opposed to 17% of hypertensive second class airmen. This is demonstrated in Table 5-1, where it can be seen that two thirds of those who are hypertensive get limited licenses, but that 31% of controllers continue with full or unlimited

Table 5-1
Frequency of License Issuance*

	License Issued			
	Unlimited	Limited	Denied	Total
No. of air traffic controllers, (%)	33 (31)	71 (66)	3 (3)	107 (100)
No. of second class airmen, (%)	13 (17)	50 (66)	13 (17)	76 (100)

*After diagnosis of hypertension is entered.

licenses, while only 17% of second class airmen are fully licensed. Furthermore, there is no evidence that there is a significantly smaller proportion of second class airmen with elevated blood pressure (systolic >140 mm Hg or diastolic >90 mm Hg) who have diagnoses of hypertension. It seems reasonable to conclude that the difference in prevalence between the two groups is exaggerated, but not enough to account for the fourfold excess of cases among the air traffic controllers.

In this connection, it should be noted that the average blood pressures by age for second class airmen closely resemble those for men accepted for ordinary insurance by the Metropolitan Life Insurance Company, though they are considerably below the averages for the general population. One recognizes, of course, that those with substantially elevated blood pressure are excluded from life insurance coverage as well as flying an airplane. The air traffic controllers' mean blood pressures significantly exceed those for second class airmen only at ages under 30. This is due, in large part, to the fact that those who are to become clearly hypertensive have not yet been weeded out or given antihypertensive medication. Despite the regulations, it would appear that men with hypertension adequately controlled by medication do from time to time receive unlimited licenses.

2. The annual incidence of hypertension in air traffic controllers is also greater than in second class airmen. As can be seen from Table 5-2, there are nearly six times as many new cases observed in the year among air traffic controllers as would be expected if the age-specific rates for second class airmen prevailed (χ^2 = 103, $P < .0001$). This cannot be explained by any differential licensing procedure, as differences in prevalence might be, but could possibly be explained by a self-selection factor. That is, second class airmen, knowing that they might not be licensed, simply would not apply for reexamination. Since it is only about one sixth of the hypertensive applicants for second class licenses who are refused, this would not seem to be very likely behavior. However, the possibility must be considered. Therefore, we looked at the inapparent cases, that is, people with blood pressures high enough to warrant treatment, but who presumably are unaware of their condition, since they are not taking relevant medication. The numbers are small but the conclusion is the same, a fourfold excess of observed cases over expected cases.

Table 5-2
Annual Incidence Rates Per 1,000 Men for Hypertension

Age Group, Yr.	Air Traffic Controllers	Second Class Airmen	
20-24	—*	—	
25-29	2	1	
30-34	2	1	
35-39	10	1	
40-44	6	—	
45-49	11	4	
50+	15	4	
		Age	
		<40	40+
Observed (O)	28.0	16.0	12.0
Expected (E)†	5.1	2.4	2.7
O/E	5.6	6.6	4.4

*The figures have been rounded off to prevent any suggestion that they are more reliable than is the case. The conventions of the National Center for Health Statistics have been used: — means the value is zero; 0 means the value is greater than zero but less than 0.5.

†Expected on the basis of multiplication of the age-specific rates for second class airmen by the relevant air traffic controller populations and summing across age groups. Statistical significance is examined by the x^2 test, assuming that the expected values represent population estimates.

3. The mean age at onset of hypertension is 41 years for this group of air traffic controllers and 48 for the second class airmen. This difference is statistically significant and is not accounted for by the difference in age between the two groups which is only four years. This same phenomenon is observable in the lower portion of Table 5-2 where it is noted that the ratio of observed to expected cases is greater for those under 40 than it is for those over 40.

4. The difference between men working at high vs low traffic density towers or centers is shown in Table 5-3. The ratio of observed to expected cases is only 1.6, but the number of cases is reasonably large, so the difference between the observed and expected cases is significant ($P < .025$). Again hypertension appears to be diagnosed at an earlier age among those under high stress as opposed to those under low stress.

In summary, it seems reasonably probable that air traffic controllers are at a higher risk of developing hypertension than are second class airmen, and that this added risk is related to working at high traffic density towers and centers. This conclusion is based on consistency of the findings, across a series of different analyses. It is also supported by the finding of Dougherty[5] that "journeyman radar ATCs" had a greater though not significantly greater

Table 5-3
Prevalence Rates Per 1,000 Air Traffic Controllers for Hypertension by Stress
Level as Measured by Traffic Density

Age Group, Yr.	High Stress	Low Stress
20-24	−*	−
25-29	4	−
30-34	6	2
35-39	12	10
40-44	26	4
45-49	51	32
50+	−	36
Observed	22.0	
Expected†	13.7	
O/E	1.6	

*See footnotes to Table 5-2.
†Expected on the basis of multiplication of the age specific rates for the low stress groups
by the relevant populations for the high stress group and summing across age groups.

prevalence of hypertension than other air traffic controllers. These findings are
all condensed in the first column of Table 5-4.

Peptic Ulcer

Duodenal ulcer, which constitutes the bulk of peptic ulcer in men, is known to
be associated with stressful circumstances such as military basic training[6] and

Table 5-4
Relation of Specified Diseases to the Demands of the Job of Air Traffic
Controller

	Hypertension	Peptic Ulcer	Diabetes
Point prevalence	*(++)4†	++2	++2
Annual incidence	++6	+2	+2
Age effect	++	+	+
Traffic density effect	++	++	NI

*++ indicates evidence is strong and significant; +, results in the predicted direction but not
statistically significant; NI, no information; (), bias may account for a portion of the effect.
†Numbers indicate the factor by which the frequency among air traffic controllers exceeds
that for second class airmen.

the role of first line supervisor.[7] The evidence from this study with respect to peptic ulcer is summarized in the second column of Table 5-4.

1. Peptic ulcer would appear to be nearly twice as prevalent among air traffic controllers as among second class airmen if there is no licensing bias (observed, 48; expected, 26.3; $P < .001$). The difference in frequency with which licenses are denied for peptic ulcer is not statistically significant, and it does not seem likely that the licensing of 99% of controllers as opposed to 96% of airmen with peptic ulcer would account for the twofold difference in prevalence. However, the estimate of the extent of licensing bias is only moderately reliable because the numbers are small.

2. The observed licensing bias is surely too small to lead second class airmen to fail to reapply for licensure because they have a known peptic ulcer. Examination of the incidence data is therefore appropriate. The numbers are too small for statistical significance, but they suggest that there is a twofold higher incidence among the controllers.

3. The bulk of the excess incidence is in the younger age groups. This implies onset at a younger age among the controllers.

4. There is a striking and statistically significant difference between the prevalence of peptic ulcer at high-stress as opposed to low-stress towers and centers (observed, 29; expected, 13.6; χ^2 = 17, $P < .001$). Again, this is particularly marked for the younger age groups.

In summary, it can be said that the evidence is consistent though not always statistically significant. It suggests that air traffic controllers are at excessive risk of developing peptic ulcer, that they develop it at a younger age than others, and that these risks are related to the stress of the job.

Diabetes Mellitus

Onsets of diabetes are reported to be associated with periods of stress,[8] particularly periods of grinding work and frustration without hope of relief.[9] The data on this subject are summarized in the last column of Table 5-4.

1. There would seem to be a threefold excess of diabetes among air traffic controllers as opposed to second class airmen, if one were to accept the simple prevalence data. In order to evaluate these data it is again necessary to investigate the licensing procedures. When this is done separately for those who have diabetes controlled by diet and for all others, it becomes clear that for those who have severe diabetes there is a serious bias, in that 80% of the second class airmen in this category are rejected while only 4% of air traffic controllers in this category are refused a license. On the other hand, for those with diabetes controlled by diet alone, the bias is trivial. For this mild form of diabetes the ratio of observed to expected cases is 2.3 (observed, 23; expected, 10; χ^2 = 17, $P < .001$).

2. The numbers are too small for the difference in annual incidence rates to be statistically significant. However, the difference is in the predicted direction and of appreciable magnitude.

3. Likewise, the age effect is in the predicted direction but not significant.

4. The numbers are much too small to permit the necessary age-specific comparison between the high- and low-density stations.

In summary, the evidence on diabetes is appreciably weaker than that on hypertension and peptic ulcer but it is sufficiently suggestive for the matter to be examined in subsequent studies.

Other

The proportion of men with any medical diagnosis other than these three diseases was examined. The ratio of observed to expected cases is 1.3 (observed, 228; expected, 179). Because the numbers are large, this difference is statistically significant. Surely some of the difference is due to some stress-related diseases that could not be separated out because of the coding procedures that were used. Though there was some evidence of a slightly greater prevalence and incidence of all disease, there was no evidence of a stress level effect among air traffic controllers. This encourages us to believe that the principal differences are among the diseases previously known to be related to social stress rather than being general across all forms of illness.

There is need for a longitudinal study that would overcome the difficulties of selective removal encountered here.

References

1. Reiser MF, Rosenbaum M, Ferris EB: Psychologic mechanisms in malignant hypertension. *Psychosom Med* 13:147-159, 1951.

2. Ruskin A, Beard OW, Schaffer RL: "Blast hypertension": Elevated arterial pressure in victims of Texas city disaster. *Am J Med* 4:228-236, 1948.

3. Graham JDP: High blood pressure after battle. *Lancet* 1:239-246, 1945.

4. Kasl SV, Cobb S: Blood pressure changes in men undergoing job loss: A preliminary report. *Psychosom Med* 32:19-38, 1970.

5. Dougherty JD: Cardiovascular findings in air traffic controllers. *Aerosp Med* 38:26-30, 1967.

6. Weiner H, et al.: Etiology of duodenal ulcer: I. Relation of specific psychological characteristics to rate of gastric secretion. *Psychosom Med* 19:1-10, 1967.

7. Dunn JP, Cobb S: Frequency of peptic ulcer among executives, craftsmen & foremen. *J Occup Med* 4:343-348, 1962.

8. Hinkle LE, Wolf S: A summary of experimental evidence relating life stress to diabetes mellitus. *J Mt Sinai Hosp* 19:537-570, 1952.

9. Dunbar F: *Psychosomatic Diagnosis.* New York, Paul B Hoeber Inc, 1943.

Stress, Acne and Skin Surface Free Fatty Acids

Stephen J. Kraus
Case Western Reserve University

Several authorities reflect the commonly held clinical impression that emotional stress exacerbates acne vulgaris.[1,2] Laboratory support for this observation, utilizing newer methods of lipid quantitation and evaluating a group of subjects large enough for statistical analysis, is not available. Therefore, the purpose of this study was to investigate the effect of one form of emotional stress on acne, by evaluating and coordinating the development of clinical acne lesions and changes in skin surface total lipids and skin surface free fatty acids (ffa). These two aspects of skin surface lipids were studied because evidence suggests that they are important in the pathogenesis of acne. For example, individuals with acne are more likely to have higher values for skin surface total lipid production than do individuals without acne.[3] Concerning the ffa, it was recently shown that improvement of acne with systemic tetracycline parallels a drop in surface ffa.[4] These fatty acids are the most irritative component of skin surface lipids and intracutaneous injection of small amounts of ffa, as compared to other surface lipids, produces a marked inflammatory response.[5]

Materials and Methods

Eight male and 1 female, first-year Case Western Reserve University medical students with a history of acne were studied. A compulsory 8-hr academic

Reprinted with permission from *Psychosomatic Medicine*, 32(5):503-508, 1970.

examination covering 10 weeks of study was used as the stressful situation. Skin surface lipids were collected before, during and after the examination period. Western Reserve students receive one examination every 10-12 weeks and are not under constant stress from frequent testing.

One student had been taking vitamin A for acne. This was stopped 2 weeks before the start of the study. No other systemic acne therapy was used prior to nor at any time during the study. No local acne therapy was used for 1 week prior to collections. The students, who washed with Ivory soap throughout the study, were instructed not to use cosmetic preparations containing antibacterial substances.

Both total lipid and ffa collections were made on 2 consecutive days 3 weeks before the examination, 2 days before the examination, 2 days before and 2 weeks after the results were published. On collection days, the students washed their faces in the morning and collections were made at the same time each evening for each subject.

The technic for collecting skin surface total lipids was adapted from the procedure used by Kirk and Chieffi.[6] A 36.4 sq cm area on the cheek was washed three times with 20 ml reagent grade acetone introduced into a glass cylinder held against the skin. The boundary of the washed area was delineated with a marker containing a lipophilic dye. This marker allowed the observer to visually detect the migration of surface lipids into the cleaned area. Three hours later, the central 27.4 sq cm of the larger area was examined for evidence of this migration; if free of such lipids, the area was washed three times with 15 ml reagent grade acetone. These latter washings were filtered through lipid-free paper, evaporated into micro weighing bottles, desiccated over $CaCl^2$ and olive oil, and then weighed to constant weight. The ability of acetone washings to remove surface lipids was shown when lipid removed by three additional acetone washings of the 27.4 sq cm area was consistently less than 3% of that removed by the first three washings.

The technic for collecting and measuring ffa has been outlined in detail.[7] A 14.5 sq cm area on the forehead was washed three times with spectroquality acetone introduced into a glass cylinder held against the skin. The boundary was outlined with the dye marker and the same precautions taken to exclude lipid migration. Three hours later, the central 5.2 sq cm area was washed twice with 3 ml of an acidified heptane-isopropyl alcohol mixture. These latter washings were combined and water soluble acids removed by aqueous extractions. The residual acids were measured by a nonaqueous titration system using tetrabutylammonium hydroxide as the titrant. The effectiveness of the heptane-isopropanol mixture in removing surface ffa was determined by applying 0.5 μEq oleate-1-^{14}C to the skin and then determining the radioactivity in the heptane-isopropanol mixture used to wash the area of oleate-1-^{14}C application. By comparing this radioactivity to that of 0.5 μEq pure oleate-1-^{14}C, the amount of ffa recovered was found to be 93 and 94% in 2 subjects studied.

Surface ffa collections were done in 7 subjects. Inability to seal the collection cylinder tightly against the forehead prevented ffa collections in the other 2 subjects.

The study was designed to fit Rothman's suggestion: if the influence of any factor on excretion of fatty acids is to be examined, tests should be done on the same individual or the same group of individuals in pre-experimental and experimental conditions.[8] The students acted as their own controls. In an attempt to minimize any effect the environment (temperature, humidity, wind, etc.) might have on skin surface lipids, there were control periods both before and after the period of stress. Controls for each subject were values obtained from two collections 3 weeks before the exam and two collections 2 weeks after test results were announced. Stress values were those obtained from collections immediately before the examination and before examination results were announced. Each subject, therefore, had four control values for skin surface total lipid production and skin surface ffa production, and four stress values for the same measure of surface lipids.

Acne lesions were clinically evaluated by counting the number of postules in a 6 X 6 cm area on both cheeks. Comedones and papules were not enumerated and cystic lesions were not encountered during the course of this study. The control value for each subject was the mean number of pustules present 3 weeks before the examination and 2 weeks after the results were announced. Stress values were the means of the number of pustules present immediately before the examination and before the results were announced.

Results

Table 6-1 presents the mean and standard deviation of each subject's four control and four stress values for skin surface total lipid and skin surface ffa production. Table 6-2 summarizes surface total lipid data; here changes are expressed as percentage increase or decrease of stress values from control values. Table 6-3 summarizes ffa data in a similar manner.

An analysis of variance was used for statistical evaluation of data. A significant increase in skin surface ffa production was observed during the period of stress ($p < 0.005$). No significant change in surface total lipid production was observed during the same period ($p > 0.1$). At the time this study was conducted, another experiment measuring the same parameters of surface lipids was being done in a group of normal adult men. The control group in this latter study received nothing known to alter surface lipids. Their surface lipid values were organized according to the same time intervals as the stress and control periods of the student experiments. No significant change in either surface ffa or surface total lipids occurred during the time surface ffa rose in the medical students.

Table 6-1

Mean Control and Stress Values for Skin Surface Total Lipid Production and Skin Surface Free Fatty Acid Production

Subject	Values	Total Lipid (mg/27.4 sq cm/3 hr) Mean (SD)	Free Fatty Acid (μEq/6.2 sq cm/3 hr) Mean (SD)
1	C	8.4 ± 0.7	.547 ± .080
	S	7.2 ± 0.3	.627 ± .101
2	C	3.9 ± 0.4	
	S	4.0 ± 0.3	
3	C	3.8 ± 0.2	.282 ± .057
	S	3.6 ± 0.5	.335 ± .037
4	C	4.2 ± 0.7	.735 ± .148
	S	4.6 ± 0.5	.911 ± .154
5	C	3.4 ± 0.3	.136 ± .025
	S	3.0 ± 0.3	.179 ± .036
6	C	3.2 ± 0.4	
	S	2.9 ± 0.1	
7	C	6.9 ± 0.4	.223 ± .055
	S	6.0 ± 0.1	.318 ± .108
8	C	5.4 ± 0.3	.708 ± .179
	S	5.4 ± 0.2	.857 ± .200
9	C	1.4 ± 0.4	.069 ± .034
	S	1.5 ± 0.3	.082 ± .037

C, control; S, stress.

Three of the 9 students had pustules during the control period of the study. These 3 had an increase in number of pustules during the period of stress. Of the 6 students free of pustules during the control period, 5 developed several pustules during the stressful period. The increase in these acne lesions was statistically significant ($p < 0.01$, Sign Test). Since this study did not follow other acne lesions, no conclusions can be drawn concerning the effect of stress on comedones and papules.

An incidental finding was the considerable variability of total lipid and ffa values from 1 subject to another. An analysis of variance showed this variation among individuals to be highly significant ($p < 0.0005$ for both ffa and total lipid).

Discussion

Academic examinations have been used in previous studies on the biologic effects of stress;[9,10,11] stressfulness of examinations is well documented in the

Table 6-2
Effect of Stress on Total Skin Surface Lipid Production

Production Change	No. of Subjects	Average Change (% of Control Values)	Range (%)
Increase	3	6	4-8
Decrease	5	11	5-14
Unchanged	1	–	–

Table 6-3
Effects of Stress on Skin Surface ffa Production

Production Change	No. of Subjects	Average Change (%)	Range (%)
Increase	7	22	19-42
Decrease	0	–	–

psychiatric literature.[12] The study reported in this paper showed such an examination was associated with increase in skin surface ffa and exacerbation of acne. Although a cause-and-effect relationship was not established, this and other indirect evidence suggest that these ffa may play a major role in acne pathogenesis. For instance, others have reported improvement of acne with systemic tetracycline which parallels a fall in skin surface ffa.[4]

The way in which ffa may exacerbate acne is unknown, but it is known that ffa are the most irritating component of skin surface lipids; intradermal injection of these acids produces a marked inflammatory response.[5] A similar phenomenon may exist in acne when rupture of the sebaceous follicle release lipids into the dermis. These follicular lipids contain ffa and possibly the greater the amount of ffa, the greater the inflammatory response.

The mechanism by which emotional stress is related to rise in skin surface ffa was not studied and cannot be determined from our data. Possible explanations may be related to other stress-induced biologic alterations such as changes in systemic lipid metabolism, changes in bacterial flora of the skin or changes in adrenal function.

Systemic lipid alterations with stress include elevation of plasma ffa.[9] This rise in plasma ffa is inhibited by ganglionic blocking agents, so it is likely that increased activity of the autonomic nervous system is involved. The relation of plasma ffa changes to skin surface ffa changes is not known.

Emotional stress is associated with increased sweating. Profuse sweating, which interferes with the self-sterilizing power of normal skin,[13] is accompanied by a transient rise in bacterial flora of normal skin.[14] Such a rise could account for increase in surface ffa since bacterial lipase activity plays a role in formation of ffa from sebum triglycerides.[15] The importance of increased bacterial flora in the increase in ffa observed in this study is difficult to ascertain since no attempts were made to evaluate changes in our subjects' skin flora.

With stress, adrenal corticosteroids are released in increasing amounts and steroid acne is a well recognized entity; however, the role of corticosteroids is unknown in ffa changes in our report.

Statistical analysis of changes in skin surface total lipid did not show a significant change during the time of stress. This finding does not necessarily contradict the data published by Wolff et al.[16] and Pochi et al.[17] The former reported 3 subjects in whom an increase of facial sebum occurred during acute periods of stress. One of these subjects demonstrated a correlation between the number of acne pustules and periods of mood alteration. The technic employed by Wolff et al. for sebum quantitation was adapted from that developed by Jones et al.[18] This method attempts to measure sebum by the degree to which it displaces a hydrocarbon film on a watery surface. Further evaluation of this procedure revealed that displacement of the hydrocarbon film was not a function of total sebum, but was directly related to the total amount of ffa in the sebum.[19] Total sebum values could be extrapolated from hydrocarbon film displacement only if the ffa content of sebum were constant; it has recently been shown that there is considerable variability in the ffa concentration of sebum.[20] The data of Wolff et al. therefore showed increase in skin surface ffa during emotional stress rather than increase in total sebum. Such an interpretation of their data makes their results consistent with the findings reported in this study.

Pochi et al.[17] found that a woman's sebum production increased after the death of her mother. In addition to increased surface lipids, they detected an increase in urinary 17-ketosteroids. The stress was felt to have increased production of adrenal corticosteroids including androgenic compounds; these in turn stimulated the sebaceous glands to produce more surface lipids. Others have documented the increase in urinary 17-ketosteroids with stress,[21] and it is known that adult female sebaceous glands will respond to increase in androgen activity.[22]

Failure of this study to demonstrate a significant alteration in surface total lipids does not necessarily contradict the finding of Pochi et al. An important difference exists between our group of students and the patient they report; their study was done on a woman and, of the 9 students in our study, 8 were men. Such a difference in sex distribution may be important, since the normal degree of androgenic stimulation for sebaceous glands to produce surface lipids is different for the two sexes. Adult male sebaceous glands are normally under maximal stimulation by androgens.[22] Skin surface lipid production of men will therefore not respond to extra androgens; in this way, surface lipid production in adult males differs from that in adult females. If increased adrenal androgen was the stimulus for increased surface lipids in the woman studied by Pochi et al., the same stimulus would not be expected to increase surface lipids in the men reported in this study. Although it is an isolated observation, the 1 female student in this study did show increase in surface total lipid production during the period of stress.

Summary

A prospective study was initiated to evaluate the commonly held clinical impression that emotional stress can exacerbate acne vulgaris. The number of experimental subjects participating in the project facilitated a statistical evaluation of observations made during the study. Emotional stress, provided by an academic examination, was accompanied by increase in number of acne lesions ($p < 0.01$). The stressful experience and acne exacerbation were associated with increase in skin surface free fatty acid production ($p < 0.005$). Although this study does not establish a cause-and-effect relationship between acne and skin surface free fatty acids, it adds to other indirect evidence which suggests that these fatty acids may play a role in the pathogenesis of acne.

References

1. MacKenna RMB, Cohen EL: Dermatology. Baltimore, Williams and Wilkins, 1964, p. 238
2. Pillsbury DM: Dermatology. Philadelphia, W.B. Saunders, 1957, p. 805
3. Pochi PE, Strauss JS, Rao GS, et al.: Plasma testosterone and estrogen levels, urine testosterone excretion and sebum production in males with acne vulgaris. J Clin Endocr 25:1660, 1965
4. Freinkel RK, Strauss JS, Yin Yip S, et al.: Effect of tetracycline on the composition of sebum in acne vulgaris. New Eng J Med 273:850, 1965
5. Strauss JS, Kligman AM: The pathologic dynamics of acne vulgaris. Arch Derm (Chicago) 82:779, 1960
6. Kirk JE, Chieffi M: The 20-minute rate of sebaceous secretion in the forehead. J Invest Derm 27:15, 1956
7. Kraus SJ: Quantitation of human skin surface total free fatty acids. J Invest Derm 51:497, 1968
8. Rothman S: Physiology and Biochemistry of the Skin: Chicago, University of Chicago Press, 1954, p. 314
9. Boddonoff MD, Estes EEH, Harlan WR, et al.: Metabolic and cardiovascular changes during a state of acute central nervous system arousal. J Clin Endocr 20:1333, 1960

10. Grundy SM, Griffin AC: Relationship of periodic mental stress to serum lipoprotein and cholesterol levels. JAMA 171:1794, 1959

11. Dreyfuss F, Czaczkes JW: Blood cholesterol and uric acid of healthy medical students under the stress of an examination. Arch Intern Med 103:708, 1959

12. Mechanic D: Students Under Stress. New York, The Free Press of Glencoe, 1952

13. Rebell G, Pillsbury DM, de Saint PM, et al.: Factors affecting the rapid disappearance of bacteria placed on the normal skin. J Invest Derm 14:247, 1950

14. Evans CA, Smith WM, Johnston EA, et al.: Bacterial flora of the normal human skin. J Invest Derm 15:305, 1950

15. Scheimann LG, Knox G, Sher D, et al.: The role of bacteria in the formation of free fatty acids on the human skin surface. J Invest Derm 34:171, 1960

16. Wolff HG, Lorenz TH, Graham DT: Stress, emotions and human sebum: their relevance to acne vulgaris. Trans Ass Amer Physicians 64:435, 1951

17. Pochi PE, Strauss JS, Mescon H: The role of adrenocortical steroids in the control of human sebaceous gland activity. J Invest Derm 41:391, 1963

18. Jones KK: A micro method for fat analysis based on formation of monolayer films. Science 111:9, 1950

19. Harber LC, Herrmann F, Mandol L, et al.: Lipid studies of the human skin surface by means of the monomolecular layer method. J Invest Derm 29:55, 1957

20. Downing DT, Strauss JS, Pochi PE: Variability in the chemical composition of human skin surface lipids. J Invest Derm 53: 322, 1969

21. Cope CL: Adrenal Steroids and Disease. Philadelphia, Lippincott, 1964, p. 225

22. Strauss JS, Kligman AM, Pochi PE: The effect of androgens and estrogens on human sebaceous glands. J Invest Derm 39:139, 1962

Social
Correlates of
Heart Disease

Commentary. Contrary to expectations, the longevity rates for males in Western industrialized societies has decreased in the last five years. This decline can be partially attributed to an increased rate of heart attacks among younger men; a rate which has been steadily rising for two decades (American Heart Association, 1972). For men between 25 and 44, the coronary death rate has increased 14 percent since 1950. The mortality for men between 45 and 64 has increased 4 percent. Thus, as Jean Mayer points out: "We are again in the age of the great pandemics. Our plague is cardiovascular."

It is clear that one major risk factor is membership in the male sex. Heart attacks are five times more common among men than women before the menopause. After the menopause coronary disease rates are only slightly less for women. Other major risk factors extensively studied are heredity, high levels of fats in the blood such as cholesterol and triglycerides, high blood pressure, cigarette smoking, obesity, and lack of exercise. Each of these variables has been shown to be related to the risk of suffering a heart attack. However, despite extensive research these variables fail to adequately predict which people are likely to develop heart disease. In an extensive review of populations having extremely low rates, for example, Bruhn and Wolfe (1970) found these risk factors high in many groups in which heart disease was rare.

What directions of research in this area are likely to bear better predictive fruit? There is a growing awareness that psychosocial factors may play a vital role in the etiology of heart disease, and thus one is beginning to find more important research in social and ecological frameworks.

One important study by Caffrey (1968) examined the social environments of Trappist and Benedictine monasteries. Ratings were based on the coronary-prone behavior pattern, to be discussed later, in which type A behavior is characterized by competitiveness, ambition, aggressiveness, and a profound sense of time urgency. Conversely, type B behavior is more relaxed and placid.

The results of this study indicated that Benedictine monasteries, in which a higher rate of coronary heart disease was found, were rated by four judges as possessing an environment that was likely to foster type A behavior. This is a particularly important finding since the results imply that there are social environments that may encourage the development of disease processes.

Among the first investigators to recognize the vital role of social factors in heart disease were Ray Rosenman and Meyer Friedman, who demonstrated that the coronary-prone behavior pattern (type A) was prevalent among heart disease victims in a ratio of 2 to 1 compared with type B subjects.

In the first chapter in this section, Rosenman and Friedman suggest that social factors operating through the central nervous system may play a significant role in coronary heart disease. They explain in detail the kinds of behavior a type A person might exhibit. The type A person, for example, is extremely punctual and greatly annoyed if kept waiting; he has few hobbies; routine jobs at home are bothersome since he feels he can spend his time more profitably. He walks rapidly and eats quickly and attempts to do several things at one time. He is impatient and often anticipates what others will say, frequently interrupting before questions or replies are fully completed. Many type Bs, of course, have some of these characteristics; however, according to Rosenman and Friedman these qualities are greatly intensified in the type A person.

In Chapter 8 John French and Robert Caplan examine some of the interactions between man and his environment, and relate them to heart disease. Among the variables studied are the relationships between person-environment fit and blood pressure. Subjects with "good fit" had low systolic and diastolic blood pressures, while "poor fit" was significantly related to high systolic and diastolic blood pressure. The authors also report significant relationships between types of job stress and other risk factors in heart disease.

If a relationship between a stressful environment and heart disease exists, what happens in a nonstressful or supportive environment? In Chapter 9, by Clarke Stout et al., the Italian-American community of Roseto, Pennsylvania was studied over a period of seven years and found to have a strikingly low death rate from heart disease. This low rate apparently occurs in spite of the "typical risk factors." In fact, obesity, a high consumption of calories, fat, and wine, was characteristic of Roseto compared with five surrounding communities where the death rate from myocardial infarction was more than twice that of Roseto.

The authors suggest that people in Roseto live in an environment with trusting and supportive neighbors and that this social milieu may be contributing to their good health. Genetic or inherited factors are also important, since good health seems to run in families. However, documented deaths from heart disease at younger ages among men born in Roseto indicated that they lived most of their lives elsewhere, suggesting again that the environment plays an important contributory role.

The last chapter in this section suggests that the social environment may play an important role in the sudden death of industrial workers. William Greene et al. obtained detailed information from many sources, including the industrial plant medical records, next of kin, and private physicians of patients who died suddenly. Analysis of the data suggests that prior depression from one week to several months were common to all subjects. In addition, subjects were exposed to increased work pressure and situations in which anger or anxiety reactions may have produced hormonal as well as central nervous system mediated behavior conducive to sudden death.

References

Bruhn, J.G., and Wolfe, S. Studies reporting "low rates" of ischemic heart disease: A critical review. *American Journal of Public Health, 60*:1477-1496, 1970.

92

Caffrey, B. Reliability and validity of personality and behavioral measures in a study of coronary heart disease. *Journal of Chronic Disease, 21*:191-204, 1968.

7

The Central Nervous System and Coronary Heart Disease

Ray H. Rosenman
Meyer Friedman
*Mount Zion Hospital and
Medical Center, San Francisco*

Q. Do you often have the feeling that time passes much too fast for you to accomplish what needs doing each day?
A. I have felt that way constantly for the past several years.

Q. Are you impatient when someone does a job slowly that you could do faster, enough to step in and try to do it yourself?
A. Always.

These two questions are among a total of about 20 or so comprising a structured interview we have been using to explore the role of certain emotions, as expressed in overt behavior, in the genesis of coronary heart disease. More from the manner of response to interview questions than from their actual content it has been possible to identify a rather specific behavioral complex that appears to enhance risk of development of premature coronary disease and that acts independently of some of the other, traditional, risk factors. (From the replies cited plus various other reactions, the respondent above could be classified as coronary-prone.)

A relationship between emotions and transient cardiovascular changes is one readily perceived by most physicians; admittedly, many find it more difficult to

Reprinted with permission from *Hospital Practice*, October, 1971, pp. 87-97.

accept the concept that lasting changes in both structure and function may also have a similar basis. Yet the evidence strongly suggests that emotional and behavioral factors operating through the central nervous system may play a major pathogenetic role in coronary heart disease. Although still under exploration, the evidence to date already indicates that this possibility must be taken into account as part of ongoing programs to control coronary risk factors. Otherwise, morbidity and mortality associated with premature coronary disease may well continue at their current high level despite measures to alter diet and lower serum lipids.

If coronary heart disease was a comparative clinical rarity until the 20th century, the probability is that the accelerated coronary atherosclerosis underlying its development was also a rarity. Epidemiologic studies have clearly shown that the increased occurrence both of severe coronary atherosclerosis and of coronary heart disease has essentially been restricted to populations both industrially and socially advanced.

The impact of traditional coronary risk factors—hyperlipidemia, hypertension, heavy cigarette smoking, and the like—is beyond dispute, and the intent here is not to minimize their importance. Their role has been demonstrated consistently in all prospective epidemiologic studies including ours, initiated a decade ago in California with more than three thousand middle-aged men (39 to 59 years old) as participants. Myocardial infarction or angina pectoris has indeed occurred with significantly increased frequency among men who at intake had elevated blood pressure, elevated serum lipid and lipoprotein levels, diabetes, and a parental history of coronary disease, and who were heavy cigarette smokers. The combination of two or more of these findings further enhanced the risk.

However, despite their acknowledged role, the traditional risk factors must not be oversold. In our prospective study population—no exception in this regard—factors such as hyperlipidemia and hypertension have been present in only a minority of subjects at intake, and also in only a minority of those who have since developed coronary heart disease. Indeed, most subjects considered at higher risk on the basis of such classic factors still remain free of clinical disease after a decade, and a considerable incidence of clinical disease has occurred in subjects not exhibiting the traditional factors at intake. In actuality, while prospective studies have permitted identification of traits that increase susceptibility to coronary disease, the findings unfortunately are predictive only for *groups* of people and lack individual specificity.

Our own interest in these questions dates back at least 15 years, to our then growing conviction that dietary patterns and serum lipids did not provide sufficient explanation by themselves for the observable rise in coronary morbidity and mortality during recent decades. For one thing, studies up to that point (and many since) had omitted consideration of other findings that might also be operative, for example, social and economic forces affecting people's lives. Actually their importance had been forecast more than 70 years ago by Osler in

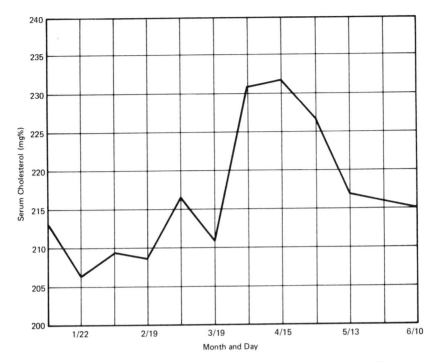

Figure 7-1. Impact of Socioeconomic and Psychological Stress Factors on Serum Cholesterol Levels is Evident in Sharply Increasing Values Recorded in a Group of Tax Accountants as April 15 Deadline Neared for Filing Tax Returns. Values Promptly Declined as Pressure Eased.

his comment that "in the worry and strain of modern life, arterial degeneration is not only very common but develops at a relatively early age. For this I believe that the high pressure at which men live and the habit of working the machine to its maximum capacity are responsible rather than excesses in eating and drinking." Since other explanations did not fully account for the increased occurrence of coronary disease, perhaps the interplay of external stresses and individual response to their challenge might prove to be a controlling factor.

To begin investigation of the role of social and environmental conditions, we measured serum cholesterol levels biweekly for six months in a group of accountants when they were beset by tax deadlines, as well as before and after when they were under far less pressure. Cholesterol levels were much higher during the period of deadline pressure, independent of changes in diet or physical activity. Serum lipid levels were later also found by others to go up in other temporarily stressful situations, for example, in medical students facing major examinations. It seemed of importance, next, to study a larger group of men not seasonally but chronically stressed, especially since clinical experience had alerted us to certain personal and behavioral traits that might increase vulnerability to external pressures. These traits were by then seen so often in middle-aged and younger coronary patients that we felt they could be considered quite typical.

The emotional interplay, subsequently termed Behavior Pattern Type A, comprises a rather specific combination of personality traits including ambition and competitive drive, aggressiveness, impatience, and a strong sense of time urgency. To be sure, these are traits present to varying degrees in most men in today's world; the type A man has them to an enhanced, often excessive, degree. Our concept, then as now, was that pattern A arises in a subject more or less perpetually involved in a struggle in which he is determined to persevere. Sometimes the struggle is with other individuals he feels are out to best him; more often he is "at war" against time, racing to attain his perhaps unattainable goals before his chance runs out. The busy clinician can understand this ongoing time pressure and sense of time urgency. The type A individual is not coronary-prone by personality alone. His problems arise because the environment presents a challenge he feels impelled to overcome. In other words, it is the interaction of the susceptible type A personality and the modern environment that evokes the specific pattern of overt behavior associated with increased risk of coronary heart disease. The type A individual's "coat of arms" might well feature a clenched fist wearing a stopwatch.

We sought to evaluate the pathogenetic effect of behavior type A in a group of men exhibiting it in extreme form. For comparison we set up a converse group, designated type B, of men who manifested extreme passivity and lack of drive, and also a group beset by chronic anxiety and insecurity because of a severe physical handicap, blindness, since these emotions are not characteristic of type A men. The first two groups were recruited at their place of employment by lay selectors asked to choose subjects most closely fitting the two contrasting patterns; 96% of the men chosen agreed to cooperate.

As a group, the type A men had much higher serum cholesterol levels, shorter blood clotting times, and increased prevalence of arcus senilis. More significant was the far greater frequency of coronary heart disease in the type A men as compared with the other two groups. Twenty-three of 83 type A men were found to have definite symptoms or ECG evidence of clinical coronary disease, as against 3 of 83 type B men and 2 of 46 in the chronically anxious group of blind men. Comparisons of dietary intake of calories and fat, smoking habits, and exercise patterns revealed little variation in any of the three groups. Moreover, whatever was responsible for the type A behavior pattern, it obviously was not confined to any single socioeconomic group since men at both high and low job levels were included among those showing typical A behavior.

As these studies proceeded, the presence of type A behavior proved to be

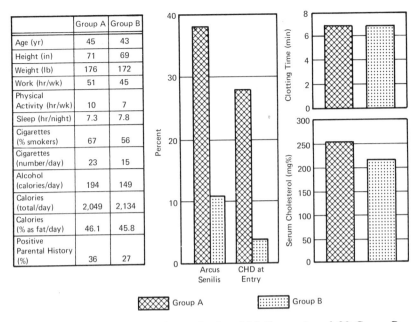

	Group A	Group B
Age (yr)	45	43
Height (in)	71	69
Weight (lb)	176	172
Work (hr/wk)	51	45
Physical Activity (hr/wk)	10	7
Sleep (hr/night)	7.3	7.8
Cigarettes (% smokers)	67	56
Cigarettes (number/day)	23	15
Alcohol (calories/day)	194	149
Calories (total/day)	2,049	2,134
Calories (% as fat/day)	46.1	45.8
Positive Parental History (%)	36	27

Figure 7-2. In 1959 Prevalence Study of 83 Group A and 83 Group B Subjects, Men in Each Group were Essentially Comparable in Age, Weight, and Dietary Habits (table at left); however, the Incidence of Pre-existing Clinical Coronary Disease and of Arcus Senilis was Significantly Higher in Group A (graph at center). On the Average, Serum Cholesterol Levels for Group A Men were also Noticeably Higher.

related to the prevalence of coronary heart disease in other groups investigated, including women as well as men, and also with other biochemical correlates of coronary heart disease, including elevated triglyceride and beta and pre-beta lipoprotein levels as well as cholesterol. Type A subjects tested during their working day also consistently showed increased catecholamine excretion.

If type A behavior and its concomitants played a significant role in the advent of coronary heart disease, then their presence in individuals free of disease should have useful predictive value. Pursuing that important question would require systematically following a large enough group of subjects classified prospectively as coronary-prone on the basis of behavior pattern. Such a study was initiated by our research group in 1960-61 with some 3,500 men aged 39 to 59 at intake, employed in 10 California companies. Collaborating investigators in Los Angeles classified the men prospectively on the basis of serum lipoproteins (beta/alpha lipoprotein ratio); data on blood coagulation were obtained by other collaborators then in San Antonio.

Our earlier work had convinced us that an oral interview administered by trained personnel would be the best approach to behavioral typing. This would

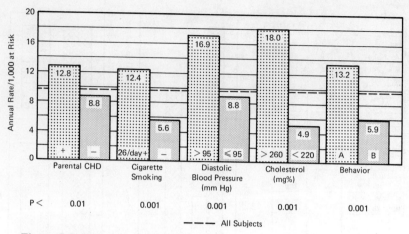

Figure 7-3. When, at the 8½ Year Mark, the Annual Incidence of Coronary Disease Among the Study Population of Approximately 3,500 Men was Classified According to Presence of Risk Factors at Entry, the Contribution of Group A Behavior Pattern does not Appear at First Glance to be Quite as Great as that of Elevations in Blood Pressure or Serum Cholesterol. However, Analysis of Incidence by Behavior Pattern in Addition to Traditional Risk Factors Yielded the Findings shown in the Graphs on Page 95.

allow assessment of both the intensity and emotional overtone of responses, usually more revealing in distinguishing A from B than the actual words used in answering the structured questions. The subject's motor behavior—gestures, grimaces, and other "body language"—is also readily evident. Emphatic, often explosive, replies are typical of the type A person; his voice, for example, is loud and at times even hostile in tone. In his impatience he anticipates what others will say, including the interviewer, and frequently interrupts to answer questions before they are fully asked.

Interview questions were designed in part to elicit angry and aggressive feelings, both past and present, as well as the degree of drive and ambition throughout a subject's working life, and above all his sense of time urgency, since this factor more than any other appears to intensify and sustain the type A pattern. As his responses indicate, the type A person is invariably punctual and greatly annoyed if kept waiting; he rarely finds time to indulge in hobbies, and when he does, he makes them as competitive as his vocation. He dislikes helping at home in routine jobs because he feels that his time can be spent more profitably. He walks rapidly, eats rapidly, and rarely remains long at the dinner table. He often tries to do several things at once and carries a second line of thought if he can possibly manage it. Admittedly, some type B subjects may reply similarly to certain interview questions, but differences in tone and mood usually are unmistakable.

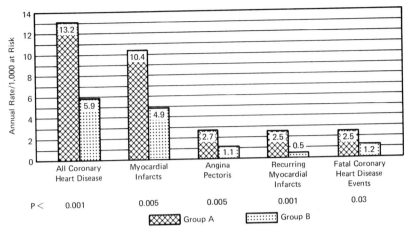

Figure 7-4. After 8½ Years of Follow-up the Incidence of New Coronary Disease Events in the Study Population was Found to Run at Least Twice as High Among Group A as Among Group B Subjects; a Similar Relationship Applies when Cases are Classified as to Type of Heart Disease. Moreover, in the Presence of Type A Behavior, the Risk of Recurrence of Myocardial Infarction is Markedly Increased; in Addition, there is a Definite Trend to Type A Behavior in Cases of Myocardial Infarction that Terminated in Death.

In the procedure followed in the prospective study, all intake interviews were tape-recorded and the recordings, plus descriptive information provided by the interviewers, were used by us for behavioral typing. To insure against bias neither of us met any of the study subjects ourselves or had access to other information about them; behavioral typing was based on interview data alone. The intent was not to single out extreme forms of the two behavior patterns, as in the earlier prevalence studies, but rather to identify type A and type B behavior more broadly as each might occur in the general population. Hence, subjects strongly exhibiting type A behavior were classified as A-1, the remainder in the A group as A-2; similarly, subjects exhibiting type B behavior in clearest form were classified as B-4, the others as B-3. As learned then, and since confirmed, some 10% of urban, employed subjects are likely to be type A-1, another 10% type B-4. The majority exhibit either type A or type B behavior to a lesser degree, but nevertheless enough for classification.

The behavioral type arrived at for each man in the prospective study, along with information on serum lipoproteins and blood coagulability obtained by the collaborating groups, was funneled directly to an independent data repository committee; other material obtained at intake, including medical and family history, diet, exercise, and smoking habits, anthropometric data, and cardiovascular findings, was also entered in the data bank.

From the outset, type A behavior proved strongly associated with clinical coronary disease. Preexisting coronary disease was found at intake in 113 of the 3,524 subjects. A type A classification had been given to 70.9% of these men (and to 52.0% of the total group). By the end of 1963 (after a mean interval of 2½ years) 70 of 3,182 subjects then at risk had developed coronary heart disease (52 were cases of myocardial infarction, 9 of them fatal; the remainder were angina pectoris). Before developing coronary heart disease these men had shared many similarities with the unaffected group, e.g., dietary and exercise patterns were similar, as were smoking habits. Mean serum cholesterol and triglyceride levels were somewhat higher in coronary cases: 249 mg% vs 224 mg% for cholesterol; 159.6 mg% vs 147.7 mg% for triglycerides. More coronary men (27.1% vs 9.4%) had an elevated diastolic blood pressure. A far greater proportion had been classified as coronary-prone on the basis of behavior pattern (85.2% vs 47.0% of all subjects aged 39 to 49 at intake and 72.1% vs 57.9% of all those aged 50 to 59). Significantly, while the presence of hypercholesterolemia or hyperbetalipoproteinemia or both clearly increased the risk of coronary disease, this effect was much less obvious in subjects who had been classified as type B in behavior. Similarly, though there was a threefold greater incidence of new coronary disease in men with preexisting hypertension, almost all hypertensives who developed heart disease had exhibited type A behavior before the latter became manifest. It became clear that elevated diastolic blood pressure or serum lipids (or both) carried major prognostic significance only when they occurred in association with type A behavior. These relationships continued to apply as the study continued.

Within a mean follow-up period of 4½ years, 133 of the men developed clinical coronary disease (acute myocardial infarction in 104). Behavior pattern proved significantly related among younger men in particular: In the 39-to-49 year age group 71.5% of the heart patients came from the type A group. In the disease-free group the two behavior types were about equally represented.

A separate analysis was done on cases of clinically unrecognized infarction, either present at intake or occurring in the follow-up period. (There had been 42 such cases detected at intake; at the 4½-year mark, 31 of the 104 new infarction cases were of the "silent" type.)

Comparison with age-paired non-coronary subjects revealed significant differences, again most marked for younger men. In the 39-to-49-year age group, men developing unrecognized infarction significantly more often reported a parental history of coronary disease, had elevated serum triglycerides and elevated systolic blood pressure, and were heavy smokers; 71.4% had been classified as type A in behavior, as compared to 46.4% of age mates without heart disease. It seemed noteworthy that in this younger age group the frequency of unrecognized infarction was not significantly increased among men exhibiting diastolic blood pressure above 94 mm Hg, nor among subjects who had serum cholesterol levels exceeding 259 mg%. Rather, the risk factor that appeared with greatest frequency was the type A behavior pattern; from the evidence, both in reference to clinically evident and silent heart disease, it appeared to operate independently of blood pressure, serum lipid or lipoprotein levels, cigarette smoking, parental history, or any of the other factors under study.

It was felt, however, that further statistical testing was necessary to ensure that the predictive power of type A behavior could not be "explained away" by its association with classic risk factors often also present. With bivariate analysis, it was shown that the impact of type A behavior remained despite statistical control of another risk factor such as elevated serum cholesterol or parental history of coronary heart disease. Subsequently, a multiple regression procedure was used to control a broad series of effective risk predictors simultaneously; the impact of the coronary-prone behavior pattern remained highly significant. In the 39-to-49 age group, the coronary disease risk of type A proved to be twice that of type B men when serum lipids, blood pressure, smoking, obesity, and several other influences were all held constant. In the older (50 to 69) group, type A men were still at increased risk, although the differences were no longer as significant.

By the 6½-year mark, clinical heart disease had developed in 195 of the 3,182 subjects; 139 of the 195 had been classified at intake as exhibiting type A behavior. The increased incidence of coronary disease in type A men continued to prevail when behavior pattern again was stratified by "high" or "low" values for other risk factors. By this study, the coronary disease incidence for type A men with a "low" value for some other risk factor was found to approximate the incidence in type B men with a "high" value for the same factor. With multiple risk factors in addition to type A behavior, the latter could still have an overriding effect.

At latest count, after 8½ years, 257 men in the prospective study have experienced clinical heart disease; the impact of type A behavior as a risk factor continues to be unmistakable. To be sure, the effect was greater in the early prevalence studies, in which the coronary disease rate was seven-fold higher among type A subjects; in the prospectively followed population, which includes a range of type A and type B behavior instead of only the extreme forms, the incidence of heart disease is two to three times higher among type A subjects, still surely enough of a difference to warrant concern.

If type A behavior were associated not only with occurrence of coronary heart disease but with risk of recurrence it would of course be important to know that too. Hence the prospective study data were analyzed to compare findings in recurring and nonrecurring infarction; the critical question of whether the risk of fatal infarction was increased was also investigated. These analyses were done at the 4½-year point; of the 104 new cases of myocardial infarction to that time, 23 had been fatal; 13 of the 104 men had had a second episode. Comparison of younger men with recurring and nonrecurring infarction showed a higher frequency of serum lipid elevation and type A behavior in the former prior to either the first or second attack; in older subjects only the higher frequency of diastolic hypertension proved statistically significant.

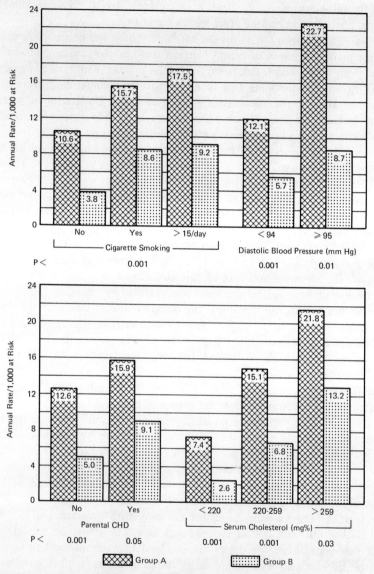

Figure 7-5. The Apparent Overriding Effect of Type A Behavior is Reflected in Coronary Disease Incidence Rates After 8½ Years of Follow-up of Subjects who had been Rated "High" or "Low" at Entry in Reference to Traditional Coronary Risk Factors. As can be seen, Incidence Rates Among Type A Men Free of One or Another Risk Factor May Approximate or Even Exceed Those Among Type B Men Rates "High" for the Same Risk Factor.

Among men with fatal vs nonfatal infarction, higher serum lipid values proved to be the chief distinguishing feature; there was a trend to more type A behavior in fatal cases but this difference was not statistically significant. Clearly, though, in both fatal and nonfatal cases, type A behavior was far more frequent than among men remaining free of heart disease.

At the 8½-year follow-up in which 257 men had experienced clinical morbidity, 41 had suffered two or more myocardial infarctions and 50 had suffered fatal coronary events. Type A behavior had been classified prospectively in 34 of the 41 subjects with recurring coronary events and in 34 of the 50 subjects suffering fatal coronary events. At this point the much higher incidences of recurring and of fatal coronary events in type A men was highly significant statistically.

From the epidemiologic evidence, then, the presence of type A behavior carries profound prognostic import, particularly for younger men, in terms of occurrence of coronary disease as well as its outcome. From what we now know it seems safe to say that serious coronary disease will occur infrequently before the age of 60 or thereabouts in the absence of type A behavior, except in subjects with diabetes, hypertension, or more marked hyperlipidemias. The behavioral assessment increases the predictive value of other risk factors; if it is not included, then no matter how large the population sample or how carefully other entities are studied, the probability exists of serious error in evaluating risk.

It must be made quite clear, however, that from a practical viewpoint the findings do not permit use of behavior typing to predict occurrence of coronary heart disease in a given patient. Type A behavior, like any of the other risk factors identified thus far, has been detected in many more subjects remaining free of heart disease than in those affected by it. Nevertheless, a considerable incidence of clinical disease still occurs in type A individuals not exhibiting any of the other classic risk factors. A physician observing these factors, behavior included, can only advise a patient that he has a higher risk of coronary disease than the average individual his age. He cannot yet be more definite.

On the other hand, one can with more certainty predict relative immunity to premature coronary heart disease in a subject with fully developed type B behavior. An analysis done after 4½ years of our prospective study convinced us that a B-4 type middle-aged man manifesting normotension and low values for two or more of the lipid entities (serum cholesterol below 226 mg% and either triglycerides below 126 mg% or a beta/alpha lipoprotein ratio below 2.01) could be given rather definite assurance that he would not incur coronary heart disease at least within the ensuing 4½ years. Subsequent follow-up studies indicate that such prediction for the type B-4 man can safely be extended for a longer period. In contrast, no combination of low lipid or blood pressure values permits similar assurance of men exhibiting type A behavior.

Our method of behavioral typing utilizing the taped personal interview has

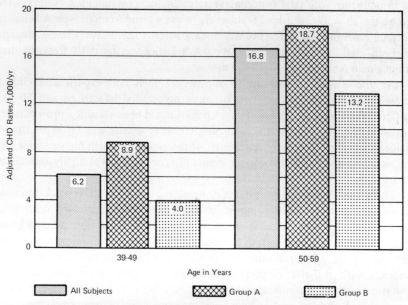

Figure 7-6. With Statistical Control of a Broad Series of Other Coronary Risk Factors by Means of a Multiple Regression Procedure, the Predictive Power of Type A Behavior Persisted, Especially Among Younger Men in the Study Group. Among Men in the 39-49 Year Age Group at Entry, the Coronary Disease Risk was at Least Twice that Among Type B Men of the Same Age. Older Men Manifesting Type A Behavior were also at Increased Risk Although the Difference here was Less Significant. The 12 Risk Factors Held Constant in this Analysis (made after 4½ years of follow-up) Included (among others) Hypercholesterolemia, Hypertension, Excessive Cigarette Smoking Obesity, and Parental History of Coronary Disease.

yielded a high degree of agreement among evaluators (in the range of 85% to 90%); moreover, results are reproducible over an extended period. Nonetheless, we have also been searching for other, more objective, methods in which the subjective role of the rater becomes less critical. One such approach is a "voice analysis" test wherein a graphic record is obtained of the rhythm, tone, and timing of the subject's speech. Most type A and type B subjects can be differentiated by use of this test and it is now considered a useful adjunct.

Until recently our work on the role of behavior and emotional factors in coronary disease had received little confirmation elsewhere; independent assessment of our approach by several other investigators has now begun to provide corroboration. For example, using our interview procedure, Quinlan, Barrow, et al. found the prevalence of myocardial infarction in Benedictine and Trappist monks to be four times higher in men classified as type A than in comparable type B men. Angina pectoris was twice as prevalent. Earlier, employing their own psychological technique, Brozek, Keys, and Blackburn could readily distinguish the potential heart disease victim among men prospectively followed during a 14-year period. The former exhibited a higher activity drive, was more likely to be "on the go" and to "speak, walk, write, drive, and eat fast even when he does not have to do so," a quite accurate description of our type A individual. In a pertinent Swedish study, Liljefors and Rahe obtained psychosocial histories on identical twins discordant for coronary disease. They found significant intrapair differences for the category of "life dissatisfactions" as well as total psychosocial score; in contrast, correlations run on subjects' medical history, smoking habits, cholesterol levels, and the like proved inconsistent and generally insignificant.

To be sure, none of the epidemiologic correlations permit conclusions as to whether the relationship between behavior and heart disease is causal or merely associative. As our prospective investigation proceeded, we attempted to answer an important basic question related to a possible causal relationship: Does type A behavior accelerate the atherosclerotic process in the coronary arteries? An autopsy study performed after 5½ years yielded relevant information on this point. By then there had been 82 deaths—40 from heart disease and 42 from other causes; coronary arteries of 51 of the victims were available for study of the relationship between the nature and severity of atherosclerosis present at death and the type of behavior manifested during life. Eighty-five percent of the men dying of heart disease were found to be type A in behavior; moreover, regardless of cause of death or age group, type A victims were found to have a greater degree of underlying coronary atherosclerosis. This was demonstrated by grading severity of coronary atherosclerosis on a 6-point scale; in younger men the average grade of atherosclerosis in the right and left coronary arteries was 2.5 and 3.1 respectively in type A and 1.8 and 2.0 in type B subjects. In the older age group, the respective averages were 3.5 and 3.8 in type A and 1.8 and 1.9 in type B.

Concerning the possible mechanisms whereby behavior pattern might accelerate atherosclerosis, our earlier findings linking fully developed type A behavior and various biochemical correlates of coronary heart disease could of course have a bearing. In further work, we have also seen that type A subjects as compared with type B manifest a significantly increased insulin response to glucose. As before, this cannot be ascribed to differences in age, weight, habits of physical activity, or dietary intake. Although the role of these abnormal lipid and insulin responses in pathogenesis is not known, other laboratory observations may have a bearing.

Earlier experiments in rabbits suggested that the hypothalamus may be the crucial area of the central nervous system through which the damaging behavior pattern is expressed; our more recent observations have strengthened our belief that this may be so. The experiments showed that electrical stimulation of the diencephalon prompted significant elevation in plasma cholesterol levels. Efforts were then made to determine the precise region of the hypothalamus responsible for the serum lipid increase by creating discrete electrolytic lesions. In rats, it was found that destruction of nuclei in the anterior portion of the hypothalamus did not alter concentration of cholesterol in plasma; neither did isolated destruction of the ventromedial, dorsomedial, or arcuate nuclei. However, chronic hypercholesterolemia almost invariably resulted from lesions involving the fornix, the medial portion of the lateral hypothalamus, and either the ventromedial or dorsomedial nucleus. Interestingly, the affected animals have been markedly altered in behavior, specifically showing greater activity and aggressiveness.

Precisely how the hypothalamic lesions induce hypercholesterolemia remains to be determined; it is notable, though, that while a diet rich in cholesterol intensified the effect, it was also seen in animals on a diet low in cholesterol.

Whether the hypothalamic lesions raise the serum cholesterol by somehow interfering with normal turnover of dietary cholesterol, or whether hormonal changes occur as the result of the effect of the hypothalamic lesions on the pituitary or other endocrine glands are questions now being explored. Whatever the basis for this type of hypercholesterolemia, clearly the experiments point up the importance of the central nervous system and in particular the hypothalamus in regulating serum cholesterol levels.

At this juncture we would conclude that the hypothalamus surely provides part of the mechanism whereby behavior alters lipid levels; however, we are not convinced that the lipid abnormalities and their atherosclerotic effects will provide the sole explanation for the cardiovascular findings observed. Conceivably the increased catecholamine discharge in type A individuals could also intensify the atherosclerotic process. Conceivably, too, the increased discharge could cause arterial damage associated with increased deposition of thrombogenic elements. The known influence of catecholamines on clotting mechanisms suggests this as a possibility.

That emotional and behavioral factors such as we have been describing lead in some way to organic changes in the coronary vasculature now seems to us well demonstrated, even if all the mechanisms involved have yet to be fully clarified. Surely from the evidence already in hand, the suggestion that such factors are of little influence in development or acceleration of coronary heart disease is no longer tenable. On the part of researchers and clinicians both, a behavioral assessment should be included in efforts to prevent coronary heart disease by controlling risk factors. As of now, more investigators are at least considering the possibility that the way a man lives may be as important as what he eats in increasing his vulnerability to heart disease. This is an encouraging sign.

8

Psychosocial Factors in Coronary Heart Disease

John R.P. French, Jr.
Robert D. Caplan
University of Michigan

Despite the seeming complexity and size of modern organizations we still find that single individuals often exercise critical influence in terms of the unique expertise and understanding they develop in their particular roles. It takes months, even years before a top administrator or a scientist fully begins to understand all of the subtle, yet important nuances that surround his work. When such a valuable person, a human asset, dies before retirement, the organization suffers a valuable loss (one that to this day we are unable to measure in dollars or in accomplishment of the mission). No amount of financial insurance can reimburse an organization against such loss, particularly under conditions where there are deadlines to be met and little time to train replacements. Under such conditions, and they appear to be more frequent in the fast-moving modern world, the best form of insurance is to prevent premature death among the members of the organization. Coronary heart disease is one of the most prevalent forms of pre-retirement death in modern organizations. The aim of our current research is to contribute to such insurance by identifying risk factors in coronary heart disease which will be useful in preventive medicine.

Over the past 20 years, evidence has mounted suggesting that the incidence of

Reprinted with permission from *Industrial Medicine*, Vol. 39, No. 9 (Sept. 1970), pp. 383-397.

heart disease varies from one broadly-defined social condition to another (socio-economic class, blue vs. white collar, rural vs. urban) and from one occupation to another. If we ever hope to be able to prevent or reduce the incidence of coronary heart disease within an organization, however, we must turn our attention to attributes of the environments that are more specific than social class or occupation. We cannot prevent heart disease by eliminating those social classes or occupations that have a high risk. However, if we can identify those particular job stresses that produce the risk, then we may be able to reduce these stresses and thus control the disease. What is called for, then, is a more sophisticated and refined look at the job environment and all of the forces that act upon the individual that may lead to certain breakdowns in his natural functions—and perhaps to illness and death.

This report of our research for NASA presents some of the more specific psychosocial factors related to heart disease. Our basic approach in carrying out this research is depicted in Diagram A. The horizontal arrows represent hypothesized causal relations. We assume that coronary heart disease, represented in the box on the right of the diagram, is caused by several factors that act upon and influence one another in a variety of ways.

We know from a wealth of medical research that there are certain well-known risk factors, closely tied in with the physiology of the person, that increase his chances of having heart disease. These are represented in the second panel from the right. Smoking, blood pressure, cholesterol, serum uric acid, and glucose have all been suggested as risk factors in heart disease. We have included heart rate, not because it is a well-known risk factor, but because it does show changes

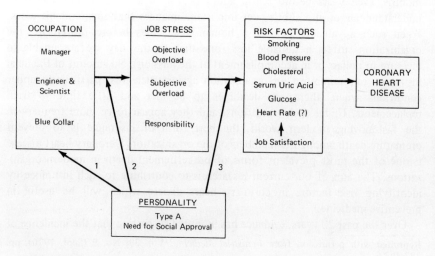

DIAGRAM A: How could we Explain the Occupational Differences in CHD?

under stress. We also include job satisfaction as a risk factor here. Its inclusion is based upon our new findings which we shall discuss shortly.

Further to the left in Diagram A we find the next panel presenting job stresses. We are hypothesizing in this model that certain types of job stresses cause certain changes in the risk factors. Thus, under stress a person may smoke more and his blood pressure and cholesterol may go up. In talking about job stress, we must differentiate between objective and subjective stress. Objective overload is stress that actually occurs in the person's external environment. For example, if a man receives too many phone calls and office visits this may constitute one sort of objective overload. Subjective overload, is a stress that exists solely within the individual—it is how much work load he *feels* he has, how much of a burden or pressure he believes he is under. Our previous research at NASA has shown that it is important to distinguish between these two types of overload. For, although subjective and objective overload are somewhat correlated (that is, people do feel overloaded when they actually have more phone calls than is normal), these two types of overload may have different effects on the risk factors listed in the adjacent panel.

As an example, in a study of 22 white collar men at NASA we found that pulse rate was primarily a function of subjective overload while cholesterol level was a function of both subjective and objective overload. To the medical practitioner this means that one must have an understanding of not only the actual work load of the patient, but of his subjective feelings about the work load as well.

Another type of stress we are considering here is responsibility. Wardwell and Bahnson (1964) have suggested that mere responsibility is not the crucial stress but responsibility for other individuals—the responsibility one has for the welfare and actions of other human beings. On the other hand, responsibility for non-person-oriented aspects of work such as for budget, equipment, and projects should not increase coronary risk according to the responsibility hypothesis.

Occupation is another major variable included in our model. As we have already noted, there have been many studies published in medical journals indicating that the incidence of heart disease tends to vary by occupation (see Marks, 1967 for an excellent review of the literature in this area). Our reason for including occupation in the far left panel of Diagram A is to indicate that different occupations may be characterized by different types of stresses. The job of administrator may have one type of responsibility while the job of engineer or scientist may have another. Similarly, we would expect that blue collar jobs also have their unique forms of occupational stress. Each of these different forms of job stress might affect the risk factors in a somewhat different manner. With this type of differentiation we can begin more specifically to explain global differences between occupational groups in incidence of coronary heart disease.

Table 8-1 presents some data that reveal the nature of such occupational

Table 8-1

Occupational Differences in Disease at Three NASA Installations Combined

Prevalence of Disease	Age 35-44			Age 45-54		
	Trade, Craft, Tech.	Manager	Engineer Scientist	Trade, Craft, Tech.	Manager	Engineer, Scientist
Size of Sample	174.0	272.0	598.0	219.0	350.0	537.0
% with Cardiovascular Disease	2.9	2.9	0.5	3.2	5.7	2.2
		n.s. P = .01			n.s. P = .02	
		P = .02			n.s.	
% with Hypertension	10.3	8.8	7.9	14.2	13.1	12.7
		n.s. n.s.			n.s. n.s.	
		n.s.			n.s.	

differences and their relationship to cardiovascular disease at NASA. These data were gathered from three NASA installations by Jean Mockbee, a statistician from the Occupational Medicine Division at NASA Headquarters.

Looking at the 35-44 year old age group we see that the trade, craft, and technician employees, who are primarily blue collar, have the same prevalence of cardiovascular disease as do managers (2.9%). Furthermore, their rate of disease is almost six times as high as it is for the engineers and scientists whose prevalence is only 0.5%. The engineers and scientists have a significantly lower rate of cardiovascular disease. Turning to the 45-54 year old age group, we again see that the engineers and scientists have the lowest prevalence (2.2%) when compared with the managers (5.7%) and the blue collar group of trades employees (3.2%). Mrs. Mockbee informs us that when the data are broken down into five-year rather than ten-year intervals, the findings remain essentially unchanged.

Table 8-1 also presents the prevalence of hypertension for each of these three occupational groups. While the differences between the groups are insignificant, it is interesting to note the trend in both age ranges. The trade, craft, and technician group has the highest prevalence of hypertension (10.3, 14.2), followed by the managers (8.8, 13.1), with the scientists and engineers being lowest (7.9, 12.7).

Now let's turn to another panel in Diagram A, the one at the bottom that refers to the individual's personality. Over the past 15 years a number of studies have been published suggesting that persons with coronary heart disease tend to differ in disposition and temperament from persons who do not have coronary heart disease. These studies have led medical researchers and psychologists to wonder whether or not such personality differences also existed in these individuals prior to the onset of myocardial infarctions and other overt manifestations of coronary heart disease. Perhaps there is a coronary-prone personality.

The most extensive and well-known studies of the coronary-prone personality to date have been carried out by Drs. Friedman, Rosenman, and their colleagues. As part of the Western Collaborative Groups they have shown that one can predict coronary heart disease on the basis of the Type A behavior pattern. The Type A personality (as contrasted to Type B) is characterized as hard-driving, ambitious, having a sense of time urgency, upwardly mobile, engaging in multiple activities, being somewhat impatient, being somewhat aggressive or hostile, and tending to prefer job pressure and deadlines.

Friedman, Rosenman et al. have shown that the Type A personality also tends to have elevated serum cholesterol levels, elevated triglycerides and beta-lipoproteins, decreased blood clotting time, elevated daytime excretion of norepinephrine, and capillary ischemia in conjunctival tissue. Such a wealth of findings makes it hard to ignore Type A as a relevant syndrome.*

Another personality variable of interest is the need for social approval. Traditionally, measures of this need have been included in psychological research in order to detect the tendency of a person to bias his response to a questionnaire by giving only socially desirable answers.

While we include the measure here for the same reasons, we also have some additional motives. First, we expect that persons high on need for social approval may experience more strain during deadlines and under heavy job pressure. Under such pressures they may feel that the opportunities for them to fail at their work are greater. Furthermore these persons high on need for social approval would feel doubly threatened by failure since it would mean to them that their superiors, colleagues, and subordinates might withhold the social approval and esteem they desire so much. Thus, our second use for this measure is as an indicator of an important need that influences the person's reactions to his social environment.

Another reason for including the measure has derived from some striking findings which suggest that (a) job stress and risk factors correlate with one another quite differently for persons who are high versus persons who are low on the need for social approval, and (b) physiological risk factors correlate with one another quite differently for persons who are high versus persons who are low on the need for social approval. As an example of the latter case, day norepinephrine and day epinephrine were correlated with one another in two groups of employed blue collar men from a company in Michigan. One group of men was high on the need for social approval (as measured by the Crowne-Marlowe scale) while the other group of men was low on the need for social approval. The

*The reader is referred to the appendix for a selected bibliography covering this and related studies of risk factors in coronary heart disease.

correlation between norepinephrine and epinephrine for the group high in need for social approval was −0.22 but the correlation between norepinephrine and epinephrine for the group low in this need was +0.32. Thus, there is a positive relation in one group and an inverse relation in the other group, and the difference between these two groups is statistically significant. At present, we can make no clear interpretation of what these differences mean, but they certainly are striking and demand further attention.

Referring to Diagram A once more, you will note that we have suggested several channels by which personality variables could lead to coronary heart disease. First of all, on the far left we note arrow Number 1 from personality to occupation. Personality may influence heart disease via occupational choice. For example, the coronary personality may be more likely to seek out the high risk administrative job rather than the job of engineer or scientist. And, perhaps, the coronary personality who finds himself in an engineering job takes steps to move into a more administrative job.

Another channel through which personality may have its effect is in mediating the relationship between one's occupation and the stress one experiences in that occupation. This effect is represented by arrow Number 2. To give an illustration, a manager when objectively overloaded may be more likely to experience subjective overload because he is a Type A personality. Similarly, Type A scientists may be more likely to experience subjective overload than Type B scientists when objectively overloaded.

A third channel by which personality might have some effect on coronary heart disease is represented by arrow Number 3. While job stress may cause changes in risk factors such as cholesterol and number of cigarettes smoked, such changes are perhaps more likely to occur if the person is Type A rather than Type B. Overall we have a picture of personality as a variable that effects many levels in our hypothesized chain of events leading to coronary heart disease.

For the physician interested in heart disease prevention, one implication of the already available research on heart disease is that it may be just as important to find out about the personality of the individual as it is to find out about his work, how he views his work, and his blood pressure, cholesterol, and glucose levels. Knowledge of the person's standing on all of the variables may allow the physician (or the personnel officer of an organization) to provide additional help and counseling to the person trying to make decisions about future steps in his career development (e.g., should he continue as a manager, or should he change jobs).

If we look back on the more conventional approaches to studying heart disease we find that when one combines information about all the physiological variables plus the Personality Type A, only about 20% of the variance in coronary heart disease is accounted for. Eighty percent of variance is still unexplained. Recently, however, we have discovered some new findings relating job satisfaction to coronary heart disease that may account for some of the unexplained variance.

As part of a dissertation carried out by Dr. Stephen Sales, subjects were experimentally subjected to conditions of overload and underload. Pre-experimental and post-experimental blood samples were taken and analyzed for serum cholesterol. One of the findings of the study was that people most dissatisfied with the task showed the highest increases in cholesterol. This suggested that job satisfaction might be related to coronary heart disease.

Support for this relationship between job satisfaction and coronary heart disease was obtained by comparing these two variables across eighteen occupational groups. For each occupation we had a mean job satisfaction score derived from previous studies of job satisfaction in these occupations. We also had for each of these occupations the standard mortality ratio of coronary heart disease. Heart disease was defined as rubric 4200 of the International Classification of Diseases. The latter figures came from Public Health Service statistics. The findings are illustrated in Figure 8-1.

These findings show that job satisfaction and coronary heart disease are correlated −0.49 across eighteen occupational groups. Furthermore, the relationship is higher and in the same direction for both the nine blue collar groups and the nine white collar groups (note that the blue collar groups tend to be less satisfied with their jobs suggesting that their rate of heart disease is higher). Of course, these correlations are based on aggregate statistics and are presumably larger than the parallel correlations for individuals might be.

Some additional research, using the same heart disease data, has been carried out by James House from The University of Michigan. His findings suggest that the type of motivation one has for working may be related to the risk of developing coronary heart disease. These latter findings are based on nine occupational groups and are illustrated in Figure 8-2. The data show that the more the members of an occupational group are motivated to work for extrinsic

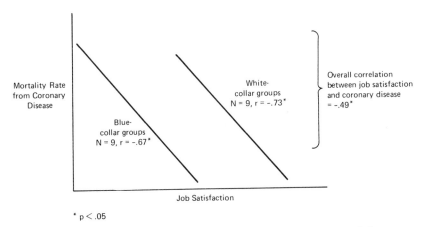

Figure 8-1. Relationship Between Job Satisfaction and Rates of Coronary Deaths (Rubric 420.0) in Eighteen Groups of Employed Men.

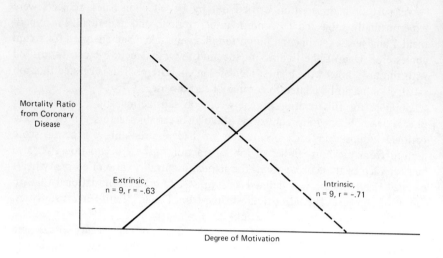

Figure 8-2. Relationship Between Motivation and Rates of Coronary Deaths in Nine Groups of Employed Men.

rewards, such as for pay and prestige, the higher is that group's mortality ratio for coronary heart disease ($r = 0.63$). This relationship between extrinsic motivation and coronary heart disease rate is represented by the solid line in the Figure. Intrinsic motivation, however, is inversely related to coronary heart disease. The higher the motivation to work for intrinsic rewards, such as for the enjoyment one gets out of the work itself, the lower the standard mortality ratio for coronary heart disease ($r = -0.71$). These findings are impressive in the sense that they account for roughly 36% to 49% of the variance in mortality ratios. They are especially relevant to occupational medicine since the findings link motives to work with coronary heart disease.*

Now let us turn to our current project at Goddard Space Flight Center. The main purpose of this project is to explain the fact, already presented in Table 8-1, that managers have higher rates of cardiovascular disease than do engineers and scientists. Our general strategy will be to describe the research methods used in our most recent studies and then present the results. Finally, we shall discuss some implications of our findings for preventive medical programs.

*We are currently carrying out studies of the relationships of extrinsic and intrinsic satisfaction to coronary heart disease. The findings are similar to those for extrinsic and intrinsic motivation although it appears that there are slightly different relationships between these satisfactions and heart disease for blue collar as compared to white collar workers.

Method

Sample

Three occupational groups of male employees from Goddard Space Flight Center—administrators, engineers, and scientists—were selected for the study. A person was initially defined as being a member of one of these three groups according to his job title in the personnel rosters of Goddard.

Next, administrators and engineers were each divided up into two additional groups. These groups were as follows:

a) Administrators in administrative environments
b) Administrators in engineering environments
c) Engineers in engineering environments
d) Engineers in administrative environments.

This breakdown was made in order to study potential fit and misfit between a person's job and the person's job environment. Where the job was similar to the job environment, as in (a) and (c) above, we said that a potential fit might be present. Where the job was different from the job environment, as in (b) and (d) above, we said that potential misfit might be present. We would then see whether the potential fit groups would report lower job stress and lower levels of cholesterol and other coronary heart disease risk factors than the potential misfit groups.

Since we formed these subgroups before actually determining the work environment of the person, we used the following definition of job environment. We defined an administrative environment as that environment where, according to the personnel records of Goddard, there existed the highest ratio of administrators to engineers using the division as the unit of environment. Likewise, we defined the engineering environment as the environment where there existed the highest ratio of engineers to administrators.

While we could find no scientists working in either administrative or engineering environments, we included the scientists in the study because of their NASA record of low rates of coronary heart disease, smoking, obesity, job absence, and other potential risk factors in heart disease.

Thus, we ended up with five groups for study: two groups of administrators, two groups of engineers, and the scientists. Our next step was to randomly sample out 70 men in each of the five groups to form a pool of potential volunteers for the study. Letters were then sent out to these 350 men informing them of the study and indicating that our laboratory assistant from The University of Michigan would probably be contacting them to see if they wished to participate.

Our assistant then visited 285 of these men in their offices asking them if they would be willing to participate in the study which required a blood sample of them, measures of blood pressure and pulse rate, and the filling out of a lengthy questionnaire. If the person agreed to volunteer, two readings of diastolic and systolic blood pressure and two readings of pulse rate were obtained. Then 30 ml of blood was drawn. The volunteer was then handed the questionnaire and told to complete it as quickly as possible and return it to The University of Michigan by mail in the enclosed stamped, pre-addressed envelope. Eighty-nine percent of those contacted agreed to participate in the study. The average age of the men who participated was forty years old with two-thirds of the group falling between thirty-four and forty-seven years of age. Eighty-three percent of those who volunteered returned the questionnaire. Thus, we have physiological data on 253 men and questionnaire data on 211 of those volunteers.

An option for all volunteers was to further participate by having their secretaries keep a tally of their phone calls, office visits, and meetings. This, we hoped, would be continued on an hourly basis for three days. Our preliminary interviews and pretests at Goddard had led us to believe that while many employees did not have their own secretaries, there was a possibility that some volunteers who did have such resources would use them in our study. Twenty-five men did agree to have such tallies taken. These men came almost exclusively from the subgroup of administrators in administration. We shall have more to say about them later.

The blood that was drawn in each volunteer's office was immediately spun to serum and frozen for subsequent shipment to The University of Michigan's Institute for Social Research. There, it was thawed and a number of analyses were carried out (cholesterol, serum uric acid, casual glucose, etc.) in a modern laboratory using automated and highly controlled analysis equipment such as the AutoAnalyzer.

The questionnaires were then coded, and all data were transferred to magnetic tape for analyses on the computer facilities of the Institute. We shall now turn to some of the results of these analyses.

Results

The findings that will now be reported should be considered preliminary because our analyses are not yet completed. First, we shall present results that bear on previous NASA findings relating overload to physiological measures of stress. Then, we shall present some of our preliminary work on personality variables that may relate to coronary heart disease. Finally, we shall consider some of the data that relate to differences between administrators, scientists, and engineers in the current study.

As already noted, in our earlier study of 22 men at NASA Headquarters, we found that objective work load as measured by the number of phone calls and office visits a person received per hour was positively correlated with subjective quantitative work load ($r = 0.64$). We then went on to relate these measures of objective and subjective work load to our physiological variables, pulse rate and serum cholesterol level. Pulse rate and cholesterol level were unrelated. We found that pulse rate was primarily related to subjective quantitative overload rather than to objective work load ($r = 0.68$). We further found that cholesterol was related to both objective and subjective work load ($r = 0.43$ and $r = 0.41$, respectively). In the current study we have measures of these same variables.

Objective quantitative overload has been measured in a similar way as in our earlier study. We have determined for each of the 25 persons on whom we have work tallies, the number of phone calls, office visits, and meetings they had per hour. Unlike the previous study, we find no correlation between this measure of objective work load and our same measure of subjective work load ($r = 0.02$, n.s.). This finding suggests that perhaps one's subjective impression regarding work load is more independent of the actual amount of work load than we had previously thought. We must, however, use caution in interpreting this finding since there are other measures of objective and subjective work load not related to one another. We shall discuss these measures shortly.

In the present study we also find that pulse rate does not correlate with objective or subjective quantitative work load although it was expected to do so ($r = 0.17$, n.s.; and $r = 0.04$,, n.s., respectively). Serum cholesterol level also fails to correlate with these objective and subjective measures of work load ($r = -0.30$, n.s.; and $r = 0.01$, n.s., respectively). Pulse rate and cholesterol are unrelated as in our previous study ($r = 0.14$, n.s.).

This failure to replicate our previous findings leads us to believe that the analyses may not have uncovered certain moderator variables that are important in distinguishing between the characteristics of the earlier sample from NASA Headquarters and the present sample of men from Goddard. For one thing, we may have a serious sampling problem regarding our measure of objective work load. In the Headquarters study, 96% of the men contacted agreed to have a tally made of their work. In this study less than 10% contacted agreed. Thus, the data relating to objective overload measures should be treated with caution.

Second, our method of obtaining pulse rate in these two studies has been markedly different. In the study of the 22 Headquarters men, pulse rate was based on averages taken over three-hour periods. In the present study, 30-second samples were taken two times within a minute or so of one another as an estimate of pulse rate. Since pulse rate is highly labile, it is conceivable that we were measuring some reaction to the test situation rather than some sample of pulse rate on the job. This suggests that we may have to return, in future studies, to the more careful measuring of pulse using our telemetry equipment.

At present we are still exploring some hypotheses about the failure of cholesterol to relate to our overload measures. These hypotheses include possibilities that seasonal variation may serve to attenuate certain relationships between cholesterol and subjective and objective quantitative work load. We have data from Goddard health examinations that show striking changes in cholesterol over the twelve months of the year with peaks in cholesterol value during November through January and troughs in March through July. The difference between peaks and troughs was 42 mb/100 ml. The present study was carried out in April and May. The previous study was carried out in June through August.

While our findings on cholesterol and pulse rate are negative so far, we do have some interesting positive findings to present with regard to cigarette smoking, a well-known risk factor in coronary heart disease.

Cigarette Smoking

Cigarette smoking has been one of the much publicized risk factors in coronary heart disease. In our study at Goddard, we asked persons to indicate the actual number of cigarettes they smoke in a typical day. The participants in the study who do smoke report smoking an average of 24 cigarettes per day. The data we shall now present are for only those persons who smoke one or more cigarettes per day. Those who smoke no cigarettes are excluded since they would skew the distributions if included.

Some interesting results present themselves when we compare the persons who had their secretaries keep a tally of their work load with those persons who did not have a secretary keep a tally. Specifically, 44 out of 189 or 23% of the non-tally volunteers returning the questionnaire smoke. By contrast, 11 out of 25 or 44% of the volunteers who had secretaries keeping tallies for them smoke. The differences in the proportions of persons who smoke in these two groups are statistically significant (x^2 = 3.94, $p < 0.05$). But, why the striking difference?

Earlier we noted that most of the volunteers for the tally part of the study are administrators. Perhaps administrators smoke more. While administrators tend to smoke more than engineers and scientists, the differences are minimal (x^2 = 2.77, n.s.).

Another possibility is that tally volunteers having secretaries, also have higher formal status with its accompanying responsibilities than do non-tally volunteers. While this may be so, we find that formal status as measured by G.S. level and salary, shows no relationship to the number of cigarettes a person smokes. Therefore, it must not be formal status which accounts for these differences in smoking among tally and non-tally volunteers.

With regard to responsibilities, however, we find quite a different picture. Table 8-2 presents the average percent of time tally and non-tally volunteers report spending in various responsibilities. We see here that on three of the responsibilities there are significant differences between the two groups. Tally

Table 8-2
Mean Percent of Time Spent Carrying Out Various Responsibilities by Tally and Non-Tally Volunteers

Type of Responsibility	Tally	Volunteer Non-Tally	$p <$
Work of others	40.2	27.4	0.01
Others' futures	15.6	7.0	0.001
Money	11.8	9.6	n.s.
Equipment	3.6	9.1	0.05
Projects	29.2	51.6	n.s.

volunteers report spending 40.2% of their time being responsible for the work of others while non-tally volunteers report that this responsibility takes up on the average only 27.4% of their time. This difference is significant at the 0.01 level. Tally volunteers also spend over twice as much time in responsibilities having to do with others' futures as do the non-tally volunteers: 15.6% compared to 7.0%. This difference is significant at the 0.001 level. While both tally and non-tally persons spend less than 10% of their time on responsibilities for equipment the tally persons do spend significantly less time: 36% of the time as compared to 9.1% of the time. These findings are interesting in light of the responsibility hypothesis we mentioned earlier. The hypothesis predicts that person-oriented responsibilities such as for another person's work and future should be related to heart disease while object-oriented responsibilities such as for budgets, equipment, etc., should be unrelated to heart disease.

Now the crucial question is do any of these responsibilities on which these two groups differ also relate to cigarette smoking? When we look at the data in Table 8-3, we find that this is indeed the case. The percent of time spent carrying out responsibility for the work of others correlates 0.31 ($p < 0.05$) with number of cigarettes smoked. The percent of time spent in responsibility for others' futures correlates non-significantly but in a positive direction, 0.08. Responsibility for money, equipment, and projects also correlates non-significantly but negatively with number of cigarettes smoked.

Overall, the set of findings suggests that the reason the tally volunteers smoke more is because they have more person-related responsibilities than the non-tally persons. Whether having more of these types of responsibilities makes one tend to volunteer more often for such tallies remains to be seen. Perhaps, having a secretary who can observe one's activities for three days is a luxury provided to persons with more of the types of responsibilities we have just been describing.

Another preliminary interpretation of these findings is that persons who do smoke do tend to volunteer for more activities. This interpretation is consistent with the notion that persons who smoke are also persons who seek stimulation

Table 8-3

Correlation Between Percent of Time Spent in Various Responsibilities and
Number of Cigarettes Smoked*

Responsibility for	r
Work of others	0.31**
Others' futures	0.08
Money	−0.22
Equipment	−0.19
Projects	−0.08

*For persons smoking 1 or more cigarettes per day.
**$p < .05$.

or arousal, smoking being an oral form of such arousal. Indeed, studies of college
students who volunteer for psychology experiments show that the volunteers
score higher on measures of arousal-seeking than non-volunteers and that
arousal-seeking is a central factor in tobacco smoking among college students
(Schubert, 1964, 1965). Such persons could be expected to take on more
activities, perhaps even overload themselves intentionally to provide more
stimulus inputs from their work environment. It is also possible that smoking
could act as a stimulant arousing the person to seek out even more stimuli and
work.

We cannot tell with the present data whether cigarette smokers are more
likely to overburden themselves with work as part of the same arousal-seeking
behavior that causes them to smoke or whether smoking causes them to seek
arousal and in the process overburden themselves. Nevertheless, we do have
additional data showing that persons who smoke more seem to be more
overloaded in their work.

Using data drawn from the tallies kept by the secretaries, we find that
objective quantitative overload and number of cigarettes smoked for persons
smoking one or more cigarettes per day are positively related ($r = 0.58$,
$p < 0.05$). In other words, persons with more phone calls, office visits, and
meetings per given unit of work time also smoke more cigarettes than persons
with fewer phone calls, office visits, and meeting per given unit of work time.

Cigarette smoking also correlates positively with the person's report of a
tendency toward environmental overburdening ($r = 0.36$, $p < 0.01$). Environmental burdening is a cluster developed in earlier research carried out by
Stephen Sales as part of a study aimed at developing a personality measure of
behavior Type A. Sales defines environmental burdening in his cluster of items
as: "The reported presence of the subject in an environment in which he
experiences chronic objective quantitative overload. Reported exposure of the

subject to constant deadlines, deadline pressures, and job responsibility." In other words, the environmental overburdening cluster from the Sales measure of Type A is a measure of subjective quantitative overload. In fact, environmental overburdening correlates 0.44 ($p < 0.01$) with our subjective quantitative overload factor.

Another interesting characteristic of smokers is that they score high on a cluster that measures their feeling of impatience about the extent to which their profession and NASA is advancing knowledge and accomplishing goals. Typical items in measuring "impatience with advancement of the profession" express dissatisfaction with statements such as (a) the *rate* at which technological developments are occurring in your field. (b) the *pace* at which the profession, field, or area is developing. Persons who feel that the rate or pace is very little smoke more than those who feel the pace is great ($r = -0.32$, $p < 0.05$). One explanation for this relationship might go as follows: (a) we have already suggested that smoking is symptomatic of arousal-seeking behavior; (b) arousal-seekers are persons who tend to perceive their environment as less stimulating than they want it to be—therefore, they seek arousal. (c) Consistent with this perceptual bias is their view of the rate at which the profession is developing. In their view, things are not happening as fast as they should, and thus, those who smoke more also report greater impatience with the rate of technological and professional development in their field.

Another finding of interest is the relationship between number of cigarettes smoked and number of reported visits to the health dispensary on the base. These two variables are inversely related ($r = -0.31$, $p < 0.05$). That is, the more people smoke, the less often they visit the dispensary. There are a number of possible interpretations we can make about this finding. First of all, smokers may be less concerned about their health than non-smokers. Thus, they not only smoke, but they also make little use of health facilities. They may show less hypochondriasis than non-smokers which accounts for their low frequency of illness behavior. Second, smokers may not visit the dispensary as often because they are already subjectively as well as objectively overloaded with work. In fact, we have just presented evidence that supports this explanation. And, of course, both explanations may jointly account for the results just presented.

While dispensary visits and cigarette smoking are negatively related, volunteering for yearly NASA health examinations and cigarette smoking are unrelated ($F = 0.19$, n.s.). Why there should be this difference in findings regarding these two types of illness behavior is not clear, but they are worth noting since physicians frequently derive health statistics on smoking in their patient population from both dispensary visits and from voluntary yearly examinations.

Finally, we find that smoking is also correlated with pulse rate ($r = 0.35$, $p < 0.05$) and with systolic blood pressure ($r = 0.32$, $p < 0.05$).

What, then, is the overall profile that we get of the heavy cigarette smoker? The findings we have just discussed are summarized in Figure 8-3. They provide

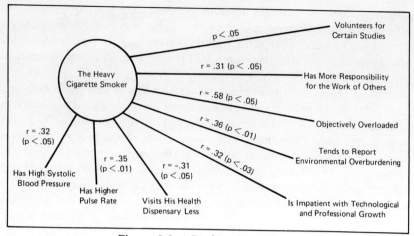

Figure 8-3. A Profile of the Cigarette Smoker.

a picture of a person who tends to volunteer for certain activities—a step towards more overload. Furthermore, the heavy smoker is more likely to be objectively overloaded and tends to characterize himself as being environmentally overburdened. He has more responsibility for the work of others, and he is impatient with the rate at which technological growth and the growth of his profession is proceeding. Perhaps ironically, while he visits his health dispensary less, he may be in poorer health having higher systolic blood pressure and higher pulse rate.

Some Differences between Administrators,
Engineers, and Scientists

Now let's turn to some data that bear on one of the central goals of our research. Namely, to account for the occupational differences in coronary heart disease noted by Dr. Carlos Villafana and Mrs. Jean Mockbee among administrators, engineers, and scientists. In Table 8-4 we find a summary of some early findings on these three occupational groups. We have defined occupation here in terms of what the Goddard volunteer labeled himself on the questionnaire.

First of all, we note that as one moves from administrators to scientists, one finds significant decreases in average age ($p < 0.001$). The administrators average about 44 years old while the engineers have an average age of 39. The scientists average slightly over 35 years of age. Since we already know that coronary heart disease appears more often in older individuals, it will be important to control on age where we feel that it is related to certain of our dependent variables such as serum cholesterol level. Surely, one could argue that

Table 8-4

Occupational Differences in Certain Background, Health, and Job Stress Variables

Measures	Administrator	Occupation Engineer	Scientist	p
Age	44.4	39.0	35.6	0.001
Average schooling	completed college	some grad. school	masters	0.001
% participate in annual NASA health exams	71.0	59.0	26.0	0.001
No. cigarettes smoked[1]	31.6	18.8	19.9	0.05
% smokers	33.0	22.0	21.0	n.s.
Systolic blood pressure	134.8	128.6	131.3	0.05[2]
Subjective quantitative overload cluster	3.7[3]	3.4	3.1	0.01
Days elapsed until questionnaire returned	19.9	13.1	14.5	0.05
Subjective qualitative overload factor	1.8	2.0	2.1	0.05
Opportunity to use administrative skills	3.6	3.0	2.6	0.001
Opportunity to use one's education, talents, and abilities	3.3	3.2	3.8	0.001
Role conflict	2.2	2.1	1.9	0.05

[1] For persons smoking one or more cigarettes per day.

[2] Significant when corrected for age differences.

[3] These values are based on a five-point rating scale where 1 = "very little" and 5 = "very great."

administrators have a higher incidence of cardiovascular disease and hypertension on the basis of age alone unless one could control on that variable while searching for other differences.

The next row in Table 8-4 shows that there is a significant increase in level of education as one moves from administrators to engineers to scientists ($p < 0.001$). Administrators on the average complete college or undergraduate school. Engineers tend to have some graduate school work, while scientists average a masters degree. Education may be a relevant variable in the study of coronary heart disease. For one thing, we can theoretically suggest that education provides an opportunity for a person to learn effective modes for coping with both quantitative and qualitative overload. Experience in colleges and universities has often been noted as providing skills and practice in handling many complex situations. Such training could provide a person with coping skills for dealing with role conflict on the job. A recent study by Hinkle and his colleagues (1968) at Bell Telephone provides some support for this hypothesis: They found in a three-year study of 1,160 male employees that myocardial infarctions were twice as prevalent among non-college educated men compared to college men. All other causes of death were evenly distributed among the two groups.

Next in Table 8-4 we see that 71% of the administrators, 59% of the engineers, and only 26% of the scientists participate in annual NASA health examinations. The differences in participation rates should be of interest to persons using the medical examinations to derive some estimates of prevalence of various coronary conditions. Data drawn from such examinations may be most valid for describing the general heatlh conditions of the administrators but could be misleading in describing the health conditions of the scientists. Perhaps only the healthiest of the scientists participate (which would provide a picture of the scientists that would underestimate the amount of obesity, silent heart pathologies, etc.). Since the volunteer rate among scientists is much higher for this study than it is for the health examination, we will be able to make some comparisons on variables such as smoking, obesity, and hypertension to see whether data derived from the yearly health examinations under-, over-, or correctly estimate the prevalence of some of these risk factors.

Continuing, we see that among those who smoke, administrators are heavier smokers than are engineers and scientists (31.6 cigarettes per day compared to 18.8 and 19.9, respectively). There is also a greater percentage of smokers among the administrators than among the engineers and scientists, although the differences are not significant.

With regard to systolic blood pressure, the administrators again score higher than the engineers and the scientists (134.8, 128.6, and 131.3, respectively, for the three groups). The difference across the three groups is significant ($p < 0.05$) when we correct for age differences between the three groups.

What about overload? How do these three occupational groups differ with regard to this variable which has often been implicated as a risk factor in heart disease? First of all, we see that administrators report being more subjectively overloaded than engineers and than scientists. The scientists are the least overloaded of all. The type of overload we are talking about here is subjective *quantitative* overload—too much work to do given the amount of time to do it in. The items in this measure are quite similar to the items in our subjective quantitative overload factor which we derived from a study of overload in university professors. In fact the subjective quantitative overload cluster we are using here correlates quite highly with the subjective quantitative overload factor from that previous study ($r = 0.66, p < 0.001$).

We get some additional insight into the nature of overload for the administrators and the other two groups when we look at how long it took each occupational group to complete and send in the questionnaire they were given for this study. Almost 20 days elapsed on the average until questionnaires were received from administrators compared to slightly over 13 days for the engineers and 14.5 days for the scientists. The differences in elapsed time across the three groups is significant ($p < 0.05$) and suggest that administrators are objectively as well as subjectively overloaded.

Now let's turn to qualitative overload. Here the picture is quite different. It is the scientists who report the most qualitative overload followed by the engineers, and then the administrators. Thus, with regard to the types of subjectively felt overload reported by different occupations, it appears that administrators suffer more from quantitative overload while scientists suffer more from qualitative overload. These findings are consistent with some earlier work on university professors and university administrators carried out here at the Institute for Social Research. In that study (French, Tupper, & Mueller, 1965) the professors (who seem analogous to our scientists) reported feeling low self-esteem due to the qualitatively overloading aspects of their work—it was important to do a professionally high quality job even if it took some time to complete it. The university administrators, on the other hand, reported feeling low self-esteem not from qualitative overload but from quantitative overload—they couldn't cope to do the best job on everything, but they were expected to handle a certain quantity of work in a given time. Perhaps we shall find that other types of job overload only constitute sources of stress for one occupational group but not for another.

Continuing down Table 8-4, we notice that administrators report more opportunity to use their administrative skills. Engineers report less opportunity, and scientists report the least opportunity. The fact that administrators do have more opportunity could suggest that they also have greater chances to become involved in role conflicts with other individuals. We note in the last line of Table 8-4 that administrators do tend to report more role conflict, followed by engineers, with scientists reporting the least amount of role conflict. The differences across the three groups are significant, and are supportive of some potentially stressful outcomes which would derive from having a lot of opportunity to use one's administrative skills.

Finally, we note that while administrators have the most opportunity to use their administrative skills, they report less opportunity to use their education, talents, and abilities than do the scientists. Both they and the engineers report being under-utilized, while the scientists report having the most opportunity to utilize all of their skills, abilities, and education.

To summarize the picture at this point, we get a view of the administrator as older, less educated, quantitatively more overloaded, and more likely to experience role conflict than the scientist. The administrator also smokes more and has a higher systolic blood pressure than the scientist. The scientist, on the other hand, is better educated, qualitatively more overloaded, and is less likely to get into role conflict. The scientist also smokes less and has lower systolic blood pressure. The engineer falls somewhere between these two occupational groups.

What About Responsibility?

We have already noted that responsibility for the work of others is correlated with number of cigarettes smoked. Do the three occupational groups differ in terms of the amount and types of responsibilities they report? Table 8-5 presents data on the three occupations which help us answer these questions.

First of all we see that an index of the overall amount of responsibility reported differs significantly across the three occupations ($p < 0.01$). Administrators report the most responsibility, followed by engineers, with scientists reporting the least.

Now let's look at the more specific types of responsibility. Administrators spend about 42% of their time carrying out responsibilities for others' work while engineers spend only about 27% of their time doing so, and scientists spend only about 17% of their time doing so. The difference across these three groups is quite significant ($p < 0.001$). Similarly administrators spend the most time of the three groups on responsibilities for others' futures—almost twice as much time as do the engineers and scientists (12.1% versus 6.3% and 6.7%, respectively). Thus, with regard to the two responsibilities for people, which we have already labeled as reflecting the "responsibility hypothesis" in coronary heart disease, the administrators report spending the greatest amount of time on the average.

With regard to responsibilities for money, administrators spend slightly more time on the average than do engineers. The scientists spend the least time of all three groups on this responsibility.

Table 8-5
Occupational Differences in Responsibility

		Occupation		
Measure	Administrator	Engineer	Scientist	p
Amount of responsibilities index	3.4	3.0	2.9	0.01
% time carrying out responsibility for:				
a) others' work	42.9	27.1	17.1	0.001
b) others' futures	12.1	6.3	6.7	0.01
c) money	11.2	10.8	6.5	0.05
d) equipment	4.4	9.3	12.0	0.05
e) projects	29.6	46.6	72.2	0.01

The pattern, however, is reversed with regard to responsibility for equipment and projects. Here the scientists spend the greatest amount of time compared to the administrators and engineers. In fact, the scientists and engineers spend, on the average, the greatest segments of their time carrying out responsibilities that should not be associated with coronary heart disease. The scientists spend 72.2% of their time in responsibility for projects while the engineers spend 46.6% of their time (and administrators spend 29.6% of their time in responsibility for projects). On the other hand, the largest segment of time for the administrators is spent carrying out responsibilities for the work of others—a responsibility that should be associated with coronary heart disease according to the responsibility hypothesis.

With regard to responsibilities then, the administrators report more of them overall, and they also report more responsibilities that are people-oriented than do the engineers and scientists. The engineers and scientists report more object-oriented responsibilities than do the administrators.

Personality Differences between
the Three Occupations

Now let's turn to Table 8-6 which presents some measures of personality on which the three occupational groups differ. First of all, we see that the administrators appear to score lower on a measure of rigid personality, while engineers fall in the middle and scientists score highest. This measure is a scale from the California Personality Inventory which characterizes a person who is

Table 8-6
Occupational Differences in Personality

| Measure | Occupation | | | p |
	Administrator	Engineer	Scientist	
Rigid personality (Flex.-rigid. scale)	2.3[1]	2.4	2.5	0.01
Involved striving	5.2[2]	4.8	5.0	0.05
Positive attitude toward pressure	5.2	4.9	4.8	0.05
Environmental overburdening	5.6	5.1	5.4	0.05
Leadership	5.0	4.3	4.2	0.05
What I Am Like (Type A)	3.5	3.3	3.2	0.05

[1] These values are based on a four-point scale where 1 = low rigid and 4 = high rigid.
[2] These values are based on a seven-point scale where 1 = low on the personality trait and 7 = high on the personality trait.

unwilling to give in to other persons' points of view, and is inflexible when it comes to compromising his own needs to meet someone else's.

This measure of personality is of interest because of some previous work done in a nationwide study of role conflict linking such conflict to the rigid personality (Kahn et al., 1964). Kahn and his colleagues found that persons who were placed in objective role conflicts were less likely to report feeling that a conflict was present if they were rigid personalities. On the other hand, if they were flexible personalities, they were more likely to feel the presence of the conflict. The explanation given was the flexible person, always bending with the wind, put himself into more conflicts by attempting to cope with all points of view by meeting them simultaneously. The rigid person, on the other hand, would shut himself off from the conflict perhaps by ignoring its existence, and thus avoid the discomfort of feeling that a conflict really existed. As we have already noted, the administrators tend to report more role conflict than do the engineers and scientists. Perhaps this is because the administrators are more flexible and thus set themselves up for such conflict.

The next five personality dimensions in Table 8-6 were all designed to measure the Type A coronary-prone personality. On all of them the administrators score the highest. Administrators seem to see themselves as higher on involved striving in what they do, higher on liking pressure and perhaps seeking it out, and higher on tending to become overburdened (this personality measure, as we have noted is positively correlated with number of cigarettes smoked) than do engineers and scientists. They also score higher on leadership, a dimension that could be viewed as a tendency to take over positions of responsibility for the welfare and work of others. Finally, there is a significant tendency for administrators to score highest on a three-item measure of Type A called "What I Am Like." This measure correlates 0.80 with the Jenkins Activity Scale, a validated measure used to predict to Type A personality (Jenkins, 1967).

In summary, then, we see that the administrators, compared to the engineers and scientists, tend to suffer more quantitative overload but less qualitative overload; and they also appear to be under more stress from responsibilities for people, but they have less responsibility for projects and equipment. Furthermore, they also seem to have more of the personality characteristics that typify the Type A coronary-prone personality. The scientists generally tend to be lowest on these potential risk factors while the engineers are somewhat intermediate.

A Brief Look at Person-environment Fit

Before concluding our presentation of data, let's turn to the notion of poor person-environment fit as a factor that could lead to coronary heart disease. We noted earlier that we had divided the administrators and the engineers into two further groups. These are administrators in administrative environments, administrators in engineering environments, engineers in engineering environments, and engineers in administrative environments. The first and third categories were labeled examples of good fit; and second and fourth categories were called examples of potentially poor fit.

We now have some preliminary data suggesting that poor fit may affect a person's health. Table 8-7 presents data on the relationships between job environment and blood pressure for administrators. We assume that an administrator is better fitted to an organizational unit primarily administrative in mission and climate but he is less well fitted to an engineering unit where most of the other personnel are engineers. To obtain a measure of environment in this case, we asked the respondent to estimate what percent of his environment was administrative and what percent was engineering. Environment was defined as follows: "Aside from your immediate job, your work life may be affected by the wider environment of your section, branch, division, or directorate. *As far as it affects your job,* is this wider environment mostly administration, engineering, or science? Considering the mission, the people, and the organizational *climate* my organizational environment is: . . . " (p. 29, questionnaire).

Table 8-7 shows that the higher the percent of environment characterized as administrative in nature, the lower both the systolic and diastolic blood pressures tended to be. Thus, good fit as defined here is related to low systolic and diastolic blood pressure ($r = -0.38$, $p < 0.01$; and $r = -0.28$, $p < 0.01$, respectively). Similarly, the higher the percent environment characterized as engineering the higher the blood pressure. Thus, poor fit for administrators associated with high systolic and diastolic blood pressure ($r = 0.28$, $p < 0.01$; and $r = 0.27$, $p < 0.01$, respectively).

Interestingly enough, this lack of fit does not serve as a source of stress for the engineers. The correlations between percent environment, either engineering or administrative, and blood pressure are close to zero and nonsignificant. This lack of correlation for the engineers, but its presence for the administrators, suggests that certain types of poor fit may serve as a source of stress for one occupational group but not for another. In our continuing analyses we shall be looking for other types of stresses that may affect one occupational group but not the other.

Table 8-7
Relationships Between Job Environment and Blood Pressure for Administrators

| Environment | Blood Pressure | |
	SBP	DBP
% Administration	−0.38	−0.28
% Engineering	0.28	0.27

Discussion

In Diagram A we presented a model of coronary heart disease implying that personality, type of occupation, various forms of responsibility and other job stresses, may affect various physiological risk factors and cause coronary heart disease. The results that we have presented so far are a long way from adequately testing the model, yet they provide a certain amount of encouragement in leading us to believe we are on the right track. We have found differences among administrators, engineers, and scientists with regard to variables that seem peculiarly associated with heart disease. These differences are in terms of physiology, personality, reported job stress, and smoking. What is lacking are the types of information needed to pin down the causal links between these various panels of variables in the manner suggested in Diagram A.

In some cases we have found administrators to be relatively high on a particular variable such as a Type A personality variable, yet have found no relationship between that variable and our physiological risk factors. In other cases, we have found some stronger links as is true of the relationship between responsibility for the work of others and cigarette smoking, and between cigarette smoking and blood pressure. What is the explanation for a failure to find relationships between some of the job stress measures that differentiate administrators from engineers and scientists and physiological measures such as cholesterol and blood pressure?

For one thing, some of these job stresses and personality variables may relate to physiological risk factors other than the ones being examined in our research. Since there is much literature linking job stress and personality to coronary heart disease, it may be wise to expand our search for related physiological risk factors in coronary heart disease.

Second, some of the relationships between job stresses and physiological risk factors may be masked by personality. As an example, we may find, upon further analysis, that job overload is likely to increase blood pressure if a person is personality Type A, but likely to decrease bood pressure if the person is Type B. Hence the relationship between overload and blood pressure would be cancelled out in a mixed group comprised of both Type A and Type B persons. To give another example, we might find that persons who are *high* on the need for social approval from others (such as measured by the Crowne-Marlowe) might show increases in cholesterol when they are overloaded with work. Persons who are low on this need for social approval might show no change in cholesterol as their work load changes. Why might this be so? We might assume that for the group of people who value social approval overload can only mean one thing—a potential opportunity to fail at their work and thus lose the social approval of others which they want so much. Thus, overload is stressful and would raise their cholesterol. On the other hand, while overload might cause the persons low on need for social approval to lose such approval, such a threatened loss in social approval would probably not cause their cholesterol to rise because they don't value social approval very highly to begin with. We are already beginning to find relationships of this type which suggest that different personalities take stress in different ways.

Overall, then, we are beginning to pick up relationships between certain types of job stress and risk factors (such as smoking) in heart disease. Furthermore, we are beginning to find differences among the three occupational groups we are studying that appear to be more than coincidentally related to coronary heart disease. An almost mandatory next step following the identification of these relevant variables, is a longitudinal study to begin a careful study of the problem of distinguishing between cause and effect in our model.

Selected Bibliography and References

I. Job Stress, Overload, and Coronary Heart Disease

French, J.R.P., Jr., and Kahn, R.L.: A programmatic approach to studying the industrial environment and mental health, *J. Social Issues*, 18:1-47, 1962

French, J.R.P., Jr., Tupper, C.J., and Mueller, E.F.: *Work load of University Professors*, University of Michigan: Cooperative Research Project No. 2171, 1965

Friedman, M., Rosenman, R.H., and Carroll, V.: Changes in serum cholesterol and blood clotting time in men subjected to cyclic variation of occupational stress, *Circulation* 17:852-861, 1958

Hinkle, L.W., Jr., Whitney, L.H., Lehman, E.W., Dunn, J., Benjamin, B., et al.: Occupation, education, and coronary heart disease, *Science* 191:238-246, 1968

Kahn, R.L., Wolfe, D.M., Quinn, R.P., Snoek, J.D., et al.: *Organizational Stress: Studies in Role Conflict and Ambiguity*, New York: Wiley, 1964

Lazarus, R.: *Psychological Stress and the Coping Process*, New York: McGraw-Hill, 1966

Lehman, E.W.: Social class and coronary heart disease—a sociological assessment of the medical literature, *J. Chronic Dis.* 20:381-391, 1967

Marks, R.U.: Factors involving social and demographic characteristics: A review of empirical findings, *Milbank Memorial Fund Quarterly*, 45:51-108, 1967

Miller, J.G.: Information input overload and psychopathology, *Amer. J. Psychiat.* 8:116, 1960

Russek, H.I.: Emotional factors in atherosclerosis, *Geriatrics* 14:479-482, 1959

Russek, H.I.: Emotional stress and CHD in American physicians, dentists, and lawyers, *Amer. J. Med. Sci.* 243:716-725, 1962

Russek, H.I., and Zohman, B.: Relative significance of heredity, diet, and occupational stress in coronary heart disease of young adults, *Amer. J. Med. Sci.* 235:266-277, 1958

Sales, S.M.: Differences among individuals in affective, behavioral, biochemical, and physiological responses to variations in work load, Unpublished doctoral dissertation, University of Michigan, 1969

Thomas, C.B., and Murphy, E.A.: Further studies on cholesterol levels in the John Hopkins medical students: The effect of stress at examinations, *J. Chronic Dis.* 8:661-668, 1958

Wardwell, W.I., Hyman, M., and Bahnson, C.B.: Stress and coronary heart disease in three field studies, *J. Chronic Dis.* 17:73-84, 1964

Wertlake, P.T., Wilcox, A.A., Haley, M.T., and Peterson, J.E.: Relationship of mental and emotional stress to serum cholesterol levels, *Proc. Soc. Exp. Biol. Med.* 97:163-165, 1958

II. Personality Factors in Coronary Heart Disease

Freidman, M., and Rosenman, R.H.: Overt behavior patterns in coronary disease: Detection of overt behavior pattern A in patients with coronary disease by a new psychophysical procedure, *J.A.M.A.* 173-1320-1325, 1960

Jenkins, C.D., Rosenman, R.H., and Friedman, M.: Components of the coronary prone behavior pattern: Their relation to silent myocardial infarction and blood lipids, *J. Chronic Dis.* 19:599-609, 1966

Keith, R.A.: Personality and coronary heart disease—A review, *J. Chronic Dis.* 19:1231-1243, 1966

Keith, R.A., Lown, B., and Stare, F.J.: Coronary heart disease and behavior patterns, *Psychosom. Med.* 27:424-434, 1965

Mordkoff, A.M., and Parsons, D.A.: The coronary personality—A critique, *Psychosom. Med.* 29:1-14, 1967

Rosenman, R.H., and Freidman, M.: Behavior pattern, blood lipids, and coronary heart disease, *J.A.M.A.* 184:934-938, 1963

Rosenman, R.H., Freidman, M., Strauss, R., et al.: Coronary heart disease in the Western Collaborative Group Study, *J.A.M.A.* 195:86-92, 1966

III. Smoking, Arousal Seeking, and Coronary Heart Disease

Jenkins, C.D., Rosenman, R.H., and Zyzanski, S.J.: Cigarette smoking: Its relationship to coronary heart disease and related risk factors in the Western Collaborative Group Study, *Circulation* 38:1140-1155, 1968

Russek, H.I.: Stress, tobacco, and coronary disease in North American professional groups, *J.A.M.A.* 192:189-194, 1965

Russek, H.I., Zohman, B.L., and Dorset, V.J.: Effects of tobacco and whiskey on the cardiovascular system, *J.A.M.A.* 57:563-568, 1955

Seltzer, C.C.: An evaluation of the effect of smoking on coronary heart disease. I. Epidemiological evidence, *J.A.M.A.* 203:127-134, 1968

Schubert, D.S.: Arousal seeking as a central factor in tobacco smoking among college students, *Int. J. Social Psychiat.* 11:221-225, 1965

Schubert, D.S.: Arousal seeking as a motivation for volunteering: MMPI scores and central-nervous-system-stimulant use as suggestive of a trait, *J. Projective Techniques & Personality Assessment* 28:337-340, 1964

9 Unusually Low Incidence of Death from Myocardial Infarction

Clarke Stout, Jerry Morrow,
Edward N. Brandt, Jr.,
and Stewart Wolf
*University of Oklahoma Medical Center
and Oklahoma Medical Research
Foundation*

Epidemiological studies of coronary artery disease in various ethnic groups have yielded a variety of interpretations. Keys et al., in several studies, have presented data suggesting that diet is important in the pathogenesis of myocardial infarction. They have inferred, for example, that there is more atherosclerosis among Japanese living in California or Hawaii than Japanese living in Japan because the former habitually eat more saturated fat than the latter.[1] Similar studies of Italians have also led to the implication that a high fat diet is important in the genesis of atherosclerosis.[2] Ethnic factors, on the other hand, were found by Dawber et al. not to be associated with differences in coronary heart disease in Framingham, Mass., where there are substantial numbers of British, Irish, and Italians.[3] Danaraj et al. report a much higher mortality from coronary disease in Indian males than in Chinese males living in Singapore under superficially similar socioeconomic conditions.[4] Whatever the relevant factors, it is evident that differences in the incidence of coronary heart disease do exist among different ethnic groups as well as among ethnically similar groups in different localities. The present study was undertaken in a nearly pure Italian community in the United States in an effort to minimize some of the variables inherent in a study involving widely differing geographical areas. The town of

Reprinted with permission from *Journal of the American Medical Association*, 188:845-849, 1964.

Roseto, Pa., was originally established in 1882. It contains first, second, and third generation Italian-Americans. The first objective of the study was to ascertain the death rate from myocardial infarction in this community as compared with other communities in the vicinity.

Mortality Statistics

The survey covered the seven-year period from 1955 to 1961. The first community surveyed was Nazareth, Pa., with a population of 6,209, predominantly German, descendants of Moravians who settled there before the American Revolution. The people continue to speak German in the home and eat a fairly typical German diet. They work mainly in steel and cement factories and on farms, but they also make musical instruments and other items requiring specialized craftsmanship. The second community was Roseto, Pa., population 1,630, which was settled in 1882 by immigrants from Roseto, Valfortore, in the province of Foggia, Italy. More than 95% of the people of Roseto are Italian, and they maintain many of the original Italian customs. Vigorous and fun-loving, the people eat a great deal and drink considerable alcohol, mainly in the form of wine. They are relatively prosperous financially due to hard work and ingenuity. Originally, most of the Rosetan men worked in the neighboring slate quarries. Today, most of the women and some of the men either own or work in small factories that manufacture shirts and blouses. Other males work in nearby steel mills and electrical industries, while only a few still work in the quarries. Bangor, Pa., only one mile from Roseto, was the third community studied. Its population is 5,766. Bangor was originally settled by Welsh quarriers who worked the nearby slate deposits. The town now contains a mixture of several ethnic types including many of German and Italian origin. The inhabitants serve the surrounding farmers as merchants and tradesmen and work in nearby construction and steel industries. The fourth community was Stroudsburg, Pa., with a population of 6,070, and the fifth, East Stroudsburg, Pa., with a population of 7,674. Both of them are composed of mixed ethnic groups. Their work is mainly to supply the nearby mountain resorts with goods and service, although many men work in nearby cement, steel, and state-operated industries.

Figure 9-1 shows the population distribution by age and sex in the five communities.

Certificates for all deaths attributed to cardiovascular disease for the five towns from 1955 through 1961 were examined. The local hospitals were then visited and the records of all admissions of these patients studied. Thereupon the family physicians were contacted personally or by mail in an attempt to verify the cause of death of each person. Particular attention was given to electrocardiographic tracings, a history of angina pectoris or previous myocardial infarction, the autopsy findings, transaminase values, and the clinical circumstances sur-

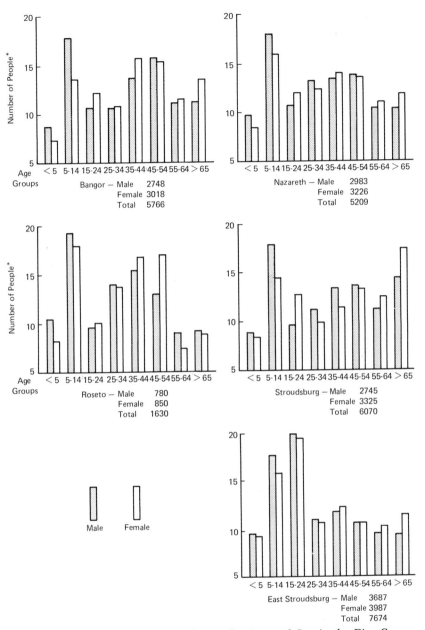

Figure 9-1. Population Distribution by Age and Sex in the Five Communities (1960 Census). Each Bar Represents Number of People in that Age Group Divided by Total Number of Same Sex.

rounding the terminal event. Also noted were the presence or absence of hypertension, diabetes, rheumatic heart disease, cerebrovascular disease, chronic pulmonary disease, and congenital heart disease.

On the basis of these data each case was placed into one of the following mutually exclusive categories: (1) Death from myocardial infarction proven anatomically. (2) Death from myocardial infarction established clinically on the basis of diagnostic electrocardiograms (ECG) and compatible symptoms. (3) Death from myocardial infarction presumed on the basis of previous history and the circumstance of death. (4) Death from arteriosclerotic heart disease without evidence of myocardial infarction. (5) Death from hypertensive heart disease not including cerebrovascular accidents, and (6) Other. This group consisted of deaths attributed to other cardiovascular diseases such as cerebrovascular accidents and congenital and rheumatic heart diseases, but also including instances in which there was evidence of emphysema or pneumonia.

Results

The death rates from myocardial infarction (proven anatomically, established clinically, and presumed) for the five towns are shown in Table 9-1. The values for Roseto were strikingly low, less than one half that of nearby Bangor. These figures were all the more impressive in view of the fact that substantially the same physicians cared for the populations of both towns, and they used the same neighboring hospitals.

When the number of deaths from myocardial infarction (proven anatomically, established clinically, and presumed) were compared by town for the seven-year period, the values for Roseto were found to be significantly lower than the values for the other four towns ($P < 0.001$). When the chi-square was partitioned[5] into four independent comparisons it was found that the only meaningful difference was between Roseto and the other four towns. This was significant ($P < 0.001$). Population values for the statistical analysis were obtained by a linear estimation utilizing the 1950 and 1960 census data summarized by age, sex, and town.

The death rates from arteriosclerotic heart disease without evidence of myocardial infarction, hypertensive heart disease, and other causes were essentially similar for the five towns (Table 9-2).

There were, in all, 938 deaths from cardiovascular disease in the five towns during the seven-year period. Information was obtained from physicians or hospitals on 704 (75%) of these, although the records did not always illuminate the cause of death. Information was available from death certificates alone on the remaining 234 (25%). Of the 938 deaths from heart disease, only 483 recorded as deaths from myocardial infarction could be verified despite the fact that earlier information from physicians and hospital records was available on a

Table 9-1
Death Rates Per 100,000 Per Year From Myocardial Infarction* by Age and
Sex, 1955-1961

				Age Groups			
Town	Sex	Under 35	35-44	45-54	55-64	65-Up	Total
Roseto	M	0	0	144	0	813	91
	F	0	0	0	0	801	66
Nazareth	M	0	0	253	1049	2545	406
	F	0	0	134	234	1309	197
Bangor	M	0	35	305	1082	1866	369
	F	0	58	64	368	1431	244
Stroudsburg	M	42	74	373	910	1980	439
	F	0	0	0	140	695	132
East Stroudsburg	M	0	32	284	705	2344	311
	F	0	0	33	144	689	94

*Proven anatomically and established clinically.

Table 9-2
Death Rates Per 100,000 Per Year From Arteriosclerotic Heart Disease (Without
Evidence of Myocardial Infarction) Hypertensive Heart Disease, and Other
Cardiovascular Diseases by Sex, 1955-1961

Town	Sex	Arteriosclerotic Heart Disease*	Hypertensive Heart Disease*	Other*
Roseto	M	127	0	91
	F	66	16	33
Nazareth	M	150	29	91
	F	179	26	62
Bangor	M	133	5	113
	F	164	18	145
Stroudsburg	M	148	25	91
	F	98	42	55
East Stroudsburg	M	105	19	66
	F	98	25	54

*For all ages.

substantially higher percentage. The ratios of verified to unverified deaths from myocardial infarction were not significantly different in the five towns. To avoid the bias of a too-low calculation of the incidence of death from myocardial infarction, all those unverified deaths were nevertheless included in the figures.

Studies on Survivors

As soon as the low death rate from myocardial infarction in Roseto became apparent, a visit was made to the community. As the first step in such a survey, the cooperation of the mayor and other leaders in the community was solicited to enable us to interview, examine, and test as many men and women over age 21 as possible. Our objectives were to ascertain whether or not the low death rate from myocardial infarction was matched by a low incidence of the disease and by relative longevity among the men. Reference to the population figures in Figure 9-1 reveals the intriguing finding that in Roseto alone among the five towns studied there were more males than females alive in the age groups over 55. During a single week, 314 (171 men and 143 women) or one third of the population over 21 were examined, weighed, tested for serum cholesterol concentration (auto analyzer), and questioned concerning dietary habits. A II-lead ECG was otained on each person. In addition, the investigators ate several meals with various of the Roseto families. These and other social contacts with the people of the community yielded preliminary observations on the attitudes and general way of life of Roseto. Other data gathered at the time included an assay for blood fibrinolytic activity, blood glucose concentration, hematocrit, serum lipoprotein electrophoresis, clotting time, thromboplastin generation time, and fibrinogen concentration. Only a few of the data from this thus far incomplete survey can be included in the present report. Ultimately data on nearly the entire adult population of Roseto will be available.

Dietary Habits

Each person completed a form which asked for usual dietary preferences as well as everything eaten in the preceding 24-hour period. A cross-check was obtained by asking in what quantities a list of 31 general food items were consumed per day, per week, per month, and per year. Several homes, bakeries, and restaurants in Roseto were visited to ascertain the nature and amounts of ingredients peculiar to local Italian cooking. Each person was then interviewed by a dietitian who assured that the questionnaire was complete and made a judgment as to its validity. The mean daily intakes of 251 of the original 314 Rosetans studied were included in the data which are shown in Table 9-3. It is apparent that in the sample studied, total fat consumption is at least equal to that of the average US

Table 9-3

Mean Daily Caloric Intake of One Fourth of the Population of Roseto Over Age 21*

	Calories	Fat		Protein		Carbohydrate		Alcohol	
		Gm	% Total Calories	Gm	% Total Calories	Gm	% Total Calories	Gm	% Total Calories
Males	3,000	125	38	98	13	315	42	34	8
Females	2,300	114	43	75	13	242	42	7	2
Both sexes	2,700	120	41	88	13	284	42	19	5

*136 males, 115 females.

citizen. Further breakdown of the diet must await refinement of and additions to our techniques and the examination of a larger segment of the population of Roseto.

It should be mentioned, however, that the impression gained from sharing meals with several families was that they eat substantially more calories and substantially more fat than the average American. Two local Italian physicians who have intimate knowledge of most of the families confirmed this impression emphatically and pointed out that a favorite dish, prosciuto, a pressed ham delicacy, has a rim of fat more than an inch thick and the Rosetans eat it whole without discarding the fat. It was also pointed out that cooking is done by most families with lard rather than olive oil as the principal shortening. Another favorite dish is fried peppers. Nearly all of the subjects interviewed acknowledged frequently eating them and most dipped their bread in the lard gravy to consume the whole dish.

Both men and women over age 21 were found to be overweight. Figures 9-2 and 9-3 illustrate the average weights of the people studied as compared to the average for the US.

Serum Cholesterol

Serum cholesterol values ranged from 136 mg% to 500+ mg% (mean 224 mg% standard deviation, 46.4) for Rosetan males; 141 mg% to 500+ mg% (mean 225 mg% standard deviation, 48.3) for Rosetan females. The mean values by age and sex corresponded closely to those reported in the Framingham Study.[6]

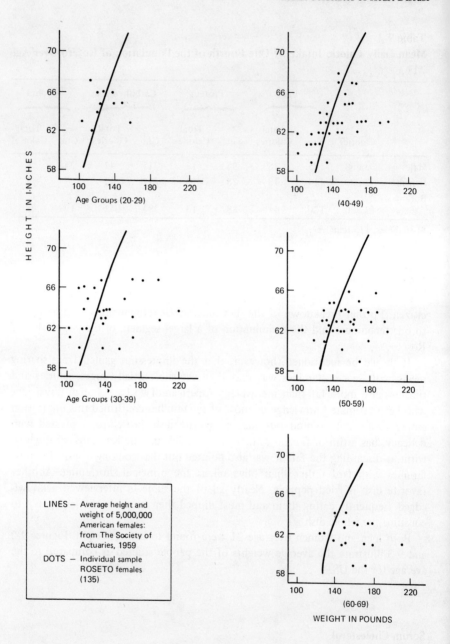

LINES — Average height and
weight of 5,000,000
American females:
from The Society of
Actuaries, 1959

DOTS — Individual sample
ROSETO females
(135)

Figure 9-2. Comparison of Height and Weight by Age and Sex of Roseto Sample Males with Average American Males.

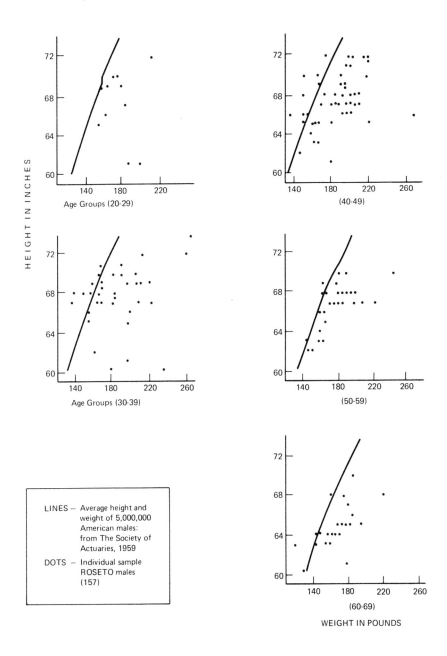

Figure 9-3. Comparison of Height and Weight by Age and Sex of Roseto Sample Females with Average American Females.

Social Behavior

The most striking feature of Roseto was the way in which the people seemed to enjoy life. They were gay, boisterous, and unpretentious. The wealthy dressed and behaved in a way similar to their more impecunious neighbors. The visitor's impression of the community was of a one-class, peasant-type society made up of simple, warm and very hospitable people. They were found to be mutually trusting (there is no crime in Roseto) and mutually supporting. There is poverty, but no real want, since neighbors provide for the needy, especially the recent immigrants who still continue to arrive in small numbers from Italy.

Comment

The reason for the relatively salubrious condition of the Rosetans is not clear at the present moment. Whether or not their sensible way of life contributes to their good health is still to be determined. Genetic and ethnic factors may be important, although it is noteworthy and deaths from myocardial infarction at relatively young ages have been documented among men born in Roseto but who lived most of their lives elsewhere in neighboring Pennsylvania, New York, or New Jersey.

University of Oklahoma Medical Center, Oklahoma City (Dr. Wolf).

This investigation was supported by Public Health Service Research Grant No. HE-06286-03 from the National Heart Institute.

Miss Lucille Boone of the Dietary Department of the University of Oklahoma Hospitals collaborated with the breakdown of the diet. Her report of the completed dietary survey will be published separately.

References

1. Keys, A., et al.: Lessons From Serum Cholesterol Studies in Japan, Hawaii, and Los Angeles, *Ann Intern Med* 48:83, 1958.

2. Keys, A., et al.: Studies on Serum Cholesterol and Other Characteristics of Clinically Healthy Men in Naples, *Arch Intern Med* (Chicago) 93:328, 1954.

3. Dawber, T.R., et al.: Some Factors Associated With Development of Coronary Heart Disease, *Amer J Public Health* 49:1349, 1959.

4. Danaraj, T.J., et al.: Ethnic Group Differences in Coronary Heart Disease in Singapore, *Amer Heart J* 58:516, 1959.

5. Kimball, A.W.: Short-Cut Formulas for Exact Partition of Chi Square in Contingency Tables, *Biometrics*, 10:452, 1954.

6. Dawber, T.R.; Moore, F.E.; and Mann, G.V.: Coronary Heart Disease in Framingham Study, *Amer J Public Health* No. 47, April, suppl, p. 4, 1957.

10 Psychosocial Aspects of Sudden Death

William A. Greene
University of Rochester
Sidney Goldstein
Strong Memorial Hospital
Arthur J. Moss
Rochester General Hospital

Meaningful information was available on 26 patients who died suddenly in a 44,000 industrial population. The data, past illnesses, prodromal symptoms, and psychosocial information were obtained from the plant medical records, the private physicians, and mainly from direct interviews with the surviving next-of-kin, usually the wife. The data suggest that the majority of these patients, all men, had been *depressed* for a week up to several months. The sudden death then occurred *in a setting of acute arousal engendered by increased work and activity or circumstances precipitating reactions of anxiety or anger.* The findings suggest that the combination of depressive and arousal psychological states or abrupt transition from one such state to another may produce disharmonious responses in the hormonal and autonomic nervous systems, as well as central nervous system mediated behavior, which are conducive to the sudden death.

The focus of my presentation is psychological variables in relation to sudden death. The patients whom I describe have already been described in some detail in Goldstein's presentation[1] since the prehospital trio involved in the study of myocardial infarction at a picturesque industrial plant in Rochester, NY, includes Dr. Goldstein, Dr. Moss, and myself. My own main concern has been with psychosocial variables in both the on-work part of the study (those

Reprinted with permission from *Archives of Internal Medicine*, Vol. 129 (May 1972), pp. 725-731. Copyright 1972, American Medical Association.

employees reporting to the industrial plant medical facility with symptoms indicating a myocardial infarction) and the so-called off-work part of the study (those reporting to nonplant medical facilities such as personal physicians, hospital emergency, or ambulance call). These two groups comprise all those with symptoms of suspect or actual myocardial infarction who get to the hospital alive. The study of this total industrial population also includes those who die suddenly, within 24 hours of onset of significant development or change of symptoms.

My interest in these psychosocial aspects evolved during a study with Dr. Moss of the adjustment of patients with cardiac pacemakers in the course of which we took note of psychological factors occurring in relation to the onset of symptoms at the time of development of varying degrees of heart block with dizziness or syncope. In many, the symptoms of heart block developed in psychologically distressful situations, chiefly those of depression.[2] A later investigation, undertaken with the cardiologists four years ago, of patients with heart disease, congenital and acquired, subjected to cardiac catheterization, showed differences in behavioral reactions to the threat of the catheterization procedure which could be correlated with variations in cortisol and growth hormone changes.[3] Such behavioral and hormonal differences in turn have recently been shown to be correlated with subsequent morbidity and mortality, especially in relation to cardiac surgery.[4] I have also had a long background of interest in problems pertaining to the psychophysiology of the cardiovascular system, having been trained under George Engel, MD, whose early investigation of the psychophysiologic aspects of fainting are well known.[5,6]

Dr. Engel has recently published papers which describe a series of cases of sudden death which he has gleaned from newspaper reports. From these accounts, he identified a number of types of dramatic life settings in which sudden death may occur. Most involved intense displeasure, as with the loss of a beloved person or conditions of profound anxiety, but a few reflected intense pleasure, as with a happy ending. Common to all was that the events were impossible for the victim to ignore and they responded with overwhelming excitation or giving up or both. He proposed that this combination may provoke neurovegetative responses, reflecting psychologic as well as physiologic uncertainty and involving both ergotrophic and trophotrophic systems which may be conducive to lethal cardiac events, especially in individuals with preexisting cardiac disease.[7,8] Part of my interest in studying in detail the patients in the Eastman Kodak Company population who have sudden deaths has been to determine whether there was any truth to what Dr. Engel has been reading in the papers, or perhaps more correctly, whether there was any appropriateness to the interpretations he was reading into what he was reading in the papers.

Material and Methods

Methods

First should be mentioned our method of obtaining psychosocial data pertaining to these patients who have died acutely. It has already been pointed out by Dr. Goldstein[1] and will be pointed out further by Dr. Moss[9] that the past illness data, as well as the prodromal pathophysiologic data on these patients, were obtained from the Eastman Kodak Company physicians as well as from the patients' private physicians, either by Dr. Moss or Dr. Goldstein. My role in the study has been to obtain data on psychological and social changes in juxtaposition to an actual myocardial infarction, episodes of prolonged ischemia from surviving hospitalized patients or from next-of-kin relatives of sudden death patients. Such psychosocial data is sometimes referred to as "soft." It has been my contention in my participation with Dr. Moss and Dr. Goldstein, as well as the other cardiologists at this medical center with whom I have worked, that psychological and social data can be as reliable as are a great deal of the so-called hard data, such as estimates of the severity of a myocardial infarction at the time certain very sophisticated measurements of pathophysiological variables are now being made. One need not be defensive about the softness of psychological data appropriately gathered, and it may be germane to be offensive at times about the fuzziness of many pertinent variables measuring the variations of pathophysiology in patients with a myocardial infarction.

Studies of sudden death have been made by a number of types of data-gathering methods[10-12] and some details of our methods should be described. Reports go to the industrial plant visiting nurses of persons who are out ill with any type of disease, and those with symptoms suggestive of a myocardial infarction are reported to this prehospital investigative group. The nurses also learn within 24 hours any circumstances of sudden death, either in the plant or out of the plant. These are reported to the prehospital study center and to me specifically.

Since the patient has died before the case is brought to our attention, the problem is whom one should approach in reference to the circumstances of the sudden death and questions about prodromal symptoms and emotional state of the patient and the family dynamics in the days, weeks, or months preceding the event. Sometimes one assumes that under such circumstances, as in many situations, it would be better if a woman did the interviewing of the responsible surviving relative (so far always the wife in our series), while at other times it would seem preferable that it be a man who does this. When it is difficult or impossible to make up one's mind about such a matter, it may be desirable to use both approaches. Fortunately, we are in a situation where both a woman, a nurse, and a man, a physician, interview in all cases.

The visiting nurse makes a courtesy call at the funeral home at the time of the funeral of the deceased, making a contact with the widow whom she frequently already knows because nearly all patients had been sick with cardiovascular disease in the past. Along with condolences, the nurse makes arrangements for a repeat call on the widow sometime in the subsequent week, mainly for the purpose of considering such things as insurance and benefits.

Within 24 hours of the sudden death, the prehospital investigation center is notified. Then a contact is made by me with the nurse to ascertain the plans for the funeral arrangements and when she will probably visit the spouse. The nurse later visits the spouse approximately a week after the funeral. Following that visit, I reconnoiter with the nurse, who has gleaned considerable information about the reaction of the spouse, as well as the spouse's description of the circumstances of sudden death, her degree of grief, and in particular, who she is angry at: fate, herself, the company, or not infrequently, the patient.

The nurses are very perceptive and frequently have had considerable association with the particular patient's family because of his previous cardiovascular symptoms related to an earlier infarction, angina, or hypertension. They informally obtain information about the circumstances, particularly the matter of prodromal or lack of prodromal symptomatology, as well as family make-up and conflicts. They also get information which is related to them by the spouse regarding the circumstances of the patient's demise. The nurses indicate that there is a special study being conducted by doctors from Strong Memorial Hospital and the Rochester General Hospital and that Dr. Greene will likely be in contact with them about the circumstances of the patient's final illness.

Initially, we had some qualms about how readily these widows would accept what might be an intrusive inquiry into the circumstances surrounding the death of their husbands. Usually between the 10th and 15th day after the death of the patient, I make a telephone call to the home, having obtained the address and telephone number from the nurses and also having called the deceased's physician and also the wife's physician, where this is different, and obtained their acquiescence. When I call the spouse, I identify myself by name, as coming from Strong Memorial Hospital, and as NOT having anything to do with the Eastman Kodak Company so that she can feel free to talk about her perception of the patient's possible work stress or dissatisfactions. I explain our general study of patients with actual or suspected heart attacks and particularly our interest in those who have died suddenly. The spouse is then given the opportunity either to refuse or for me to meet with her directly for an interview at her home, in my office, or over the telephone, the preference of all of them so far. Much to our surprise, these spouses have been only too willing to talk about the circumstances leading up to their husbands' deaths. Some of this I am sure is motivated by their current grief and their wish to talk over the situation with someone. I should point out that I have had long experience and toleration in interviewing people in grieving situations and obtaining psychological data.

During such data gathering I may be therapeutically supportive, I think, without contaminating appreciably the information obtained. Most of the widows indicate their wish to go over the circumstances of the death of their spouse with the idea that it may be of benefit to someone else. Some of their participation is obviously motivated by their need to express their sadness and, at times, their fury at the plant, at the personal physician, at fate, and, not infrequently, at the patient whom they may describe in various ways as stupid and stubborn at not having gone to a physician sooner. It has been surprising how many of these women indicate, at least after the fact, that they had assumed and felt for days or weeks that the patient was going to have another myocardial infarction and frequently they had predicted the several circumstances in which this might occur.

We had assumed that the emotional distress of the relative would be a problem in conducting these interviews. The interviews are semi-structured and include essentially the same information that is obtained in interviews of patients who develop actual or suspected infarctions, turn in on-work or off-work, and are interviewed directly in the hospital. Rather than being reluctant, the spouse has usually been very willing to talk and the problem has been one of terminating the interview after an hour or more. The extent to which these widows are able to talk, at times with considerable distress, but with reasonable coping resources has been quite touching. Particularly this seems so since they talk to someone that they do not know over the telephone. It may be that this mode of interview data gathering has certain advantages, as well as some disadvantages and may engender positive or negative contaminating influences on the validity of the information obtained.

Subjects

The particular patients about whom I am reporting today include the 22 sudden deaths that Dr. Goldstein[1] has already referred to, and an additional four patients. Two of these were deaths on-work prior to our beginning the total work study in June of 1970 and were sudden deaths on-work during 1969 after the on-work phase began in December 1968. Another additional patient was in the on-work study when he developed a severe myocardial infarction and survived but then died suddenly by carbon monoxide suicide three months later. He is included mainly to highlight the occurrence of actual suicide among persons who have the disability often associated with myocardial infarction. The fourth patient, in addition to those covered by Dr. Goldstein, was a retired employee who died at the plant and is considered because he died in a situation of apparent success and elation as will be described more in detail later.

The next-of-kin interviewed regarding these sudden death patients has been the widow except in four circumstances: once where it was the father, another in which it was the sibling, and in two circumstances in which it was an extramarital girlfriend.

Preliminary Findings

Past Illnesses

A history of the patient's past health is obtained after the spouse is asked to give an account of the acute prodromal symptoms and the social circumstances leading up to the patient's death. In all, except three patients, there was evidence that there were some prodromal symptoms and this may have been 100% if one includes increasing patient fatigue, quite evident to the spouse. In nearly all of these sudden death patients, as indicated by Dr. Goldstein, there had been a history of previous myocardial infarction or known cardiovascular disease making them high-risk patients.

We have also been particularly interested in eliciting information about the incidence of past peptic ulcer, hiatus hernia, gallbladder disease, or evidence of vasodepressor syncope. One of our hypotheses has been that these categories of past illness might predict those in the population who are vagal reactors and therefore might be candidates for arrhythmias and sudden death. These 26 sudden death patients are not a large enough number to make meaningful comparisons with the group of patients reaching the hospital alive and surviving 24 hours after infarction. None of the patients with sudden death, at least according to the private physician or the spouse, had ever had any episodes of what were interpreted by us as vasodepressor syncope. However, at least a third of them had had well-documented peptic ulcer, gallbladder disease, or hiatus hernia.

We are also gathering from the next-of-kin, as we do with the patients who reach the hospital alive, the incidence of vascular disease, particularly myocardial infarction, angina, cerebrovascular ("stroke") episodes, and peripheral vascular insufficiency in the parents and siblings, regardless of whether the relatives are still alive or dead and the age at death where this has occurred. This pertains to one of our hypotheses that there may be an inverse relationship between the presence of a familial or constitutional factor and the occurrence of prodromal psychological precipitating factors. This has been indicated in certain other diseases, particularly rheumatoid arthritis.

Psychosocial Data

The spouses are asked to give their perceptions of the patient's psychological state on the day of the sudden death and in the 3- to 18-month prodromal period. As mentioned before, it has been of particular interest how frequently the spouse has been afraid that a recurrence of a myocardial infarction or of a catastrophic illness including death was going to occur and the inability that she has had in getting the patient to seek medical help. She usually based this assumption on her awareness of his tension due to increased pressure at work, actual longer hours at work,[13] and on family or other socially precipitated emotional distress for the patient. Even so, approximately half of these patients had seen a physician, generally for a scheduled routine check-up or for symptoms of epigastric or chest discomfort or increase in anginal symptoms, within the preceding ten days.

For all of the patients, the interview included the family make-up, whether the patient had changed his place of residence recently, whether the wife is aware of any recent work change, and in particular, whether there has been any change in the status of the household: parents dying, moving into another home, and in particular, family social transitions which have been a focus of interest to the group at Rochester for some time. This includes the health of the spouse, whether or not there are offspring, and whether the children have moved out of the home recently. In particular, among these men who develop myocardial infarction, we have found considerable psychological distress evoked by circumstances in which there were departures or current disappointing conflicts between the patient and a son or daughter, especially a son.

Circumstances of departure of a child from the home or disappointment of parental expectations appear to be the most commonly reported acute precipitating factor in the patients who reached the hospital, as well as in those with sudden death as reported by the spouse. It may be that this is a commonplace dilemma and occurrence among 50- to 60-year-old men with their offspring in the culture of our times. There is some evidence that this may be a problem peculiar to an industrial plant population where there has been for years considerable conflict between employee-patients who have worked over the years without going to college and other employees who have been to college, where both have the same job classification, for instance as an engineer. It appears to have been particularly important for the one who went to college to have his son emulate him by going to college and for the man who only went to high school or less that his son become one of the college men as he would like to have been in the cultural hierarchy of the plant.

The spouse is asked directly whether there have been any current conflicts between herself and the patient. Generally, I think, the spouses have been reasonably open and accurate in their statements about these matters, including the adequacy or inadequacy of sexual relationships. Sexual incompatibility or impotence has been surprisingly infrequent in these men who are often depressed, at least as far as the data we have obtained is concerned, and has not so far been reported as a source of conflict or as the activity occurring at the time of the patient's final acute illness with sudden death.

Of particular interest to us has been whether the week or the day of the patient's sudden death has any particular significance as far as the patient or the family is concerned. Was this an anniversary of the death of any parent, of a marriage, of a birth, or any significant event in the life of the patient or the family as a group such as the age or date of death of the parents? I described the emotional significance of such anniversaries, conscious or unconscious, as determinants of distressing affective reaction of patients developing relapses in leukemias and lymphomas several years ago.[14] Anniversary reaction as used here is not the same phenomena described originally by Hilgard pertaining to a parent's reaction to a distressing event in his own life as a child when his child in turn reaches the same age.[15] Such age-related reactions between parent and child I term "generation reactions" rather than "anniversary reactions." These factors have been stressed particularly by Fischer and Dlin[16,17] in their studies of patients with myocardial infarctions as "emotionally invested deadlines" and have also been noted by Wolf[13] in his appreciation of the significance of anniversary reactions. These are the main areas that we cover in the interview and there are other details which I will not go into at the present time.

Age and Socioeconomic Status

In my presentation, I am going to hazard committing two taboos. One is not to present any tables or figures and the other is to be somewhat anecdotal about four of the 26 patients to whom I am making reference in this presentation. But I have to give some figures. The mean age of the 25 patients dying suddenly, most likely from myocardial infarction or arrhythmia, or both, (I am not counting the man who committed suicide) was 55.6 years with a median of 56.5 years. Mean age of the patients who reported into the medical facilities on work with suspect or actual myocardial infarction was also 55.7 and a median of 57 years. Those who reported off work, to their own physician or directly to a hospital, were somewhat younger: mean age, 52 years, with a median of 54 years, and they had worked at the plant a somewhat shorter period of time. Combined on-work and off-work age groups showed a mean age of 54 years, so there is no significant difference in age of the sudden death patients compared to the total group of suspect or actual myocardial infarcts. There is also no difference in socioeconomic status between the sudden death patients and those who reached the hospital alive, at least within this industrial population which is probably not representative, being of somewhat higher socioeconomic rank as compared to the total population of Rochester. During the period of the occurrence of the 22 sudden deaths, out of a total of 200 suspect or actual infarctions, there were also six suicides, all among men, with a mean age of 46 years (median, 50.5 years). So the deaths by suicide occurred in men nearly a decade younger than the members of the population dying suddenly or those hospitalized with myocardial infarctions.

Representative Patient Summaries

Psychological factors seemed to play a precipitating factor in the time of development of the event in four categories of sudden death circumstances. It should be pointed out that among 40% to 50% of these patients no evidence was obtained that acute psychological factors were of significance in the time of the patient's death, although such factors may have been a factor in the patient's tardiness in getting to medical help. From the data available, via the sources available, at least 80% of these 26 patients had symptoms which could be construed as depression. They were and had been "running sad."

One 55-year-old man had worked for many years at the plant and had always been quite disorganized and irresponsible in reference to his family as well as his work. Over the course of the summer months, he began putting everything in order both at home and at work. At least in retrospect, his wife felt he knew something was going to happen to him and he wanted to have things in order, including insurance policies, his accounts at home, and his correspondence at work. According to his wife, he had been depressed due to conflicts with his son because the 18-year-old boy had been in court for stealing and had had to serve out his time in jail on weekends for several months. In addition, there was a severe disappointment for both the patient and his wife who had saved for this oldest son to go to college. However, the son had actually had to repeat two years in grammar school, again failed, and was having to repeat another year of high school. On the day after the son was again caught stealing and held for petit larceny, the patient had a massive myocardial infarction at work and died in spite of attempts at resuscitation at the plant.

Representative of the circumstance of a number of patients was the departure of the last or only child in the family for college or marriage, in response to which the patient had been depressed. However, according to his wife, he had not been able to express these feelings and compensated by overextending himself by working harder at home or at the plant or shoveling snow vigorously and developed a sudden cardiovascular collapse.

A unique tale is that of a 50-year-old man who for a year had multiple abscesses of his right breast, not the left, which had required incision and drainage over a period of some eight months, keeping him off from work an appreciable amount of time. He finally agreed to go to the hospital and had a mastectomy in August. He had no previous history of cardiovascular disease, but the evening after his surgery and recovery from anesthesia he developed a myocardial infarction. Following this he did quite well in recovering from his infarction in the hospital and at home. According to his wife, however, he was increasingly depressed and particularly upset that he was not able to be active and return to work. In late October, he had become "not angry," she said, but just "feeling he couldn't do anything about it" when a group of local youngsters blew up a fire cracker damaging their mailbox on the night of Halloween. Three days later his wife persuaded him to take their first stroll in his convalescence into the garden of their home hoping to cheer him up a little. They walked into the back garden and noted for the first time that an arborway, which he had built early that summer and of which he was very proud, had been sprayed with tar paint. The patient apparently just looked at this while his wife expressed her anger. At this, the patient said he did not feel well and wanted to return to the house. He got 20 yards, as far as the kitchen side door, and collapsed. As he did so she asked him whether he was having any pain to which he replied, "No." He died within five minutes. The wife added the fact that she was so relieved that they had not gone further out into the back yard where they had a new trailer which had also been tar spray-painted as a Halloween prank.

It happened on this occasion, since it was unusual for a man to have a mastectomy, that I asked whether having a mastectomy was of any particular significance to this man. To this his wife replied, "It's strange you should ask that question." She then gave an account that her sister had died two years before on Nov. 12 with a carcinoma of the breast after a mastectomy. This man's death actually occurred on Nov. 6. His wife then indicated that on Nov. 3, one year before, the patient's sister, who had had a carcinoma of the breast and a mastectomy, had died, Also on Nov. 12, one year ago, his older and favorite brother had dropped dead of a myocardial infarction.

An additional example is a retired 66-year-old employee who is not in the employee total group, but who is included because of the circumstances of his death and because he happened to be in the company plant at the time of his sudden death. This occurred when he was playing in a billiard tournament in the retirees recreation facility in which he had become very much involved as one of the compensations for his retirement the year before. In the particular league match in which he was playing, he was up against a partner with whom he was especially competitive. This patient also had been depressed since his wife had recently come home from the hospital having suffered a myocardial infarction and his only child, a 40-year-old daughter, had been sick and was in the hospital for evaluation of multiple congenital, including cardiac, anomalies. The course of this match which went evenly back and forth came down to the last two balls on the table. The patient's opponent had an easy shot and the patient said to him, "Well, I guess that's it." Whereupon the opponent took his shot and missed. This left the patient an equally easy shot which he made. He stood up, manifesting his relief and pleasure, and then collapsed on the billiard table and could not be resuscitated. To the knowledge of friends who had been with him for the previous two hours, he had been having no symptoms and had been playing well and accurately without discomfort.

Comments

From this preliminary report, our data suggest that in at least 50% of the patients with sudden death, psychological and social factors are associated with the time of sudden death. It is likely that the frequency of this association might be higher if more specific subjective information were available from the deceased, which is of course impossible. The psychological setting is multifactorial, usually a setting in which the patient has been depressed and expressed this according to another person's observation and a sudden reaction precipitating arousal, such as increased work, anxiety, or anger occurs.

It appears to me that there is some wisdom in the lore which Engel has read into the reports in the newspapers.[8] The data suggest that a combination of depressive and arousal affects may together be conducive in engendering sudden death. Perhaps these combinations of affect states and their physiologic concomitants produce a disharmonious variety of reactions implemented by autonomic and hormonal reactions and central nervous system-mediated behavior. Most attractive is the hypothesis that sudden death occurs in a basically depressed man with high physiological coronary disease risk who for some reason experiences high arousal. On return to his baseline ongoing depressive state after arousal, there may be a decrement in pulse rate and blood pressure in relationship to which there may develop arrhythmia or infarction, or *both*. The report by Hinkle of relative bradycardia and disordered conduction as predictors of sudden death in his population would support this conjecture.[19]

I see no reason to assume from the data we have so far on this group of 26 sudden deaths plus superficially screened data we have on an additional 20 patients that any type of telephone heart attack service or mobile coronary care ambulance would have made any difference. It has been my interpretation that the patients I have seen, both those reaching the hospital as well as the sudden death patients, would have been reluctant to turn to someone for assistance even when appreciating the likelihood that they are having a heart attack of significance. They repress this perception and rationalize its significance rather than face the prospect of the helplessness of being sick. This I expressed at the first Prehospital Conference in 1969, in contrast to Hackett's assumption of the patient's use of denial to defend against the anxiety of the threat of death.[20] It has seemed to me, as I stated at the 1969 Prehospital Conference, that some type of buddy system should be worked out for the high-risk patient. The buddy would most logically be his spouse, a sibling, a friend at home, or a fellow worker. Both patient and buddy should be instructed by the physician with a definite, non-alarming statement that the patient is liable to have a subsequent myocardial infarction and that the patient should turn to the person who has been designated as his buddy. They should both be told what to do if the physician is not immediately available, such as to go to the nearest hospital emergency room or call the local ambulance. This proposal is related to the fact that I think the main problem in the long delay period of patients with myocardial infarction has little to do with anxiety about a heart attack per se or anxiety about dying, so-called denial. The patient is more concerned with a reluctance to admit being helpless or sick and he can only turn to somebody with whom he has previously lived or worked and feels it is permissible to be helpless. Even so, I doubt that this type of preparation would have made an appreciable difference in more than six of these 26 patients with acute sudden death.

It is also likely that the most reliable opportunity for gathering data on the relevance of psychosocial circumstances surrounding sudden death in patients will accrue from a study of patients who do die suddenly but do not actually die, that is to say patients who have potentially lethal arrhythmias and are resuscitated. From such patients one can get prodromal data, including patients' actual behavior, thoughts, and affects prior to the event requiring resuscitation. This approach may present a problem because a few of these patients are amnesic for the immediate prodromal period, but this is not so in most cases. Robert Klein, MD, Dr. Moss, and I are currently getting such information from these patients as they become available in the emergency department and on the coronary care units. Most focus of studies on such patients has instead been on the psychological *effects* of arrest and resuscitation.

In this connection it is germane to mention one patient of Dr. Moss's in which the circumstances precipitated a ventricular tachycardia were certainly closely associated with psychologically distressful occurrences of considerable idiosyncratic emotional significance to this man. He was interviewed by me since he worked at the company and was admitted as a patient of Dr. Moss with a recent obvious myocardial infarction. He requested Dr. Moss as his physician since he had taken such thoughtful and effective care of the patient's wife four years before when she was terminally ill with a cardiomyopathy associated with disseminated carcinoma of the breast. The patient who had no previous significant cardiovascular illness had not seen Dr. Moss, nor had he been in Strong Memorial Hospital since the death of his wife.

While being cared for acutely in the emergency department and without discomfort with his infarction, he was approached about being a research patient on the Inhospital Myocardial Infarction Research Unit (MIRU) study, the investigative purpose of which was explained to him. He agreed since he felt his role as research subject might be beneficial to someone else. He was therefore asked to sign the customary consent form. As he was about to sign, it occurred to him that he might be too weak and not attentive enough in his state of illness to sign his name correctly. This immediately reminded him of the evening four years before when his dying wife had to sign a legal document the night before she died and bemoaned the fact that she was not sure she had the strength or was enough in her right mind to sign her name properly. The patient did sign his name appropriately but was aware of acute grief feelings touched off by this association of his own situation and that of his wife. He was then taken to the third floor of the hospital, the floor he recalled where his wife had been, and he was prepared to the usual MIRU investigative procedures. Still thinking of his wife, he was aware of increased anxiety about what procedures he was going to have to undergo even though he had complete confidence in Dr. Moss and the

MIRU staff. Before any manipulative procedure such as venipunctures or catheterizations were initiated, he developed acute ventricular tachycardia and severe hypotension requiring resuscitation. This recurred three times in the next 15 minutes until the patient was stabilized with lidocaine hydrochloride therapy. This is an instance of an acute arrhythmia which could likely have heralded sudden death and was perhaps precipitated by the patient's idiosyncratic circumstances in association with his wife's death which engendered, quite privately, feelings of intense grief as well as anxiety. Such types of data were available because the patient himself could be interviewed after the event.

References

1. Goldstein S, Moss AJ, Greene WA: Sudden death in acute myocardial infarction: Relationship to factors affecting delay in hospitalization. *Arch Intern Med* 129:720-724, 1972.

2. Greene WA, Moss AJ: Psychosocial factors in the adjustment of patients with permanently implanted cardiac pacemakers. *Ann Intern Med* 70:897-902, 1969.

3. Greene WA, Conron G, Schalch DS, et al.: Psychologic correlates of growth hormone and adrenal secretory responses of patients undergoing cardiac catheterization. *Psychosom Med* 32:599-614, 1970.

4. Greene WA, Sweeney DR, Schreiner BF: Psychological and hormonal characteristics and outcome of patients considered for cardiac surgery, abstracted. *Psychosom Med* 33:475, 1971.

5. Engel GL: Mechanisms of fainting. *J Mt Sinai Hosp* 12:170-190, 1945.

6. Engel GL: *Fainting–Physiological and Psychological Considerations.* Springfield, Ill., Charles C Thomas Publisher, 1950.

7. Engel GL: Sudden death and the "medical model" in psychiatry. *Canad Psychiat Assoc J* 15:527-537, 1970.

8. Engel GL: Sudden and rapid death during psychological stress—folklore or folk wisdom? *Ann Intern Med* 74:771-782, 1971.

9. Moss AJ, Goldstein S, Greene WA, Decamilla J: Prehospital precursors of ventricular arrhythmias in acute myocardial infarction. *Arch Intern Med* 129:756-762, 1972.

10. Kuller L, Lilienfeld A, Fisher R: An epidemiological study of sudden and unexpected deaths in adults. *Medicine* 46:341-361, 1967.

11. Fulton M, Julian DG, Oliver MF: Sudden death and myocardial infarction. *Circulation* 39(suppl):IV-182-IV-193, 1969.

12. Chiang BN, Perlman LV, Fulton M, et al.: Predisposing factors in sudden cardiac death in Tecumseh, Michigan: A prospective study. *Circulation* 41:31-38, 1970.

13. Sales SM, House J: Job dissatisfaction as a possible risk factor in coronary heart disease. *J Chron Dis* 23:861-873, 1971.

14. Greene WA, Young LE, Swisher SN: Psychological factors and reticulo-endothelial disease: II. Observations on a group of women with lymphomas and leukemias. *Psychosom Med* 18:284-303, 1956.

15. Hilgard JR: Anniversary reaction in parents precipitated by children. *Psychiatry* 16:73-80, 1953.

16. Weiss E, Dlin B, Rollin HR, et al.: Emotional factors in coronary occulsion: I. Introduction and general summary. *Arch Intern Med* 99:628-641, 1957.

17. Fischer HK, Dlin BM: Man's determination of his time of illness or death: Anniversary reactions and emotional deadlines. *Geriatrics* 25:89-94, 1971.

18. Earls JH, Wolf S: A report of multiple periodic anniversary reactions in one individual. *Ann Intern Med* 58:530-533, 1963.

19. Hinkle LE, Caver ST, Plakun A: Slow heart rates and increased risk of cardiac death in middle-aged men. *Arch Intern Med* 129:732-748, 1972.

20. Hackett TP, Cassem NH: Factors contributing to delay in responding to the signs and symptoms of acute myocardial infarction. *Amer J Cardiol* 24:651-658, 1969.

IV

Social Processes and Immunity

158

Commentary. The immune system operates by resisting such microscopic invaders as bacteria, viruses, and fungi, as well as malignant transformations of cells that result in diseases such as cancer. This complex system recognizes anything that is "nonself," and repels or destroys the foreign body or antigen through elaborate defenses. These defenses involve lymphocytes and antibodies that are dispersed through most of the tissues of the body. Like most organs, the immune system works most efficiently when it is least burdened. A person already suffering from an infectious disease is much more vulnerable to other invading organisms. A man constantly subjected to a stressful social environment may not have the benefit of an adequate immune response to successfully deal with an invading organism, since hormones activated to deal with stress also suppress the immune response (Selye, 1956).

Thus, the ability of an organism's immune system to resist illness or disease appears to vary with both physical and emotional states and social situations. In an early classic study by Renée Spitz (1949), the mortality rates of infants in two institutions were compared. In institution A the children were raised by their mothers. In institution B the children were cared for by overworked nursing personnel. The institutions were similar in that the infants received adequate food. Hygiene and cleanliness were strictly enforced. The housing of the children was excellent and medical care was equally good. In spite of these similarities, institution B had an infant mortality of 37 percent over a period of two years, while A did not lose a single child through death during a similar period.

Spitz attributes these effects to the social or ecological environment, and specifically to the mother-child interaction, the absence of which is likely to increase the child's vulnerability to illness. While this study has many methodological weaknesses, it is important as an early inquiry into the role the social environment plays with respect to immunological competence. There is still a paucity of research in this area, particularly with human subjects, although more recent investigations have at least indirectly explored the problem (Yarrow, 1963; Rahe et al., 1964; Solomon, Levine and Kraft, 1968).

In Chapter 11 Jonas Salk discusses social factors which may influence disease processes. He suggests that forms of cancer are associated with social, industrial, or environmental influences, and that by altering certain behaviors or habits (i.e., smoking) of the population much can be done to reduce the frequency of some cancers. Salk feels that biological explanations and models of disease must be broadened to include more aspects of human behavior. And from this more encompassing point of view a more insightful understanding of disease processes might arise.

Few people exposed to disease-causing organisms actually contract the disease. Thus it appears that particular individuals are more susceptible than others. In Chapter 12 Stanford Friedman and Lowell Glasgow argue convincingly that psychological stress determines not only who contracts a disease but also who recovers from its effects and gains immunity. They review the relationship between psychosocial situations and the physiologic response to stress, and suggest that the most important stimulus to the activity of some glands are psychological in nature. For example, mild environmental stimulation may change adrenocortical functioning. One study cited by the authors compared corticosteroid levels in adult subjects watching films: the corticosteroid levels in adult subjects watching a Disney nature film were lowered, compared to usual basal levels. In contrast, corticosteroid levels were elevated in subjects watching a war film.

The authors conclude that although it may be possible to demonstrate that a given environmental stress may modify the immunological response to an infectious agent, it is difficult to compare experimenter results, and therefore to generalize about the precise physiological mechanisms involved. They also suggest that investigators have exclusively focused on adrenocortical functioning, whereas the study of other hormones or physiologic processes might yield important new information about the relationship between immunological competence and social phenomena.

The final chapter in this section, by George Solomon and Alfred Amkraut, examines in detail some other social factors that affect the immune response. The authors suggest that personality factors are related to the presence and progression of cancer. Four important attributes are discussed: the loss of a relationship prior to the development of a tumor; the patient's inability to express hostile feelings and emotion; unresolved tension concerning a parental figure; and sexual disturbance. They describe social factors linking susceptibility to and recovery from infectious diseases. They cite one study, for example, which compared families whose children were ill with families of healthy children. The results indicated that families whose children were ill exposed their children to a greater number of social changes which were threatening and disruptive.

References

Rahe, R.H., Meyer, M., Smith, M., Kjaer, G., and Holmes, T.H. Social stress and illness onset. *Journal of Psychosomatic Research, 8*:35-44, 1964.

Selye, H. *The Stress of Life.* New York: McGraw-Hill, 1956.

Solomon, G., Levine, S., and Kraft, J. Early experience and immunity. *Nature, 220:* 821-822, November 23, 1968.

Spitz, Renée. The role of ecological factors in emotional development in infancy. *Child Development, 20*:145-155, 1949.

Yarrow, L.J. Research in dimensions of early maternal care. *Merrill-Palmer Quarterly, 9*:101-114, 1963.

11

Biological Basis of Disease and Behavior

Jonas E. Salk
Salk Institute
La Jolla, California

Attitude toward the Nature of Disease

We are a long way beyond the days when disease was interpreted as the act of a vengeful god or retribution for having sinned. We now look upon disease as something over which man should exercise control; we believe that illness and premature death represent evidence of man's failure either to understand adequately the nature of a disease or to act when specific knowledge is available.

The extent to which life can now be prolonged increases the importance of concern with the meaningfulness and effectiveness of living. The possibilities are now greatly augmented for enrichment of life through wisdom that could accrue to many more whose life span will reach long beyond the minimum necessary to perpetuate the species—and could be used in the service of the generations to follow.

The concept of the biological basis of disease has been so well established and so fruitful that it would seem to be unnecessary to dwell upon the subject. However, I have chosen to do so because I have the feeling that it bears repetition, and especially because the phrase "biological basis of disease and behavior" indicates how this concept serves as a guide in seeking solutions of man's problems.

Reprinted with permission from *Perspectives in Biology and Medicine*, Winter, 1962, pp. 198-206.

We are all aware of the extent to which advancing clinical knowledge and diagnostic skills can reduce suffering and save many from premature death. We are also aware that ultimate solutions to problems of human disease come from understanding the relevant biological mechanisms that become disordered, giving rise to disease. Understanding of this kind leads inevitably to insights into the development of means for treatment and, sometimes, prevention.

You will observe that I am leading you to the familiar position of all who try to spread the gospel that the development of a useful practice or procedure for the control of disease comes through knowledge and understanding that is built by a great many who, like those who fashion bricks or girders, often do not see the ultimate structure to which they have contributed essential parts. I am certain that you know this and that you are aware of the importance of basic and unrelated observations often made without any idea of the place they may later have in solutions that are soon taken for granted.

Among those who possess the means to make it possible for free and uninhibited imaginative work to be done, there are few who become enthusiastic without a promise that the work in question does have a defined relation to the solution of some immediate problem. I say this because I have in recent months been in touch with men of means and with those who are intrusted with disbursing funds for foundations. The conservatism that prevails in the face of the obvious need to continue to experiment in new and bold ways convinces me that our errors are more often those of omission than of commission. I mention this personal experience to draw your attention to the possibilities ahead through the recognition of the biological nature of disease and behavior. These possibilities can be realized only by deeper and broader exploration of biological systems and the construction of biological concepts that may serve to unify knowledge and understanding of the organization and processes of life—that such knowledge and understanding may then be applied to the art of living as well as to problems of disease.

Biological Basis of Neoplastic Disease

I want to illustrate the idea behind the term "biological basis of disease." A question-asking attitude as well as an answer-finding attitude is implied in it. A question must be asked before it can be answered. To discover the right question may be the secret. The right answer may already have been found but, since the question has not been asked, the answer cannot be given. It might almost be said that all answers pre-exist; the questions do not. How does one go about asking questions that are interesting to try to answer?

I believe I can illustrate this by beginning with such popular questions as: "What is the cause of cancer?" . . . "Is it caused by a virus?" . . . "Will we ever have a cancer vaccine?" It may be of interest to use these as a background and see whether there are any other questions that might be asked.

Let us begin by thinking of a cancer cell as a normal cell that has been "bewitched"; one that now behaves very much like a free-living microorganism not unlike a tubercle bacillus or a staphylococcus, for example, or some other microbe that multiplies by cell division.

For a moment let us imagine that a cell which is normally part of a totally integrated organism becomes altered, by any one of a number of different factors, until it possesses properties characteristic of a microbial parasite. Such a cell then metabolizes, multiplies, and metastasizes without the limiting influences that apply to cells which normally remain within the limits of the body economy. It becomes a cell that does not contribute in a useful way but draws upon the economy of the host for nourishment as would an unwelcome guest.

An immunological defense is the most common one against bacterial cells—the tubercle bacillus, for example—that derive nourishment from the host in the same unwelcome way as does a cancer cell. After an initial period of multiplication of tubercle bacilli, or other bacteria, the body recognizes the existence of a foreign invader and the appropriate defensive cells come into play. These react appropriately by producing one or more forms of antibody to curtail and then destroy the invading organism. Under normal circumstances the body does not react this way to its own cells; if it did, vital cells and organs would be destroyed. (Occasionally this does happen, but only under unusual circumstances of disease involving the immunological mechanism.) Thus, when one of its own cells goes "berserk," as may be said of the cancer cell, the body does not normally react to this immunologically by some kind of antibody formation unless the cancer cell is sufficiently different in the immunological sense to be recognized as "not-self."

Let us develop these thoughts a bit further. But we will not concern ourselves for the moment with what sets in motion the neoplastic process, whether it be a virus or hormones or the spontaneous occurrence of a mutation or exposure to tars or to radioactivity. We will consider merely that "a cell has been born" that has altered properties in which the multiplication shut-off mechanism has been lost or in some way removed. Unless the cell is sufficiently different immunologically to be recognized as foreign, or "not-self," then we can see the "helplessness" on the part of the body to restrict growth or to destroy the "lawless cell" which it does not recognize as foreign. It is as if the defensive cells of the body cannot destroy one of their own flesh and blood, even though one of their own flesh and blood is destroying the whole economy and will, in the process, eventually destroy itself.

How can one cope with such a situation? One school of thought believes that chemicals will be found that have a selectively poisonous effect upon cancer cells, advantage being taken of the fact that cancer cells are somewhat different metabolically from normal cells. While this approach toward treatment clearly has been successful in a number of neoplastic diseases, it has, in general, been less rewarding than the search for chemical agents for bacterial diseases. The bacterial cell and the host cell are quite different metabolically and immunologically. The limitation in cancer chemotherapy is similar to that in chemotherapy of virus diseases, the degree of difference between the substance of the virus and the host's substance from which it must be distinguished metabolically being not so different as in the case of bacteria and host. The possibility of devising additional toxic chemicals that differentiate between virus and host or between cancers and host is by no means impossible or inconceivable, but it is much more difficult than for bacterial diseases.

The problem for cancer can be more clearly illustrated by viruses or bacteria that can "hide away" inside a host's cell and remain protected and out of contact with the immunological system. Under such circumstances, either the immunological system fails to be stimulated or it is unable to exercise an effective attack. Such viruses and bacteria are camouflaged in the cloak of the population they have invaded; they have developed the most perfect protective coloration conceivable. This essentially is also the nature of the cancer cell.

If any immunological difference that exists between cancer and host cells could be exposed to the defensive cells of the immunological system, then it is conceivable that an active defense would develop and regression or cure would come about.

Is it conceivable that some instances of spontaneous regression and cure observed under natural circumstances, or regression under certain coincidental or therapeutic circumstances, may have been due not to loss of vitality of the tumor cell but to an antigenic change in the cell expressed in a way that permitted the immunological defense of the host to come into play and bring about a sequence of events not unlike that occurring in the course of cure of a microbial disease, as in tuberculosis, for example?

Might some of the procedures which are believed to be responsible for inducing regression of neoplastic disease have activated the immunologic mechanism of the host, not directly, but rather by altering the proteinsynthesizing system within the neoplastic cell, especially for the surface antigens, in a way that increased the degree of recognizable immunological difference between cancer cell and host so that the normal graft-rejection phenomenon could come into play? It appears from histologic examination of biopsy or surgical specimens from neoplastic disease that some degree of immunological intolerance exists in many instances; it is a clinical-pathologic axiom that the clinical course is more favorable when a surgical or biopsy specimen reveals a strong lymphocytic reaction in the periphery of a tumor. It may be concluded from this and other relevant information that where tumor persists, sufficient immunological difference does not exist to effect rejection.

Observations from many sources as well as some made in our laboratory over the past several years have led us to explore the possibility that agents may exist that could act upon neoplastic cells, not by destroying them directly, but by so altering such cells antigenically that the host may then react immunologically and destroy such cells through its normal graft-rejection mechanism, as if the tumor belonged to another host.

If such a mechanism is in fact operative, then a systematic search will be of value, not only for cell poisons that have a differential effect upon cancer and normal cells, but for agents that induce differential alterations in the protein-synthesizing information system of the cell, possibly affecting synthesis of surface antigens especially. A limitation in potential clinical usefulness of such agents would be that the effects are not sufficiently differential on normal versus neoplastic cells. This would also be true for protein-altering agents unless a large enough proportion of the normal cell population were not affected so that sufficient regeneration could occur.

Recent studies in our laboratory suggest that the essential component of the immunological system for tumor rejection is not that primarily engaged in the formation of humoral antibody but that associated with cellular antibody, such as is involved in both the delayed hypersensitivity reaction and the homograft reaction. The failure, or limited usefulness, of serum from immunized animals or of active immunization procedures, except where large enough immunological differences exist between cell and host, is understandable in the light of the investigations leading to these tentative conclusions.

I will not go into discussion of the technical aspects of the experimental approach to test some of the hypotheses that I have referred to since it is my intention primarily to illustrate the meaning of the term "biological nature of disease" by discussing cancer in terms of understanding the problem in its many ramifications rather than in terms of a single cause or single cure. There is more than one approach to devising a means of control.

Many laboratories are concerned with investigating the immunological aspects of neoplastic disease, and I would like to be able to put the various ideas and approaches into perspective, but this occasion does not allow more than a hint of the diversity.

Viruses and Cancer

Before concluding these remarks on cancer, I would like to touch upon one way viruses in general may be studied to arrive at further understanding of their role as a cause of neoplasia.

There is increasing evidence that viruses can initiate a neoplastic process, but demonstrable proof in man is still forthcoming. There is reason to believe that viruses may initiate such a process but may then disappear in the cell so altered, thus resulting in a fruitless search for a criminal that has committed the perfect crime. It would be the equivalent of murder with an icicle that then melted away. The mutagenic effect of radiation or radioactive substances or of certain chemical mutagens would be analogous.

It is conceivable that some neoplastic processes could be initiated in unusual instances by certain of the common viruses. Therefore, if viruses can be controlled generally by immunologic means—as has been shown to be possible, by vaccines made of viruses that have been rendered non-infectious, such as the killed-virus vaccines for influenza and for polio, for example—then, in retrospect, some neoplastic processes may be observed to be reduced in frequency and possibly to disappear. An analogy may be the control of such diseases as rheumatic fever and the secondary and tertiary consequences of syphilis, etc., which have followed as a consequence of the primary control of certain bacterial and other microbial diseases.

It may be of value to speculate about the possible relationship of common viruses to neoplasia. But even if the hypothesis that some neoplastic diseases may be initiated by commonly prevalent viruses proved to be of limited value, or of no value whatever, in respect to the control of cancer, the consequences of a course of conduct that would lead to the control of virus diseases generally would be advantageous. Such lines of pursuit would have one benefit, and possibly more.

Thus, we see the complex cause-and-effect inter-relationships implied by disease. A given cause, such as a virus, can induce different effects, and a given effect, such as cancer, can be induced by diverse causes. For some diseases, we think not of the "cause" but of the "biological nature," thus encompassing the application of many disciplines rather than the techniques and understanding of only one. Control will come from direct empirical approaches only if based upon biologically sound hypotheses, or at least upon hypotheses that can be tested. It is clear that, henceforth, understanding and control of the still unsolved problems of disease require the development of unifying biological concepts and principles.

Social Factors in the Control of Cancer

With respect to the control of cancer now, it is believed that whatever may be the precise mechanisms involved, cancer of the lung and cancer of the lip and tongue could be reduced in frequency by altered smoking habits of the population. It has been shown that other forms of cancer are associated with certain social, industrial, or environmental influences, the elimination of which can affect the incidence of these diseases. It is also known that routine examination can favorably influence the outcome of cancers accessible to simple methods of examination.

While much can now be done by eliminating or reducing known hazards, and by early diagnosis and treatment, the fascinating biological problem of cancer still remains. Through the study of cancer much will be learned about biology, and from the study of biology much will be learned that will be of value in the further control of cancer. Even studies in social biology will reveal why people expose themselves to clear and apparent risk and why they do not exercise the self-control necessary to *not* do something hazardous, or fail to exercise the self-control necessary *to do* something beneficial, preventive, or protective.

Biological Basis of Behavior

This leads me to a few concluding remarks about the "behavior" part of the title of this discussion against the background that has been laid, although time will not permit as full elaboration of the idea as I will develop for another occasion. The word is intended to include disease expressed in behavior.

The essential idea, which I have touched upon elsewhere,* is that the cells of the central nervous system basically resemble cells of the reticuloendothelial system—i.e., the immunological system—even though they are, of course, obviously different in many details. It is tempting to apply concepts of both genetics and immunology to the development and maturation of some CNS functions. If we can study CNS phenomena according to those biological principles that have been shown to be applicable to other systems, a basis for reconsidering behavior in biologically meaningful terms may emerge, which then by empirical means may expand further our understanding of the CNS of man and all that flows therefrom: behavior, creative activity, motivation, values, responsibility, and the intangible qualities of personality reflected in reactions, choices, aptitudes, and attitudes.

The suggestion in the title of this paper is that biological ideas can give birth to new ideas, which, in turn, will suggest methods to develop means whereby man can control not only his physical diseases but diseases of unreasonableness, prejudice, and selfishness. In time these will be the most common, as they are now amongst the most serious.

We continue to witness startling evidences of the enormity of man's inhumanity, even as its level is being reduced—but by measures that neither adequately nor appropriately match the problem, for we do not yet fully or correctly understand its nature. As we see the successes that have been scored by an approach to man's problems through deeper understanding of the science of biology, we have reason to hope that our way into the future will be found by following the broad path of biology.

Man's view of himself and of the diseases that afflict him has only relatively recently in human history become biologically oriented. His sense of security derives from the discovery and understanding of cause-and-effect relationships. What man now knows is but a small fraction of what he will know. His understanding will deepen as he accepts a realistic conceptual structure for the facts he learns. Therefore, biological explanations and models must be developed to encompass as broadly as possible the various manifestations of human behavior. The application of biological principles and concepts for an interpretation of behavior can revolutionize man's thought beyond anything that has yet been realized.

This is the direction of change, but how the new knowledge will contribute to man's control over himself individually and over the human condition generally remains to be seen.

*"Biology in the Future," presented April 8, 1961, at Massachusetts Institute of Technology Centennial.

12

Psychologic Factors and Resistance to Infectious Disease

Stanford B. Friedman
Lowell A. Glasgow
University of Rochester Medical Center

Only a small percentage of persons who become colonized or infected by a parasite actually acquire disease. The production of disease by a microorganism, then, is only one of the possible outcomes of a relation between that organism and a host. Since infectious *disease* is a product of a host-parasite relation, it is apparent that to understand the disease process one must examine both the factors which determine the capacity of the microorganism to invade and initiate infection, and those which affect the response of the host to that infection. The rapid advances in control and treatment of infectious diseases in recent years have resulted primarily from the focus of attention on the microorganism, and only more recently has the necessity for further elucidation of the host response become apparent. Thus both in practice and in the laboratory we must try to find better ways of defining the "determinants of disease" of which Dubos[17] spoke, i.e. the physiologic and environmental factors concerned with resistance to infection.

The purpose of this paper is to consider briefly the complexity of the factors associated with host resistance and to examine the evidence concerning one aspect of environmental influence: namely, the possibility that psychologic influences contribute to the process of infection and the production of disease in

Reprinted with permission from *Pediatrics Clinics of North America*, Vol. 13, No. 2 (May 1966), pp. 315-335. Published by W.B. Saunders Company.

man. Although at present the concepts to be presented are intended primarily to provide working hypotheses for the development of experimental models, it is hoped that this discussion also will stimulate the reader to be cognizant of the possible influence psychologic factors have upon resistance to microbial disease and to look for and consider these factors in the daily practice of medicine.

Determinants of Disease

The broad scope of factors influencing the individual in his interaction with the microbial population of his environment, and the possible outcomes of such interactions, are schematically illustrated in Figure 12-1. In any given situation the relation of an individual host and any of the numerous microorganisms to which he is exposed may be determined by one or, more likely, by a number of the exogenous and endogenous influences presented in this diagram.

There seems little question that only a small minority of persons exposed to potentially pathogenic organisms actually contract clinical disease. It has been estimated, for example, that nearly 100 percent of the population may become

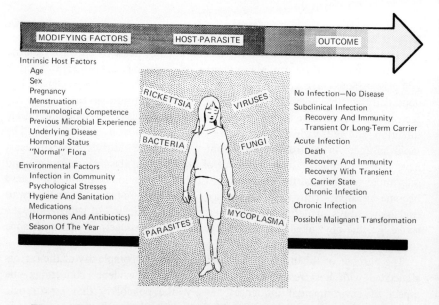

Figure 12-1. Schematic Illustration of Intrinsic Host and Environmental Factors which may Interact to Influence the Host's Response to Potentially Pathogenic Microbial Organisms, and the Possible Outcomes of the Resulting Host-Parasite Relations.

transiently colonized with meningococci (*N. meningitidis*), yet only a tiny fraction of such infected persons suffer disease.[67] This pattern is repeated in many host-parasite relations. The pediatrician frequently cultures beta hemolytic streptococcus from the throats of asymptomatic children and from children with diseases unrelated to this organism. Carrier rates during streptococcal epidemics may reach 40 percent of a school population, again with only a portion of these actually manifesting symptoms. What is critical in our developing concept of host-parasite relations is that the occurrence of disease in this small fraction of infected persons does not happen in a random fashion. Or, more simply expressed, certain persons are more susceptible to infectious diseases than others.

The question we are considering is: What factors are responsible for this phenomenon? In some host-parasite relations, specific factors may be defined which increase the probability of infection progressing to disease. Many such examples might be drawn from the experiences of medical practice and from animal experiments. Only one model, however, of host-parasite relations will be discussed to illustrate the complexity of host resistance: namely, the factors involved in modifying host resistance to the Coxsackie B viruses. At the same time this example will provide background information for the evidence to be presented that factors which could be considered psychologically stressful might be expected to influence host-parasite relations in man.

The changing pattern of infectious diseases with maturation of the host is readily apparent to physicians, particularly to pediatricians, and a greatly increased susceptibility to many forms of infection due to viral and bacterial agents is characteristic of premature and newborn infants. The Coxsackie B viruses produce a number of usually benign clinical syndromes in older children and adults, including pleurodynia and aseptic meningitis. These same viruses in the infant, however, may take a much more fulminant course, with rapid dissemination and multiple organ involvement including liver, pancreas, heart and brain.[70] The marked susceptibility of suckling mice, in contrast to adult mice, to the Coxsackie B viruses parallels these human observations, and investigation of this phenomenon has served to define a number of determinants which may contribute to this age-related difference in susceptibility.

A significant body of evidence has implicated interferon as being involved in host resistance to viral infections.[3,28] Recently Heineberg and co-workers[31] demonstrated that in suckling mice Coxsackie B virus multiplication stimulates little interferon production by host tissues. In contrast, infections with this virus in older, resistant animals are characterized by restricted viral replication and a significantly greater interferon response. These data, then, would suggest that the capacity of the host to respond to viral infection with production of interferon is one determinant of resistance to virus infection, and that in the "mouse-Coxsackie B" model this response is related to the age of the host.

In another interesting investigational approach to this problem Behbehani et al.[5] demonstrated increase of susceptibility in older suckling mice if newly parturient foster mothers are substituted for the original mothers. These results suggested to the authors the presence of a factor in the newly postpartum milk of mice which, in this situation, increased the susceptibility of the suckling animals. This finding is particularly interesting since gravid female mice are themselves more susceptible to infection with Coxsackie viruses,[14] suggesting the speculation that the hormonal levels observed during pregnancy might be related to the susceptibility of suckling mice to this virus.

The interaction between different microorganisms infecting man has been long recognized, and has found expression in such practices as feeding lactobacilli in the treatment of diarrhea and, more recently, in the use of an attenuated strain of staphylococci to prevent colonization by a more virulent one. Viral interference, i.e. the ability of one virus to inhibit the replication of a second virus either in vitro or in vivo, has been an extensively investigated phenomenon. That viral-bacterial interactions not only may occur, but also may have clinical implication, has been demonstrated in the "cloud babies" described by Eichenwald et al.,[19] in that infants have an increased capacity to disseminate staphylococci into their environment in the presence of dual infection with staphylococcus and a virus. Recent evidence suggests that viral-bacterial interaction also may be a factor in resistance to Coxsackie B virus. Schaffer and co-workers[65] have shown that contamination of germ-free suckling mice with a strain of staphylococci increased resistance to lethal infection with Coxsackie B virus. Thus resistance to disease in certain instances would appear related not only to host factors themselves, but also to the presence or absence of other host-parasite relations.

The course of many infectious diseases may be influenced by endogenous or exogenously supplied corticosteroids,[42,43] including the Coxsackie virus-host model that we have been considering. Kilbourne and Horsfall[44] and Boring and co-workers[7] have presented evidence that adult mice, normally resistant to Coxsackie B virus infections, may be rendered susceptible after treatment with adrenal cortical steroids. If exogenous corticosteroids produce such an alteration of host resistance, then it would appear reasonable to postulate that some of the many factors, including psychologic stress, which are known to affect the pituitary-adrenal cortical axis and endogenous corticosteroid levels may concomitantly influence susceptibility to infectious diseases.

There is little doubt that a given host-parasite relation is influenced by many factors. In considering the Coxsackie B viruses, it is apparent that age, interferon production, pregnancy, other microbial flora, and hormonal status are some of the determinants of disease "due to" this viral agent. Likewise, in clinical medicine, many of the determinants of the outcome of host-parasite relations are known, but these known determinants do not fully explain the observed nonrandom distribution of disease.

Psychologic Factors in the Etiology of Disease

Until recently those interested in psychosomatic medicine have paid little attention to infectious diseases. This is somewhat surprising, for in our everyday life we often explain decreased resistance as the result of unusual fatigue or emotional stress. Thus both the professional and the lay person may connect emotional stresses in an individual's life to increased susceptibility, explaining that his "general resistance" was lowered and he was "run-down."

Commonly, and perhaps traditionally, psychogenic diseases are often thought of as those in which psychologic factors *directly cause* a diseased state. Thus a given emotional crisis, or series of psychologic upheavals, might be sought for in a patient whose symptoms could not be explained on an "organic" basis. Furthermore, it has been proposed that particular personality types, or patterns of behavior, might predispose a person to specific diseases, hence designating someone as the "peptic ulcer type." Clinical studies continue to suggest that such formulations have a strong element of truth to them, but the practitioner may not often observe this direct and specific relation between psychologic behavior and clinical disease. To a large degree, the problem is that such psychogenic explanations of disease are greatly oversimplified and have led more recent investigators such as Engel[21] to propose a "multi-factorial approach" to the causation of disease, including many of the factors already illustrated in Figure 12-1. Furthermore, it is not sufficient merely to enumerate the possible etiologic factors, but it is important to realize that these multiple factors may interact with each other in ways that are not merely additive. Indeed, it is the study of these interactions that truly defines the present field of psychosomatic medicine.[1]

It is necessary, therefore, when evaluating the importance of psychologic factors in the causation of a disease to examine concurrently constitutional and nonpsychologic environmental influences. Thus in a study of young adults[58] it was possible to predict accurately who would acquire peptic ulcers—a lesion considered often to be associated with emotional distress—by using *both* psychologic and physiologic data, the latter being the plasma pepsinogen levels of the men under study. Nevertheless this concept of a psychologic *and* a constitutional etiologic influence is in itself a vast oversimplification. It may be that the pepsinogen levels themselves are not entirely genetically determined and are, to some degree, modified by later psychologic experiences or eating patterns. In turn, there is increasing evidence that newborns differ in their behavior patterns and that these inborn differences may significantly influence later psychologic and emotional development.[48] It is also obvious that there is no reason to consider only two etiologic factors, and the clinician and the investigator both have the task of defining those influences that have a significant or measurable effect upon the host from a seemingly infinite number of genetic and environmental possibilities.

With these views in mind, is it reasonable to think that psychologic factors might influence the acquisition or course of a disease "caused" by an infectious agent? Our thesis is that it would be surprising if this were *not* so, taking into account the delicate balance that often exists between the host's physiologic defenses and the pathogenicity of the microorganism. Again we quote Dubos:[18]

Any event in the outer world which impinges on an individual modifies, however indirectly and slightly, the balance between his various organs and functions. In reality, therefore, the internal environment should not be considered apart from the external environment. Shivering or pallor, brought about either by exposure to cold or by a sudden fear, is but the outward manifestation of a physiological disturbance which may alter indirectly the performance of many essential body mechanisms. . . . Thus, the internal environment is constantly responding to the external environment, and history—racial, social, as well as individual—conditions the manner of response just as much as does the intrinsic nature of the stimulus.

Psychologic Stress

For the purpose of this discussion, "stress" is defined as any environmental stimulation that is noxious to the organism or would be if physiologic processes were not activated to prevent injury; such stimuli have also been termed stressors. *Psychologic* stress may be further defined as having to be mediated by the central nervous system, in contrast to the direct injury caused by noxious stimulation such as excessive heat or physical trauma. As will be brought out later in this section, the central nervous system may augment physiologic reactivity in other organs or systems (such as the pituitary-adrenocortical axis) by relating past experiences to the stress, and in man intrapsychic processes may actually initiate such responses. On the other hand, the central nervous system may diminish the responsiveness of other systems by successfully coping with the threatening nature of the stimulus.

There is no *a priori* reason to assume that psychologic stress is necessarily detrimental to the organism in a specific situation. As an analogy, one has only to recall that certain nutritional deficiencies lead to decreased resistance to some types of microorganisms, while increasing resistance to others.[68] Furthermore, continuous nutritional deprivation may lead to a "series of reproducible phases of increased and decreased resistance" to viral agents.[69] Likewise, the influence of a defined psychologic stress may well depend upon the nature of the offending microorganism, as well as the prestress physiologic status of the host and the time relation between the stress and exposure to the infectious agent.

The mechanisms which may link psychologic stresses to host resistance are poorly defined at present and probably are multiple. It is known from both animal and human experiments that the emotional state of the organism can affect heart and respiratory rates, blood pressure, peripheral vascular tone, renal blood flow, rate of perspiration, and many other metabolic processes.

Under hypnosis either an increased or decreased inflammatory reaction to standard noxious stimulation could be produced, depending on the nature of the hypnotic suggestion.[12] All these, and other, physiologic responses to psychologic stress might well influence systemic or local resistance to specific infectious agents. Indeed, epinephrine injected into skin or muscle has been observed to increase the susceptibility of these tissues to a number of bacterial agents.[22] Section of the sciatic nerve also has been shown to increase the ability of the involved muscle to support the growth of Coxsackie A viruses in adult mice, whereas under normal conditions only muscle from suckling mice has this property.[63]

Those interested in the possible relation of psychologic factors and modified susceptibility to microorganisms have been particularly interested in the central nervous system's influence upon the secretion rate of various hormones. The reason for this focus upon endocrine function is twofold. First, as has already been mentioned, it has been repeatedly demonstrated that hormones, particularly the adrenal hormones, modify susceptibility to a great number of microorganisms in both the experimental animal and in man. Second, as will be discussed, there is now abundant evidence that psychologic stress has a profound influence upon a number of endocrine glands, though the majority of studies have been concerned specifically with adrenocortical function. Thus there has been the speculation that the adrenocorticosteroids, and probably other hormones, might act either alone or in conjunction with other physiologic processes to modify host susceptibility as a result of psychologic stress. It has been further proposed that the modified resistance might be related to the known influence of the adrenocortical hormones upon antibody levels[55] and interferon production.[45]

Physiologic Response to Psychologic Stress

Adrenocortical function appears extremely sensitive to psychologic influences and may be reflected in altered serum corticosteroid levels, urinary excretion rates, or disruption of the normal diurnal rhythm of steroid secretion. The very sensitivity of the anterior pituitary-adrenocortical axis led Mason et al.[54] to discard the concept of "normal" values, since in the monkey it was found that corticosteroid levels consistently reflected such subtle changes as the decreased activity in the laboratory over the weekend. Likewise in the rate, "resting" corticosterone levels were related to such equally subtle factors as how the animals were housed.[4] In man, 17-hydroxycorticosteroid levels were depressed, as compared to usual basal levels, in adult subjects watching a Disney nature movie, and were elevated in subjects watching a war movie.[75] These are just a few examples of how, in many species, extremely mild environmental stimulation may change adrenocortical function.

Further studies in human subjects are reviewed by Hamburg,[30] who concludes that elevated 17-hydroxycorticosteroid levels are particularly noted in the presence of disintegrative anxiety, clinical depressive disorders, and situations characterized by a high degree of novelty and ambiguity. A number of recent studies have related adrenocortical function to the *effectiveness* of coping behavior or ego defense structure, and the breakdown of such adaptive psychologic functioning has been associated with elevated corticosteroid levels. For instance, in a group of parents of children with leukemia, the higher 17-hydroxycorticosteroid excretion rates were observed in those parents judged to be relatively *ineffective* in coping with the problems of caring for a fatally ill child.[26,77]

Numerous studies have partially elucidated how the central nervous system may exert an influence upon the pituitary-adrenocortical system. It has been observed in monkeys[52] and in man[49] that stimulation of certain areas of the amygdala results in increased levels of blood corticosteroids, whereas stimulation of the hippocampal area appears to inhibit adrenocortical function. Destructive lesions in these portions of the brain seem to have the opposite effect.[46] It is thought that the limbic system influences ACTH secretion by way of connections with hypothalamic areas. It is in the hypothalamus, particularly the median eminence, that ACTH-releasing factors appear to be secreted and are carried to the anterior lobe of the pituitary by a portal system.[62] Bush[10] has emphasized the importance of psychologic stress in activating such a system:

It is probable that very severe burns, and large doses of certain agents such as bacterial pyrogens, histamine, and peptones, cause a brisk release of ACTH that is independent of any emotional concomitants; but it is extremely doubtful whether any of the physical stimuli which are commonly supposed to be "stresses" are effective in causing the increased secretion of ACTH at all. Thus, severe exercise, cold and fasting produce little or no effect on the secretion and metabolism of cortisol in man unless they are part of a situation that provokes emotion. On the other hand, strong emotion in the absence of any recognizable physical stimuli or "stresses" regularly cause maximal increases in the secretion rate of cortisol and its concentration of peripheral blood. . . . Our whole concept of the adrenal cortex as a gland the secretions of which regulate an as yet undiscovered metabolic process that affects the metabolism of carbohydrate, protein, and other substances is thrown into confusion by the suggestion that the most important natural stimulus to the activity of the gland is psychological in character.

Another reason for the focus upon the adrenal cortex is that much of the work relating infectious diseases to psychologic stress has been stimulated by the known effect of exogenous adrenocorticosteroids upon host resistance, and often it has been hypothesized that the findings in these experiments are dependent upon intrinsic changes in adrenocortical function. But it has *not* yet been demonstrated that corticosteroids secreted as a physiologic response to stress can directly influence the acquisition or course of a disease associated with a known infectious agent; this is in contrast to the dramatic effect that exogenous ACTH or corticosteroid has on a large number of infectious processes due to fungal, bacterial and viral agents. Attention also should be directed to the fact that in many experimental studies the administered adrenal steroid has not been that naturally secreted by the animal; for instance, cortisone often augments infection in the mouse, but the primary adrenal steroid in this species appears to be corticosterone.[76]

This emphasis on adrenocortical function is somewhat arbitrary, and due in part to our relatively greater knowledge about the effect of stress upon this particular gland. It is becoming increasingly clear, however, that psychologic stress influences the secretion of other hormones, including epinephrine, norepinephrine, thyroid hormone and the sex hormones. Mason[53] has discussed the advantages of simultaneously measuring several hormones in situations of stress, and stated that one must entertain the possibility that these hormones are acting in synergetic and antagonistic relations.

Clinical Studies

As suggested earlier in this paper, certain persons appear more susceptible to infectious agents than others. Hinkle, Wolff and their colleagues[32-35] present the most convincing clinical data that emotional factors may in fact influence the distribution and course of infectious diseases. They found in a large group of telephone company employees that absenteeism was not equally distributed, but concentrated in one segment of the working population. In their study of over 1000 telephone operators[35] they noted that one third of this group accounted for two thirds of the days absent from work, and that infectious respiratory illnesses accounted for a large proportion of all reported disease. These investigators then selected a subsample composed of 20 women with a high absentee rate and 20 with an extremely low rate, and studied these 40 subjects intensively. It was found that, in general, the women who were often absent from work were "dissatisfied, discontented, unhappy and resentful at their lot in life and that throughout their working years they were loaded with outside responsibilities, worries and frustrations . . . " Of interest is that the family histories and childhood experiences were similar for both groups of women, and the outstanding difference appeared to be that the "high absentee" group were subsequently exposed to many more life stresses. The 20 "high absentee" women reported 12 times as many minor respiratory illnesses and many more instances of abdominal pain than the "low absentee" group. All the menstrual and menopausal symptoms were found in the "high absentee" group.

In a subsequent study of displaced Chinese graduate students[34] it was shown that 25 percent of them experienced 50 percent of all illnesses, and two subsamples were again selected from the total group, namely, those "rarely ill" and those "frequently ill." In this study it was observed that members of both groups had faced many difficult life experiences, but those "rarely ill" *viewed* their lives as interesting, varied and relatively satisfying. Those "frequently ill" were described as being more inner-directed, more self-absorbed, and more highly aware of emotional and interpersonal problems, than those "rarely ill." Thus, in this more recent study, it would appear that "the actual life situations encountered are less important in this respect than the way in which these situations are perceived."[34]

The data reviewed have related to the reporting of symptoms and absentee rates, which may not reflect the actual incidence of illness as much as how one reacts to disease. Certainly there is a great deal of variation in individual response to both minor and major illness, and this has been the expressed interest of many studies. Yet in their study of telephone operators, Hinkle and Plummer[35] point out that even major illnesses appeared to concentrate in the same relatively small group of individuals and that these same individuals accounted for most of the minor and major accidents. This suggests that the true incidence of disease actually did differ in the two groups under study as variations in reporting might be assumed to be of less import in major illness and accidents.

Some interesting data regarding the reporting of "cold" symptoms were included in a study by Jackson et al.[37] on susceptibility and immunity to common viral respiratory infections. As part of their investigation, a control group of volunteers were given, as nasal drops, uninfected material. A direct relation was noted between the number of colds per year reported by the subject and the likelihood of his developing symptoms after the uninfected inoculum. Thus, of the 23 subjects who reported a usual history of five or more colds per year, 26 percent developed a "cold" according to the criteria used in the experiments, whereas in those reporting only one to two colds per year less than 10 percent developed a "cold" after the benign inoculum. The more susceptible persons were found, as a group, to believe that emotional factors influenced physical status, and tended to report worry or concern about some problem existing at the time of the experimental challenge. It should be noted, however, that though personality factors influenced the reporting of symptoms after a placebo inoculum, such factors did not appear to influence the acquisition of symptoms after an inoculation of infected material.

Meyer and Haggerty[57] attempted to look more directly at the possible influence of family crises upon resistance to infection, and, in particular, the evaluation of factors that might modify susceptibility to streptococcal disease. In 16 families observed for a 12-month period, each family member was followed with periodic throat cultures, antistreptolysin O titers, and clinical evaluation of all illnesses. Certain environmental factors, such as close contact with infected family members and season of the year, were noted to influence whether a given person would acquire the streptococcal organism. Furthermore, both streptococcal and nonstreptococcal respiratory illnesses were about four times as frequent after family episodes judged to be stressful. The authors then utilized a rating scale of chronic stress and noted a definite increase in acquisition rate, prolonged carrier states, streptococcal illness rate and anti-streptolysin O response as the chronic stress score increased. These findings probably represent the best clinical data available directly relating psychologic and social factors to susceptibility to an infectious agent. The findings are also consistent with those of Schottstaedt et al.,[66] who noted that streptococci were isolated most often in children insecure in their parental relationships.

In a well designed study[29] 38 students at the University of Wisconsin were judged as to their rate of recovery from infectious mononucleosis by an internist using hematologic data as criteria. The subjects were then divided into a "long-recovery" and a "short-recovery" group. Approximately six months later the subjects were administered the Minnesota Multiphasic Personality Inventory, and two scales were used to assess psychologic health (ego-strength). There was a statistically significant positive association of these measures of psychologic health and rate of recovery from infectious mononucleosis. Other studies have also dealt with recovery rate from various illnesses, but typically have been concerned primarily with personality disturbances influencing the individual's reaction to his illness and medical management,[8,36] rather than whether psychologic factors might directly influence a physiologic or recovery process.

Investigators have been impressed with the association of stressful emotional experiences and the development of lesions due to herpes simplex.[6,27] This virus has been of particular interest, since a large number of nonspecific physical stresses are known to be precipitate typical herpetic lesions, presumably by upsetting the equilibrium between host and parasite, thus activating the "latent" virus, and it has been speculated that psychologic stresses might act in a similar manner.

It has been noted that the distribution of somatic complaints and illnesses in patients hospitalized for psychiatric reasons differs from that in the general population.[16] It has, however, been extremely difficult to interpret such findings, including incidences of infectious diseases, since many variables are difficult or impossible to control. An often quoted study is that of Vaughan et al.,[73] in which schizophrenic patients developed lower antibody titers to pertussis vaccine than control subjects. Yet the authors themselves point out that the patient population had been institutionalized from four months to 12 years, but not the control subjects, and this obviously raises certain method-ological problems. In another study[25] acutely psychotic patients were investi-gated in terms of their response to cholera vaccine, and it was found that schizophrenic patients developed significantly higher antibody titers than patients judged to be primarily depressed. It will be impossible to interpret such findings until further work is done in this area.

Experimental Studies

There appears to be only a limited number of studies directly concerned with the possible relation of psychologic stress to infectious processes. Rasmussen and his colleagues at the University of California in Los Angeles have truly pioneered in this area of investigation, and thus far have produced the most extensive evidence that such a relation might exist.[11,38-40,50,51,59-61,78] In most of their published work this group has utilized three techniques to stress their experimental animals: avoidance-learning, loose restraint, and high-intensity sound.

In 1957 Rasmussen et al.[60] reported that both avoidance-learning and restraint had the effect in mice of increasing susceptibility to herpes simplex virus. The avoidance situation was produced in a two-compartment "shuttle-box" type of cage. The floor of both compartments consisted of stainless steel grids which could be alternately electrified, and the compartments were separated by a low barrier. A five-second warning signal (conditioned stimulus) preceded the presentation of electric current (unconditioned stimulus) to one of the two compartments, and every five minutes for six hours each day the current would be switched to the alternate compartment after the warning signal. The mice in these experimental cages learned to avoid the electric shock by jumping over the barrier to the nonelectrified compartment upon presentation of the conditioned stimulus. Control animals were placed in identical cages, subjected to the warning signal (a buzzer and cue light), deprived of food during the six-hour experimental period, but not subjected to electric shock. The investigators demonstrated that mice experiencing either 14 or 21 days of avoidance-learning were significantly more susceptible to an inoculation of herpes simplex virus at the end of this experimental period than control animals, as measured by mortality.

The above-noted experiments did not eliminate the possibility that the shock itself could have physically injured the animal and thereby modified its resistance, rather than the effect being mediated by way of the central nervous system. In subsequent experiments the authors utilized confinement as a way to stress their experimental group, and each mouse was loosely wrapped in fine copper screen. A similar trend was noted, the animals stressed (confined) six hours a day for 28 days dying in significantly greater numbers than control animals.

The role of multiple factors influencing the host-parasite relation in Coxsackie B infection has been discussed in a previous section. Johnsson et al.[40] used this model to show that avoidance-learning increased the susceptibility of *adult* mice to this virus. This change in susceptibility was manifested by increased weight loss in those mice that were stressed and inoculated with virus, as compared to control animals subjected only to virus inoculation. It was also noted that a significantly higher virus titer could be demonstrated in the pancreas, liver, heart and muscle of stressed mice as compared to unstressed animals. In discussing their findings in more detail, the authors state that the time relations suggest that it was not interference with antibody response that made the stressed mice more susceptible, but "rather the known antiphlogistic effect of corticoids." Such an interpretation was thought to be consistent with the results of previous experiments[51] which demonstrated that both avoidance-learning and restraint were associated with adrenal cortical hypertrophy occurring in three to seven days. In this latter publication, it is further stated that the results suggest that "neither electric shock nor physical activity is crucial but that fear produced in both situations is the important factor in changes observed."

It has already been mentioned that, theoretically, stress need not be detrimental to the host, and that one must consider the nature of the stress and the physiologic response it provokes in the host, the nature of the challenging infectious agent and the time relations. Thus monkeys subjected to avoidance stress displayed increased *resistance* to poliomyelitis virus.[50] The authors note that, compared to their previous work with herpes simplex and Coxsackie B viruses in mice, these latter experiments consisted of a single stressful procedure. In this context, it is interesting that a single dose of corticosteroids increases in-vivo interferon response to virus infection, while repeated chronic steroid administration suppresses interferon production.[56]

In mice the avoidance-learning technique was again utilized to examine the effect that stress might have upon susceptibility to passive anaphylaxis.[61] Mice were subjected to either one day or four weeks of stress, consisting of six hours a day in the avoidance situation, and then inoculated with a "shocking" dose of antigen-antibody mixture. The severity of the anaphylactic reaction was graded, and both the acute and chronically stressed mice proved to be more resistant to this challenging dose than controls. The authors then cite evidence which led them to believe that this increased resistance was probably due to increased adrenocortical activity caused by the avoidance-learning stress.

In two further papers Jensen and Rasmussen[38,39] used high-intensity sound as a stress and observed its effect upon resistance to the intranasal inoculation of vesicular stomatitis virus. It was noted that animals subjected to a single three-hour period of high-intensity sound displayed an increased susceptibility to this virus, and this effect was noted whether the virus was inoculated before or after the stress period. Perhaps of most interest was the finding that if these stress periods were continued on subsequent days, the susceptibility was biphasic. Animals inoculated just before being subjected to the high-intensity sound on a more chronic basis were more susceptible than controls, while those inoculated after the stress period were less susceptible. The *increased* susceptibility was thought to be independent of adrenal cortical activity, though the data suggested that the *decreased* susceptibility might be related to adrenal function. A further study[78] with vesicular stomatitis virus involved mice inoculated intramuscularly and subjected to the avoidance-learning paradigm. In these experiments it was noted that the virus disappearance rate in the stressed animals was significantly retarded, though no differences were noted in serum-neutralizing antibody levels.

Work with polyoma virus by Rasmussen et al.[59] demonstrated that a combination of avoidance-learning and high-intensity sound did not modify the "incidence, extent or location of tumors," nor were there differences in median survival times. In this study the mice were inoculated shortly after birth and subjected to stress at approximately 40 days of age. In a subsequent study[11] the virus inoculation was delayed until two to three weeks of age, and the mice were then subjected to these stresses without a lag period; in this instance the stressed mice had a higher incidence of tumors. These results were thought to be possibly related to an observed suppression of interferon in mice subjected to high-intensity sound.

In reviewing the foregoing work, there appears to be little doubt that the stress situations utilized influenced susceptibility to a number of viruses and to at least one type of anaphylactic reaction. Yet the reader is impressed with the importance of the time relation, i.e. the acuteness or chronicity of the stress and the relation between the stress and time of inoculation. Furthermore, the presence or absence of modified resistance is to a large degree dependent upon the measurement used to reflect resistance—weight loss, mortality, virus multi-plication or disappearance rate, survival time, and so forth. A further question is how "psychologic" are stresses such as avoidance-learning, restraint and high-intensity sound. Though the authors present convincing data that the observed effects are related to central nervous system functioning, the separation of physical versus psychologic stress has remained a methodological problem.

This last issue has interested the present writers, and, in collaboration with Robert Ader, a series of experiments were undertaken.[23] Mice were subjected for seven days to one of nine possible combinations of a periodically occurring, an aperiodically occurring, or absence of shock stimulation, preceded by a paired, unpaired or absence of a warning light (Figure 12-2). A tenth group of mice were left undisturbed in standard laboratory cages to serve as controls. It was noted that merely moving mice from standard laboratory cages to the experimental cages resulted in a significant decrease in weight gain, and that mice subjected to periodic shock preceded by a stimulus light lost a greater amount of weight than mice subjected to any of the other experimental conditions. These results are shown in Figure 12-3, and it was concluded that the stimulus light acted as a warning, which in turn allowed the animal to "anticipate" the coming of the noxious shock stimulus.

These results were used to devise more refined schedules in an attempt to show that psychologic stress produced by the anticipation of shock might modify resistance to a Coxsackie B virus, whereas shock alone would not have this effect.[24] Mice were stressed for three days, inoculated with Coxsackie virus,

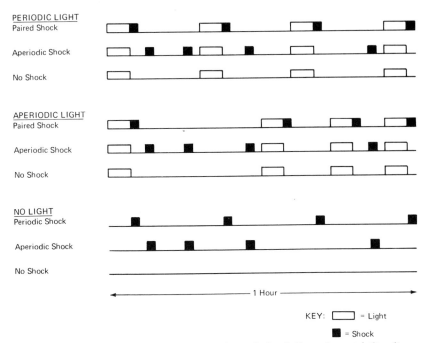

Figure 12-2. Schematic Representation of the 9 Experimental Conditions Described in the Text. (From Friedman and Ader.[23])

and then stressed for four additional days. Change in body weight *following virus inoculation* was used as an index of viral disease. Figure 12-4 shows the data obtained in one such experiment, in which it was shown that neither psychologic stress nor the inoculation of virus, acting independently, was sufficient to cause manifest disease, but the combination of stress and the pathogenic agent resulted in disease as reflected by a significant loss of body weight. It was suggested that this type of interaction, between an environmental stress and an infectious agent, is an illustration of the "multifactorial approach to etiology."

Other studies also have been concerned with the possible influence of emotional or environmental factors upon host resistance. Some have taken advantage of a predominant behavior pattern in a given species; for instance, the characteristic tendency for male mice to fight and develop a dominance hierarchy, or "pecking order," and that such fighting has physiologic correlates.[9] In one such investigation Davis and Read[15] showed that resistance to *Trichinella spiralis* was decreased in previously isolated male mice subsequently allowed the opportunity to fight. The authors suggest that this effect might be related to the increase in adrenocortical function, which has also been noted in mice allowed to interact. Examining a similar type of social situation, Vessey[74] has demon-

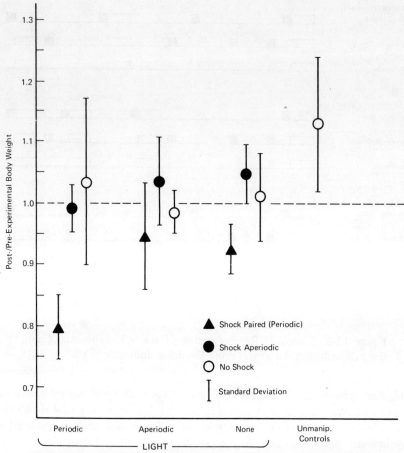

Figure 12-3. Effect of Experimental and Control Conditions on Body Weight. (From Friedman and Ader.[23])

strated that in male mice housed in groups, the dominant animals respond with higher antibody titers after an antigenic stimulus than those mice judged to be submissive.

It now appears clear that housing arrangements, independent of fighting behavior, may have profound influences upon resistance. Christian[13] has well documented the physiologic changes involving the pituitary-adrenocortical axis, reproductive organs, and other endocrine functions that take place in animals housed in various social groupings. The placement of many animals in a single cage has often been termed "crowding," and under such conditions increased resistance has been noted to tuberculosis in mice.[72] Preliminary findings in our laboratory suggest that the group-housed animals do not necessarily have to be "crowded" or allowed to fight in order for resistance to be modified. Female mice (which normally do not fight if grouped as weanlings) were housed in

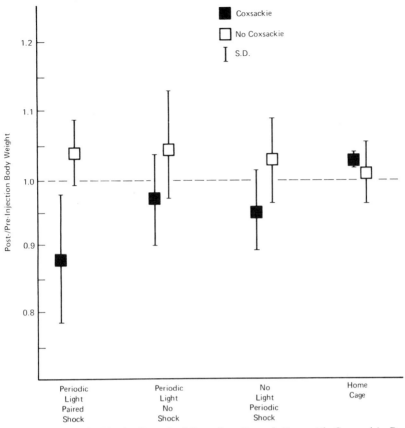

Figure 12-4. Weight Loss in Mice after Inoculation with Coxsackie B Virus. (From Friedman Ader and Glasgow.[24])

groups of five in cages routinely used to house up to 10 to 12 mice, and other animals were housed one to a cage. It was observed that the animals housed alone died at a significantly greater rate when inoculated with encephalomyocarditis virus than those housed in groups, and current work is aimed at determining the possible physiologic basis for this difference in resistance. Though housing appears to be a rather subtle, and often ignored, influence upon host susceptibility, the mere daily examination of experimental animals was noted to increase the susceptibility of hamsters to poliomyelitis virus.[71] The physiologic effects of merely picking up an animal ("handling" or "gentling") have been studied[47,64] and have been related to noninfectious disease processes,[2] though no published studies known to the authors have examined the effects of "handling" upon resistance to infectious agents. In our laboratory this technique has not been successful in modifying resistance to encephalomyocarditis virus or to a murine leukemia virus (Rauscher agent), though further studies are currently in progress.

In reviewing these studies, it is difficult to come to any generalizations, except to say that relatively subtle psychologic and environmental factors appear to influence susceptibility to a wide range of infectious and parasitic agents. Although there is a paucity of studies, there are several obvious problems worth discussing. First, as previously alluded to, there is no *a priori* reason to assume that a given psychologic stress would modify resistance at all times or in the same direction, or to all infectious agents, or in all species. Indeed, the whole concept of multiple etiologic factors implies that it may be necessary for conditions—in the host, in the microorganism, and in the environment—to be "just right" for disease to develop. It is therefore difficult, at our present state of relative ignorance, to design studies that will best allow us to measure the effects of psychologic stress upon host resistance.

The investigator in this area of research must make three decisions: the animal he chooses to study (the host), the psychologic or environmental phenomenon he wishes to examine, and the infectious agent that will be used. Obviously, there has been no systematic attempt among investigators to keep any one of these variables constant. Hence the difficulty in comparing the results of one experimenter with those of another, and the inability to proceed much beyond merely demonstrating, once again, that a *given* environmental stress may modify resistance to a *particular* infectious agent in a *particular* species. At present it is therefore impossible to come to any general conclusions about the physiologic processes that may underlie the findings just reviewed, and findings that superficially appear contradictory may merely reflect our lack of knowledge about species and strain differences, the physiologic correlates of various types of stress, and other factors related to the complexity of host-parasite inter- actions. Also, as previously mentioned, there has been an almost all-inclusive focus upon adrenocortical function, and investigators may be thereby missing the importance of other hormones or physiologic processes in relating psycho- logic stress and resistance to infectious diseases. It is hoped that there will be an increasing emphasis upon defining any relevant physiologic mechanism, which in turn will be dependent upon finding a host-parasite system that will optimally reflect the influences of psychologic and social phenomena. Such a "model" might then point the way for more sophisticated clinical investigations and a better understanding of the intriguing balances seen between the host and the microorganism in man.

Conclusions

An attempt has been made to offer illustrative evidence that the balance between the host and infectious agent is usually a tenuous one. It has been further proposed that anatomic relationships and physiologic mechanisms exist that would allow for the possibility of psychologic and social factors influencing this host-parasite relation. Supporting data from both clinical and animal studies have been reviewed, though it must be admitted that conclusive evidence relating psychologic factors and host resistance in man is still lacking.

References

1. Ader, R.: Training for Psychosomatic Research: Some Views of an Experimental Psychologist. *Adv. in Psychosom. Med.* Basel, Switzerland, and New York, S. Karger (in press).
2. Ader, R., and Friedman, S.B.: Psychological Factors and Susceptibility to Disease in Animals; D. McK. Rioch (Ed.): *Medical Aspects of Stress in the Military Climate.* Washington, D.C., Walter Reed Army Institute of Research, 1965.
3. Baron, S.: Mechanism of Recovery from Viral Infections; in *Advances in Virus Research.* New York, Academic Press, 1963, p. 39.
4. Barrett, A.M., and Stockham, M.A.: The Effect of Housing Conditions and Simple Experimental Procedures upon the Corticosterone Level in the Plasma of Rats. *J. Endocrinol.*, 26:97, 1963.
5. Behbehani, A.M., Sulkin, S.E., and Wallis, C.: Factors Influencing Susceptibility of Mice to Coxsackie Virus Infection. *J. Infect. Dis.*, 110:147, 1962.
6. Blank, H., and Brody, M.W.: Recurrent Herpes Simplex, *Psychosom. Med.*, 12:254, 1950.
7. Boring, W.D., Angevine, D.M., and Walker, D.L.: Factors Influencing Host-Virus Interactions, I. A Comparison of Viral Multiplication and Histopathology in Infant, Adult, and Cortisone-Treated Adult Mice Infected with the Conn-5 Strain of Coxsackie Virus. *J. Exper. Med.*, 102:753, 1955.
8. Brodman, K., Mittelmann, B., Wechsler, D., Weider, A., and Wolff, H.G.: The Relation of Personality Disturbances to Duration of Convalescence from Acute Respiratory Infections. *Psychosom. Med.*, 9:37, 1947.
9. Bronson, F.H., and Eleftheriou, B.E.: Chronic Physiological Effects of Fighting in Mice. *Gen. & Comp. Endocrinol.*, 4:9, 1964.
10. Bush, I.E.: Chemical and Biological Factors in the Activity of Adrenocortical Steroids. *Pharmacol. Rev.*, 14:317, 1962.
11. Chang, S., and Rasmussen, A. F., Jr.: Stress-Induced Supression of Interferon Production in Virus-Infected Mice. *Nature*, 205:623, 1965.
12. Chapman, L.F., Goodell, H., and Wolff, H.G.: Changes in Tissue Vulnerability Induced During Hypnotic Suggestion. *J. Psychosom. Res.*, 4:99, 1959.
13. Christian, J.J., and Davis, D.E.: Endocrines, Behavior, and Population. *Science*, 146:1550, 1964.

14. Dalldorf, G., and Gifford, R.: Susceptibility of Gravid Mice to Coxsackie Virus Infection. *J. Exper. Med.*, 99:21, 1954.

15. Davis, D.E., and Read, C.P.: Effect of Behavior on Development of Resistance in Trichinosis. *Proc. Soc. Exper. Biol. Med.*, 99:269, 1958.

16. Doust, J.W.L.: Psychiatric Aspects of Somatic Immunity Differential Incidence of Physical Disease in the Histories of Psychiatric Patients. *Brit. J. Soc. Med.*, 6:49, 1952.

17. Dubos, R.: Unsolved Problems in the Study and Control of Microbial Diseases. *J.A.M.A.*, 157:1477, 1955.

18. Idem: *Mirage of Health*. Garden City, N.Y., Doubleday & Company, 1961, pp. 107, 112.

19. Eichenwald, H.G., Kotsevalov, O., and Fasson, L.A.: The "Cloud-Baby" an Example of Bacterial-Viral Interaction. *Am. J. Dis. Child.*, 100:161, 1960.

20. Ely, N.E., Verhey, J.W., and Holmes, T.H.: Experimental Studies of Skin Inflammation. *Psychosom. Med.*, 25:264, 1963.

21. Engel, G.L.: Selection of Clinical Material in Psychosomatic Medicine. *Psychosom. Med.*, 16:368, 1954.

22. Evans, D.G., Miles, A.A., and Niven, J.S.F.: The Enhancement of Bacterial Infections by Adrenaline. *Brit. J. Exp. Path.*, 29:20, 1948.

23. Friedman, S.B., and Ader, R.: Parameters Relevant to the Experimental Production of "Stress" in the Mouse. *Psychosom. Med.*, 27:27, 1965.

24. Friedman, S.B., Ader, R., and Glasgow, L.A.: Effects of Psychological Stress in Adult Mice Inoculated with Coxsackie B Viruses. *Psychosom. Med.*, 27:361, 1965.

25. Friedman, S.B., Cohen, J., and Iker, H.: Antibody Response to Cholera Vaccine in Depressed, Schizophrenic, and Normal Subjects. (Unpublished.)

26. Friedman, S.B., Mason, J.W., and Hamburg, D.A.: Urinary 17-Hydroxycorticosteroid Levels in Parents of Children with Neoplastic Disease. *Psychosom. Med.*, 25:364, 1963.

27. Geocaris, K.: Circumoral Herpes Simplex and Separation Experiences in Psychotherapy. *Psychosom. Med.*, 23:41, 1961.

28. Glasgow, L.A.: Interferon: A Review. *J. Pediat.*, 67:104, 1965.

29. Greenfield, N.S., Roessler, R., and Crosley, A.P.: Ego Strength and Length of Recovery from Infectious Mononucleosis. *J. Nerv. & Ment. Dis.*, 128:125, 1959.

30. Hamburg, D.A.: Plasma and Urinary Corticosteroid Levels in Naturally Occurring Psychologic Stresses; in *Ultrastructure and Metabolism of the Nervous System. Proc. A. Res. Nerv. & Ment. Dis.*, 40:406, 1962.

31. Heineberg, H., Gold, E., and Robbins, F.C.: Differences in Interferon Content in Tissues of Mice of Various Ages Infected with Coxsackie B1 Virus. *Proc. Soc. Exp. Biol. Med.*, 115:947, 1964.

32. Hinkle, L.E.: The Doctor, His Patient, and the Environment. *Am. J. Pub. Health*, 54:11, 1964.
33. Hinkle, L.E., Jr., Christenson, W.N., Benjamin, B., Kane, F.D., and Wolff, H.G.: Observations on the Role of Nasal Adaptive Reactions, Emotions and Life Situations in the Genesis of Minor Respiratory Illnesses. *Psychosom. Med.*, 24:515, 1962 (Abst.).
34. Hinkle, L.E., Jr., and others: An Investigation of the Relation Between Life Experience, Personality Characteristics, and General Susceptibility to Illness. *Psychosom. Med.*, 20:278, 1958.
35. Hinkle, L.E., Jr., and Plummer, N.: Life Stress and Industrial Absenteeism. *Indust. Med. & Surg.*, 21:363, 1952.
36. Holmes, T.H.: Psychosocial and Psychophysiological Studies of Tuberculosis; in R. Roessler and N.S. Greenfield (Eds.): *Psychological Correlates of Psychological Disorders*. Madison, University of Wisconsin Press, 1962.
37. Jackson, G.G., and others: Susceptibility and Immunity to Common Upper Respiratory Viral Infections—The Common Cold. *Ann. Int. Med.*, 53:719, 1960.
38. Jensen, M.M., and Rasmussen, A.F.: Stress and Susceptibility to Viral Infection. I. Response of Adrenals, Liver, Thymus, Spleen and Peripheral Leukocyte Counts to Sound Stress. *J. Immunol.*, 90:17, 1963.
39. Idem: Stress and Susceptibility to Viral Infections. II. Sound Stress and Susceptibility to Vesicular Stomatitis Virus. *J. Immunol.*, 90:21, 1963.
40. Johnsson, T., Lavender, J.F., Hultin, E., and Rasmussen, A.F., Jr.: The Influence of Avoidance-Learning Stress on Resistance to Coxsackie B Virus in Mice. *J. Immunol.*, 91:569, 1963.
41. Kaplan, S.M., Gottschalk, L.A., and Fleming, D.E.: Modifications of Oropharyngeal Bacteria with Changes in the Psychodynamic State. *A.M.A. Arch. Neurol. & Psychiat.*, 78:656, 1957.
42. Kass, E.H.: Resistance to Infection; in J. Brown and C.M. Pearson (Eds.): *Clinical Uses of Adrenal Steroids*. New York, McGraw-Hill Book Company, Inc., 1962.
43. Kass, E.H., and Finland, M.: Corticosteroids and Infections. *Adv. in Intern. Med.*, 9:45, 1958.
44. Kilbourne, E.D., and Horsfall, F.L.: Lethal Infection with Coxsackie Virus of Adult Mice Given Cortisone. *Proc. Soc. Exp. Biol. & Med.*, 77:135, 1951.
45. Kilbourne, E.D., Smart, K.M., and Pokorny, B.A.: Inhibition by Cortisone of the Synthesis and Action of Interferon. *Nature*, 190:650, 1961.
46. Knigge, K.M.: Adrenocortical Response to Stress in Rats with Lesions in Hippocampus and Amygdala. *Proc. Soc. Exper. Biol. Med.*, 108:18, 1961.
47. Levine, S.: Psychophysiological Effects of Infantile Stimulation; in E.L. Bliss (Ed.): *Roots of Behavior*, New York, Harper, 1962.
48. Lipton, E.L., Steinschneider, A., and Richmond, J.B.: The Autonomic Nervous System in Early Life. *New England J. Med.*, 273:147, 1965.

49. Mandell, A.J., Chapman, L.F., Rand, R.W., and Walter, R.D.: Plasma Corticosteroids: Changes in Concentration After Stimulation of Hippocampus and Amygdala. *Science*, 139:1212, 1963.
50. Marsh, J.T., Lavender, J.F., Chang, S., and Rasmussen, A.F.: Poliomyelitis in Monkeys: Decreased Susceptibility After Avoidance Stress. *Science*, 140:1414, 1963.
51. Marsh, J.T., and Rasmussen, A.F., Jr.: Response of Adrenals, Thymus, Spleen and Leucocytes to Shuttle Box and Confinement Stress. *Proc. Soc. Exper. Biol. Med.*, 104:180, 1960.
52. Mason, J.W.: The Central Nervous System Regulation of ACTH Secretion: in *Recticular Formation of the Brain*. Boston, Little, Brown & Company, 1958, p. 645.
53. Idem: Psychological Influences on the Pituitary-Adrenal Cortical System. *Recent Prog. Hormone Res.*, 15:345, 1959.
54. Mason, J.W., Harwood, C.T., and Rosenthal, N.R.: Influence of Some Environmental Factors on Plasma and Urinary 17-Hydroxycorticosteroid Levels in the Rhesus Monkey. *Am. J. Physiol.*, 190:429, 1957.
55. McMaster, P.D., and Franzl, R.E.: The Effects of Adrenocortical Steroids upon Antibody Formation. *Metabol.*, 10:990, 1961.
56. Mendelson, J., and Glasgow, L.A.: Unpublished data.
57. Meyer, R.J., and Haggerty, R.J.: Streptococcal Infections in Families: Factors Altering Individual Susceptibility. *Pediatrics*, 29:539, 1962.
58. Mirsky, I.A.: Physiologic, Psychologic, and Social Determinants in the Etiology of Duodenal Ulcer. *Am. J. Digest. Dis.* 3:285, 1958.
59. Rasmussen, A.F., Hildemann, W.H., and Sellers, M.: Malignancy of Polyoma Virus Infection in Mice in Relation to Stress. *J. Nat. Cancer Inst.*, 30:101, 1963.
60. Rasmussen, A.F., Jr., Marsh, J.T., and Brill, N.Q.: Increased Susceptibility to Herpes Simplex in Mice Subjected to Avoidance-Learning Stress or Restraint. *Proc. Soc. Exper. Biol. Med.*, 96:183, 1957.
61. Rasmussen, A.F., Jr., Spencer, E.S., and Marsh, J.T.: Decrease in Susceptibility of Mice to Passive Anaphylaxis Following Avoidance-Learning Stress. *Proc. Soc. Exp. Biol. Med.*, 100:878, 1959.
62. Reichlin, S.: Neuroendocrinology. *New England J. Med.*, 269:1182, 1963.
63. Rowe, W.P.: Propagation of Group A Coxsackie Viruses in Denervated Adult Mouse Muscle. *Science*, 117:710, 1953.
64. Ruegamer, W.R., Bernstein, L., and Benjamin, J.D.: Growth, Food Utilization, and Thyroid Activity in the Albino Rat as a Function of Extra Handling. *Science*, 120:184, 1954.
65. Schaffer, J., Beamer, P.R., Trexler, P.C., Breidenbach, G., and Walcher, D.N.: Response of Germ-Free Animals to Experimental Virus Monocontamination. I. Observation on Coxsackie B Virus. *Proc. Soc. Exp. Biol. Med.*, 112:561, 1963.

66. Schottstaedt, W.W., Krause, J.H., Foerster, D.W., Dooley, R.T., and Kelly, F.C.: Host Factors Affecting Growth of B-Hemolytic Streptococci in the Human Pharynx: A Pilot Study. *Am. J.M. Sc.*, 235:23, 1958.

67. Shaw, E.B.: Editorial–The Outbreak of Meningitis. *Calif. Med.*, 102:234, 1965.

68. Sprunt, D.H., and Flanigan, C., Jr.: The Effect of Nutrition on the Production of Disease by Bacteria, Rickettsiae, and Viruses. *Adv. in Veterinary Sci.*, 6:79, 1960.

69. Sprunt, D.H., and Flanigan, C.C.: The Effect of Malnutrition on the Susceptibility of the Host to Viral Infection. *J. Exper. Med.*, 104:687, 1956.

70. Sussman, M.L., Strauss, L., and Hodes, H.L.: Fatal Coxsackie Group B Virus Infection in the Newborn. *Am. J. Dis. Child.*, 97:483, 1959.

71. Teodoru, C.V., and Shwartzman, G.: Endocrine Factors in Pathogenesis of Experimental Poliomyelitis in Hamsters. Role of Inoculatory and Environmental Stress. *Proc. Soc. Exper. Biol. Med.*, 91:181, 1956.

72. Tobach, E., and Bloch, H.: Effect of Stress by Crowding Prior to and Following Tuberculous Infection. *Am. J. Physiol.*, 187:399, 1956.

73. Vaughan, W.T., Jr., Sullivan, J.C., and Elmadjian, F.: Immunity and Schizophrenia. *Psychosom. Med.*, 11:328, 1949.

74. Vessey, S.H.: Effects of Grouping on Levels of Circulating Antibodies in Mice. *Proc. Soc. Exper. Biol. Med.*, 115:252, 1964.

75. Wadeson, R.W., Mason, J.W., Hamburg, D.A., and Handlon, J.H.: Plasma and Urinary 17-OHCS Responses to Motion Pictures. *Arch. Gen. Psychiat.*, 9:146, 1963.

76. Wilson, H., Borris, J.J., and Bahn, R.C.: Steroids in the Blood and Urine of Female Mice Bearing an ACTH-Producing Pituitary Tumor. *Endocrinol.*, 62:135, 1958.

77. Wolff, C.T., Friedman, S.B., Hofer, M.A., and Mason, J.W.: Relationship Between Psychological Defenses and Mean Urinary 17-Hydroxycorticosteroid Excretion Rates. *Psychosom. Med.*, 26:576, 1964.

78. Yamada, A., Jensen, M.M., and Rasmussen, A.F., Jr.: Stress and Susceptibility to Viral Infections. III. Antibody Response and Viral Retention During Avoidance Learning Stress. *Proc. Soc. Exper. Biol. Med.*, 116:677, 1964.

13 Emotions, Stress, and Immunity

G.F. Solomon
A.A. Amkraut
Stanford University
School of Medicine

Hypotheses

Stress and emotional distress may influence the function of the immunologic system via central nervous system and endocrine mediation. Thus, environmental factors might in some circumstances be implicated as aspects of the pathogensis of cancer, the resistance to which growing evidence finds immunologic in nature, and of infections as well as of autoimmune diseases, which seem to have an association with states of relative immunologic incompetence. There are considerable data to link personality factors, stress, and, particularly, failure of psychologic defenses or adaptations to the onset and course of cancer and of infectious and autoimmune diseases, particularly rheumatoid arthritis. I am concerned especially with physiologic mechanisms, nervous and humoral, by which emotions and stress may relate to the diseases associated with dysfunction and hypofunction of the immunologic system. Illness may concern genetic, behavioral, social, and immunologic relationships [39]. One link between experience and disease is the effect of stress-responsive adrenal cortical steroid hormones, which may be immunosuppressive. A logical consequence of this view is that stress effects on immunologic response would be expected to be observed

Reprinted with permission from *Frontiers of Radiation Therapy and Oncology*, Vol. 7, 1972, pp. 84-96 (Karger, Basel and University Park Press, Baltimore, 1972).

under clinical conditions of gross failure to psychologic defenses, as generally occurs during acute mental illness.

Infectious Diseases and Emotions

Clinicians have long been aware of the importance of host resistance in the etiology of infectious diseases. Osler is supposed to have commented on the importance of knowing what is going on in a man's head in order to predict the outcome of his tuberculosis. The British authority, Day [3], stated, 'To develop chronic active pulmonary tuberculosis a person needs some bacilli, some moderately inflammable lungs (not celluloid like the guinea pig's nor asbestos like the elephant's) and some internal or external factor which lowers the resistance to the disease', and he went on to say that unhappiness is a cause of lowered resistance. In research studies, emotions, especially depression [40], and social factors [35] have been linked to susceptibility to, and recovery from, infectious diseases. Families of ill children were found to have been more disorganized during the prior six-month period and to have exposed their children to a greater number of psychologic and social changes, which were threatening and had a disruptive impact, than was the case with a comparison group of healthy children. Delayed recovery from infectious mononucleosis has been correlated with deficient ego strength [16], and prolonged convalescence from brucellosis [20] and influenza [21] correlated with depression. Experimentally, avoidance learning and restraint lead to increased susceptibility to herpes simplex virus in mice. Though neither stress nor Coxsackie B virus alone is sufficient to produce disease in mice, the combination results in a loss of body weight [37]. Disappearance of vesicular stomatitis virus from the site of inoculation is retarded in stressed mice [49].

Cancer and Emotions

Personality factors have been tied to the presence and the rapidity of dissemination of cancer in a large number of studies, rapid progression of cancer being associated with unsuccessful psychologic defenses and psychic distress. (Even Galen considered that melancholy women suffer from cancer more frequently than sanguine women!) Four consistent factors are found in reports of personality studies on some patients with cancer [27] : (1) the patient's loss of an important relationship prior to the development of a tumor, (2) the cancer patient's inability to express hostile feelings and emotion, (3) the cancer patient's unresolved tension concerning a parent figure, (4) sexual disturbance. As will be seen, these are very similar to the factors that have been described in patients with autoimmune diseases. In a predictive study, Klopfer [22] related long survival either to successful denial of reality or, more rarely, to a mature, calm acceptance of reality, and rapid death to ego defensiveness with a high degree of subjective distress. Bahnson [2] theorizes that the cancer patient regresses somatically rather than behaviorally in the face of depression or breakdown of psychologic defenses.

Cancer and Stress

Effects of stress on induction and course of growth of a variety of experimental tumors in animals without reference to immunologic factors have recently been reviewed by LaBarba [26]. Studies have included virus and methylcholanthrene-induced tumors as well as Walker carcinoma. Ehrlich ascites, spontaneous mammary tumors and leukemias. Increase as well as decrease in disease induction and tumor growth were found, and a number of experiments failed to show any effect of stress on the particular system under study. The wide variation in results may be ascribable to the multiplicity of tumor systems and the different species and stress procedures used in the experiments or to viscissitudes in stress effects on immunologic resistance. LaBarba concludes that scientific evidence strongly supports the notion that cancer in animals can be influenced by experimental manipulation.

Cancer and Immunity

The evidence of immunologic resistance to cancer need not be reviewed here. Habel's [17] statement in regard to an experimental tumor is relevant:

'Perhaps the only way in which the mouse, naturally infected as an adult or with a small amount of virus as a newborn, can develop a polyoma tumor is by *the chance occurrence of some event which temporarily reduces its immunologic competence at the proper time* after virus transformation of normal cells to tumor cells'.

In regard to stress effects on tumor immunity, the concept of 'immunologic balance' may be important, taking into account factors in addition to cellular immunologic rejection mechanisms. For example, stress-induced suppression of blocking (enhancing) antibody might increase tumor resistance. Influence of stress on humoral immunity might also affect cytotoxic antibodies or 'de-blocking' antibodies recently described by the Hellströms [19]. In the case of virus-induced tumors, stress-caused changes in interferon induction may play a role. Solomon *et al.* [47] found that acute stress prior to virus inoculation *enhanced* interferon production. That immunologic competence of the host is

crucial to tumor resistance is suggested by Fefer and co-workers' [6, 7] finding
that all immunologically immature mice inoculated with murine sarcoma virus
before two weeks of age succumb; whereas, those injected at four weeks or older
develop sarcomas that grow for about 15 days and then are rejected rapidly.

Autoimmune Diseases and
Immunologic Incompetence

Though the etiologic significance of autoantibodies themselves remains uncertain, relative immunologic incompetence may be related to the pathogenesis of
autoimmune diseases such as rheumatoid arthritis, systemic lupus erythematosus, myasthenia gravis, acquired hemolytic anemia and pernicious anemia. These
diseases occur with relative frequency in patients and experimental animals with
immunologic deficiency states and with neoplastic diseases of immunologically
competent cells. The mechanism tying autoimmunity to immunologic deficiency
is unclear. Dixon *et al.* [4] relate autoimmune disease to the presence of
circulating antigen-antibody complexes, which occur when antibody appears in
an environment of antigen excess. In rabbits injected daily with small amounts
of purified serum proteins, only those animals with a *poor* antibody response, in
contrast to those with an absent or with a vigorous antibody response, develop
chronic glomerulonephritis. Immunologic complexes can produce chronic degenerative tissue change, and the injured tissue needs no immunologic relationship to the antigen involved. Antigen-antibody complexes inactivate comple-
ment, release amines from mast cells, may produce disseminated inflammatory
lesions, and also activate the proteolytic enzyme plasmin, which has been noted
to be elevated in conditions of emotional stress. It is conceivable that *in vivo*
denaturation of body constituents by proteolytic activity might lead to autoimmunity. Weigle [48] has shown that administration of proteins modified *in
vitro* and given to animals tolerant to that protein breaks the tolerance for the
original protein. Also, antigen-antibody complexes themselves might act as new
antigens for formation of new antibody. Rheumatoid factor is probably such an
autoantibody. Another hypothetical mechanism by which immunologic incompetence, perhaps based partly on genetic predisposition, might relate to autoimmunity is the failure to eliminate by rejection mechanisms abnormal clones of
immunologically competent cells reactive against self. Another possibility is that
a bacterium or virus, ordinarily readily handled by the immune system, may
attack a specific tissue and alter it immunologically to induce autoimmunity.

Emotions and Social Factors in the Onset
and Course of Autoimmune Diseases

In view of evidence that relative immunologic incompetence, which may be
stress-induced, may be important in the pathogenesis of autoimmune disease,

our findings in regard to emotional factors in the autoimmune diseases seem pertinent. As we shall see, these factors are similar to those cited for infectious disease and cancer.

Moos' [30] review of the literature of over 5,000 patients with rheumatoid arthritis found that investigators agreed that arthritics, when compared with various control groups, tend to be self-sacrificing, masochistic, conforming, self-conscious, shy, inhibited, perfectionistic, and interested in sports. Moos and Solomon [34] found that female rheumatoid patients were nervous, tense, worried, moody, depressed, concerned with the rejection they perceived from their mothers and the strictness they perceived from their fathers, and showed denial and inhibition of the expression of anger in contrast to their healthy sisters. Women with definite or classical rheumatoid arthritis scored higher than healthy female family members on Minnesota Multiphasic Personality Inventory scales reflecting inhibition of anger, anxiety, depression, compliance-subservience, conservatism, security-seeking, shyness and introversion [31]. We related rapidity of progression of disease [32], relatively high degrees of functional incapacity [33], and lack of response to medical treatment in rheumatoid arthritis [44], to an inability to utilize previously successful ego adaptations. Arthritics who did poorly were more anxious and depressed, were more isolated, introverted and alienated, and were more unable to maintain compulsive defenses and suppression of anger than were those with a more benign course. These findings are quite analogous to those already cited in the cases of infectious disease and cancer. We [45] compared two groups of *healthy* female relatives of rheumatoid arthritic patients, one group having, and the other lacking rheumatoid factor in their sera, since there is some evidence that the presence of rheumatoid factor in the serum may predispose to arthritis. Psychologic test results indicated that there was a greater incidence of emotional decompensation—anxiety, depression, low self-esteem, alienation, fear and worry, and lack of impulse control and ego mastery—in those relatives *lacking* rheumatoid factor. It seemed as if the occurrence of psychic disequilibrium in the presence of rheumatoid factor might lead to overt rheumatoid disease, so that physically healthy persons with rheumatoid factor, to remain so, need by psychologically healthy as well. Thus, emotional decompensation in the predisposed individual might result in a specific physical illness. Interestingly, the rheumatoid factor-*positive* relatives were more similar to the arthritic patients in their *type* of character structure defense and adaptation, but were distinguished from the patients by the *success* of these adaptations.

Recently, Rimón's [38] clinical research in Finland provided evidence for two types of rheumatoid arthritis (analogous to the process and reactive forms of schizophrenia).

'In the first one, the disease begins suddenly and the symptoms appear distinct and even fierce. The onset of the disease is most often associated with a significant psychodynamic conflict situation, and a hereditary predisposition for rheumatoid arthritis is obviously lacking. In the other type, the onset of the disease is slow and the progression of the symptoms retarded. A correlation to an actual psychodynamic conflict situation is absent; whereas, a hereditary predisposition for rheumatoid arthritis does exist, judging by the relatively great number of other affected members of the family.'

Rimón's 'non-conflict group' did not differ from a series of ordinary medical patients in direct expression of aggression.

It is of considerable interest that personality data similar to those we and others have reported for patients with rheumatoid arthritis have been published for patients with other autoimmune diseases. Engel [5], in his classical studies of ulcerative colitis, a disease often associated with anticolon antibodies, refers to obsessive-compulsive character traits of conscientiousness, neatness, indecision, conformity, overintellectualization, rigid morality, and worrying. Engel's colitis patients, as arthritics have been described, could not directly express hostility, and seemed basically immature and dependent. Colitis patients' mothers were controlling and had a propensity to assume the role of martyr, again as arthritics' mothers have been described. McClary et al. [29] speak of the role of the mechanism of depression in patients with disseminated lupus erythematosus. They observed an unusual need for activity and independence, which they consider a denial of the guilt-provoking wish for maternal affection. McClary, like Otto and Mackay [36], found that onset of lupus frequently followed major life stress situations.

The Central Nervous System and Immunity

Several lines of evidence point to a direct role of the central nervous system in control of immunogenesis. Fessel [9] demonstrated that mental stress produces a rise in 19S γ-globulin. Fessel and Forsyth [11] demonstrated alteration in γ-globulin levels by electrical stimulation of the lateral hypothalamus of rats. Korneva and Khai [25] found that a destructive lesion in a specific portion of the dorsal hypothalamus led to complete suppression of primary antibody response and prolonged retention of antigen in the blood, prolonged graft retention, and inability to induce streptococcal antigen myocarditis in rabbits. Korneva has some evidence that these effects can be reversed by growth hormone, which is now being implicated in antibody synthesis [personal communication]. Electrical stimulation of the same hypothalamic region enhanced antibody response [24]. In new work, these Soviet workers found that ablation of the hypothalamic region augmented experimental allergic polyneuritis, related to the absence of complement-fixing antibodies against myelin or nerve fibers, which play a protective role [23]. Macris et al. [28] found protection against lethal anaphylaxis, low antibody titers, and decreased cutaneous delayed hypersensitivity in guinea pigs with symmetrical lesions in the anterior basal hypothalamus.

Immunologic Abnormalities and Mental Illness

A relationship among immunoproteins, stress, and central nervous system is suggested by the findings of various dysproteinemias and autoimmune agglutination reactions in conjunction with schizophrenic illnesses. Elevation of γ-globulin levels and of macroglobulin as well as qualitative disturbances in the electrophoretic patterns of γ-globulin have been reported in various groups of patients with functional psychoses [12]. An increased incidence of positive FII (rheumatoid factor) and lupus factor tests has been found in the sera of psychotic state hospital patients [8]. Using various agglutination techniques, antibrain antibody activity has been reported in the sera of acutely and chronically ill mental patients [10]. Heath and Krupp [18] claimed that the substance 'taraxein' derived from the serum of disturbed schizophrenic patients, which is reputedly capable of eliciting psychotic symptoms upon injection into normal volunteers and monkeys and of producing eletroencephalographic spike activity in the septal region similar to that he found in schizophrenic patients, is a specific IgG antibrain antibody. The presence of abnormal globulins in schizophrenic patients may be related to the findings of abnormal lymphocytes in schizophrenics and in their family members reported by Fessel and Hirata-Hibi [13] and Fessel et al. [14].

Early work of ours suggested a positive correlation between severity of general psychotic symptoms and 19S macroglobulin levels and a negative correlation of these symptoms with overall γ-globulin levels in schizophrenic patients [46]. More recently, we found psychiatric patients show significant elevations of immunoglobulins IgA and IgM [42].

Work on Stress and Immunity from our Laboratory

(1) Stress and antibody response: Some forms of stress, especially overcrowding, significantly reduce primary and secondary antibody response to flagellin, a potent bacterial antigen [41].

(2) Early experience and antibody response: early experience alters adult immunologic responsivity in the rat. Fischer rats were handled from birth by being picked up and placed in a small box for 3 min and then returned to the nest. Handled rats respond more vigorously to primary challenge with flagellin at 9 weeks, particularly in the 19S globulin, and also show somewhat higher titers, which are sustained longer, after booster immunization 4 weeks following primary than unhandled controls [43].

(3) Stress and adjuvant-induced arthritis (an immunologic disease, considered by some an experimental model of rheumatoid arthritis): Mixed-sex group housing a high male-female ratios instituted a week prior to inoculation and continued during the course of disease significantly increases the clinical rating of intensity of adjuvant arthritis in the male Fischer rat, regardless of the

presence of overcrowding. Stress may accelerate the time of maximal disease and rate of recovery. Daily handling for the first 21 days of life does not alter disease in the adult animal [1].

(4) Dose and time relationships: Stress administered both prior to, and immediately subsequent to inoculation with flagellin is immunosuppressive. Stress applied several days subsequent to inoculation is ineffective. Thus, stress seems to act over a short period of time. Giving a high dose of flagellin eliminates differences between stressed and control animals. We have other evidence that stress is immunosuppressive only in the face of stimulation by small amounts of antigen, since other high dose systems, including sheep red blood cells and hapten-hemocyanin, do not show significant stress effects.

(5) Autoimmune anemia in NZB mice (which spontaneously develop auto-immune hemolytic anemia): Apprehension-electric shock stress variably results in acute drop in the hematocrit (packed red cell %). Earlier appearance of autoantibody is unclear. Sex-segregated animals show consistently lower hema-tocrits through age 14 months than controls and have a higher death rate.

(6) Reaginic antibody (implicated in allergic disorders): We are inducing formation of low levels of skin-sensitizing antibody using DNP-KLH and pertussis vaccine. This system should reflect the production of reaginic antibody, which is supposed to be stress-related in humans and has been shown to be steroid-dependent in animals. Food deprivation and electric shock stress *increase* the titer of reaginic antibody; whereas, overcrowding and ACTH are less effective.

(7) Graft versus-host reactions: Parental lymphocytes are injected into first generation (F_1) hybrid recipients either intradermally or into the footpad. Seven days later, the animal is either injected intravenously with Evans blue dye (following intradermal lymphocyte administration) and the size of the skin spot resulting from dye leakage measured, or the weight of the popliteal lymph node draining the injected footpad is measured with the animal serving as its own control. Both Norwegian Brown X Fischer (a strongly histo-incompatible system) and Buffalo X Fischer (a weakly incompatible system) have been used. Crowding and food deprivation stresses of the recipient reduce the magnitude of the reaction significantly. Stress immediately following lymphocyte injection appears most critical. Stress to donors is under study.

(8) Experimental tumor system—Moloney murine sarcoma virus (MSV): A variety of stresses has been studied in order to establish reliable effects on an experimental tumor system, for which immunologic resistance has been demon-strated, in order to be able further to explore mediating immunologic mecha-nisms. Group-housed female Balb/c mice that spontaneously develop fighting behavior shortly following weaning show significantly greater resistance to MSV, including both a lower incidence and smaller size of tumors. Male mice segregated by sex and group-housed at weaning show no difference in MSV susceptibility at three months of age from males housed individually with two or

more females. At six and more markedly at nine months sex-segregated groups show an increase in tumor size. The stress of 4-hour/day periods of random brief electric shocks administered only for three days prior to inoculation with virus *reduces* the incidence and size of tumors. When shock is continued during the course of tumor growth and regression (whether or not fighting is induced) onset is somewhat retarded, but both incidence and size eventually equal that of controls. Five-month-old females subjected to three days of electric shock stress *following* virus inoculation show significantly *increased* tumor size.

(9) Immunoglobulins and schizophrenia (with Mathea Allansmith, Maurice Rappaport and Julian Silverman): The purpose of this study is to determine the correlation of increases of specific immunoglobulins with clinical features, course, treatment and cognitive-perceptual features of schizophrenia; to attempt to determine the presence of any immunoglobulin specific to schizophrenia; and to elucidate the immune mechanisms underlying the immunologic abnormalities found. Elevations of and abnormalities of distribution of IgA and IgM and, to a lesser degree, of IgG are found in schizophrenic patients. Average IgA and IgM levels are lower in patients who improve during hospitalization, low IgA correlating with improvement specifically in phenothiazine-treated patients. So far, neither an immunoglobulin specific to schizophrenia nor antibrain antibody activity have been found. Elevations of creatine phosphate kinase and evoked cortical response variables have not correlated with immunoglobulins.

(10) Central nervous system and immunity (with Phyllis Kasper-Pandi): Attempts to replicate Dr. Korneva's work on suppression of humoral immunity by hypothalamic lesions appear encouraging, but extra-hypothalamic pathways may also be involved. Ablation of specific hypothalamic centers in the recipient seems to alter graft-versus-host reactions.

Summary

Stress and emotional distress may influence the function of the immunologic system. Thus, environmental and psychologic factors might in some circumstances be implicated in the pathogenesis of cancer, the resistance to which growing evidence finds immunologic in nature, as well as of infections and of autoimmune diseases, which seem to have an association with states of relative immunologic incompetence. There are considerable data to link personality factors, stress, and, particularly, failure of psychologic defenses to the onset and course of cancer and of infectious and autoimmune diseases. Clinical situations of emotional decompensation and mental illness appear to be associated with immunologic disturbances. We are concerned with nervous and hormonal mechanisms by which emotions and stress may relate to specific dysfunctions of the immunologic system.

We have experimental evidence that some forms of stress reduce primary and secondary antibody response to low dose antigen stimulation in rats and that adult immunologic responsivity may be altered by early infantile experience. Mixed-sex group housing at high male-female ratios increases severity of adjuvant-induced arthritis in the male rat. Spontaneous autoimmune hemolytic anemia in NZB mice is aggravated by sex-segregated housing. Skin-sensitizing ('allergic', reaginic type) antibody titers are *increased* by stress. Graft-versus-host reactions are diminished by stress to recipient animals. Sex-segregated group-housed mice show larger murine virus-induced sarcomas when inoculated at 6 and 9 months of age than males housed individually with two or more females. Electric shock stress for three days prior to inoculation with virus reduces incidence and size of MSV tumors, while shock administered three days following inoculation increases tumor size. Female mice that develop spontaneous fighting behavior show significantly greater resistance to MSV tumors.

References

1 Amkraut, A.; Solomon, G.F., and Kraemer, H.C.: Stress, early experience and adjuvant-induced arthritis in the rat. Psychosom. Med. *33*:203-214 (1971).
2 Bahnson, C.B. (ed.): Second Conference on Psychophysiological Aspects of Cancer. Ann. N.Y. Acad. Sci. *164:* 307-634 (1969).
3 Day, G.: The psychosomatic approach to pulmonary tuberculosis. Lancet 6663 (1951).
4 Dixon, F.J.; Feldman, J., and Vasquez, J.: Experimental glomerulonephritis. J. exp. Med. *113:* 899 (1961).
5 Engel, G.L.: Studies of ulcerative colitis. III. The nature of the psychologic processes. Amer. J. Med. *19:* 231 (1955).
6 Fefer, A.; McCoy, J.L., and Glynn, J.P.: Induction and regression of primary Moloney sarcoma virus-induced tumors in mice. Cancer Res. *27:* 1626 (1967).
7 Fefer, A.; McCoy, J.L.; Perk, K., and Glynn, J.P.: Immunologic, virologic and pathologic studies of regression of autochthonous Moloney sarcoma virus-induced tumors in mice. Cancer Res. *28:* 1577 (1968).
8 Fessel, W.J.: Disturbed serum proteins in chronic psychosis. Arch. gen. Psychiat. *4:* 154 (1961).
9 Fessel, W.J.: Mental stress, blood proteins, hypothalamus: experimental results showing effect of mental stress upon 4S and 19S proteins; speculation that functional behavior disturbances may be expressions of general metabolic disorder. Arch. gen. Psychiat. *7:* 427 (1962).
10 Fessel, W.J.: 'Antibrain' factors in psychiatric patient's sera. I. Further studies with hemagglutination technique. Arch. gen. Psychiat. *8:* 614 (1963).
11 Fessel, W.J. and Forsyth: Hypothalamic role in control of γ-globulin levels. Abstract. Arthritis Rheum. *6:* 770 (1963).

12 Fessel, W.J. and Grunbaum, B.W.: Electrophoretic and analytical ultracentrifuge studies in sera of psychotic patients: elevation of γ-globulins and macroglobulins and splitting of α_2-globulins. Ann. intern. Med. *54:* 1134 (1961).

13 Fessel, W.J. and Hirata-Hibi, M.: Abnormal leukocytes in schizophrenia. Arch. gen. Psychiat. *9:* 601 (1963).

14 Fessel, W.J.; Hirata-Hibi, M., and Shapiro, I.M.: Genetic and stress factors affecting the abnormal lymphocyte in schizophrenia. J. Psychiat. Res. *3:* 275 (1965).

15 Fudenberg, H.H.: Are autoimmune diseases immunologic deficiency states? Hosp. Pract. *3:* 43 (1968).

16 Greenfield, N.S.; Roessler, R., and Crosley, A.P., jr.: Ego strength and length of recovery from infectious mononucleosis. J. nerv. ment. Dis. *128:* 125 (1966).

17 Habel, K.: Immunologic aspects of oncogenesis by polyoma virus; in Conceptual advances in immunology and oncology (Hoeber, New York 1963).

18 Heath, R.G. and Krupp, I.M.: Schizophrenia as an immunologic disorder. Arch. gen. Psychiat. *16:* 1 (1967).

19 Hellström, K.-E. and Hellström, I.: Personal commun. (1971).

20 Imboden, J.B.; Carter, A.; Leighton, E.C., and Trevor, R.W.: Brucellosis. III. Psychologic aspects of delayed convalescence. Arch. intern. Med. *103:* 406 (1959).

21 Imboden, J.B.; Carter, A., and Leighton, E.C.: Convalescence from influenza: a study of the psychological and clinical determinants. Arch. intern. Med. *108* (1961).

22 Klopfer, B.: Psychological variables in human cancer. J. Project Techn. *21:* 331 (1957).

23 Konovalov, G.V.; Korneva, E.A., and Khai, L.M.: Effect of destruction of the posterior hypothalamic area on experimental allergic polyneuritis. Brain Res. *29:* 383-386 (1971).

24 Korneva, E.A.: The effect of stimulating different mesencephalic structures on protective immune response patterns. Fiziol. Zh. SSSR Sechenov *53:* 42 (1967).

25 Korneva, E.A. and Khai, L.M.: Effect of destruction of hypothalamic areas on immunogenesis. Fiziol.Zh. SSSR Sechenov *49:* 42 (1963).

26 LaBarba, R.C.: Experimental and environmental factors in cancer: a review of research with animals. Psychosom. Med. *32:* 259 (1970).

27 Leshan, L.L. and Worthington, R.E.: Personality as factor in pathogenesis of cancer: review of literature. Brit. J. med. Psychol. *29:* 49 (1956).

28 Macris, N.T.; Schiavi, R.C.; Camerino, M.S., and Stein, M.: Effect of hypothalamic lesion on immune processes in the guinea pig. Amer. J. Physiol. *219:* 1205-1209 (1970).

29 McClary, A.R.; Meyer, E., and Weitzman, D.J.: Observations on role of mechanisms of depression in some patients with disseminated lupus erythematosus. Psychosom. Med. *17:* 311 (1955).

30 Moos, R.H.: Personality factors associated with rheumatoid arthritis: a review. J. chron. Dis. *17:* 41 (1963).

31 Moos, R.H.: Minnesota Multiphasic Personality Inventory response patterns in patients with rheumatoid arthritis. J. Psychosom. Res. *8:* 17 (1964).

32 Moos, R.H. and Solomon, G.F.: Personality correlates of the rapidity of progression of rheumatoid arthritis. Ann. rheum. Diss. *23:* 145 (1964).

33 Moos, R.H. and Solomon, G.F.: Personality correlates of the degree of functional incapacity of patients with physical disease. J. chron. Dis. *18:* 1019 (1965).

34 Moos, R.H. and Solomon, G.F.: Psychologic comparisons between women with rheumatoid arthritis and their non-arthritic sisters. I. Personality test and interview rating data. Psychosom. Med. *27:* 135 (1965); II. Content analysis of interviews. Psychosom. Med. *27:* 150 (1965).

35 Mutter, A.Z. and Schleifer, M.J.: The role of psychological and social factors in the onset of somatic illness in children. Psychosom. Med. *28:* 333 (1966).

36 Otto, R. and Mackay, I.I.: Psychosocial and emotional disturbance in systemic lupus erythematosus. Med. J. Austr. *2:* 488 (1967).

37 Rasmussen, A.F., jr.; Spencer, E.S., and Marsh, J.T.: Increased susceptibility to herpes simplex in mice subjected to avoidance-learning stress or restraint. Proc. Soc. exp. Biol. Med. *96:* 183 (1957).

38 Rimón, R.: A psychosomatic approach to rheumatoid arthritis: a clinical study of 100 female patients. Acta rheum. scand., suppl., vol. 13 (1969).

39 Salk, J.: Biological basis of disease and behavior. Perspect. Biol. Med. *5:* 198 (1962).

40 Schmale, A.H., jr.: The relation of separation and depression to disease. Psychosom. Med. *20:* 259 (1958).

41 Solomon, G.F.: Stress and antibody response in rats. Int. Arch. Allergy *35:* 97 (1969).

42 Solomon, G.F.; Allansmith, M.; McClellan, B., and Amkraut, A.: Immunoglobulins in psychiatric patients. Arch. gen. Psychiat. *20:* 272 (1969).

43 Solomon, G.F.; Levine, S., and Kraft, J.: Early experience and immunity. Nature, Lond. *220:* 821 (1968).

44 Solomon, G.F. and Moos, R.H.: Psychologic aspects of response to treatment in rheumatoid arthritis. GP *32:* 113 (1965).

45 Solomon, G.F. and Moos, R.H.: The relationship of personality to the presence of rheumatoid factor in asymptomatic relatives of patients with rheumatoid arthritis. Psychosom. Med. *27:* 350 (1965).

46 Solomon, G.F.; Moos, R.H.; Fessel, W.J., and Morgan, E.E.: Globulins and behavior in schizophrenia. Int. J. Neuropsychiat. *2:* 20 (1966).

47 Solomon, G.F.; Merigan, T.; and Levine, S.: Variation in adrenal cortical

hormones within physiologic ranges, stress and interferon production in mice. Proc. Soc. exp. Biol. Med. *126:* 74 (1967).

48 Weigle, W.O.: The antibody response in rabbits to previously tolerated antigens. Ann. N.Y. Acad. Sci. *124:* 133 (1965).

49 Yamada, A.; Jensen, M.M., and Rasmussen, A.F., jr.: Stress and susceptibility to viral infections. III. Antibody response and viral retention during avoidance-learning stress. Proc. Soc. exp. Biol. Med. *116:* 677 (1964).

V

Social
Dimensions in
Obesity

Commentary. Obesity, a major health problem in our society, is characterized by an excess accumulation of body fat. Obesity is more than a cosmetic problem: it is associated with coronary heart disease, high blood pressure, diabetes, and other disorders. Unfortunately, millions of Americans are obese.

What is the difference between being obese and just overweight? One common method of determining obesity is the thickness of the fat layer underneath the skin, known as *subcutaneous fat*. Approximately half the total body fat is located in this layer. If a person were to pinch a roll of skin between two fingers, he would be compressing a double thickness of subcutaneous fat. This double thickness can be measured with *skinfold thickness calipers*. Skinfold thickness can be measured at various sites of the body. It is often measured at the tip of the shoulder blade and the triceps (the muscle at the back of the upper arm that extends the forearm which contracted). A skinfold thickness measured at the triceps exceeding 16 millimeters (6.4 inches) for males and 28 millimeters (11.2 inches) for females is frequently a criterion for obesity. (Seltzer and Mayer, 1965).

While obesity may be unhealthy it is not always viewed negatively. In some cultural groups obesity is regarded as a sign of social influence and power. In the first chapter in this section Philip Goldblatt, Mary Moore, and Albert Stunkard suggest that obesity may be a normal response in particular subgroups of society to the "perceived expectations of their social milieu." Their findings indicate that obesity is six times more common among women of low socioeconomic status than among those of high status; that upwardly mobile women are less obese than downwardly mobile women; and that the longer a woman's family has been in the United States the less likely she is to be obese.

In Chapter 15 Albert Stunkard and his colleagues extend previous work to include the problem of obesity in children. Most obese children become obese adults, so this problem is particularly relevant: in fact, this chapter indicates that the odds against an obese child becoming a normal weight adult are 28 to 1 if weight has not been reduced by the end of adolescence. Because of the early onset of class-related differences in the prevalence of obesity, the authors suggest, it is important to focus attention on the problem in childhood.

Apart from social class, other distinctions have been observed between obese and normal persons. It appears that the eating behavior of obese people is not initiated by the same internal stimuli as that of persons of normal weight. While hunger and satisfaction, for example, shape the eating patterns of persons of normal weight, obese people seem to be much more at the mercy of environmental cues. Regardless of how recently or extensively they have eaten, they may be prompted to eat again simply by the sight or smell of food (Schachter, 1971). Thus, in the last chapter in this section Richard Stuart emphasizes the importance of environmental controls in treating obesity. He uses three procedures: *cue elimination*, e.g., restricting eating activity to one place; *cue suppression*, e.g., preparing and serving small quantities only; and *cue strengthen-*

ing, e.g., maintaining weight charts and displaying pictures of desired clothing, appearance, and activities.

Another approach to the treatment of obesity combines behavior modification and group therapy procedures. Penick et al. (1971) carried out a program of three months' duration, consisting of once-a-week sessions from 10:30 A.M. to 3:00 P.M. Activities included an exercise period, preparation and eating of a low-calorie lunch, and a group therapy period. Results indicated that 13 percent of the subjects lost more than forty pounds each, and 53 percent lost more than twenty pounds each. While these early results are encouraging, the long-term effectiveness of this program cannot be determined without follow-up studies.

Medical approaches to the treatment of obesity have apparently met with little success. The use of appetite-dulling drugs to reduce a person's food intake, for example, are usually only temporarily effective. The lost weight is eventually regained unless a change in eating behavior takes place. Surgical procedures to reduce absorption and food intake have also been shown to be risky (Mason and Ito, 1969).

References

Mason, E.E., and Ito, C. Gastric bypass. *Annals of Surgery, 170*:329-339, 1969.

Penick, S., Filion, R., Fox, S., and Stunkard, A.J. Behavior modification in the treatment of obesity. *Psychosomatic Medicine, 33*:(1)49-55, 1971.

Schachter, S. Some extraordinary facts about obese humans and rats. *American Psychologist, 26*:129-144, 1971.

Seltzer, C.C., and Mayer, J. A simple criterion of obesity. *Postgraduate Medicine, 38*:101-106, 1965.

14 Social Factors in Obesity

Phillip B. Goldblatt, Mary E. Moore,
and Albert J. Stunkard*
University of Pennsylvania

This report is an extension of our previous finding that social factors play an important role in human obesity.[1] Current theories as to the etiology of obesity, whether behavioral, biochemical, or physiological, have directed their attention to the individual. We were, therefore, very much interested in a finding incidental to our earlier study, which was undertaken to assess the relationship of mental health to obesity in a large, representative, urban population.[1] Parental social class, introduced as a controlling variable, showed a high correlation with the prevalence of obesity and was a more powerful predictor of overweight than a number of psychological measures. The present study, undertaken to investigate this relationship further, showed obesity to be related to each of the following additional social variables: the respondent's own socioeconomic status, social mobility, and generation in the United States.

Methods and Materials

The data reported here were collected as part of the Midtown Manhattan Study, a comprehensive survey of the epidemiology of mental illness. The details of the

Reprinted with permission from *Journal of American Medical Association,* 192(12):1039-1044, June 1965.
*Currently Chairman, Department of Psychiatry, Stanford University School of Medicine.

sample and the data collection techniques have been fully described else-where.[2,3] The data in the present analysis were obtained from the Midtown Home Survey of 1,660 adults, consisting of 690 males and 970 females between the ages of 20 and 59. One female in the Home Survey was omitted from our study because she was under four feet (122 cm) in height. The population was divided into three weight categories—"obese," "normal," and "thin"—based upon the self-reported heights and weights as described in our previous paper. The validity of such reports has been attested to by an independent survey.[4]

The relationships of these categories to the widely accepted standards for "desirable" weight of the Metropolitan Life Insurance Company[5] is shown in Table 14-1. The "desirable" weights are those for which the mortality rates are lowest, so that even the group which we have designated "normal" exceeds their "desirable" weight by about 10%. The means for our "obese" groups were 34% and 44% above the "desirable" weight, indicating a significant degree of overweight. The corresponding means for the "thin" groups were 13% and 16% below the "desirable" weight.

The respondent's own socioeconomic status (SES) at the time of the interview was rated by a simple score devised by Srole et al.[2] based upon the respondent's occupation, education, weekly income, and monthly rent. Each of these four variables was subdivided into six categories. In the scoring, each variable was given equal weight. Thus, an individual in the lowest category of each variable (unskilled labor, no schooling, income less than $49 per week, and monthly rent less than $30) received a score of four. Conversely, an individual in all of the highest categories (high white collar, graduate school education, income over $300 per week, and monthly rent greater than $200) received a score of 24. (Unmarried working women were rated on the basis of their own occupation. Unmarried nonworking women were classified by their fathers' occupation. Married women, whether working or not, were rated on the basis of their husbands' occupation.) In order to obtain subgroups of sufficient size to permit control by variables which the analysis showed to be relevant, the

Table 14-1

Relationship of Midtown Home Survey Weight Categories to Standards of "Desirable" Weight*

Midtown Weight Category	Average % Over (+) or Under (−) Desirable Weight	
	Females	Males
Thin	−13	−16
Normal	+11	+ 9
Obese	+44	+34

*Standards of Metropolitan Life Insurance Company for desirable weight.

population was divided into three socioeconomic groups as nearly equal in number as feasible. Individuals with scores of 4 to 10 were designated low status; those with scores of 11 to 16 were middle status; and those with 17 to 24 points were high status.

In our first paper we used the respondent's social class of origin as a controlling variable. This measure was employed so as to avoid any reciprocal relationship that might exist between a respondent's present SES and his obesity. Obesity may in part depend on social status but, at the same time, social status may in part depend on obesity. The SES of origin is a measure of important social influences on a respondent which are in no sense a product of his obesity. The social class or origin was based on the education and occupation of the respondent's father when the respondent was 8 years old.

The scores for SES of origin were divided into "low," "medium" and "high" socioeconomic categories in a manner analogous to that used for the respondent's own SES. These two sets of scores permitted us to study the relationship of obesity to social mobility by comparing the socioeconomic status of the respondent at the age of 8 with that at the time of the interview.

Results

The present analysis extended in a most dramatic way our previous finding of the importance in the understanding of human obesity of one socioeconomic variable—socioeconomic status of origin. Every one of the three additional social factors investigated was also strongly related to obesity. Furthermore, each was more strongly related to obesity among women than among men. The analysis of the data for women will be presented first.

Obesity Among Women

Own Socioeconomic Status.—There was a marked inverse relationship between the prevalence of obesity and the respondent's own SES. Figure 14-1 shows that the prevalence of obesity among lower SES women was 30%, falling to 16% among the middle SES, and to only 5% in the upper SES. A chi-square test of the relationship between socioeconomic status and the three weight categories was significant at the 0.001 level ($X^2 = 120.7$).

Socioeconomic Status of Origin.—Just as the respondent's own socioeconomic status was inversely related to her obesity, so also was her socioeconomic status of origin ($X^2 = 66.5, P < 0.001$). This latter finding, reported in greater detail in our earlier study, is also shown in Figure 14-1. Note that the relationship between this factor and obesity was nearly as strong as that between the respondent's own socioeconomic status and her weight category.

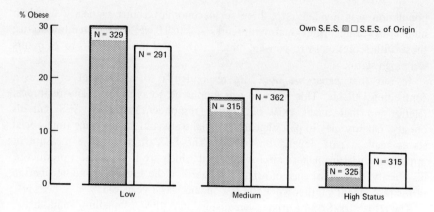

Figure 14-1. Decreasing Prevalence of Obesity with Increasing Socioeconomic Status (SES). Data Exclude One Female about Whom no Information on the Socioeconomic Status of Origin was Available.

Social Mobility.—The close correspondence between the results for the respondent's own SES and SES of origin suggested the possibility that these two variables were measuring the same underlying dimension. This would be the case in a society in which the vast majority of people lived out their entire lives in the same social class into which they were born. Such was not the case, however, in Midtown Manhattan which showed a high degree of social mobility. Indeed, 44% of the women belonged to a different social class from that of their parents. In other words, many people were classified differently by our two indices of social status, and these two variables did not measure the same underlying dimension. A measure of this discrepancy between the respondent's own SES and the SES of her origin is given by our index of social mobility.

Figure 14-2 shows the relationship of social mobility to obesity. Of women who remained in the socioeconomic status into which they were born 179 were obese, whereas among women who moved down in social status there was a higher prevalence of obesity (22%), while among those who moved upwards there was a lower prevalence (12%) (X^2 = 20.5, $P < 0.001$). Thus, movement *among* the social classes as well as membership in a social class was predictive of obesity.

Generation in the United States.—The fourth variable, generation in the United States, was also strongly linked to obesity. To assess this variable respondents were divided into one of four groups on the basis of the number of generations their families had been in this country. Generation I consisted of foreign-born immigrants; generation II, of all those native-born respondents with at least one

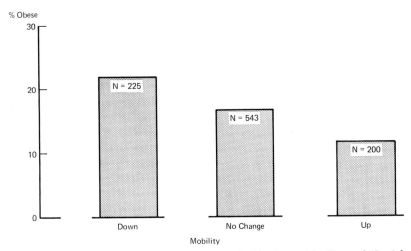

Figure 14-2. Decreasing Prevalence of Obesity with Upward Social Mobility. Data Exclude One Female about Whom no Information on Mobility was Feasible.

foreign-born parent; generation III, of all those who were native-born of native-born parents but had at least one foreign-born grandparent; and generation IV, of all those who had no foreign-born grandparents and who otherwise met the qualifications for generation III.

Figure 14-3 shows that the longer a woman's family had been in this country, the less likely she was to be obese. Of first generation respondents 24% were overweight, in contrast to only 5% in the fourth generation (X^2 = 56.5, $P < 0.001$).

It seemed probable that generation in the United States was closely related to socioeconomic status, and that the longer a family had been in this country, the higher its status was likely to be. The data in Table 14-2 show that this is indeed the case. Thus, in the first generation, 194 out of 365 respondents were of low SES, while in the fourth generation, 102 out of 140 were of high SES (X^2 = 235.6, $P < 0.001$).

To determine whether this phenomenon accounted for the finding that obesity was less common the longer a respondent's family had been in the country, we examined the prevalence of obesity for each SES within each generation. Table 14-2 clearly demonstrates that the inverse relation between obesity and generation was independent of socioeconomic status. Of the

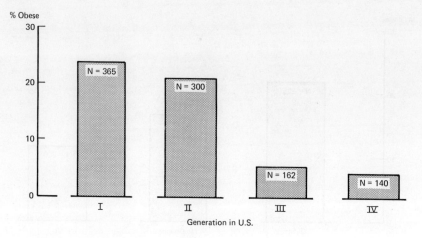

Figure 14-3. Decreasing Prevalence of Obesity with Increasing Length of Time of Respondent's Family in United States. Data Exclude Two Women about Whom no Information on Generation in United States was Available.

generation I respondents who were of low status 30% were obese, but only 13% of generation IV low-status females were overweight. This trend obtained in all the social classes (X^2 for low SES = 21.5, $P < 0.01$; X^2 for middle SES = 18.1, $P < 0.01$; X^2 for high SES = 21.5, $P < 0.01$).

Table 14-2

Percentage of Obese Females by Generation in United States—Controlling the Factor of Socioeconomic Status (SES)

	Generation											
	I			II			III			IV		
	Own SES Low	Own SES Med	Own SES High	Own SES Low	Own SES Med	Own SES High	Own SES Low	Own SES Med	Own SES High	Own SES Low	Own SES Med	Own SES High
Obese, %	30	21	7	34	19	6	22	6	2	13	4	4
N (100%)*	194	113	58	96	126	78	23	52	87	15	23	102

*N = Number in sample falling into particular category, e.g., 30% of 194 first generation low SES females are obese. Excludes two females about whom no information on generation is available.

Obesity Among Men

The relationship between social factors and the prevalence of obesity among males paralleled that among the women, but in each instance was less marked.

Own Socioeconomic Status.—There was an inverse relationship between his own SES and obesity. Figure 14-4, however, shows that the effect was far weaker than in the case of females (X^2 = 17.4, $P < 0.01$). Whereas obesity was six times more common among women of lower socioeconomic status than among those of high status, the corresponding ratio among men was only 2:1.

Socioeconomic Status of Origin.—Socioeconomic status of origin had an effect upon the prevalence of overweight among men, although, as was true for women, the effect was weaker than that of the respondent's own SES. Furthermore, the influence of SES of origin was far weaker among men than among women. Whereas obesity was four times more common among women of lower socioeconomic status of origin than among those of high status, the corresponding ratio among males was less than 2:1.

Social Mobility.—Social mobility was even more common among the men in our sample than among the women, with 47% of the males belonging to a different social class than their parents. Figure 14-5 shows the prevalence of obesity among those men who moved downward, stayed in the same class, or moved upward. Once again the same trend obtained as for females; in this instance, however, the chi-square did not reach a level of statistical significance.

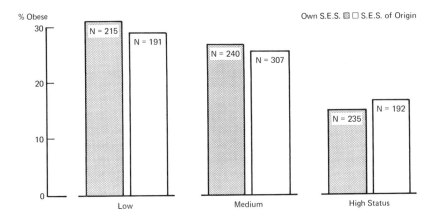

Figure 14-4. Decreased Prevalence of Obesity with Increased Socioeconomic Status (SES).

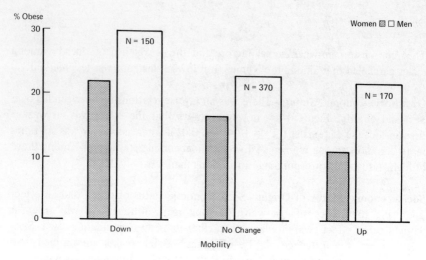

Figure 14-5. Slight Trend Toward Decreased Prevalence of Obesity with Upward Mobility Among Men as Constrasted to Significant Trend Among Women.

Generation in the United States.—Among the men as among the women the percentage of obese respondents decreased as the number of generations in the United States increased. Figure 14-6 reveals that obesity was three times more common among the males in the first generation as compared to those in the fourth generation ($X^2 = 18.7, P < 0.001$). There was, however, no sharp drop in the percentage of obese between generation II and III, as was the case among females. As among women, these findings resulted even when socioeconomic status was held constant.

The Thin Category

At the beginning of the analysis of the weight categories, we expected that "thinness" would behave as though it were the opposite of obesity. We found, however, a striking difference in this regard between men and women. With increasing status, women moved from the "obese" to the "thin" category, whereas men moved from the "obese" to the "normal." Thus, thinness did operate as the opposite of obesity for women, but not for men. Table 14-3 shows that there were four times as many thin respondents among women of high status as there were among those of low status. Among men, however,

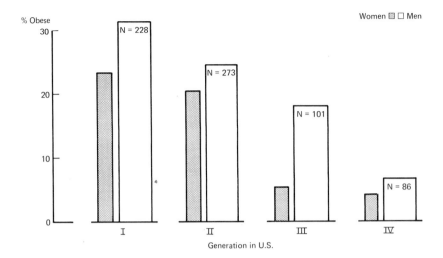

Figure 14-6. Decreasing Prevalence of Obesity with Increasing Length of Time of Respondent's Family in United States. Data Exclude Two Men about Whom no Information on Generation in United States was Available.

about 10% were thin in all classes, and it was the percentage of normal-weight respondents that increased with increasing status.

Comment

The most important finding of this study was the remarkable consistency with which social factors correlated with body weight. Such a strong correlation, appearing in all the factors investigated, is highly significant. The only other attempt to study obesity as a social phenomenon, that by Pflanz[6] in Germany, has reported similar findings. It is now apparent that obesity can no longer be viewed as simply an abnormal characteristic of the individual. It must also be viewed as one of the possible, and not too infrequent, normal responses of persons in certain subgroups of society to the perceived expectations of their social milieu.

Although not being obese, indeed, being thin, seems culturally desirable for the women of Midtown, almost one out of three lower class females was obese. Such a high percentage implies that in this subgroup of Midtown society, overweight is common enough that it need not be viewed as abnormal.

Table 14-3
Weight Categories by Respondent's Own Socioeconomic Status (SES)

| | % of Each Weight Category in Each SES | | | | | |
| | Low SES | | Middle SES | | High SES | |
Weight Categories	Males	Females	Males	Females	Males	Females
Thin	10%	9%	9%	19%	12%	37%
Normal	59	61	64	65	73	58
Obese	31	30	27	16	15	5
N (100%)*	215	329	240	315	235	325

*Number of individuals in sample falling into particular category.

In the Midtown society we do not have to look far to see the image of the slim, attractive female as portrayed throughout the popular culture. Motion picture stars, television personalities, women in advertisements, fashion models, and, indeed, the fashionable clothes themselves, all reflect the definition of the beautiful female as the one who is thin. How does such an ideal of beauty exert its impact on the body weight of persons in the different elements of society? At least two mechanisms seem plausible.

First, a selection process may operate so that in any status-conferring situation, such as a promotion at work or marriage to a higher status male, thinner women may be preferentially selected over their competitors.

Second, an acculturation phenomenon may be operating. For example, an individual's adult weight can be seen to be partly a product of social influences operating in his childhood. That this occurred in Midtown is demonstrated by our finding of a marked relationship between obesity and the SES of one's origin. A similar process may also be operating throughout life. Thus a female who acquires upper socioeconomic status for desirable attributes other than thinness will perceive that among her new peers more emphasis is placed upon being slim than was true in her old environment. She is likely, therefore, to make a greater effort to lose weight than she might previously have done.

The lesser importance of social factors as related to body weight among men, as contrasted to women, may arise from a lesser importance that society attaches to the physical appearance of men, as well as from a different definition of culturally desirable weight for them. In advertisements, for example, men are as likely to be exhorted to avoid being "97-lb weaklings," as to avoid being obese. It is, perhaps, not surprising that the normal weight category correlates so highly with upper socioeconomic status.

The extent to which a respondent has adopted the Midtown values about body weight apparently depends upon at least two factors: first, on the length of his family's exposure to these values (as measured by number of generations in the United States) and second, the amount of pressure to conform to these values, which is a function of his proximity to the upper classes where the values are most strongly exemplified.

Although generation and socioeconomic status are related to each other, it has been shown in this study that each makes an independent contribution to the prevalence of obesity. It is unfortunate that the size of the sample precluded more precise estimates of their relative contributions.

It is obvious that there were important differences among our respondents besides those of class and generation. The Midtown sample included nine ethnic groups (British, Russian-Polish-Lithuanian, German-Austrian, Irish, Puerto Rican, Italian, Hungarian, Czech, and fourth generation American) as well as many religions and sects. We discovered several relationships between ethnic and religious backgrounds and obesity. These were so intertwined with each other and with other social factors, such as generation and socioeconomic status, that we were unable to control all of the relevant factors simultaneously. Nevertheless, some of the data are worth describing briefly.

For example, only 9% of female respondents of British descent were obese, whereas 27% of those of Italian extraction were in this weight category. These differences diminished when social class was the control. Thus, for example, when only the upper classes of both ethnic groups were contrasted, the prevalence of obesity was 10% for the British and 20% for the Italian. Such differences can be related to what is known about the traditional diets and social implications of eating of these two ethnic groups. Joffe,[7] for example, has reported that first generation Italian mothers regard obesity in their children as protection against tuberculosis. Childs[8] found the basic diet of Italian-Americans to have a high fat content. Finally, a recent study in a small Pennsylvania town inhabited almost entirely by Italian-Americans revealed that the diet had a greater proportion of fat than that of the average American diet and that the prevalence of obesity was also significantly above average.[9]

Another example of such a phenomenon may be found among our data for Americans of eastern European extraction. Joffe notes that the Czechs love food and are less Americanized than the Poles as far as cooking habits are concerned. Among the Czechs, there is a great deal of visiting on Sundays during which time large quantities of food are consumed. Refusing a second or even a third helping of food is considered impolite. Our data reflect the results of these customs. Of the lower-class Czechs 41% were obese as compared with only 18% of the lower-class Polish-Russian-Lithuanians that were obese.

We also found differences among respondents of different religions. Lutherans, for example, were more often obese (24%) than Episcopalians (3%), but any statement made about the Lutherans and Episcopalians reflects also the difference between respondents of German and of British extraction. Unfortunately, we did not have enough cases to sift out the effects of religion per se.

What has been reported in this study about obesity in Midtown in 1954 is not necessarily applicable in toto to any other country, or any other urban area, or even to the Midtown of today. Indeed, Pflanz found an increased incidence of obesity among upwardly mobile German men and a decreased incidence among German women; in contrast, a decreased incidence among the upwardly mobile of both sexes was found in the present study. It thus appears that the same social mechanisms which discourage obesity among the socially mobile in this country may encourage it among German men. Even though Pflanz's specific findings differed from ours, his conclusion was the same: human obesity must be understood in part as a social phenomenon.

Many of the present theories about human obesity were formulated by psychiatrists on the basis of their treatment of middle and of upper class women, for whom obesity was a severe social liability. In other segments of society, however, obesity appears to be by no means such a handicap. Future researchers will have to explore the ways in which some respondents in all classes develop the attitude that a slim appearance is very important. Studies will be needed to determine the reasons why certain subgroups have a higher incidence of this belief than others, the mechanisms by which this belief is inculcated, and the ages at which it appears with differing frequencies in differing social classes. Future theories will have to take into account the differing implications of overweight for the different social classes.

It seems quite possible that the lack of success in the control and treatment of obesity stems from the fact that until now physicians have thought of obesity as always being abnormal. This is certainly not true for persons in the lower socioeconomic population. Obesity may always be unhealthy, but it is not always abnormal.

Unfortunately, our weight control programs have directed their appeals in a nonspecific way to rich and poor alike. The present study reveals an unexpected opportunity for increasing the selectivity of public health measures for the control of obesity. Would it not be more effective to initiate programs tailored specifically for subgroups of society where obesity is most common? The success of a similar approach has been demonstrated by Johnson et al.,[10] who studied the epidemiology of polio vaccine acceptance in Dade County, Fla. They pointed up the importance of ethnic background and social class as an index of commonly held beliefs, shared feelings, group values and attitudes, and social participation. Utilizing such information in work with a high-risk population (lower class, Spanish-speaking residents of Dade County), they significantly increased the percentage of respondents who took polio vaccine over the percentage who had done so in previous campaigns.

The present study shows the feasibility of identifying obese populations at high risk. Such identification has generally been a prerequisite for effective public health programs. Recognition of the significance of social factors in obesity may lay the foundation for our first effective public health program for the control of obesity.

References

1. Moore, M.E.; Stunkard, A.; and Srole, L.: Obesity, Social Class, and Mental Illness, *JAMA* 181:962-966 (Sept 15) 1962.

2. Srole, L., et al.: *Mental Health in the Metropolis: Midtown Manhattan Study*, New York: McGraw-Hill Book Co., Inc., vol 1, 1962.

3. Langner, T.S., and Michael, S.T.: *Life Stress and Mental Health: Midtown Manhattan Study*, New York: The Free Press of Glencoe, Inc., vol 2, 1963.

4. Perry, L., and Learnard, B.: Obesity and Mental Health, *JAMA* 183:807-808 (March 2) 1963.

5. New Weight Standards for Men and Women, *Statist Bull Metrop Life Insur Co* 40:2-3 (Nov-Dec) 1959.

6. Pflanz, M.: Medizinische-soziologische Aspekte der Fettsucht, *Psyche* 16:575-591, 1962-1963.

7. Joffe, N.F.: Food Habits of Selected Subcultures in United States, *Bull Nat Res Council* 108:97-103 (Oct) 1943.

8. Childs, A.: Some Dietary Studies of Poles, Mexicans, Italians, and Negroes, *Child Health Bull* 9:84-91, 1933.

9. Stout, C., et al.: Unusually Low Incidence of Death From Myocardial Infarction: Study of Italian American Community in Pennsylvania, *JAMA* 188:845-849 (June 8) 1964.

10. Johnson, A.L., et al.: *Epidemiology of Polio Vaccine Acceptance–Social and Psychological Analysis*, monograph No. 3, Florida State Board of Health, 1962.

15

Influence of Social Class on Obesity and Thinness in Children

Albert Stunkard*, Eugene D'Aquili,
Sonja Fox, and Ross D.L. Filion
*University of Pennsylvania
and Philadelphia General Hospital*

This report continues our assessment of the influence of social factors on obesity in man. In earlier studies, carried out in New York City, we demonstrated a strong inverse relationship between socioeconomic status and obesity. Obesity was six times more prevalent among women of lower than among women of upper socioeconomic status.[1,2] Correlation between parental socioeconomic status and prevalence of obesity was nearly as strong, indicating that socioeconomic status was cause as well as correlate (Figure 15-1). We also demonstrated significant inverse relationships between social mobility and obesity, and between number of generations in this country and obesity. In addition, several ethnic and religious variables appeared related to the prevalence of obesity.[3,4] Subsequently, we found similar results in a study in London.[5] In all these investigations, the relationship between social factors and prevalence of obesity among men paralleled that in women but in each instance was less marked.

The present study was designed to establish the age at which the influence of socioeconomic status on body weight becomes apparent. We also wanted to delineate the subsequent evolution of the relationship between socioeconomic status and obesity and thinness.

Reprinted with permission of *Journal of the American Medical Association*, 221(6):579-584, 1972.
*Currently Chairman, Department of Psychiatry, Stanford University School of Medicine.

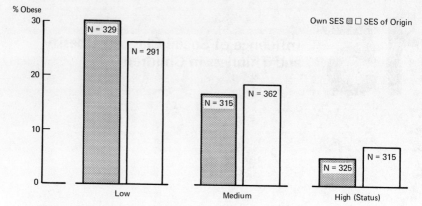

Figure 15-1. Decreasing Prevalence of Obesity with Increasing Socioeconomic Status (SES) Among Women in an Eastern City.

Materials and Methods

To assess the prevalence of obesity we measured the skin-fold thicknesses of 3,344 white school children in three Eastern cities. The 11 schools in the study were chosen so as to provide a population of both upper- and lower-class children. The respondent's socioeconomic status was determined on the basis of the father's occupation, according to *Intermediate Occupational Classification for Males*, a 1950 publication of the Bureau of the Census. The respondents were 5 to 18 years old.

We decided on the use of the triceps skin-fold thickness as the best index of obesity for a large field study on the basis of Seltzer and Mayer's extensive work with this measure,[6-9] as well as the view of Dugdale et al.[10] that it is the best anthropometric measure of adiposity. Furthermore, Shephard et al.[11] have presented evidence that the triceps skin-fold provides an especially accurate assessment of obesity in children and adolescents. To avoid interobserver error, all measurements were made by the same observer (S.F.), using the Lange skin-fold calipers. Reliability coefficient of the measurements was 0.93.

Since there is no generally accepted criterion for obesity in children, we chose two criteria that had been utilized in other studies and that seemed reasonable. The first criterion was the values for skin-fold thickness reported by Seltzer and Mayer in their study of Boston school children. They defined as obese those children whose skin-fold thickness exceeded one standard deviation from the mean for their age and sex. Table 15-1 shows the minimum triceps skin-fold thickness indicating obesity according to Seltzer and Mayer.[7]

Malina has criticized the Seltzer-Mayer criterion as inapplicable to other

Table 15-1
Obesity Standards in White Americans According to Seltzer and Mayer

Age (Yr)	Minimum Triceps Skin-Fold Thickness Indicating Obesity (mm)	
	Males	Females
5	12	14
6	12	15
7	13	16
8	14	17
9	15	18
10	16	20
11	17	21
12	18	22
13	18	23
14	17	23
15	16	24
16	15	25
17	14	26
18	15	27
19	15	27
20	16	28

populations[12] and, indeed, the standard deviation for some age groups in our population differed from that of Seltzer and Mayer. Accordingly, we subjected our data to a second criterion of obesity. We also defined as obese the 10% of each sex in the total population that had the thickest skin-folds; and we used the minimum skin-fold thickness of this group to define obesity within each age group. Hampton et al. effectively used a similar percentile criterion to define obesity and leanness.[13] In fact, according to Dr. Joseph Brozek, the percentile criterion is favored by many physical anthropologists, in part, at least, because it has the advantage of showing that obesity increases with age, a trend that is obvious in the raw data. Furthermore, by using percentiles we were able to define thinness in children, for whom no such standard is now available. We defined as thin the 10% of each sex with the thinnest skin-folds and analyzed the data as for the obese group. These empirically derived values for obesity were 23 mm for girls and 18 mm for boys. For thinness they were girls, 8 mm, and boys, 6 mm.

In the course of studying the 3,344 white children we measured also the skin-fold thicknesses of 1,903 black and Puerto Rican children. Since blacks, Puerto Ricans, and whites have different distributions of skin-fold thickness, it was not possible to analyze all 5,247 respondents as a single population.

Hampton et al. had also found significant differences in anthropometric measurements among teen-agers of different racial origins and cautioned against using the same standards for different races. Furthermore, the small number of upper-class blacks and Puerto Ricans made it impossible to run separate analyses of blacks and Puerto Ricans relating socioeconomic status to obesity. For these reasons the analysis reported here was confined to the 3,344 white respondents. Of these, 2,310 were classified in the upper socioeconomic status (occupational categories I and II by 1950 Bureau of Census listing); 857 were classified as of lower socioeconomic status (occupational categories III and IV); the remaining 167 could not be clearly classified. Table 15-2 shows the number of respondents at each age according to socioeconomic status and sex.

Results

We found marked differences in the prevalence of obesity between the upper- and lower-class children. Moreover, these differences were apparent by age 6.

Obesity in Girls

Figure 15-2 shows the relationship between socioeconomic status and prevalence of obesity for girls, using the Seltzer-Mayer criterion. At age 6, 29% of the

Table 15-2
Number of Respondents in Each Age Group by Socioeconomic Status (SES) and Sex

Age (Yr)	Upper SES		Lower SES	
	Boys	Girls	Boys	Girls
5	47	5	21	25
6	67	34	27	24
7	71	40	17	16
8	79	56	24	32
9	80	54	16	17
10	90	52	26	32
11	107	56	31	21
12	74	77	33	32
13	84	76	38	31
14	103	66	44	44
15	167	84	42	53
16	216	80	48	55
17	206	80	29	43
18	114	33	19	15

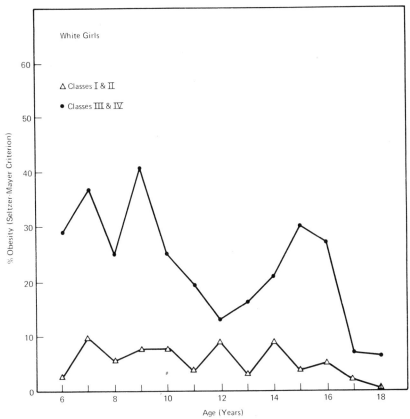

Figure 15-2. Socioeconomic Status and Obesity by Social Class Among Girls (Seltzer-Mayer Criterion). Lower Class Girls Show Far Higher Prevalence Than Upper Class Girls, Especially During Younger Years.

lower-class girls were obese as compared with only 3% of the upper-class girls. This class-linked difference continued through age 18, but fell to a minimum at age 12, when 13% of lower-class and 9% of upper-class girls were obese. Table 15-3 shows the four-fold contingency table relating high and lower social class obesity or its absence.

When we applied the percentile criterion, we also demonstrated the marked difference in the prevalence of obesity between social classes (X^2 = 70.838, $P < 0.001$). At age 6, the lower socioeconomic group contained 8% obese girls, while the upper-class group had no obese girls at either age 6 or 7. This difference was maintained until age 18, as with the Seltzer-Mayer criterion. In addition, the percentile criterion demonstrated an increase in the prevalence of

Table 15-3
Distribution of Obesity by Socioeconomic Status (SES) (Girls)*

	Upper SES	Lower SES
Obese	41	93
Nonobese	747	332

$*X^2 = 81.367, P < 0.001.$

obesity as a function of increasing age in both socioeconomic groups. Figure 15-3 shows further that the slopes for the upper and lower classes differ, with a greater yearly increment in the percentage of obese in the lower class. Obesity is not only more prevalent among poor girls, but this greater prevalence is established earlier and increases at a more rapid rate than among upper-class girls.

Obesity in Boys

Lower-class boys showed a greater prevalence of obesity than did those of the upper class, although here the differences were not as striking as among the girls. Figure 15-4 shows the data for boys as analyzed by the Seltzer-Mayer criterion. At age 6, a marked difference between the two socioeconomic groups is already established, with 40% of the lower socioeconomic group classified as obese, compared with 25% of the upper-class group. Unlike the pattern among the girls, however, the difference between the boys is not continuous to age 18. Note the reversal at age 12, when the upper-class group has a greater percentage of obese. But by age 14 the lower-class group again shows a greater prevalence of obesity, and this difference is maintained until age 18. These data are summarized in Table 15-4.

Figure 15-5 shows the data for boys analyzed by the percentile criterion. Although the profile differs from that in Figure 15-4, where the Seltzer-Mayer criterion was utilized, the basic trend is similar ($X^2 = 40.439, P < 0.001$). Once again a significant difference between social classes is apparent by age 6. This inverse relationship between social status and obesity is maintained, except for the previously noted reversal at age 12.

Our earlier studies had shown a positive correlation between socioeconomic status and prevalence of thinness among women. We found four times as many thin women among those of high status as among those of low status. In the present study, applying the percentile criterion, we found a similar pattern among girls. Figure 15-6 shows that there was more leanness among girls of upper socioeconomic status. At age 6, 15% of the upper-class girls were thin as compared to only 4% of the lower-class. This difference continued until age 12,

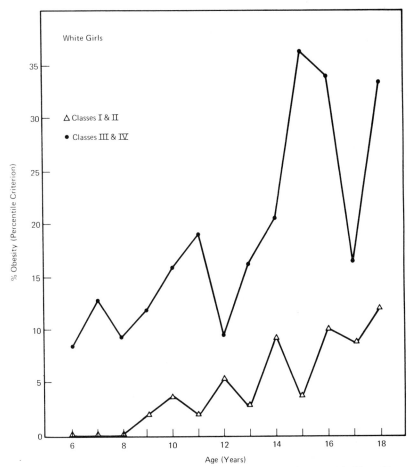

Figure 15-3. Socioeconomic Status and Obesity by Social Class (Percentile Criterion). Apparent Increase in Prevalence of Obesity with Age Probably Reflects Physiological Facts.

at which point the two groups converged and showed decreasing prevalences of thinness. Table 15-5 shows the relationship between high and low socioeconomic status and leanness or its absence.

Thinness in Boys

Our earlier studies had shown no association between socioeconomic status and leanness among men. About 10% of each group was lean. The data on boys

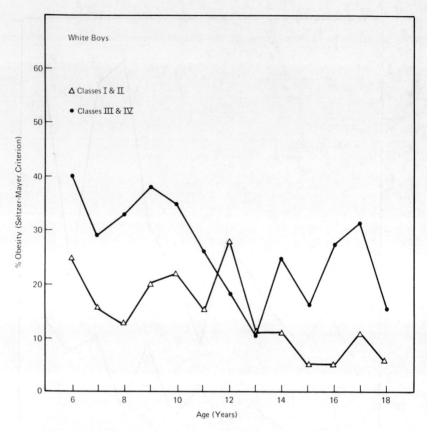

Figure 15-4. Socioeconomic Status and Obesity by Social Class for Boys (Seltzer-Mayer Criterion). Lower Class Boys Show Greater Prevalence of Obesity Than Upper Class Boys, but Differences are Less Striking Than Among Girls.

Table 15-4
Distribution of Obesity by Socioeconomic Status (SES) (Boys)*

	Upper SES	Lower SES
Obese	187	100
Nonobese	1,269	294

$^*X^2 = 37.210, P < 0.001.$

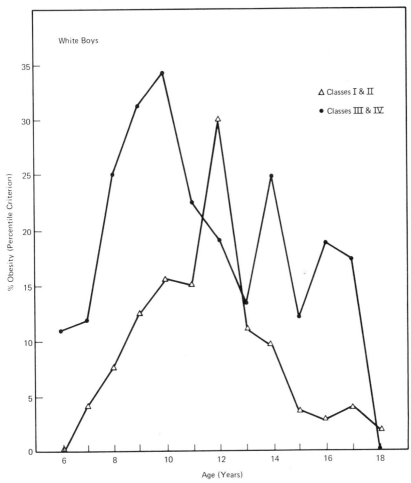

Figure 15-5. Socioeconomic Status and Obesity by Social Class for Boys (Percentile Criterion).

similarly failed to show such an association. Figure 15-7 demonstrates this absence of any clear trend.

Comment

During the past ten years, we have learned a great deal about obesity in the United States, and the results have been a surprise. Our conception of the nature of obesity, based in large part on the results of treating members of the upper

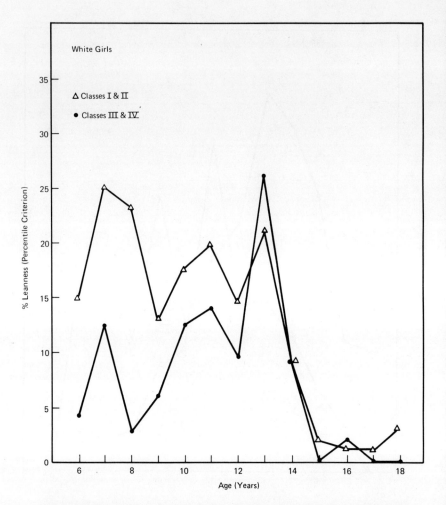

Figure 15-6. Socioeconomic Status and Thinness by Social Class for Girls (Percentile Criterion). Upper Class Girls Show Greater Prevalence of Leanness Until Age 12 when Condition Essentially Disappears for Both Groups.

Table 15-5
Distribution of Thinness by Socioeconomic (SES) Status*

	Upper SES	Lower SES
Thin	88	28
Nonthin	700	387

*$X^2 = 6.078, P < 0.02$.

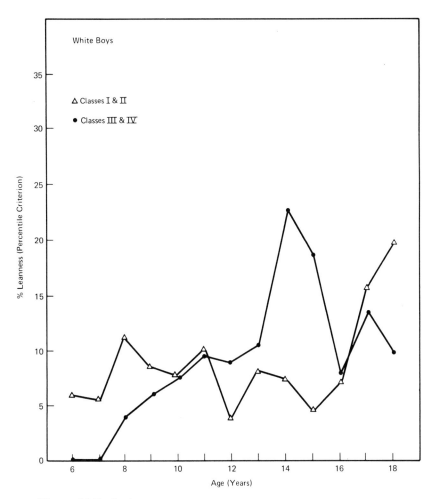

Figure 15-7. Socioeconomic Status and Thinness by Social Class for Boys (Percentile Criterion). Lack of Association Apparent.

and middle classes, has been shaken by the discovery that obesity is largely a problem of the lower classes. It now appears that socioeconomic status and related social factors have more to do with determining whether a person will be obese than does individual psychopathology.[1,14] The implications of these findings are far reaching. For one, they suggest that we need not be constrained by current psychodynamic formulations of obesity and their pessimistic outlook for treatment, when dealing with the group most afflicted with the disorder. Instead, an educational approach that recognizes the importance of social factors and is designed to influence the values and life-styles of large groups, may be more appropriate and more effective than conventional psychotherapeutic techniques.

The study reported here extends previous work and defines a discrete and particularly vulnerable group within the high-risk population—the children of the poor. Not only is childhood obesity a major problem in its own right, but the prognosis for the obese child magnifies the over-all problem for obese children become obese adults. The most authoritative estimate is that 85% of obese children follow this course.[15] Furthermore, the odds against an obese child becoming a normal-weight adult, which are more than 4:1 at age 12, rise to 28:1 if weight has not been reduced by the end of adolescence.[16]

Recent research into juvenile-onset obesity in laboratory animals adds to these actuarial cautions a possible explanation and a cause for further concern. In rats, the cellularity of adipose tissue, and consequently its lipid storage capacity, is determined very early—probably during the first three weeks of life—and primarily by the animal's level of food intake.[17] Over-nutrition during this critical period leads to marked increase in the cellularity of adipose tissue, increased body size, and obesity; undernutrition has the opposite effect. Nor do changes in diet after infancy have any effect on the number of adipose cells. Caloric restriction reduces weight solely by reducing the lipid content of these cells, often to an abnormally low level. The depleted cells then remain ready to return to their initial levels of adiposity whenever sufficient lipids are available. By contrast, adult-onset obesity is produced by cellular hypertrophy, and weight loss returns the adipose tissue cells to a more normal size.

Although data of comparable precision for man are lacking, available information strongly suggests a similar pattern.[18,19] And the mechanism described offers a convincing biologic explanation for the remarkable tendency of juvenile-onset obesity to persist into adult life. We still do not know precisely what period in human development corresponds to the critical first three weeks in the rat's life. However, the fact that such a large percentage of lower-class children is obese by age 6 suggests that hypercellular adipose tissue accounts for at least part of this increased incidence of obesity.

While we know that childhood obesity tends to persist into adulthood, we do not know what proportion of obese adults has juvenile-onset obesity. Even if the contribution is not greater than the one third that has been suggested, however, juvenile-onset obesity remains a serious problem. For all the pathologic correlates and sequelae of obesity are more prevalent and more severe in adults with juvenile-onset obesity, from diabetes and atherosclerosis to emotional disturbance. Furthermore, the juvenile-onset obese have special problems. Any psychopathology is likely to be related to obesity, and fully half of persons with juvenile-onset obesity suffer from body-image disturbances.[20] In persons with adult-onset obesity, on the other hand, psychopathology is usually coincidental and disturbance in body image rare.

One aspect of these findings deserves special note. The prevalence of thinness among the lower-class children was very low despite the poverty in which they lived. This finding surprised us, coming as it did in the midst of reports of widespread hunger among the poor, and its significance is unclear. Perhaps skin-fold calipers failed to detect evidence of undernutrition. However, they have proved adequate to the task of assessment of the undernutrition of anorexia nervosa. Perhaps the level of poverty associated with frank undernutrition is lower than that of the children we studied. But we sought out the children with the lowest level of socioeconomic status that could be found in New York, Philadelphia, and Wilmington. It may be that white children, at least, in these cities do not suffer from undernutrition.

Conclusion

Before we can institute effective measures to prevent or treat a disorder, it is helpful to define the population at high risk. This all-important step has now been taken for obesity. The lower socioeconomic class is the one with by far the greatest prevalence of obesity. Some of the preventive and therapeutic measures that this finding suggests have already been described.[1]

We have now taken a second step and pinpointed a discrete population at particularly high risk—the children of the poor. As early as age 6, the prevalence of obesity is far higher among the lower classes, particularly among girls, than it is among those of higher socioeconomic status. Furthermore, application of the percentile criterion, as illustrated in Figure 15-3, demonstrates that obesity is not only more prevalent in poor girls, but this prevalence is established earlier and increases at a more rapid rate than among upper-class girls.

These findings help define our task, and they should encourage us in the fight against obesity. For the remarkably early age at which obesity begins among so many of the poor bespeaks faulty nutritional practices by parents. We do not yet know to what extent these faulty nutritional practices result from lack of information or from lack of appropriate food. An effective program of obesity control among poor children requires that we distinguish between these two causes. Research that will enable us to determine more precisely what causes poor nutrition among the poor—nutritional misinformation or economic deprivation—is sorely needed. We have recently embarked upon such a project. One final note—Despite the poverty in which our lower-class children lived, they were no more likely to be thin than were the upper-class children.

References

1. Goldblatt PB, Moore ME, Stunkard AJ: Social factors in obesity. *JAMA* **192**:1039-1044, 1965.

2. Moore ME, Stunkard A, Srole L: Obesity, social class, and mental illness. *JAMA* **181**:962-966, 1962.

3. Stunkard AJ: Environment and obesity: Recent advances in our understanding of regulation of food intake in man. *Fed Proc* **27**:1367-1373, 1968.

4. Stunkard AJ: Obesity, in Freedman AM, Kaplan HI (eds), *Comprehensive Textbook of Psychiatry*. Baltimore, Williams & Wilkins Co, 1967, pp 1059-1062.

5. Silverstone JT, Gordon RP, Stunkard AJ: Social factors in obesity in London. *Practitioner* **202**:682-688, 1969.

6. Seltzer CC, Goldman, RF, Mayer J: The triceps skinfold as a predictive measure of body density and body fat in obese adolescent girls. *Pediatrics* **136**:212-218, 1965.

7. Seltzer CC, Mayer J: A simple criterion of obesity. *Postgrad Med* **38**:A101-107, 1965.

8. Mayer J: Some aspects of the problem of regulation of food intake and obesity. *New Eng J Med* **274**:610-616, 1966.

9. Seltzer CC, Mayer J: Greater reliability of the triceps skinfold over the subscapular skinfold as an index of obesity. *Amer J Clin Nutr* **20**:950-953, 1967.

10. Dugdale AE, Chen ST, Hewitt G: Patterns of growth and nutrition in childhood. *Amer J Clin Nutr* **23**:1280-1287, 1970.

11. Shephard RJ, Jones G, Ishii, et al.: Factors affecting body density and thickness of subcutaneous fat. *Amer J Clin Nutr* **22**:1175-1189, 1969.

12. Malina RM: Patterns of development of skinfolds of negro and white Philadelphia children. *Human Biology* **38**:89-103, 1966.

13. Hampton MC, Hueneman RL, Shapiro LR, et al.: A longitudinal study of gross body composition and body conformation and their association with food and activity in a teen-age population. *Amer J Clin Nutr* **19**:422-435, 1966.

14. Holland J, Masling J, Copley D: Mental illness in lower class normal, obese and hyperobese women. *Psychosom Med* **32**:351-357, 1970.

15. Abraham S, Nordsieck M: Relationship of excess weight in children and adults. *Public Health Rep* **75**:263-273, 1970.

16. Stunkard AJ, Burt V: Obesity and the body image: II. Age at onset of disturbances in the body image. *Amer J Psychiat* **123**:1443-1447, 1967.

17. Knittle JL, Hirsch J: Effect of early nutrition on the development of rat epididymal fat pads: Cellularity and metabolism. *J Clin Invest* **47**:2091-2098, 1968.

18. Salans LB, Knittle JL, Hirsch J: Role of adipose cell size and adipose tissue insulin sensitivity in the carbohydrate intolerance of human obesity. *J Clin Invest* **47**:153-165, 1968.

19. Hirsch J, Knittle JL: Cellularity of obese and nonobese human adipose tissue. *Fed Proc* **29**:1516-1521, 1970.

20. Stunkard AJ, Mendelson M: Obesity and body image: I. Characteristics and disturbances in the body image of some obese persons. *Amer J Psychiat* **123**:1296-1300, 1967.

16 A Three-Dimensional Program for the Treatment of Obesity

Richard B. Stuart
The University of Michigan

Whether overweight is determined by gross body weight (Metropolitan Life Insurance Company, 1969) or skin-fold measurement (Seltzer and Mayer, 1965) even when differences in fat as a proportion of body weight are controlled (Durnin and Passmore, undated, p. 137), at least one in five Americans is found to be overweight (United States Public Health Service, undated). The social and economic costs of being overweight are staggering and are complicated by greatly increased vulnerability to a broad range of physical diseases, including cardiovascular and renal diseases, maturity-onset diabetes, cirrhosis of the liver, and gall bladder diseases, among many others (Mayer, 1968).* Despite the history of concern with obesity and the magnitude of the problem, little uncontested knowledge has been accumulated with respect to its etiology and treatment. Mayer (1968) has suggested that genetic factors may contribute to the onset of a small number of cases, while an additional small number of cases

Reprinted from *Behavior Research & Therapy*, 9:177-186, 1971, with the permission of Microform International Marketing Corporation, exclusive copyright licensee of Pergamon Press journal back files.

*It has been argued that the relationship between obesity and such illnesses as cardiovascular diseases depends in part on the way in which fat is accumulated. For example, "People who become fat on a high carbohydrate, low fat diet are much less prone to develop atherosclerotic and thrombotic complications than those on a high fat diet (Cornell Conferences on Therapy, 1958, p. 87)."

can be explained on the basis of injury to the hypothalamus, hormonal imbalance and other threats to normal metabolism. The exact role of genetic and physiological factors has, however, remained a mystery, and there has been little evidence to countermand an early observation by Newburgh and Johnston (1930) that most cases of obesity are:

> ... never directly caused by abnormal metabolism but (are) always due to food habits not adjusted to the metabolic requirement—either the ingestion of more food than is normally needed or the failure to reduce the intake in response to a lowered requirement (p. 212).

Therefore most obesities can be attributed to an excess of food intake beyond the demands of energy expenditure, and a major objective in treating obesity is a reduction in the amount of excess food consumed.

Just as there is uncertainty concerning the etiology of obesity, there is great confusion over the role of psychological factors in overeating and its management. Some authors have contributed various useful typologies; for example, Stunkard (1959a) classified eating patterns as night eating, binge eating and eating without satiation, while Hamburger (1951) classified the triggers of excessive eating as either external or intrapsychic. Despite Suczek's (1957) observation that "single psychologic factors may not relate to either degree of obesity or ability to lose weight (p. 201)," other authors have sought to identify specific psychological mechanisms associated with obesity. For example, Conrad (1954) postulates that specific intrapsychic factors, such as efforts to prevent loss of love and to express hostility or efforts to symbolically undergo pregnancy and to ward off sexual temptations, underlie obesity. In a similar vein, while eating has been seen as a means of warding off anxiety (Kaplan and Kaplan, 1957), it has also been seen as a depressive equivalent (Simon, 1963). Furthermore, while writers have suggested that "depression, psychosis . . . suicide (Cappon, 1958, p. 573)" and other stress reactions have accompanied weight loss (Cornell Conferences on Therapy, 1958; Glucksman et al., 1968), other studies have shown that: (a) the so-called "depression" associated with weight loss by some people is actually just a function of lowered energy due to reduced food consumption (Bray, 1969); (b) negative psychological reactions are frequently not found (Cauffman and Pauley, 1961; Mees and Keutzer, 1967); and (c) a reduction in anxiety and depression may actually accompany weight loss (Shipman and Plesset, 1963). Despite this evidence, Bruch's (1954) admonition that treatment of overeating which does not give "psychologic factors . . . due consideration (can lead) at best to a temporary weight reduction (while being) considered dangerous from the point of view of mental health (p. 49)" is still influential in dissuading experimenters and therapists from undertaking parsimonious treatment of overeating.

While the research pertaining to physiological and psychological concomitants of obesity has led to some paradoxical conclusions, Stunkard's (1968) review of environmental factors related to obesity has demonstrated a clear-cut connection between obesity and socioeconomic status, social mobility and ethnic variables. It is interesting to note, however, that where comparative data are available, the differences ascribed to each of these factors are stronger for women than men. One explanation of this sex difference may be that the physical expenditure of energy in work may reduce the tendency toward adiposity of lower class, socially nonmobile men while the women, faced with relative inactivity, may show a more direct effect of high carbohydrate, low protein diets common at lower socioeconomic strata (Select Committee on Nutrition and Human Needs, 1970).

The literature describing the treatment of obesity is dismal and confusing. One authoritative group noted:

. . . most obese patients will not remain in treatment. Of those who do remain in treatment, most will not lose significant poundage, and of those who do lose weight, most will regain it promptly. In a careful follow-up study only 8 percent of obese patients seen in a nutrition clinic actually maintained a satisfactory weight loss (Cornell Conferences on Therapy, 1958, p. 87).

Failure has been reported following some of the most ambitious and sophisticated treatments (e.g. Mayer, 1968, pp. 1-2; Stunkard and McLaren-Hume, 1959), while success has been claimed for some of the more superficial "diet-clinic"-type approaches (e.g. Franklin and Rynearson, 1960). The role of drugs has been extolled by many writers, while others have cautioned that their side effects strongly contraindicate their use (American Academy of Pediatrics, 1967; Gordon, 1969; Modell, 1960). Fasting has been shown to have a profound effect upon weight loss (e.g. Bortz, 1969; Stokes, 1969), but the results have been shown to be short-lived as the patient is likely to quickly regain lost weight when he leaves the hospital setting (MacCuish et al., 1968). Claims of success have also been advanced for individual and group psychotherapy (e.g. Kornhaber, 1968; Mees and Keutzer, 1967; Stanley et al., 1970; Stunkard et al., 1970; Wagonfield and Wolowitz, 1968) and hypnosis (Hanley, 1967; Kroger, 1970), although these reports are typically not supported by controlled investigation. Finally, positive outcomes have been reported for behavior therapy techniques ranging from token reinforcement (Bernard, 1968), aversion therapy (Mayer and Crisp, 1964) and covert sensitization (Cautela, 1967) through complex contingency management procedures. Illustrative of the latter approaches are the work of Stuart (1967), which has been replicated in controlled studies by Ramsay (1968) and Penick and his associates (Penick et al., 1970), and the work of Harris (1969), which included control-group comparisons in the original research.

It is probably true that behavior therapy has offered greater promise of positive results than any other type of treatment. This paper will present a rationale of and description for the treatment of overeating based upon behavioral principles.

Rationale

The treatment of obesity has typically attempted to stress the development of "self-control" by the overeater whose self-control deficit is often regarded as a personal fault. Conceding that behavior modifiers recognize first that self-control is merely the emission of one set of responses designed to alter the probability of occurrence of another set of responses (Bijou and Baer, 1961, p. 81; Ferster, 1965, p. 21; Holland and Skinner, 1961, Chapter 47; Homme, 1965, p. 504), and second, that self-controlling responses are acquired through social learning (e.g. Bandura and Kupers, 1964; Kanfer and Marston, 1963), most behaviorists still appear to regard self-control as a personal virtue and its absence a personal deficit (Stuart, 1971). For example, Cautela (1969, p. 324) is concerned with the individual's ability to manipulate the contingencies of his own behavior while Kanfer (1971) offers among other explanations for the breakdown of self-control "the patient's commitment to change," a presumed index of the patient's degree of motivation, or "the patient's prior skill in use of self-reward or self-punishment responses for changing behavior," a presumed index of the patient's capacity to utilize treatment.

In any event, the relevance of the concept of self-control to the management of over-eating may be questioned in the light of many recent studies. The most basic of these is the work of Stunkard (1959b) who demonstrated that in comparison with nonobese subjects, obese subjects are far less likely to report hunger in association with "gastric motility." Thus the cues for hunger experiences of the obese may be tied to external events. Several ingenious studies have contributed to this possibility. First, Schacter and his associates demonstrated that obese subjects are less influenced than nonobese subjects by manipulated fear and deprivation of food (Schacter et al., 1968), while they are more influenced by the time they think it is than by the actual time (Schacter and Gross, 1968). In addition it was shown that when the cues of eating are absent, as on religious fast days, obese subjects are more likely to observe dietary restrictions than nonobese subjects (Schacter, 1968). In a similar vein, Nisbett (1968) and Hashim and Van Itallie (1965) showed that obese subjects are more influenced by the taste of food than are nonobese subjects when the duration of food deprivation is controlled. These varied studies and others suggested that the first of two requirements for the treatment of overeating must stress environmental management rather than self-control because the cues of overeating are environmental rather than intrapersonal.

The second requirement for the management of obesity must be a manipulation of the energy balance–the balance between the consumption of energy as food and the expenditure of energy through exercise. If all of the energy which is derived from the consumed food is expended in exercise, then gross body weight will remain constant. Any excess of food energy consumption over energy expenditure, however, is stored as adiposity at the rate of approximately one pound of body fat for each excessive 3500 kcal (Gordon, 1969, p. 148; Mayer, 1968, p. 158). Weight can therefore be lost through: (1) an increase in the amount of exercise, holding food intake constant; (2) a decrease in the amount of food intake, holding exercise constant; or (3) both an increase in exercise and a decrease in food intake.

It has been well-demonstrated that the rising problem of obesity is associated with decreasing demands for exercise. Mayer (1968) suggested that "inactivty is the most important factor explaining the frequency of 'creeping' overweight in modern societies (p. 821)," while Durnin and Passmore (undated, p. 143) revealed that food intake is typically not adjusted to reduced exercise. Recent evidence adduced by the Agricultural Research Service (1969, pp. 22-24) demonstrated that the diets of young men in higher-income brackets include 20 percent more kcal than the diets of those with smaller incomes and presumably more physically taxing occupations, and this is most likely to result in some measure of obesity among middle-class males. Increase in the rate of exercise can, however, have a profound effect upon body weight although the amount of exercise necessary is greater than generally expected.* Furthermore, given the fact that an obese person actually expends *less* energy than a nonobese person doing the same amount of work (e.g. a 250-pound man walking 1.5 mph expends 5.34 kcal per min, while a 150-pound man walking at the same rate and carrying a 100-pound load expends 5.75 kcal per min [Bloom and Eidex, 1967, p. 687]), planned programs for exercise are particularly important. In addition to aiding in the management of gross body weight, exercise programs for the thin as well as the obese seem definitely to reduce the risk of certain cardiovascular diseases (Mayer, 1967).

Just as it is important systematically to increase the amount of exercise, so too is it important to reduce the amount of food or change the nature of foods eaten. Mayer (1968) recommends:

A balanced diet, containing no less than 14 percent of protein, no more than 30 percent of fat (with saturated fats cut down), and the rest carbohydrates (with sucrose–ordinary sugar–cut down to a low level) . . . (p. 160).

---

*Stuart (unpublished data) asked a group of obese women to estimate the amount of exercise required to work off the weight gain attributable to such common foods as donuts, ice cream sodas and potato chips. Comparing their answers with the estimates based upon Konishi's (1965) figures for a 150-pound man walking at the rate of 3.5 miles per hr (29, 49 and 21 min respectively), they were found to underestimate the true work required by from 200 to 300 percent.

Apart from its nutritional advantages, it is important to include a substantial amount of protein in the diet because smaller amounts of protein as opposed to carbohydrates produce satiety and because a portion of the caloric content of protein is used in its own metabolism (Gordon, 1969, p. 149), leaving a smaller proportion as a possible contributor to adiposity. Conversely, it is important to reduce the amount of carbohydrates consumed because a higher proportion of its caloric content is available for adiposity, because at least certain carbohydrates—e.g. sucrose (Yudkin, 1969)—are associated with increased incidence of certain cardiovascular diseases to which obese persons are vulnerable, and because "carbohydrate food causes the storage of unusually large amounts of water (Gordon, 1969, p. 148)"—typically a special problem faced by obese individuals.

The foregoing observations lead to several basic considerations for weight reduction programs. First, it is essential to design an environment in which food-relevant cues are conducive to the maximal practice of prudent eating habits. This is required by the fact that overeating among obese persons appears to be under enviornmental control. Also, training the patient in the techniques of environmental control will probably reduce the gradual loss of therapeutic effect found in certain (e.g. Silverstone and Solomon, 1965) but not all (Penick et al., 1970) other programs. Second, it is essential to plan toward a negative energy balance. In doing this, however, it is essential to avoid exercise or dietary excesses. They are unlikely to be followed, and if they are followed each may result in iatrogenic complications. Excessive exercise might lead to overexertion or serious cardiovascular illness. Unbalanced diets might lead to physiological disease, while insufficient diets might lead to enervation and physiologically produced depression. It is therefore essential to plan gradual weight-loss programs associated with progressive changes in the energy balance, as these are both safer and more likely to meet with success (Wang and Sandoval, 1969, p. 220). The exact determination of these levels must be empirically determined for each patient, beginning with tables of recommended dietary allowance (e.g. Mayer, 1968, pp. 168-169), adjusting these for the amount of exercise, carefully monitoring weight and mood changes as time on the program progresses, and being careful to make certain that the degree of weight loss provides sufficient motivation for the patient to continue using the program.

Treatment

Translation of the above rationale into a set of specific treatment procedures sometimes requires an arbitrary selection of intervention alternatives derived from contrary or contradictory conclusions in the basic research literature. For example, while Gordon, (1969) repudiated his earlier contention that a patient's eating several smaller meals each day would necessarily result in greater weight loss than his eating only the three traditional meals, others (e.g. Debry *et al.*, 1968) have shown that *with caloric intake held constant* patients who eat three meals daily may not only maintain their weight but may actually gain weight, while the same patients dividing their caloric allowance into seven meals lose weight precipitously. As another example, Nisbett and Kanouse (1969) demonstrated that obese food shoppers actually buy less the more deprived of food they are while nonobese shoppers increase their food buying as a function of the extent of food deprivation. In contrast, Stuart (unpublished data) demonstrated that when a group of obese women confined their food shopping to the hours of 3:30-5:00 p.m., they purchased 20 percent more food than when they postponed their food shopping until 6:30-8:00 p.m. Thus the therapist reading the Gordon and Nisbett studies would have his patients eat three meals and delay their food shopping until they were at least moderately deprived of food, while the therapist familiar with the work of Debry *et al.* and Stuart would do just the reverse. The therapist familiar with both must decide which recommendations to follow, framing his decision as a reversible hypothesis which can be invalidated in response to patient-produced data.

The treatment procedures which have been used in this investigation fall into three broad categories. First, an effort is made to establish firm control over the eating environment. This requires: (a) the elimination or suppression of cues associated with problematic eating while strengthening the cues associated with desirable eating patterns; (b) planned manipulation of the actual response of eating to accelerate desirable elements of the response while decelerating undesirable aspects; and (c) the manipulation of the contingencies associated with problematic and desirable eating patterns. A sample of the procedures used in the service of each of these objectives is presented in Table 16-1.

Second, an effort is made to establish a dietary program for each patient on an individual basis. The first step in the development of a diet is completion by the patient of a self-monitoring food intake form. Because patients frequently claim to exist on unbelievably small quantities of food, only to lose weight rapidly when their diet is regulated at amounts two or three times greater than originally claimed, it is helpful to provide some social monitoring of the use of the monitoring sheets to ensure accuracy. Procedures such as those employed by Powell and Azrin (1968) have proven helpful. When validated eating records have been obtained for a 14-day period, adjustments in food intake can be planned based upon recommended caloric levels, balanced diet planning and adjustments for the level of food intake in light of the patient's exercise. In dietary planning, "food exchange" recommendations are made (Stuart and Davis, 1971) rather than recommendations for specific food choices. In food exchange dieting, foods in each of six food categories (e.g. milk, fruit, meat, etc.) are grouped according to similar caloric levels (e.g. one egg has approximately the same caloric value as one slice of bread). Selections are made according to food exchanges and this greatly increases the ease and precision of

Table 16-1
Sample Procedures Used to Strengthen Appropriate Eating and to Weaken Inappropriate Eating

Cue Elimination	Cue Suppression	Cue Strengthening
1. Eat in one room only	1. Have company while eating	1. Keep food, weight chart
2. Do nothing while eating	2. Prepare and serve small quantities only	2. Use food exchange diet
3. Make available proper foods only: (a) shop from a list; (b) shop only after full meal	3. Eat slowly	3. Allow extra money for proper foods
4. Clear dishes directly into garbage	4. Save one item from meal to eat later	4. Experiment with attractive preparation of diet foods
5. Allow children to take own sweets	5. If high-calorie foods are eaten, they must require preparation	5. Keep available pictures of desired clothes, list of desirable activities
Reduced Strength of Undesirable Responses		Increase Strength of Desirable Responses
1. Swallow food already in mouth before adding more		1. Introduce planned delays during meal
2. Eat with utensils		2. Chew food slowly, thoroughly
3. Drink as little as possible during meals		3. Concentrate on what is being eaten

Provide Decelerating
Consequences

1. Develop means for display of caloric value of food eaten daily, weight changes

2. Arrange to have deviations from program ignored by others except for professionals

3. Arrange to have overeater re-read program when items have not been followed and to write techniques which might have succeeded

Provide Accelerating Consequences

1. Develop means for display of caloric value of food eaten daily, weight changes

2. Develop means of providing social feedback for all success by: (a) family; (b) friends; (c) co-workers; (d) other weight losers; and/or (e) professionals

3. Program material and/or social consequences to follow: (a) the attainment of weight loss subgoals; (b) completion of specific daily behavioral control objectives

meal planning. Furthermore, when this is done as a means of increasing the probability that the diet will be followed, the unavailability of specific foods frequently leads to a termination of the entire dietary program.

Third, an effort is made to develop an individualized aerobics exercise program based upon walking in most cases (Cooper, 1968). In introducing the need for exercise, the patient is offered a choice between adherence to a punishing diet which may lead to chronic discomfort throughout the day and a more permissive diet coupled with exercise which may lead to discomfort for an hour or less per day. When an exercise program is developed, an effort is made to weave the exercise activity into the normal fabric of the patient's day to increase the likelihood that it will be followed. For example, a patient might be asked to park his car 10 blocks from the home of friends he is about to visit, to avoid elevators and walk up to his destinations, and to carry each item upstairs as needed—rather than allowing several items to accumulate—as a means of increasing the number of steps necessary.

Results

The pilot investigation reported here reflects the treatment of six overweight, married, middle-class women (171-212 pounds) between the ages of 27 and 41. Each woman requested treatment on a self-referred basis. Treatment was offered on an individual basis, but women were randomly assigned to one of two cohorts. Both groups of three patients were asked to complete the Sixteen Personality Factor Questionnaire (Cattell and Eber, 1967) and to keep a 5-week baseline of their weight and food intake. The first group was then offered treatment twice weekly (average 40 min per session) for a 15-week period, while the second group was asked to practice "self-control" of eating behavior. The self-control subjects were given the same diet planning materials and exercise program that the treatment group was offered. They were not, however, given instruction for the management of food in the environment. At the conclusion of the 15-week period, the treated group was asked to continue the treatment program and the second group was offered 15 weeks of the same treatment. Approximately 6 months following the termination of treatment of Group 1 and 3 months following the termination of treatment of Group 2, follow-up data were collected including weight, eating patterns and the readministration of the Cattell 16 P.F. The results including follow-up data are presented in Figure 16-1. It will be seen that patients in Group 1 lost an average of 35 pounds while those in Group 2 lost an average of 21 pounds. These results are consistent with the objective set for gradual weight loss approximating one pound per week. It will also be seen that the mere collection of baseline self-monitoring data was associated with mild weight loss in both groups, although these gains were dissipated as time progressed for the second group. Finally, comparison of the

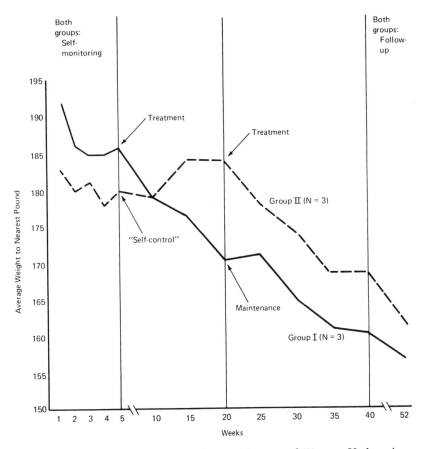

Figure 16-1. Weight Changes in Two Groups of Women Undergoing Behavior Therapy for Overeating.

pre- and post-test personality test results reveal little change other than small improvement in "ego stability" and tension (Factors C and Q4) of the 16 P.F.

The results provide suggestive evidence for the usefulness of a threefold treatment of obesity stressing environmental control of overeating, nutritional planning and regulated increase in energy expenditure. The sample size was too small to permit generalization, and the superiority of the initially treated (Group 1) over the initially untreated (Group 2) patients may be due to an inclination among the latter group to be casual about weight reduction. To forestall this possibility, every effort was made to make the treatment appear "official" but no validation of the success of this effort was undertaken. Furthermore, it is perhaps noteworthy that the results were obtained with no evidence of psychological stress in a patient population which was regarded as "well-adjusted" at the start and termination of treatment.

To validate these procedures in any definitive manner, extensive replication is needed using careful experimental control procedures applied to a far more diverse population than was used in this pilot study. Research such as that recently completed by Penick *et al.* (1970) has made important strides in this direction. It is only through such experimentation that the vast amount of "faddism and quackery (Gordon, 1969, p. 148)" which characterizes the broad field of obesity control can be replaced by a scientifically validated set of procedures.

References

Agricultural Research Service, U.S. Department of Agriculture (1969) *Food Intake and Nutritive Value of Diets of Men, Women, and Children in the United States, Spring 1965: A Preliminary Report.* (ARS 62-18), Washington, D.C.: United States Government Printing Office.

American Academy of Pediatrics, Committee on Nutrition (1967) Obesity in childhood. *Pediatrics* **40**, 455-465.

Bandura A. and Kupers C.J. (1964) Transmission of patterns of self-reinforcement through modeling. *J. abnorm. soc. Psychol.* **69**, 1-9.

Bernard J.L. (1968) Rapid treatment of gross obesity by operant techniques. *Psychol. Rep.* **23**, 663-666.

Bijou S.W. and Baer D.M. (1961) *Child Development I: A Systematic and Empirical Theory.* Appleton-Century-Crofts, New York.

Bloom W.L. and Eidex M.F. (1967) The comparison of energy expenditure in the obese and lean. *Metabolism* **16**, 685-692.

Bortz W. (1969) A 500 pound weight loss. *Am. J. Med.* **47**, 325-331.

Bray G.A. (1969) Effect of caloric restriction on energy expenditure in obese patients. *Lancet* **2**, 397-398.

Bruch H. (1954) The psychosomatic aspects of obesity. *Am. Practnr Dig. Treat.* **5**, 48-49.

Cappon D. (1958) Obesity. *Can. Med. Assoc. Jl* **79**, 568-573.

Cattell R.B. and Eber H.W. (1957) *Handbook for the Sixteen Personality Factor Questionnaire.* The Institute for Personality and Ability Testing, Champaign, Ill.

Cauffman W.J. and Pauley W.G. (1961) Obesity and emotional status. *Penn. Med. Jl* **64**, 505-507.

Cautela J.R. (1967) Covert sensitization. *Psychol. Rep.* **20**, 459-468.

Cautela J.R. (1969) Behavior therapy and self-control: Techniques and implications. In *Behavior Therapy: Appraisal and Status* (Ed. C.M. Franks). McGraw-Hill, New York.

Conrad S.W. (1954) The problem of weight reduction in the obese woman. *Am. Practnr. Dig. Treat.* **5**, 38-47.

Cooper K.H. (1968) *Aerobics.* Bantam Books, New York.

Cornell Conferences on Therapy (1958) The management of obesity. *N.Y.S.J. Med.* **58**, 79-87.

Debry G., Rohr R., Azouaou G., Vassilitch I. and Mottaz G. (1968) Study of the effect of dividing the daily caloric intake into seven meals on weight loss in obese subjects. *Nutritio Dieta* **10** 288-296.

Durnin J.V.G.A. and Passmore R. (undated) The relation between the intake and expenditure of energy and body weight. *Problèmes Actuels D'Endocrinologie et de Nutrition* (Serie No. 9), 136-149.

Ferster C.B. (1965) Classification of behavior pathology. In *Research in Behavior Modification* (Eds. L. Krasner and L.P. Ullmann). Holt, Rinehart & Winston, New York.

Franklin R.E. and Rynearson E.H. (1960) An evaluation of the effectiveness of diet instruction for the obese. *Staff Meet. Mayo Clin.* **35**, 123-124.

Glucksman M.L., Hirsch J., McCully, R.S., Barron B.A. and Knittle J.L. (1968) The response of obese patients to weight reduction: A quantitative evaluation of behavior. *Psychosom. Med.* **30**, 359-373.

Gordon E.S. (1969) The present concept of obesity: Etiological factors and treatment. *Med. Times* **97**, 142-155.

Hamburger W.W. (1951) Emotional aspects of obesity. *Med. Clin. N. Am.* **35**, 483-499.

Hanley, F.W. (1967) The treatment of obesity by individual and group hypnosis. *Can. Psychiat. Ass. J.* **12**, 549-551.

Harris M.B. (1969) Self-directed program for weight control—A pilot study. *J. abnorm. Psychol.* **74**, 263-270.

Hashim S.A. and Van Itallie T.B. (1965) Studies in normal and obese subjects with a monitored food dispensary device. *Ann. N.Y. Acad. Sci.* **131**, 654-661.

Holland J.G. and Skinner B.F. (1961) *The Analysis of Behavior.* McGraw-Hill, New York.

Homme L.E. (1965) Perspectives in psychology: XXIV. Control of coverants, the operants of the mind. *Psychol. Rec.* **15**, 501-511.

Kanfer F.H. (1971) Self-monitoring: Methodological limitations and clinical applications. *J. consult. clin. Psychol.* in press.

Kanfer F.H. and Marston A.R. (1963) Conditioning of self-reinforcement responses: An analogue to self-confidence training. *Psychol. Rep.* **13**, 63-70.

Kaplan H.I. and Kaplan H.S. (1957) The psychosomatic concept of obesity. *J. nerv. ment. Dis.* **125**, 181-201.

Konishi F. (1965) Food energy equivalents of various activities. *J. Am. Diet. Ass.* **46**, 186-188.

Kornhaber A. (1968) Group treatment of obesity. *G.P.* **5**, 116-120.

Kroger W.S. (1970) Comprehensive management of obesity. *Am. J. clin. Hypnosis* **12**, 165-176.

MacCuish A.C., Munro J.F. and Duncan L.J.P. (1968) Follow-up study of refractory obesity treated by fasting. *Br. Med. J.* **1**, 91-92.

Mayer J. (1967) Inactivity, an etiological factor in obesity and heart disease. In *Symposia of the Swedish Nutrition Foundation, V: Symposium on Nutrition and Physical Activity* (Ed. G. Blix). Almqvist & Wiksells, Uppsala, Sweden.

Mayer J. (1968) *Overweight: Causes, Cost and Control.* Prentice-Hall, Englewood Cliffs, N.J.

Mees H.L. and Keutzer C.S. (1967) Short term group psychotherapy with obese women. *NW Med.* **66**, 548-550.

Metropolitan Insurance Company (1969) New weight standards for men and women. *Statistical Bulletin* **40**, 1-8.

Meyer V. and Crisp A.H. (1964) Aversion therapy in two cases of obesity. *Behav. Res. & Therapy* **2**, 143-147.

Modell W. (1960) Status and prospect of drugs for overeating. *J. Am. Med. Ass.* **173**, 1131-1136.

Newburgh L.H. and Johnston M.W. (1930) The nature of obesity. *J. clin. Invest.* **8**, 197-213.

Nisbett R.E. (1968) Taste, deprivation, and weight determinants of eating behavior. *J. person. soc. Psychol.* **10**, 107-116.

Nisbett R.E. and Kanouse D.E. (1969) Obesity, food deprivation, and supermarket shopping behavior. *J. person. soc. Psychol.* **12**, 289-294.

Penick S.B., Filion R., Fox S. and Stunkard A. (1970) Behavior modification in the treatment of obesity. Paper presented at the annual meeting of the Psychosomatic Society, Washington, D.C.

Powell J. and Azrin N. (1968) The effects of shock as a punisher for cigarette smoking. *J. appl. Behav. Anal.* **1**, 63-71.

Ramsay R.W. (1968) Vermageringsexperiment, Psychologisch Labratorium van de Universiteit van Amsterdam, *Researchpracticum* **101**, voorjaar 1968.

Schachter S. (1968) Obesity and eating. *Science* **161**, 751-756.

Schachter S., Goldman R. and Gordon A. (1968) Effects of fear, food deprivation, and obesity on eating. *J. person. soc. Psychol.* **10**, 91-97.

Schachter S. and Gross L.P. (1968) Manipulated time and eating behavior. *J. person. soc. Psychol.* **10**, 98-106.

Seltzer C.C. and Mayer J. (1965) A simple criterion of obesity. *Postgrad. Med.* **38**, A101-A106.

Shipman W.G. and Plesset M.R. (1963) Anxiety and depression in obese dieters. *Archs gen. Psychiat.* **8**, 26-31.

Silverstone J.T. and Solomon T. (1965) The long-term management of obesity in general practice. *Br. J. clin. Pract.* **19**, 395-398.

Simon R.I. (1963) Obesity as a depressive equivalent. *J. Am. Med. Ass.* **183**, 208-210.

Stanley E.J., Glaser H.H., Levin D.G., Adams P.A. and Cooley I.C. (1970) Overcoming obesity in adolescents: A description of a promising endeavour to improve management. *Clin. Pediat.* **9**, 29-36.

Stokes S.A. (1969) Fasting for obesity. *Am. J. Nurs.* **69**, 796-799.

Stuart R.B. (1967) Behavioral control of overeating. *Behav. Res. & Therapy* **5**, 357-365.

Stuart R.B. (1971) Situational versus self control. In *Advances in Behavior Therapy* (Ed. R.D. Rubin). Academic Press, New York, in press.

Stuart R.B. and Davis B. (1971) *Behavioral Techniques for the Management of Obesity.* Research Press, Champaign, Ill, in press.

Stunkard A. (1959a) Eating patterns and obesity. *Psychiat. Q.* **33**, 284-295.

Stunkard A. (1959b) Obesity and the denial of hunger. *Psychosom. Med.* **21**, 281-289.

Stunkard A. (1968) Environment and obesity: Recent advances in our understanding of regulation of food intake in man. *Fed. Proc.* **6**, 1367-1373.

Stunkard A., Levine H. and Fox S. (1970) The management of obesity. *Archs intern. Med.* **125**, 1067-1072.

Stunkard A. and McLaren-Hume M. (1959) The results of treatment for obesity. *Archs intern. Med.* **103**, 79-85.

Suczek R.F. (1957) The personality of obese women. *Am. J. Clin. Nutr.* **5**, 197-202.

United States Public Health Service (undated) *Obesity and Health.* (Publication No. 1495), United States Department of Health, Education and Welfare, Washington, D.C.

United States Senate, Select Committee on Nutrition and Human Needs (1970) *Nutrition and Human Needs–1970.* Parts I, II & III. U.S. Government Printing Office, Washington, D.C.

Wagonfield S. and Wolowitz H.M. (1968) Obesity and self-help group: A look at TOPS. *Am. J. Psychiat.* **125**, 253-255.

Wang R.I.H. and Sandoval R. (1969) Current status of drug therapy in management of obesity. *Wis. Med. J.* **68**, 219-220.

Yudkin J. (Spring, 1969) Sucrose and heart disease. *Nutrition Today* **4**, 16-20.

VI

The Social Environment and Mental Health

Commentary. The view that the social milieu can have an important impact on mental health can be traced back to the end of the eighteenth century. This approach emanated from the work of Pinel, Tuke, and Chiarugi, who viewed the "insane" as essentially normal people who could profit from a favorable social environment. Moral therapy, as it was called at the time, is described by Rees:

The insane came to be regarded as normal people who had lost their reason as a result of having been exposed to severe psychological and social stresses. These stresses were called the moral causes of insanity, and moral treatment aimed at relieving the patient by friendly association, discussion of his difficulties, and the daily pursuit of purposeful activity; in other words, social therapy, individual therapy, and occupational therapy. (1957)

It is interesting to note that during the first half of the nineteenth century, when moral therapy reached its peak as the primary method of treatment, records show that at least 70 percent of mental hospital patients who had been ill for less than one year were discharged as recovered. Some recovery rates were reported to be as high as 90 percent (Tourney, 1967).

Despite impressive evidence of its effectiveness, moral therapy was abandoned in the latter part of the nineteenth century. Subsequent data by Bockoven (1956) from the Worcester State Hospital indicated that recovery rates declined over 90 percent after 1860, reaching their lowest point between 1923 and 1950. Although one may question old statistics and the conclusions drawn from them, the results of moral therapy have not been surpassed during contemporary periods despite the advances made by physical medicine (Adams, 1964).

Adams has suggested that moral therapy was abandoned because it was regarded as "unscientific" in accordance with medical doctrine of the time. In addition, it was thought that the procedures found effective with physical illness could be carried over unchanged into the treatment of mental illness.

A return and extension of the underlying assumptions of the "moral therapy era" is very much in evidence today, and is put forth by Alexander Leighton in the first chapter in this section. He suggests that mental illness is a social environmental problem, and that it is much more tenable to work on symptoms of psychiatric disorder than to attempt to restructure or change personality. He further suggests that problems such as obsessive-compulsive neurosis can be modified to the extent that the individual can function on a day-to-day basis. This point of view is supported by the learning or behavior theorists, who assert that the symptom *is* the disorder without any particular underlying cause (Ullmann and Krasner, 1969; Eysenck and Rachman, 1965). Leighton feels that one of the important issues in mental health is "socio-cultural disintegration." This term refers to a social system with specific malfunctions, such as defective communication among its members; lack of leadership and followership; inability to arrive at group decisions; defective child rearing, training, and education; deficiencies in work and productivity; lack of recreation; and weak control over hostile impulses. Leighton suggests that raising and lowering the level of disintegration is related to the prevalence of psychiatric disorders.

In Chapter 18 D.L. Rosenhan describes an intriguing study in which eight "sane" people simulated mental illness to gain admission to twelve different mental hospitals, in order to assess the salient characteristics of a psychiatric diagnosis and to observe and experience the environment of a psychiatric institution.

The author reports several disturbing conclusions from the experiences of the pseudopatients:

1. Behaviors that are stimulated by the environment are commonly mis-attributed to the patient's disorder;

2. A psychiatric label has a life of its own—once the impression has been formed that the patient is schizophrenic, the expectation is that he will continue to be schizophrenic; and

3. Unlike medical diagnoses, psychiatric diagnoses carry with them personal, legal, and social stigma.

Rosenhan's study has been criticized on the grounds that physicians must rely heavily on what a patient tells them and do not assume that patients who seek help are lying. While this is a valid criticism, it doesn't lessen the total impact and contribution that Rosenhan's study makes. The same behavior is evaluated differently depending on the social milieu. For example, if a normal person spends much of his time writing in his living room or in his office he might be viewed as "productive," whereas this behavior on a psychiatric ward might be labeled as negativistic, seclusive, and interpersonally isolating. In addition, diagnoses may affect patients as self-fulfilling prophecies, so that the patient himself accepts the diagnosis with all its expectations and behaves accordingly.

In the final chapter in this section Richard Price reviews various assumptions about the nature of abnormal behavior. Price argues that people who identify themselves with one point of view tend to view abnormal behavior simplistically as caused by a single variable. The consequences of this view relate directly to the kind of intervention seen as appropriate. Thus, if the causes of abnormal behavior are seen as residing in the individual, treatment should focus on the individual. Alternatively, if the causes are seen as arising from the environment, the emphasis of action would be environmental. Price suggests that the rapidly growing field of environmental psychology may provide some of the answers to preventive mental health efforts.

References

Adams, H.B. "Mental illness" or interpersonal behavior? *American Psychologist, 19*:191-197, 1964.

Bockoven, J.S. Moral treatment in American psychiatry. *Journal of Nervous and Mental Disease, 124*:292-321, 1956.

Eysenck, H.J., and Rachman, S. *Causes and Cures of Neurosis.* San Diego, R.R. Knapp, 1965.

Rees, T.P. Back to moral treatment and community care. *Journal of Mental Science, 103*:303-313, 1957.

Tourney, G. A history of therapeutic fashions in psychiatry, 1800-1966. *American Journal of Psychiatry, 124*:784-796, 1967.

Ullmann, L.P., and Krasner, L. *A Psychological Approach to Abnormal Behavior.* Englewood Cliffs, N.J.: Prentice-Hall, 1969.

17

Is Social Environment a Cause of Psychiatric Disorder?

Alexander Leighton
Harvard School of Public Health

As a beginning, may I apologize for the title of my talk? I see now that there are certain minor obscurities in it, such as the meaning of "social environment," "cause," and "psychiatric disorders." The "a" and the "of," however, are relatively clear.

Let me see if I can restate the topic. Given that each human society constitutes a dynamic system, and given that individual members occupy various positions in this system during the course of their lives, it would seem inevitable that relationships must exist between kind of system and kind of position on the one hand, and mental health and mental illness on the other. If this is so, then the question arises as to the nature of the relationship. My plan tonight is to focus on this issue and to touch four clusters of ideas.

The first deals with a major change going on regarding our ways of thinking about psychiatric disorder. This includes a shift of emphasis from pathological dynamics to control of disability, and a rethinking of the approach to nomenclature.

The second suggests that as part of the rethinking we shall move away from preoccupation with *the* cause of psychiatric disorder and in its place develop what may be called the *concept of salient cause.*

The third predicts that as a trend interlinked with the above we shall see more

Reprinted with permission from *Psychiatric Research Reports*, 22:337-345, 1965.

attention given to a widespread social phenomenon which may be designated as *sociocultural disintegration.* We shall be concerned with this because of its relationship to mental health.

The fourth and last set of notions deals with the possibility that the current world-wide increase of sociocultural disintegration can be countered by a process to which the title *congruent programming* may be attached.

I am going to suggest that *sociocultural disintegration* is a *salient cause* of psychiatric disorder and that preventive psychiatry must concern itself with *congruent programming.*

You can see from this forecast that my approach is not scientific, but speculation, impression, and guess. Perhaps because of this it will be a welcome relief from the strenuous fielding of hard facts you have had to do in previous Conference sessions. If you doze quietly now, you may rest assured you are not missing any facts.

My first proportion, then, is that increasingly evidence will show that in many kinds of psychiatric disorders it is more feasible to modify impairment and disability than it is to restructure the personality and effect a cure from within. For example, in the case of a person with an obsessive compulsive neurosis, it will be more feasible to reduce the symptoms so that they are less interfering with life functioning than it will be to effect a reorganization of the personality and so eliminate the symptoms altogether. The same will be true of depression, anxiety, and many other conditions. This trend will be fostered by the fact that techniques of disability reduction and disability prevention will advance rapidly and become more and more widely used.

In saying this I do not wish to imply the elimination of the psychodynamic approach, nor to down-grade its importance as a frame of reference, but I do think its position in the practice of American psychiatry is in the process of alteration.

The rethinking of nomenclature is closely linked to the shift of attention toward disability and impairment. Dissatisfaction with the way we name psychiatric disorders is of course an old, old story, but no accepted solution has so far emerged. It is probably fair to say that in the past there have been two main orientations: (1) the psychodynamic, and (2) the view that mental illness is a disease. These have sometimes been treated as in conflict and sometimes as congruent. Depression comes to mind as an example. My suggestion is that we are going to move away from both these orientations; we shall take something of value from each with us, and certain disorders such as some types of schizophrenia may turn out to be diseases, but eventually we shall for the most part replace these orientations with a focus on symptoms.

After this, at a later date, we shall move again beyond symptoms, since the word implies underlying disease and therefore contradicts the step it is intended to accomplish, to a still more phenomenal labelling, to something that might be called *behaviours of psychiatric interest,* such as fears, depressions, and delusions. These are, of course, symptoms, but they will be redefined so as to avoid built-in etiological concepts and the phenomena they represent will be systematically investigated for the factors and circumstances that lead to their appearance and disappearance, both "normal" and "abnormal." By "factors" I mean recurrent psychological, biochemical, social, cultural, and situational events. This notion of *behaviours of psychiatric interest* touches on what I think Dr. Bahn[1] had in mind this morning when she spoke of multi-dimensional nomenclature. For example, the day is probably coming when we shall do away with the present clinical distinction between anxiety and fear because it is incapable of precise definition; we shall abandon distinctions between "normal" and "abnormal" states of fear with their underlying assumptions and instead develop operational definitions for dealing with a variety of types of fear, each of which will be investigated for the various causal factors that enter into its appearance.

The road then is from diagnostic entities to symptom patterns to behaviours of psychiatric interest. But why would one suggest that this might happen? Mainly because it is happening, and because the reasons behind it are durable. Take, for one example, the advent of modern chemotherapy: the effective drugs bear more on symptoms than on diagnostic entities, more on depressed moods, fears, and tension states, than on neuroses, or personality disorders, or psychoses.

In an entirely different mode comes evidence from certain kinds of epidemiological research. Attempts at true prevalence studies indicate that symptom patterns can be identified and counted by independent psychiatric evaluators more readily than can diagnostic entities or "reaction types." Furthermore, these studies are flooding us with new information about subclinical disorders that do not fit very well into any of the more traditional categories, but are manageable with a typology based on symptoms.

Typologies of this sort are able to handle the complex continuity that appears to exist between patterns of health and patterns of illness. One can picture this, diagrammatically, as comprising two extremes in a field: one side, health behaviours, is a dense population of white dots, and the other, psychiatric behaviours (symptoms) is a dense population of black dots. As one looks across the field from light to dark, the whites grow less and less and the blacks become thicker and thicker.

A third body of evidence supporting an approach which focuses on behaviours of psychiatric interest comes from certain clinical investigations. I have in mind here the "social breakdown syndrome" long discussed under a variety of names such as institutional neurosis, but recently reviewed and formulated by Gruenberg and his colleagues.[2] This syndrome, first identified, as you may know, in the wards of chronic hospitals, consists in marked withdrawal or hostility, or some combination of the two. The condition is exceedingly resistant to individual therapy but is believed modifiable by change in ward regime. The point for our purposes here is that the syndrome is defined in behavioural terms, and is identified independently of whatever other traditional psychiatric disorder the patient is thought to have.

So much then for the first major point, a new look at psychiatric disorders with emphasis on disability and on taking behaviour patterns as the unit of investigation.

The second point is the notion of *salient cause*. Although multiple causality is a commonplace in psychiatry, we often act as if we did not really accept it. We talk about *the* cause rather than the *causes* and one still hears "either-or" arguments about organic, hereditary, psychodynamic, and social factors. But while it is evident that these are unprofitable issues revolving around wrong questions, they are not easy to drop. The difficulty is that as we come to accept genuinely and to act on the principle of multiple causality and to unravel the webs of complex relationships, we become lost unless we have some guiding concept of saliency.

Let me illustrate what I mean from outside the field of psychiatry. In the mid-nineteenth century, Rudolf Virchow was sent by the Prussian Government to Upper Silesia to investigate a typhus epidemic.[3] In his report he said that while it was quite likely that there was an agent, as yet unidentified, involved in this disease, the way to eliminate typhus was to eliminate poverty, overcrowding, and lack of adequate food. In putting his finger on the social conditions he was singling out for attention what he considered the most salient cause.

A salient cause is one that is critical in terms of some particular orientation. In most of our concerns in preventive psychiatry this will be for the years to come the causes about which something can be done to improve health. Thus, social conditions may be the salient cause in one situation, a virus in another, diet in a third, birth traumata in another, and so on. Much of future research will concern mapping out the networks of causal factors, and then, further, identifying certain particular items as, in this sense, salient. Arguments about which cause is the most important will fade. We will know that the importance of one cause as compared to another depends on the purpose of the questioner. If the purpose is treatment or preventive action, then the salient cause, from among all the causes in the complex, is the one about which we can do something. In the case of the social breakdown syndrome, for instance, the salient cause is the social system of the chronic wards. When these are changed, mental health is apparently improved.

Reference to social system brings us to my third point: *sociocultural disintegration*. Several instances of this have been under study by my colleagues and myself in small communities over a period of years. A disintegrated community is basically one that is no longer a community, being crippled with regard to most of the processes upon which group survival depends. This general property is manifest in a plurality of specific malfunctions such as defective communication among the members of the group; lack of leadership and followership; inability to arrive at group decisions; defective child rearing, training and education; deficiencies in work and productivity; lack of recreation, and weak control of hostile impulses.

The importance for mental health is that epidemiological research reveals a much higher prevalence of psychiatric disorders in the disintegrated groups than in others. This is probably a good example of multiple factors at work, much as was the case with regard to typhus in Upper Silesia. It is also very likely that the relationship of behaviour, mental health, and sociocultural disintegration is reciprocal—each to some extent causing the other. There are, however, theoretical reasons and some evidence to suggest that raising and lowering the level of disintegration can raise and lower the prevalence of psychiatric disorders. In one particular instance under study a community was seen to change over a ten year period from an extreme of disintegration to a level of integration that approaches its regional average. The fact that mental health moved clearly in the predicted direction suggests that sociocultural disintegration is a salient cause of psychiatric disorder.

You will note that I speak of sociocultural disintegration rather than poverty, although the communities in question are poor. This is a distinction worth making because it draws attention away from poverty as such to a more fundamental underlying process. Poverty is undoubtedly a common causal factor in the emergence of sociocultural disintegration but it is not the only one. Its opposite, sudden affluence, can have similar effects, and so can rapid social change, as in developing countries.

Some years ago, Dr. Tom Sasaki, of the Cornell Southwest Project, was studying a Navaho Indian community in New Mexico comprised of about 200 families.[4] They lived with a very low income, not more than a few hundred dollars a year. Only a few families in 200, for example, owned any kind of car, and these were pick-up trucks, for the most part, beaten up and second hand. The aim of Sasaki's study was to provide a base-line description of the community before introducing agricultural techniques calculated to lift economic and educational levels and to motivate the members toward adjustment to modern American life.

After the base-line study, but before much of the action could be started, natural gas, then uranium and oil, were discovered in the vicinity. The nearest town, Farmington, grew in a matter of months from 3,500 to 12,000 people. In the Navaho community, within a short time there were 150 cars and trucks, some families owning two. Wage work paid $1.50 to $2.70 an hour and there was time-and-a-half for overtime. All kinds of secondary developments occurred in the area, so that women could earn almost as much as the men in restaurants, laundries, etc. Thus a family in which two adults worked could earn $600.00 a month—more than they had previously earned in a year. Many families had more than two adult workers.

Sudden poverty could not have blasted a community into a state of disintegration any more effectively than did this abrupt opulence. Broken families, divorces, and neglected children emerged, accompanied by alcoholism, fights, and lawlessness. Such reactions make the point that sociocultural disintegration can arise from poverty's remedies as well as from poverty, and they direct attention to the importance of understanding these relationships.

As noted earlier, one of the characteristics of a disintegrated system is that social and psychological pathology reinforce each other, constituting a downward spiral, or, as the case may be, maintaining each other at a low functional level. Much evidence points to the probability that this phenomenon is expanding in human society all over the world, spreading like a fungus on top of a spreading population. Among the reasons for this, one may be identified as what sociologists and psychologists call "relative deprivation."[5] In former times, although many people lived in miserable circumstances they did so without realizing that there could be any other way. Further, however miserable they might be, they enjoyed a measure of local autonomy. Except for paying taxes to some central authority and in some instances providing soldiers when needed, towns, villages, and tribes were pretty well able to control their own affairs. This was probably a matter of some psychological importance.

A few years ago a group of us at Cornell made a comparative study of seven small communities in widely different parts of the world.[6] These included groups in rural Nova Scotia, Navaho country, Peru, Burma, India, Thailand and Japan. One of the findings throughout was an increase in expectation and the shrinking of autonomy. Fifty years ago the rural Nova Scotian community, for example, determined its own teachers, health regulations, care of the poor, means of maintaining law and order, and much else. Today, these determinations are made largely by professionals who come from a distance. The standards of service are higher and there is better education, better health and welfare, but the sense of control of one's own destiny in the community and being able to do things that make a difference has receded. At the same time there has developed a much greater appreciation of the advantages people have who live in other places, particularly cities, and with this has come a sense of being deprived, of being out of the main stream, and hence at a disadvantage.

Thus, while in our time the ideal of individual worth and of democracy have been increasing, many an individual's perception of his own actual worth (economic, political, and social) has been on the decline. People recognize the discrepancy between their lot and what might be, partly due to better communication, and partly due to moving around more and being able to see the contrasts. Television, radio, and educational systems all tell the individual that there is a difference between his condition and that enjoyed by many others. They also keep suggesting to him that the gap ought not to exist.

The process of disintegration, therefore, is not only a matter of poverty, starvation, poor health, and short life expectancy, important as these are; it is also a matter of a sentiment system which says that the situation is unjust and needless—an outrage. When such a state of mind persists without change of conditions it brings about deterioration in zestful attitudes and a blunting of ability to cope. Withdrawal and hostility emerge instead, very much as in the social breakdown syndrome on the back ward, and from this follows progressive disintegration of the social system. Psychiatric symptoms then occur such as irrational fears, depressions, delusions, mental dullness, psychophysiological disturbances, and much else.

At least this is what the first readings of comparative epidemiological studies suggest. They indicate that it is important for sociocultural disintegration to be defined in operational terms and attacked with programs for its modification. If such environmental control can be achieved in psychiatry, it will bring us at last to something which may with truth be called primary prevention.

Prevention is the fourth and last point. Here I am rash enough to say that wherever it is a question of sociocultural disintegration, only one approach will work and that is *congruent programming*. This means reversing the downward spiral of sociocultural disintegration and converting it into an upward spiral through the joint effort of professions—specifically: education, welfare, economics, health, and especially, mental health.

While it is sure that psychiatrists alone are unable to control sociocultural disintegration, however important it may be for mental health, the same applies equally to the educator, the economist, and the others. It is not enough to offer jobs, it is not enough to provide educational opportunities. Despite common belief, these moves are not sufficient to renovate a social system once it has passed beyond a certain threshold of disintegration, nor to engage the motivations of its component members.

There is a parallel here to a person who has become dehydrated. Beyond a certain point it does him no good to offer a drink of water. More drastic measures, intermuscular or intravenous injections of fluid, are required. These have to be maintained until his system recovers to the point where it can take over again, and he can once more drink for himself. In a similar way, the disintegrated social system requires special measures to get it moving. It does not have the social structure necessary for helping itself when given opportunity. Further, the individuals of the group are handicapped by their psychological condition and characteristic state of mind, and this does not go away over night simply because somebody has an educational or economic program under way. A group in a state of sociocultural disintegration has its lack of communication and its lack of structure for achieving group decision reinforced by psychological attitudes of depression, apathy, and anxiety. Hence, psychiatric rehabilitation has a part to play along with economic development, welfare, education, and general health programming.

Despite relative deprivation—or possibly because of it—the trend of our time is toward a better way of life for more people. In this context the pull of preventing psychiatric disorders is bound to lead psychiatry into community projects in which the profession will be a partner in congruent development. But accomplishing this requires preparation and we are not now prepared. By "we" I mean the majority of people working in the mental health field. Preparedness will take training and realignments and there are going to be difficulties.

One set of difficulties arises from the fact that functions in large societies such as ours tend to become the charges of bureaucracies. Bureaucracies in turn mean fences and fences have a way of interfering with co-operation. This is apt to be most manifest at the local level. Health, education, welfare, and economic development are likely to stand in a community as the separate feet of long columns reaching up out of sight to some high central throne of policy. The result all too often is non-congruent development; that is, conflict, things done out of phase with each other—job opportunities for which nobody has any training or training for which there are no jobs.

This is an old, old story. We as a nation have had a hundred years of it in our efforts to deal helpfully with the American Indian. Yet, in spite of its age the problem is current today and little closer to solution. Programs are very often fragmented and disarticulated in their impact at the level where the services are received. Individually admirable, their joint effect can be, not integration, but more disintegration.

Can we find a patterning for local coordination? Is it possible to have a group that can coordinate at the community level? A local authority with power to bind? Is this a function toward which mental health centers might evolve?

Whatever the means (county authority, ombudsman, or mental health center), a pattern must be found, for nothing otherwise will work, and the old errors will go on being new errors. It has to be a pattern that binds the different professional activities at the surface where they have interaction with the community. From somewhere must emerge the social structure necessary for congruent programming in communities.

From where? This is not a rhetorical question, but one for the mental health professions.

References

1. Bahn, Anita K. Some methodologic issues in psychiatric epidemiology. Chapter II, this publication (Psychiatric Research Report No. 22).
2. Gruenberg, E. Identifying cases of social breakdown syndrome. Milbank Memorial Fund Quarterly. Vol. XLIV, No. 1, Jan., 1966. Part 2.
3. Ackerknecht, Erwin H. Rudolf Virchow. Madison, Wisc. University of Wisconsin Press, 1953. esp. pp. 123-137.
4. Sasaki, Tom T. Fruitland, New Mexico: A Navaho Community in Transition. Ithaca, N.Y. Cornell Univ. Press, 1960.
5. Stouffer, Samuel A., et al. The American Soldier. Vol. I. Princeton, N.J. Princeton Univ. Press, 1949. pp. 124-130.
6. Leighton, Alexander H., and Smith, Robert J. A comparative study of social and cultural change. In: Proceedings of the American Philosophical Society. Vol. 99, No. 2, April 1955.

18

On Being Sane in Insane Places

D.L. Rosenhan
Stanford University

If sanity and insanity exist, how shall we know them?

The question is neither capricious nor itself insane. However much we may be personally convinced that we can tell the normal from the abnormal, the evidence is simply not compelling. It is commonplace, for example, to read about murder trials wherein eminent psychiatrists for the defense are contradicted by equally eminent psychiatrists for the prosecution on the matter of the defendant's sanity. More generally, there are a great deal of conflicting data on the reliability, utility, and meaning of such terms as "sanity," "insanity," "mental illness," and "schizophrenia."[1] Finally, as early as 1934, Benedict suggested that normality and abnormality are not universal.[2] What is viewed as normal in one culture may be seen as quite aberrant in another. Thus, notions of normality and abnormality may not be quite as accurate as people believe they are.

To raise questions regarding normality and abnormality is in no way to question the fact that some behaviors are deviant or odd. Murder is deviant. So, too, are hallucinations. Nor does raising such questions deny the existence of the personal anguish that is often associated with "mental illness." Anxiety and

Reprinted with permission from *Science*, 179:250-258, 1973. Copyright 1973 by the American Association for the Advancement of Science.

depression exist. Psychological suffering exists. But normality and abnormality, sanity and insanity, and the diagnoses that flow from them may be less substantive than many believe them to be.

At its heart, the question of whether the sane can be distinguished from the insane (and whether degrees of insanity can be distinguished from each other) is a simple matter: do the salient characteristics that lead to diagnoses reside in the patients themselves or in the environments and contexts in which observers find them? From Bleuler, through Kretchmer, through the formulators of the recently revised *Diagnostic and Statistical Manual* of the American Psychiatric Association, the belief has been strong that patients present symptoms, that those symptoms can be categorized, and, implicitly, that the sane are distinguishable from the insane. More recently, however, this belief has been questioned. Based in part on theoretical and anthropological considerations, but also on philosophical, legal, and therapeutic ones, the view has grown that psychological categorization of mental illness is useless at best and downright harmful, misleading, and pejorative at worst. Psychiatric diagnoses, in this view, are in the minds of the observers and are not valid summaries of characteristics displayed by the observed.[3-5]

Gains can be made in deciding which of these is more nearly accurate by getting normal people (that is, people who do not have, and have never suffered, symptoms of serious psychiatric disorders) admitted to psychiatric hospitals and then determining whether they were discovered to be sane and, if so, how. If the sanity of such pseudopatients were always detected, there would be prima facie evidence that a sane individual can be distinguished from the insane context in which he is found. Normality (and presumably abnormality) is distinct enough that it can be recognized wherever it occurs, for it is carried within the person. If, on the other hand, the sanity of the pseudopatients were never discovered, serious difficulties would arise for those who support traditional modes of psychiatric diagnosis. Given that the hospital staff was not incompetent, that the pseudopatient had been behaving as sanely as he had been outside of the hospital, and that it had never been previously suggested that he belonged in a psychiatric hospital, such an unlikely outcome would support the view that psychiatric diagnosis betrays little about the patient but much about the environment in which an observer finds him.

This article describes such an experiment. Eight sane people gained secret admission to 12 different hospitals.[6] Their diagnostic experiences constitute the data of the first part of this article; the remainder is devoted to a description of their experiences in psychiatric institutions. Too few psychiatrists and psychologists, even those who have worked in such hospitals, know what the experience is like. They rarely talk about it with former patients, perhaps because they distrust information coming from the previously insane. Those who have worked in psychiatric hospitals are likely to have adapted so thoroughly to the settings that they are insensitive to the impact of that experience. And while there have been occasional reports of researchers who submitted themselves to psychiatric hospitalization,[7] these researchers have commonly remained in the hospitals for short periods of time, often with the knowledge of the hospital staff. It is difficult to know the extent to which they were treated like patients or like research colleagues. Nevertheless, their reports about the inside of the psychiatric hospital have been valuable. This article extends those efforts.

Pseudopatients and Their Settings

The eight pseudopatients were a varied group. One was a psychology graduate student in his 20's. The remaining seven were older and "established." Among them were three psychologists, a pediatrician, a psychiatrist, a painter, and a housewife. Three pseudopatients were women, five were men. All of them employed pseudonyms, lest their alleged diagnoses embarrass them later. Those who were in mental health professions alleged another occupation in order to avoid the special attentions that might be accorded by staff, as a matter of courtesy or caution, to ailing colleagues.[8] With the exception of myself (I was the first pseudopatient and my presence was known to the hospital administrator and chief psychologist and, so far as I can tell, to them alone), the presence of pseudopatients and the nature of the research program was not known to the hospital staffs.[9]

The settings were similarly varied. In order to generalize the findings, admission into a variety of hospitals was sought. The 12 hospitals in the sample were located in five different states on the East and West coasts. Some were old and shabby, some were quite new. Some were research-oriented, others not. Some had good staff-patient ratios, others were quite understaffed. Only one was a strictly private hospital. All of the others were supported by state or federal funds or, in one instance, by university funds.

After calling the hospital for an appointment, the pseudopatient arrived at the admissions office complaining that he had been hearing voices. Asked what the voices said, he replied that they were often unclear, but as far as he could tell they said "empty," "hollow," and "thud." The voices were unfamiliar and were of the same sex as the pseudopatient. The choice of these symptoms was occasioned by their apparent similarity to existential symptoms. Such symptoms are alleged to arise from painful concerns about the perceived meaninglessness of one's life. It is as if the hallucinating person were saying, "My life is empty and hollow." The choice of these symptoms was also determined by the *absence* of a single report of existential psychoses in the literature.

Beyond alleging the symptoms and falsifying name, vocation, and employment, no further alterations of person, history, or circumstances were made. The significant events of the pseudopatient's life history were presented as they had actually occurred. Relationships with parents and siblings, with spouse and children, with people at work and in school, consistent with the aforementioned exceptions, were described as they were or had been. Frustrations and upsets were described along with joys and satisfactions. These facts are important to remember. If anything, they strongly biased the subsequent results in favor of detecting sanity, since none of their histories or current behaviors were seriously pathological in any way.

Immediately upon admission to the psychiatric ward, the pseudopatient ceased simulating *any* symptoms of abnormality. In some cases, there was a brief period of mild nervousness and anxiety, since none of the pseudopatients really believed that they would be admitted so easily. Indeed, their shared fear was that they would be immediately exposed as frauds and greatly embarrassed. Moreover, many of them had never visited a psychiatric ward; even those who had, nevertheless had some genuine fears about what might happen to them. Their nervousness, then, was quite appropriate to the novelty of the hospital setting, and it abated rapidly.

Apart from that short-lived nervousness, the pseudopatient behaved on the ward as he "normally" behaved. The pseudopatient spoke to patients and staff as he might ordinarily. Because there is uncommonly little to do on a psychiatric ward, he attempted to engage others in conversation. When asked by staff how he was feeling, he indicated that he was fine, that he no longer experienced symptoms. He responded to instructions from attendants, to calls for medication (which was not swallowed), and to dining-hall instructions. Beyond such activities as were available to him on the admissions ward, he spent his time writing down his observations about the ward, its patients, and the staff. Initially these notes were written "secretly," but as it soon became clear that no one much cared, they were subsequently written on standard tablets of paper in such public places as the dayroom. No secret was made of these activities.

The pseudopatient, very much as a true psychiatric patient, entered a hospital with no foreknowledge of when he would be discharged. Each was told that he would have to get out by his own devices, essentially by convincing the staff that he was sane. The psychological stresses associated with hospitalization were considerable, and all but one of the pseudopatients desired to be discharged almost immediately after being admitted. They were, therefore, motivated not only to behave sanely, but to be paragons of cooperation. That their behavior was in no way disruptive is confirmed by nursing reports, which have been obtained on most of the patients. These reports uniformly indicate that the patients were "friendly," "cooperative," and "exhibited no abnormal indications."

The Normal Are Not Detectably Sane

Despite their public "show" of sanity, the pseudopatients were never detected. Admitted, except in one case, with a diagnosis of schizophrenia,[10] each was discharged with a diagnosis of schizophrenia "in remission." The label "in remission" should in no way be dismissed as a formality, for at no time during any hospitalization had any question been raised about any pseudopatient's simulation. Nor are there any indications in the hospital records that the pseudopatient's status was suspect. Rather, the evidence is strong that, once labeled schizophrenic, the pseudopatient was stuck with that label. If the pseudopatient was to be discharged, he must naturally be "in remission"; but he was not sane, nor, in the institution's view, had he ever been sane.

The uniform failure to recognize sanity cannot be attributed to the quality of the hospitals, for, although there were considerable variations among them, several are considered excellent. Nor can it be alleged that there was simply not enough time to observe the pseudopatients. Length of hospitalization ranged from 7 to 52 days, with an average of 19 days. The pseudopatients were not, in fact, carefully observed, but this failure clearly speaks more to traditions within psychiatric hospitals than to lack of opportunity.

Finally, it cannot be said that the failure to recognize the pseudopatients' sanity was due to the fact that they were not behaving sanely. While there was clearly some tension present in all of them, their daily visitors could detect no serious behavioral consequences—nor, indeed, could other patients. It was quite common for the patients to "detect" the pseudopatients' sanity. During the first three hospitalizations, when accurate counts were kept, 35 of a total of 118 patients on the admissions ward voiced their suspicions, some vigorously. "You're not crazy. You're a journalist, or a professor [referring to the continual note-taking]. You're checking up on the hospital." While most of the patients were reassured by the psuedopatient's insistence that he had been sick before he came in but was fine now, some continued to believe that the pseudopatient was sane throughout his hospitalization.[11] The fact that the patients often recognized normality when staff did not raise important questions.

Failure to detect sanity during the course of hospitalization may be due to the fact that physicians operate with a strong bias toward what statisticians call the type 2 error (5). This is to say that physicians are more inclined to call a healthy person sick (a false positive, type 2) than a sick person healthy (a false negative, type 1). The reasons for this are not hard to find: it is clearly more dangerous to misdiagnose illness than health. Better to err on the side of caution, to suspect illness even among the healthy.

But what holds for medicine does not hold equally well for psychiatry. Medical illnesses, while unfortunate, are not commonly pejorative. Psychiatric diagnoses, on the contrary, carry with them personal, legal, and social stigmas.[12] It was therefore important to see whether the tendency toward diagnosing the sane insane could be reversed. The following experiment was arranged at a research and teaching hospital whose staff had heard these findings but doubted that such an error could occur in their hospital. The staff was informed that at some time during the following 3 months, one or more pseudopatients would attempt to be admitted into the psychiatric hospital. Each staff member was asked to rate each patient who presented himself at admissions or on the ward according to the likelihood that the patient was a pseudopatient. A 10-point scale was used, with a 1 and 2 reflecting high confidence that the patient was a pseudopatient.

Judgments were obtained on 193 patients who were admitted for psychiatric treatment. All staff who had had sustained contact with or primary responsibility for the patient—attendants, nurses, psychiatrists, physicians, and psychologists—were asked to make judgments. Forty-one patients were alleged, with high confidence, to be pseudopatients by at least one member of the staff. Twenty-three were considered suspect by at least one psychiatrist. Nineteen were suspected by one psychiatrist *and* one other staff member. Actually, no genuine pseudopatient (at least from my group) presented himself during this period.

The experiment is instructive. It indicates that the tendency to designate sane people as insane can be reversed when the stakes (in this case, prestige and diagnostic acumen) are high. But what can be said of the 19 people who were suspected of being "sane" by one psychiatrist and another staff member? Were these people truly "sane," or was it rather the case that in the course of avoiding the type 2 error the staff tended to make more errors of the first sort—calling the crazy "sane"? There is no way of knowing. But one thing is certain: any diagnostic process that lends itself so readily to massive errors of this sort cannot be a very reliable one.

The Stickiness of Psychodiagnostic Labels

Beyond the tendency to call the healthy sick—a tendency that accounts better for diagnostic behavior on admission than it does for such behavior after a lengthy period of exposure—the data speak to the massive role of labeling in psychiatric assessment. Having once been labeled schizophrenic, there is nothing the pseudopatient can do to overcome the tag. The tag profoundly colors others' perceptions of him and his behavior.

From one viewpoint, these data are hardly surprising, for it has long been known that elements are given meaning by the context in which they occur. Gestalt psychology made this point vigorously, and Asch[13] demonstrated that there are "central" personality traits (such as "warm" versus "cold") which are so powerful that they markedly color the meaning of other information in forming an impression of a given personality.[14] "Insane," "schizophrenic," "manic-depressive," and "crazy" are probably among the most powerful of such central traits. Once a person is designated abnormal, all of his other behaviors and characteristics are colored by that label. Indeed, that label is so powerful that many of the pseudopatients' normal behaviors were overlooked entirely or profoundly misinterpreted. Some examples may clarify this issue.

Earlier I indicated that there were no changes in the pseudopatient's personal history and current status beyond those of name, employment, and, where necessary, vocation. Otherwise, a veridical description of personal history and circumstances was offered. Those circumstances were not psychotic. How were they made consonant with the diagnosis of psychosis? Or were those diagnoses modified in such a way as to bring them into accord with the circumstances of the pseudopatient's life, as described by him?

As far as I can determine, diagnoses were in no way affected by the relative health of the circumstances of a pseudopatient's life. Rather, the reverse occurred: the perception of his circumstances was shaped entirely by the diagnosis. A clear example of such translation is found in the case of a pseudopatient who had had a close relationship with his mother but was rather remote from his father during his early childhood. During adolescence and beyond, however, his father became a close friend, while his relationship with his mother cooled. His present relationship with his wife was characteristically close and warm. Apart from occasional angry exchanges, friction was minimal. The children had rarely been spanked. Surely there is nothing especially pathological about such a history. Indeed, many readers may see a similar pattern in their own experiences, with no markedly deleterious consequences. Observe, however, how such a history was translated in the psychopathological context, this from the case summary prepared after the patient was discharged.

This white 39-year-old male . . . manifests a long history of considerable ambivalence in close relationships, which begins in early childhood. A warm relationship with his mother cools during his adolescence. A distant relationship to his father is described as becoming very intense. Affective stability is absent. His attempts to control emotionality with his wife and children are punctuated by angry outbursts and, in the case of the children, spankings. And while he says that he has several good friends, one senses considerable ambivalence embedded in those relationships also. . . .

The facts of the case were unintentionally distorted by the staff to achieve consistency with a popular theory of the dynamics of a schizophrenic reaction.[15] Nothing of an ambivalent nature had been described in relations with parents, spouse, or friends. To the extent that ambivalence could be inferred, it was probably not greater than is found in all human relationships. It is true the pseudopatient's relationships with his parents changed over time, but in the ordinary context that would hardly be remarkable—indeed, it might very well be expected. Clearly, the meaning ascribed to his verbalizations (that is, ambivalence, affective instability) was determined by the diagnosis: schizophrenia. An entirely different meaning would have been ascribed if it were known that the man was "normal."

All pseudopatients took extensive notes publicly. Under ordinary circumstances, such behavior would have raised questions in the minds of observers, as, in fact, it did among patients. Indeed, it seemed so certain that the notes would elicit suspicion that elaborate precautions were taken to remove them from the ward each day. But the precautions proved needless. The closest any staff member came to questioning these notes occurred when one pseudopatient asked his physician what kind of medication he was receiving and began to write down the response. "You needn't write it," he was told gently. "If you have trouble remembering, just ask me again."

If no questions were asked of the pseudopatients, how was their writing interpreted? Nursing records for three patients indicate that the writing was seen as an aspect of their pathological behavior. "Patient engages in writing behavior" was the daily nursing comment on one of the pseudopatients who was never questioned about his writing. Given that the patient is in the hospital, he must be psychologically disturbed. And given that he is disturbed, continuous writing must be a behavioral manifestation of that disturbance, perhaps a subset of the compulsive behaviors that are sometimes correlated with schizophrenia.

One tacit characteristic of psychiatric diagnosis is that it locates the sources of aberration within the individual and only rarely within the complex of stimuli that surrounds him. Consequently, behaviors that are stimulated by the environment are commonly misattributed to the patient's disorder. For example, one kindly nurse found a pseudopatient pacing the long hospital corridors. "Nervous, Mr. X?" she asked. "No, bored," he said.

The notes kept by pseudopatients are full of patient behaviors that were misinterpreted by well-intentioned staff. Often enough, a patient would go "berserk" because he had, wittingly or unwittingly, been mistreated by, say, an attendant. A nurse coming upon the scene would rarely inquire even cursorily into the environmental stimuli of the patient's behavior. Rather, she assumed that his upset derived from his pathology, not from his present interactions with other staff members. Occasionally, the staff might assume that the patient's family (especially when they had recently visited) or other patients had stimulated the outburst. But never were the staff found to assume that one of themselves or the structure of the hospital had anything to do with a patient's behavior. One psychiatrist pointed to a group of patients who were sitting outside the cafeteria entrance half an hour before lunchtime. To a group of young residents he indicated that such behavior was characteristic of the oral-acquisitive nature of the syndrome. It seemed not to occur to him that there were very few things to anticipate in a psychiatric hospital besides eating.

A psychiatric label has a life and an influence of its own. Once the impression has been formed that the patient is schizophrenic, the expectation is that he will continue to be schizophrenic. When a sufficient amount of time has passed, during which the patient has done nothing bizarre, he is considered to be in remission and available for discharge. But the label endures beyond discharge, with the unconfirmed expectation that he will behave as a schizophrenic again. Such labels, conferred by mental health professionals are as influential on the patient as they are on his relatives and friends, and it should not surprise anyone that the diagnosis acts on all of them as a self-fulfilling prophecy. Eventually, the patient himself accepts the diagnosis, with all of its surplus meanings and expectations, and behaves accordingly.[5]

The inferences to be made from these matters are quite simple. Much as Zigler and Phillips have demonstrated that there is enormous overlap in the symptoms presented by patients who have been variously diagnosed,[16] so there is enormous overlap in the behaviors of the sane and the insane. The sane are not "sane" all of the time. We lose our tempers "for no good reason." We are occasionally depressed or anxious, again for no good reason. And we may find it difficult to get along with one or another person—again for no reason that we can specify. Similarly, the insane are not always insane. Indeed, it was the impression of the pseudopatients while living with them that they were sane for long periods of time—that the bizarre behaviors upon which their diagnoses were allegedly predicated constituted only a small fraction of their total behavior. If it makes no sense to label ourselves permanently depressed on the basis of an occasional depression, then it takes better evidence than is presently available to label all patients insane or schizophrenic on the basis of bizarre behaviors or cognitions. It seems more useful, as Mischel[17] has pointed out, to limit our discussions to *behaviors*, the stimuli that provoke them, and their correlates.

It is not known why powerful impressions of personality traits, such as "crazy" or "insane," arise. Conceivably, when the origins of and stimuli that give rise to a behavior are remote or unknown, or when the behavior strikes us as immutable, trait labels regarding the *behaver* arise. When, on the other hand, the origins and stimuli are known and available, discourse is limited to the behavior itself. Thus, I may hallucinate because I am sleeping, or I may hallucinate because I have ingested a peculiar drug. These are termed sleep-induced hallucinations, or dreams, and drug-induced hallucinations, respectively. But when the stimuli to my hallucinations are unknown, that is called craziness, or schizophrenia—as if that inference were somehow as illuminating as the others.

The Experience of Psychiatric Hospitalization

The term "mental illness" is of recent origin. It was coined by people who are humane in their inclinations and who wanted very much to raise the station of (and the public's sympathies toward) the psychologically disturbed from that of witches and "crazies" to one that was akin to the physically ill. And they were at least partially successful, for the treatment of the mentally ill *has* improved considerably over the years. But while treatment has improved, it is doubtful that people really regard the mentally ill in the same way that they view the physically ill. A broken leg is something one recovers from, but mental illness allegedly endures forever.[18] A broken leg does not threaten the observer, but a crazy schizophrenic? There is by now a host of evidence that attitudes toward the mentally ill are characterized by fear, hostility, aloofness, suspicion, and dread.[19] The mentally ill are society's lepers.

That such attitudes infect the general population is perhaps not surprising, only upsetting. But that they affect the professionals—attendants, nurses, physicians, psychologists, and social workers—who treat and deal with the mentally ill is more disconcerting, both because such attitudes are self-evidently pernicious and because they are unwitting. Most mental health professionals would insist that they are sympathetic toward the mentally ill, that they are neither avoidant nor hostile. But it is more likely that an exquisite ambivalence characterizes their relations with psychiatric patients, such that their avowed impulses are only part of their entire attitude. Negative attitudes are there too and can easily be detected. Such attitudes should not surprise us. They are the natural offspring of the labels patients wear and the places in which they are found.

Consider the structure of the typical psychiatric hospital. Staff and patients are strictly segregated. Staff have their own living space, including their dining facilities, bathrooms, and assembly places. The glassed quarters that contain the professional staff, which the pseudopatients came to call "the cage," sit out on every dayroom. The staff emerge primarily for caretaking purposes—to give medication, to conduct a therapy or group meeting, to instruct or reprimand a patient. Otherwise, staff keep to themselves, almost as if the disorder that afflicts their charges is somehow catching.

So much is patient-staff segregation the rule that, for four public hospitals in which an attempt was made to measure the degree to which staff and patients mingle, it was necessary to use "time out of the staff cage" as the operational measure. While it was not the case that all time spent out of the cage was spent mingling with patients (attendants, for example, would occasionally emerge to watch television in the dayroom), it was the only way in which one could gather reliable data on time for measuring.

The average amount of time spent by attendants outside of the cage was 11.3 percent (range, 3 to 52 percent). This figure does not represent only time spent mingling with patients, but also includes time spent on such chores as folding laundry, supervising patients while they shave, directing ward cleanup, and sending patients to off-ward activities. It was the relatively rare attendant who spent time talking with patients or playing games with them. It proved impossible to obtain a "percent mingling time" for nurses, since the amount of time they spent out of the cage was too brief. Rather, we counted instances of emergence from the cage. On the average, daytime nurses emerged from the cage 11.5 times per shift, including instances when they left the ward entirely (range, 4 to 39 times). Late afternoon and night nurses were even less available, emerging on the average 9.4 times per shift (range, 4 to 41 times). Data on early morning nurses, who arrived usually after midnight and departed at 8 a.m., are not available because patients were asleep during most of this period.

Physicians, especially psychiatrists, were even less available. They were rarely seen on the wards. Quite commonly, they would be seen only when they arrived and departed, with the remaining time being spent in their offices or in the cage. On the average, physicians emerged on the ward 6.7 times per day (range, 1 to 17 times). It proved difficult to make an accurate estimate in this regard, since physicians often maintained hours that allowed them to come and go at different times.

The hierarchical organization of the psychiatric hospital has been commented on before,[20] but the latent meaning of that kind of organization is worth noting again. Those with the most power have least to do with patients, and those with the least power are most involved with them. Recall, however, that the acquisition of role-appropriate behaviors occurs mainly through the observation of others, with the most powerful having the most influence. Consequently, it is understandable that attendants not only spend more time with patients than do any other members of the staff—that is required by their station in the hierarchy—but also, insofar as they learn from their superiors' behavior, spend as little time with patients as they can. Attendants are seen mainly in the cage, which is where the models, the action, and the power are.

I turn now to a different set of studies, these dealing with staff response to patient-initiated contact. It has long been known that the amount of time a person spends with you can be an index of your significance to him. If he initiates and maintains eye contact, there is reason to believe that he is considering your requests and needs. If he pauses to chat or actually stops and talks, there is added reason to infer that he is individuating you. In four hospitals, the pseudopatient approached the staff member with a request which took the following form: "Pardon me, Mr. [or Dr. or Mrs.] X, could you tell me when I will be eligible for grounds privileges?" (or " . . . when I will be presented at the staff meeting?" or " . . . when I am likely to be discharged?"). While the content of the question varied according to the appropriateness of the target and the pseudopatient's (apparent) current needs the form was always a courteous and relevant request for information. Care was taken never to approach a particular member of the staff more than once a day, lest the staff member become suspicious or irritated. In examining these data, remember that the behavior of the pseudopatients was neither bizarre nor disruptive. One could indeed engage in good conversation with them.

The data for these experiments are shown in Table 18-1, separately for physicians (column 1) and for nurses and attendants (column 2). Minor differences between these four institutions were overwhelmed by the degree to which staff avoided continuing contacts that patients had initiated. By far, their most common response consisted of either a brief response to the question, offered while they were "on the move" and with head averted, or no response at all.

The encounter frequently took the following bizarre form: (pseudopatient) "Pardon me, Dr. X. Could you tell me when I am eligible for grounds

Table 18-1
Self-initiated Contact by Pseudopatients with Psychiatrists and Nurses and Attendants, Compared to Contact with Other Groups

| Contact | Psychiatric Hospitals | | University Campus (Nonmedical) | | University Medical Center | |
	(1) Psychiatrists	(2) Nurses and Attendants	(3) Faculty	(4) "Looking for a Psychiatrist"	Physicians (5) "Looking for an Internist"	(6) No Additional Comment
Responses						
Moves on, head averted (%)	71	88	0	0	0	0
Makes eye contact (%)	23	10	0	11	0	0
Pauses and chats (%)	2	2	0	11	0	10
Stops and talks (%)	4	0.5	100	78	100	90
Mean number of questions answered (out of 6)	*	*	6	3.8	4.8	4.5
Respondents (No.)	13	47	14	18	15	10
Attempts (No.)	185	1283	14	18	15	10

*Not applicable.

privileges?" (physician) "Good morning, Dave. How are you today?" (Moves off without waiting for a response.)

It is instructive to compare these data with data recently obtained at Stanford University. It has been alleged that large and eminent universities are characterized by faculty who are so busy that they have no time for students. For this comparison, a young lady approached individual faculty members who seemed to be walking purposefully to some meeting or teaching engagement and asked them the following six questions.

1) "Pardon me, could you direct me to Encina Hall?" (at the medical school: " . . . to the Clinical Research Center?").

2) "Do you know where Fish Annex is?" (there is no Fish Annex at Stanford).

3) "Do you teach here?"

4) "How does one apply for admission to the college?" (at the medical school: " . . . to the medical school?").

5) "Is it difficult to get in?"

6) "Is there financial aid?"

Without exception, as can be seen in Table 18-1 (column 3), all of the questions were answered. No matter how rushed they were, all respondents not only maintained eye contact, but stopped to talk. Indeed, many of the respondents went out of their way to direct or take the questioner to the office she was seeking, to try to locate "Fish Annex," or to discuss with her the possibilities of being admitted to the university.

Similar data, also shown in Table 18-1 (columns 4, 5, and 6), were obtained in the hospital. Here too, the young lady came prepared with six questions. After the first question, however, she remarked to 18 of her respondents (column 4), "I'm looking for a psychiatrist," and to 15 others (column 5), "I'm looking for an internist." Ten other respondents received no inserted comment (column 6). The general degree of cooperative responses is considerably higher for these university groups than it was for pseudopatients in psychiatric hospitals. Even so, differences are apparent within the medical school setting. Once having indicated that she was looking for a psychiatrist, the degree of cooperation elicited was less than when she sought an internist.

Powerlessness and Depersonalization

Eye contact and verbal contact reflect concern and individuation; their absence, avoidance and depersonalization. The data I have presented do not do justice to the rich daily encounters that grew up around matters of depersonalization and avoidance. I have records of patients who were beaten by staff for the sin of having initiated verbal contact. During my own experience, for example, one patient was beaten in the presence of other patients for having approached an attendant and told him, "I like you." Occasionally, punishment meted out to patients for misdemeanors seemed so excessive that it could not be justified by the most radical interpretations of psychiatric canon. Nevertheless, they appeared to go unquestioned. Tempers were often short. A patient who had not heard a call for medication would be roundly excoriated, and the morning attendants would often wake patients with, "Come on, you m-----f-----s, out of bed!"

Neither anecdotal nor "hard" data can convey the overwhelming sense of powerlessness which invades the individual as he is continually exposed to the depersonalization of the psychiatric hospital. It hardly matters *which* psychiatric hospital—the excellent public ones and the very plush private hospital were better than the rural and shabby ones in this regard, but, again, the features that psychiatric hospitals had in common overwhelmed by far their apparent differences.

Powerlessness was evident everywhere. The patient is deprived of many of his legal rights by dint of his psychiatric commitment.[21] He is shorn of credibility by virtue of his psychiatric label. His freedom of movement is restricted. He cannot initiate contact with the staff, but may only respond to such overtures as they make. Personal privacy is minimal. Patient quarters and possessions can be entered and examined by any staff member, for whatever reason. His personal history and anguish is available to any staff member (often including the "grey lady" and "candy striper" volunteer) who chooses to read his folder, regardless of their therapeutic relationship to him. His personal hygiene and waste evacuation are often monitored. The water closets may have no doors.

At times, depersonalization reached such proportions that pseudopatients had the sense that they were invisible, or at least unworthy of account. Upon being admitted, I and other pseudopatients took the initial physical examinations in a semipublic room, where staff members went about their own business as if we were not there.

On the ward, attendants delivered verbal and occasionally serious physical abuse to patients in the presence of other observing patients, some of whom (the pseudopatients) were writing it all down. Abusive behavior, on the other hand, terminated quite abruptly when other staff members were known to be coming. Staff are credible witnesses. Patients are not.

A nurse unbuttoned her uniform to adjust her brassiere in the presence of an entire ward of viewing men. One did not have the sense that she was being seductive. Rather, she didn't notice us. A group of staff persons might point to a patient in the dayroom and discuss him animatedly, as if he were not there.

One illuminating instance of depersonalization and invisibility occurred with regard to medications. All told, the pseudopatients were administered nearly 2100 pills, including Elavil, Stelazine, Compazine, and Thorazine, to name but a few. (That such a variety of medications should have been administered to patients presenting identical symptoms is itself worthy of note.) Only two were swallowed. The rest were either pocketed or deposited in the toilet. The pseudopatients were not alone in this. Although I have no precise records on how many patients rejected their medications, the pseudopatients frequently found the medications of other patients in the toilet before they deposited their own. As long as they were cooperative, their behavior and the pseudopatients' own in this matter, as in other important matters, went unnoticed throughout.

Reactions to such depersonalization among pseudopatients were intense. Although they had come to the hospital as participant observers and were fully aware that they did not "belong," they nevertheless found themselves caught up in and fighting the process of depersonalization. Some examples: a graduate student in psychology asked his wife to bring his textbooks to the hospital so he could "catch up on his homework"—this despite the elaborate precautions taken to conceal his professional association. The same student, who had trained for quite some time to get into the hospital, and who had looked forward to the experience, "remembered" some drag races that he had wanted to see on the weekend and insisted that he be discharged by that time. Another pseudopatient attempted a romance with a nurse. Subsequently, he informed the staff that he was applying for admission to graduate school in psychology and was very likely to be admitted, since a graduate professor was one of his regular hospital visitors. The same person began to engage in psychotherapy with other patients—all of this as a way of becoming a person in an impersonal environment.

The Sources of Depersonalization

What are the origins of depersonalization? I have already mentioned two. First are attitudes held by all of us toward the mentally ill—including those who treat them—attitudes characterized by fear, distrust, and horrible expectations on the one hand, and benevolent intentions on the other. Our ambivalence leads, in this instance as in others, to avoidance.

Second, and not entirely separate, the hierarchical structure of the psychiatric hospital facilitates depersonalization. Those who are at the top have least to do with patients, and their behavior inspires the rest of the staff. Average daily contact with psychiatrists, psychologists, residents, and physicians combined ranged from 3.9 to 25.1 minutes, with an overall mean of 6.8 (six pseudopatients over a total of 129 days of hospitalization). Included in this average are time spent in the admissions interview, ward meetings in the presence of a senior staff member, group and individual psychotherapy contacts, case presentation conferences, and discharge meetings. Clearly, patients do not spend much time in interpersonal contact with doctoral staff. And doctoral staff serve as models for nurses and attendants.

There are probably other sources. Psychiatric installations are presently in serious financial straits. Staff shortages are pervasive, staff time at a premium.

Something has to give, and that something is patient contact. Yet, while financial stresses are realities, too much can be made of them. I have the impression that the psychological forces that result in depersonalization are much stronger than the fiscal ones and that the addition of more staff would not correspondingly improve patient care in this regard. The incidence of staff meetings and the enormous amount of record-keeping on patients, for example, have not been as substantially reduced as has patient contact. Priorities exist, even during hard times. Patient contact is not a significant priority in the traditional psychiatric hospital, and fiscal pressures do not account for this. Avoidance and depersonalization may.

Heavy reliance upon psychotropic medication tacitly contributes to depersonalization by convincing staff that treatment is indeed being conducted and that further patient contact may not be necessary. Even here, however, caution needs to be exercised in understanding the role of psychotropic drugs. If patients were powerful rather than powerless, if they were viewed as interesting individuals rather than diagnostic entities, if they were socially significant rather than social lepers, if their anguish truly and wholly compelled our sympathies and concerns, would we not *seek* contact with them, despite the availability of medications? Perhaps for the pleasure of it all?

The Consequences of Labeling
and Depersonalization

Whenever the ratio of what is known to what needs to be known approaches zero, we tend to invent "knowledge" and assume that we understand more than we actually do. We seem unable to acknowledge that we simply don't know. The needs for diagnosis and remediation of behavioral and emotional problems are enormous. But rather than acknowledge that we are just embarking on understanding, we continue to label patients "schizophrenic," "manic-depressive," and "insane," as if in those words we have captured the essence of understanding. The facts of the matter are that we have known for a long time that diagnoses are often not useful or reliable, but we have nevertheless continued to use them. We now know that we cannot distinguish insanity from sanity. It is depressing to consider how that information will be used.

Not merely depressing, but frightening. How many people, one wonders, are sane but not recognized as such in our psychiatric institutions? How many have been needlessly stripped of their privileges of citizenship, from the right to vote and drive to that of handling their own accounts? How many have feigned insanity in order to avoid the criminal consequences of their behavior, and, conversely, how many would rather stand trial than live interminably in a psychiatric hospital—but are wrongly thought to be mentally ill? How many have been stigmatized by well-intentioned, but nevertheless erroneous, diagnoses? On the last point, recall again that a "type 2 error" in psychiatric diagnosis does not have the same consequences it does in medical diagnosis. A diagnosis of cancer that has been found to be in error is cause for celebration. But psychiatric diagnoses are rarely found to be in error. The label sticks, a mark of inadequacy forever.

Finally, how many patients might be "sane" outside the psychiatric hospital but seem insane in it—not because craziness resides in them, as it were, but because they are responding to a bizarre setting, one that may be unique to institutions which harbor nether people? Goffman[4] calls the process of socialization to such institutions "mortification"—an apt metaphor that includes the processes of depersonalization that have been described here. And while it is impossible to know whether the pseudopatients' responses to these processes are characteristic of all inmates—they were, after all, not real patients—it is difficult to believe that these processes of socialization to a psychiatric hospital provide useful attitudes or habits of response for living in the "real world."

Summary and Conclusions

It is clear that we cannot distinguish the sane from the insane in psychiatric hospitals. The hospital itself imposes a special environment in which the meanings of behavior can easily be misunderstood. The consequences to patients hospitalized in such an environment—the powerlessness, depersonalization, segregation, mortification, and self-labeling—seem undoubtedly countertherapeutic.

I do not, even now, understand this problem well enough to perceive solutions. But two matters seem to have some promise. The first concerns the proliferation of community mental health facilities, of crisis intervention centers, of the human potential movement, and of behavior therapies that, for all of their own problems, tend to avoid psychiatric labels, to focus on specific problems and behaviors, and to retain the individual in a relatively nonpejorative environment. Clearly, to the extent that we refrain from sending the distressed to insane places, our impressions of them are less likely to be distorted. (The risk of distorted perceptions, it seems to me, is always present, since we are much more sensitive to an individual's behaviors and verbalizations than we are to the subtle contextual stimuli that often promote them. At issue here is a matter of magnitude. And, as I have shown, the magnitude of distortion is exceedingly high in the extreme context that is a psychiatric hospital.)

The second matter that might prove promising speaks to the need to increase the sensitivity of mental health workers and researchers to the Catch 22 position of psychiatric patients. Simply reading materials in this area will be of help to some such workers and researchers. For others, directly experiencing the impact of psychiatric hospitalization will be of enormous use. Clearly, further research into the social psychology of such total institutions will both facilitate treatment and deepen understanding.

I and the other pseudopatients in the psychiatric setting had distinctly negative reactions. We do not pretend to describe the subjective experiences of true patients. Theirs may be different from ours, particularly with the passage of time and the necessary process of adaptation to one's environment. But we can and do speak to the relatively more objective indices of treatment within the hospital. It could be a mistake, and a very unfortunate one, to consider that what happened to us derived from malice or stupidity on the part of the staff. Quite the contrary, our overwhelming impression of them was of people who really cared, who were committed and who were uncommonly intelligent. Where they failed, as they sometimes did painfully, it would be more accurate to attribute those failures to the environment in which they, too, found themselves than to personal callousness. Their perceptions and behavior were controlled by the situation, rather than being motivated by a malicious disposition. In a more benign environment, one that was less attached to global diagnosis, their behaviors and judgments might have been more benign and effective.

References

1. P. Ash, *J. Abnorm. Soc. Psychol.* 44, 272 (1949); A.T. Beck, *Amer. J. Psychiat.* 119, 210 (1962); A.T. Boisen, *Psychiatry* 2, 233 (1938); N. Kreitman, *J. Ment. Sci.* 107, 876 (1961); N. Kreitman, P. Sainsbury, J. Morrisey, J. Towers, J. Scrivener, *ibid.*, p. 887; H.O. Schmitt and C.P. Fonda, *J. Abnorm. Soc. Psychol.* 52, 262 (1956); W. Seeman, *J. Nerv. Ment. Dis.* 118, 541 (1953). For an analysis of these artifacts and summaries of the disputes, see J. Zubin, *Annu. Rev. Psychol.* 18, 373 (1967); L. Phillips and J.G. Draguns, *ibid.* 22, 447 (1971).
2. R. Benedict, *J. Gen. Psychol.* 10, 59 (1934).
3. See in this regard H. Becker, *Outsiders: Studies in the Sociology of Deviance* (Free Press, New York, 1963); B.M. Braginsky, D.D. Braginsky, K. Ring, *Methods of Madness: The Mental Hospital as a Last Resort* (Holt, Rinehart & Winston, New York, 1969); G.M. Crocetti and P.V. Lemkau, *Amer. Sociol. Rev.* 30, 577 (1965); E. Goffman, *Behavior in Public Places* (Free Press, New York, 1964); R.D. Laing, *The Divided Self: A Study of Sanity and Madness* (Quadrangle, Chicago, 1960); D.L. Phillips, *Amer. Sociol. Rev.* 28, 963 (1963); T.R. Sarbin, *Psychol. Today* 6, 18 (1972); E. Schur, *Amer. J. Sociol.* 75, 309 (1969); T. Szasz, *Law, Liberty and Psychiatry* (Macmillan, New York, 1963); *The Myth of Mental Illness: Foundations of a Theory of Mental Illness* (Hoeber-Harper, New York, 1963). For a critique of some of these views, see W.R. Gove, *Amer. Sociol. Rev.* 35, 873 (1970).
4. E. Goffman, *Asylums* (Doubleday, Garden City, N.Y., 1961).

5. T.J. Scheff, *Being Mentally Ill: A Sociological Theory* (Aldine, Chicago, 1966).

6. Data from a ninth pseudopatient are not incorporated in this report because, although his sanity went undetected, he falsified aspects of his personal history, including his marital status and parental relationships. His experimental behaviors therefore were not identical to those of the other pseudopatients.

7. A. Barry, *Bellevue Is a State of Mind* (Harcourt Brace Jovanovich, New York, 1971); I. Belknap, *Human Problems of a State Mental Hospital* (McGraw-Hill, New York, 1956); W. Caudill, F.C. Redlich, H.R. Gilmore, E.B. Brody, *Amer. J. Orthopsychiat.* 22, 314 (1952); A.R. Goldman, R.H. Bohr, T.A. Steinberg, *Prof. Psychol.* 1, 427 (1970); unauthored, *Roche Report* 1 (No. 13), 8 (1971).

8. Beyond the personal difficulties that the pseudopatient is likely to experience in the hospital, there are legal and social ones that, combined, require considerable attention before entry. For example, once admitted to a psychiatric institution, it is difficult, if not impossible, to be discharged on short notice, state law to the contrary notwithstanding. I was not sensitive to these difficulties at the outset of the project, nor to the personal and situational emergencies that can arise, but later a writ of habeas corpus was prepared for each of the entering pseudopatients and an attorney was kept "on call" during every hospitalization. I am grateful to John Kaplan and Robert Bartels for legal advice and assistance in these matters.

9. However distasteful such concealment is, it was a necessary first step to examining these questions. Without concealment, there would have been no way to know how valid these experiences were; nor was there any way of knowing whether whatever detections occurred were a tribute to the diagnostic acumen of the staff or to the hospital's rumor network. Obviously, since my concerns are general ones that cut across individual hospitals and staffs, I have respected their anonymity and have eliminated clues that might lead to their identification.

10. Interestingly, of the 12 admissions, 11 were diagnosed as schizophrenic and one, with the identical symptomatology, as manic-depressive psychosis. This diagnosis has a more favorable prognosis, and it was given by the only private hospital in our sample. On the relations between social class and psychiatric diagnosis, see A. deB. Hollingshead and F.C. Redlich, *Social Class and Mental Illness: A Community Study* (Wiley, New York, 1958).

11. It is possible, of course, that patients have quite broad latitudes in diagnosis and therefore are inclined to call many people sane, even those whose behavior is patently aberrant. However, although we have no hard data on this matter, it was our distinct impression that this was not the case. In many instances, patients not only singled us out for attention, but came to imitate our behaviors and styles.

12. J. Cumming and E. Cumming, *Community Ment. Health* 1, 135 (1965); A. Farina and K. Ring, *J. Abnorm. Psychol.* 70, 47 (1965); H.E. Freeman and O.G. Simmons, *The Mental Patient Comes Home* (Wiley, New York, 1963); W.J. Johannsen, *Ment. Hygiene* 53, 218 (1969); A.S. Linsky, *Soc. Psychiat.* 5, 166 (1970).

13. S.E. Asch, *J. Abnorm. Soc. Psychol.* 41, 258 (1946); *Social Psychology* (Prentice-Hall, New York, 1952).

14. See also I.N. Mensh and J. Wishner, *J. Personality* 16, 188 (1947); J. Wishner, *Psychol. Rev.* 67, 96 (1960); J.S. Bruner and R. Tagiuri, in *Handbook of Social Psychology*, G. Lindzey, Ed. (Addison-Wesley, Cambridge, Mass., 1954), vol. 2, pp. 634-654; J.S. Bruner, D. Shapiro, R. Tagiuri, in *Person Perception and Interpersonal Behavior*, R. Tagiuri and L. Petrullo, Eds. (Stanford Univ. Press, Stanford, Calif., 1958), pp. 277-288.

15. For an example of a similar self-fulfilling prophecy, in this instance dealing with the "central" trait of intelligence, see R. Rosenthal and L. Jacobson, *Pygmalion in the Classroom* (Holt, Rinehart & Winston, New York, 1968).

16. E. Zigler and L. Phillips, *J. Abnorm. Soc. Psychol.* 63, 69 (1961). See also R.K. Freudenberg and J.P. Robertson, *A.M.A. Arch. Neurol. Psychiatr.* 76, 14 (1956).

17. W. Mischel, *Personality and Assessment* (Wiley, New York, 1968).

18. The most recent and unfortunate instance of this tenet is that of Senator Thomas Eagleton.

19. T.R. Sarbin and J.C. Mancuso, *J. Clin. Consult. Psychol.* 35, 159 (1970); T.R. Sarbin, *ibid.* 31, 447 (1967); J.C. Nunnally, Jr., *Popular Conceptions of Mental Health* (Holt, Rinehart & Winston, New York, 1961).

20. A.H. Stanton and M.S. Schwartz, *The Mental Hospital: A Study of Institutional Participation in Psychiatric Illness and Treatment* (Basic, New York, 1954).

21. D.B. Wexler and S.E. Scoville, *Ariz. Law Rev.* 13, 1 (1971).

I thank W. Mischel, E. Orne, and M.S. Rosenhan for comments on an earlier draft of this manuscript.

19

Etiology, the Social Environment, and the Prevention of Psychological Dysfunction

Richard H. Price
Indiana University

Currently there is considerable controversy in the mental health field concerning the most suitable theoretical approach or perspective for understanding abnormal behavior. I have argued elsewhere (Price, 1972) that the current state of the field of psychopathology bears certain similarities to what Kuhn (1962) has described as a "paradigm clash." In a field undergoing such a conflict over paradigms, a variety of fundamentally different viewpoints compete for ascendancy. Previously unquestioned assumptions about the nature and etiology of abnormal behavior may be under attack from a variety of different quarters. Only in a field undergoing this kind of scientific revolution could a proponent of one view assert that "mental illness is a myth" (Szasz, 1961), while another could argue that "personality disorder *is* disease" (Ausubel, 1961).

Although Szasz and Ausubel made these assertions about the nature of abnormal behavior over ten years ago, the controversy is far from over. Kuhn (1962) has argued that the examination of textbooks in any given field is a fairly good indication of the state of generally accepted knowledge in that field. By that standard, the field of abnormal psychology continues to be in a state of conceptual conflict. The conflict is clearly acknowledged in many recent texts by the dutiful inclusion of separate sections on biological, socio-cultural, and learning viewpoints.

Biotropes and Sociotropes

One dominant theme that runs through the current controversy involves the relative importance of biological versus social determinants of abnormal behavior. That we could be arguing about the relative importance of these two classes of determinants instead of asking the more reasonable question, "What role does each of these sets of determinants play in the ultimate expression of abnormal behavior?" is an indication of the level of thinking in this field.

If we can step back from the conflict for a moment, we can see two camps of advocates. One camp wishes to make strong claims for the importance of biological determinants in abnormal behavior, while steadfastly minimizing evidence implicating the role of social factors. The other asserts the importance of social factors, while systematically ignoring the role of biologically determined individual differences. We have become what Meehl (1972) has called "biotropes" or "sociotropes." These "tropisms" serve to impede rather than to advance our understanding of the nature of the development of psychological dysfunction, and frequently, as we shall see, produce confusion about the nature of appropriate interventions.

There are a variety of reasons for this polarization. It is worthwhile to examine some of these reasons, since they help to illuminate the context in which persons in the mental health field do their research and treatment.

The first class of reasons can be described roughly as conceptual. Sociologists and other researchers principally concerned with the social reaction to various forms of deviant behavior have come to conceive of the problem of abnormal behavior in a very different way from psychologists and psychiatrists, who have emphasized the role of individual differences. Thus, students of society have quite understandably come to assume that the variables with which they are most concerned, such as those of social power, status, and community norms, are of great importance in the expression and maintenance of psychopathology.

Psychologists and psychiatrists, on the other hand, who are typically concerned with the experiential and genetic determinants of individual differences, have come to consider these variables as the most important determinants of abnormal behavior. Consequently, proponents of each point of view have come to "see" the problem of abnormal behavior quite differently (Price, 1972). At their worst, such differences in emphasis result in the advocacy of simplistic single-cause conceptions of abnormal behavior.

A second reason for the biotrope-sociotrope polarization is ideological, and revolves around the question of the rights of the individual as opposed to those of society (Price & Denner, 1973; Denner & Price, 1973). Strong proponents of the defense of individual rights tend to argue that nearly any form of social intervention in response to the behavior of an individual represents a threat to the right of self-determination of that individual. On the other hand, defenders of the rights of society argue that society has the right to protection, and that treatment is merely for the individual's own good. Becker (1964) has described these ideological differences in terms of what he calls "conventional and unconventional sentimentality." These ideological positions are also often tied to preconceptions about the etiology of mental illness. Champions of individual rights tend to attribute the major causes of psychopathology to unjust or capricious social forces, while supporters of the rights of society usually attribute abnormal behavior to individual failings.

A third reason for the biotrope-sociotrope polarization is methodological. Almost invariably we observe abnormal behavior after it has already developed. In the laboratory or the clinic both biological and social variables have produced the behavioral end state that we observe, but at this stage it is very difficult to disentangle the effects of one set of determinants from the other. Thus, in our current state of relative ignorance, it is all too easy for proponents of the biological or the social view to regard the already developed dysfunction as an exclusive product of either biological or social factors.

Assumptions About Etiology and Intervention

The biological-sociological conflict currently existing in the field of psycho-pathology primarily concerns the question of etiology. That is, differences among theoreticians largely revolve around the question of "the cause" of abnormal behavior. Aside from presupposing an unworkably simple causal model for the development of abnormal behavior, this conflict has another extremely important effect: *Our assumptions about etiology strongly condition our notions of appropriate intervention.*

This point is brought forceably home in a recent article by Caplan and Nelson (1973). They argue:

What is done about a problem depends on how it is defined. The way a social problem is defined determines the attempts at remediation—or even whether such attempts will be made—by suggesting both the *foci* and the *techniques* of intervention and by ruling out alternative possibilities. More specifically, problem definition determines the change strategy, the selection of a social action delivery system, and the criteria for evaluation.

Problem definitions are based on assumptions about the causes of the problem and where they lie. If the causes of delinquency, for example, are defined in *person-centered* terms (e.g., inability to delay gratification, or incomplete sexual identity), then it would be logical to initiate *person-change* treatment techniques and intervention strategies to deal with the problem. . . . If, on the other hand, explanations are *situation centered*, for example, if delinquency were interpreted as the substitution of extralegal paths for already preempted, conventionally approved pathways for achieving socially valued goals, then efforts toward corrective treatment would logically have a *system-change* orientation. Efforts would be launched to create suitable opportunities for success and achievement along conventional lines; thus existing physical, social, or economic arrangements, not individual psyches, would be the targets for change (p. 200-201).

Of course Caplan and Nelson's argument does not hold only for delinquency. They note, "whether the social problem to be attacked is delinquency, mental health, drug abuse, unemployment, ghetto riots or whatever, the significance of the defining process is the same: *the action (or inaction) taken will depend largely on whether causes are seen as residing within individuals or in the environment.*" (p. 201)

Although our notions about the etiology of a particular disorder will strongly condition our ideas about the "most appropriate" intervention for that disorder, it does *not* follow that these ideas about intervention are necessarily correct. That is, it is quite possible that social interventions would be highly appropriate for disorders having a substantial biological substrate, and vice versa.

In order to illustrate this point more clearly let us take as an example Meehl's (1962) theoretical account of the broad outlines of the development of schizophrenia. Meehl suggests that we consider seriously the concept of *specific etiology*. Briefly, this concept refers to that causal condition which is necessary but not sufficient for an illness to occur. Thus, the causal factor which is designated as the specific etiology must be present for the illness to occur, but may not by itself produce the illness. The specific etiology, whatever it may be, is the essential condition, however, for the occurrence of the disorder.

Meehl uses the whimsical analogy of a "color psychosis" to illustrate the concept of specific etiology. He points out that the specific etiology of color blindness is known to involve a mutated gene on the X chromosome. If an individual who possessed this specific etiology and who therefore was color blind grew up in a society that was entirely oriented around making fine color discriminations, he might develop a "color psychosis." Cultural and social factors would inevitably play a role in the development of his disorder. Nevertheless, if we ask what is the specific etiology of color psychosis, the answer must be the mutated gene on the X chromosome.

Meehl has been careful to point out, however, that when the concept of specific etiology is applied to a disorder such as schizophrenia, a number of misunderstandings may arise. In particular, he notes that the presence of the etiological factor does *not* necessarily produce the clinically observed disorder, and that the course of the disorder is not treatable only by procedures which are directed against the specific etiology itself. Furthermore, the largest source of variance in symptoms is not necessarily due to the specific etiology. These qualifications make it clear that the notion of specific etiology does not imply a simple cause-effect relationship between etiological factors and symptoms. In fact, there may be a large number of links in the causal chain—and a correspondingly large number of points for intervention—between the specific etiology and the symptoms ultimately displayed by the individual.

The point here is straightforward. Clearly, even for disorders which may have a specific etiology of genetic origin, social factors may still determine to a very large degree whether the disorder in question actually occurs or not. This last point is crucial, especially in the case of the prevention of psychological disorders.

Let us consider for a moment the remarks of an epidemiologist concerned with the questions of disease and its prevention.

In recent decades, epidemiologists who have worked on noninfectious diseases have found the one-agent disease model less and less useful, and the term "multi-factorial causation" has been adopted. The phrase is lacking in grace, but expresses a concept that more nearly approaches reality. Indeed, the notion that an illness results from a complex net of antecedent events and circumstances is very useful to epidemiologists in dealing with both infectious and noninfectious processes. The key is that epidemiology is directed toward prevention, rather than therapy, and whereas therapy tends strongly to become more effective as it becomes more specific, *prevention may be accomplished by altering environmental circumstances far removed from a particular host-parasite interaction.* We may even suggest, tentatively, that prevention becomes more powerful as procedures are less disease-specific, but this is so heretical an idea that it must be handled very gingerly (Stallones, 1973, p. 29, italics added).

Research on the Social Environment and Its Role in the Prevention of Psychological Dysfunction

In the past, the principal efforts of mental health practitioners have been directed at the treatment of mental dysfunction rather than at its prevention. There are compelling reasons to believe, however, that this strategy will in the long run be a losing battle. Even leaving aside the question of the effectiveness of current therapies, the allocation of resources to treat psychological dysfunctions is limited and will surely not grow as rapidly as the incidence of psychological dysfunction itself. Thus, there promises to be an ever widening gap between the need for treatment resources, however effective, and our ability to deliver them.

Consequently, many workers in the general field of community mental health have argued that primary prevention, that is, attempts to prevent psychological dysfunction and therefore to reduce the rates of occurrence of disorder in the population at large, is in the long run the only acceptable strategy that we have available to us. Primary prevention activities are aimed at groups and communities of individuals who have not yet shown signs of psychological dysfunction. The purpose of these activities is to prevent the occurrence of dysfunction rather than to merely limit its duration once it has already occurred (Bloom, 1968).

Within those efforts that can be identified as primary prevention, a further distinction is often made between systems-centered and person-centered efforts

(Cowen, 1973; Caplan, 1964). Person-centered preventive approaches usually are directed at individuals who may be at risk for the development of psychological disorder. Once individuals at risk for psychological disorder are identified, attempts are then made to intervene with these individuals via special training or education in order to reduce the risk of disorder among those individuals. Systems-centered approaches, on the other hand, are directed at key social institutions and settings in the environment which are presumed to affect human functioning for better or for worse. As Moos (1973) has argued:

Essentially, every institution in our society is attempting to set up conditions that it hopes will maximize certain types of behaviors and/or certain factors of development. Families, hospitals, prisons, business organizations, secondary schools, universities, communes, groups, and, for that matter, entire societies are all engaged in setting up environmental conditions which will have certain effects. In this sense it may be cogently argued that the most important task for the behavioral and social sciences should be the systematic description and classification of environments and their differential costs and benefits to adaptation. (p. 662)

One rapidly growing field that may provide the answers to system-centered preventive mental health efforts is that of environmental psychology (Moos, 1973; Craik, 1973; Barker, 1968; Proshansky, Ittleson & Rivlin, 1970). But to develop a system-centered primary prevention technology, fundamental research will be required that is directed at the description of those key social settings presumed to effect psychological development. As Cowen (1973) remarks, "To understand the effects of settings on growth requires that we first develop systematic frameworks for *describing* settings—something we currently lack." Accordingly, some of the recent efforts that have been made to describe social settings will now be reviewed and their implications for a systems-centered preventive effort will be considered.

Dimensional Description of Settings

There have been a number of recent efforts to develop dimensions for the description of settings. These efforts include the work of Sells (1963) which provides an extremely comprehensive set of categories concerned with the physical, social, and behavioral characteristics of settings. Krause (1970) has offered a more abstract theoretical set of seven subclasses of dimensions which are interactional in nature and include such behaviors as joint working, trading, fighting, sponsored teaching, and self-disclosure. Astin (1962) has factor-analyzed a large number of college environments based on items obtained from public sources. Astin's analysis provided five factors: affluence, size, masculinity, homogeneity of offerings and technical emphasis.

Moos and his associates (1968a,b, 1972, 1973) have developed a number of instruments to measure the perceived climates of psychiatric treatment programs, educational environments, correctional environments, and, more recently, family settings. Although the specific dimensions developed depend upon the nature of the setting being examined, the basic dimensions fall into three general types: relationship dimensions; personal development dimensions; and systems maintenance and systems change dimensions.

In addition, Price and Bouffard (1974) have developed techniques for measuring the degree of situational constraint existing in various settings using a behavior-situation matrix. This measurement technique promises to provide information about the range and type of response hierarchies considered appropriate in various situational contexts and to provide information concerning the degree of causal attribution to the person in the setting for any given behavior. (Price & Bouffard, 1973) The attribution of the cause of behavior may be particularly important, since the strong dispositional statements inherent in psychiatric diagnoses or in the attribution of mental illness may be controlled to a substantial extent by situational variables. Goffman (1963) has noted that, in diagnosing psychological disorders, psychiatrists frequently cite aspects of the patient's behavior that are "inappropriate to the situation." Thus, such variables as situational constraint may not only affect the behavior of persons in various settings, but may also affect one's perception of others in the setting.

Another important dimensional approach to the description of settings is derived from the work of Barker (1968) and Barker and Gump (1964). Barker (1968) has outlined a theory discussing the effects of behavior setting size which was stimulated in part by a comparison of two small towns, one in Kansas and one in Yorkshire, England. The population of the Midwestern town tended to perform at least three times as often in their settings as did the residents in the English town. Barker reasoned that in order to maintain the more numerous settings in the Midwestern town, the residents were required to accept more positions of responsibility and to include in the settings larger proportions of people who are only marginally qualified to function in those settings. Thus, Barker argued that the behavior settings of the Midwestern town were "undermanned," at least compared with those of the English town.

In fact, according to Barker's theory, a number of behavioral consequences should occur for those individuals participating in undermanned settings. Thus, undermanned settings should make a greater claim on individual occupants, both by requiring greater effort and by assigning relatively more difficult and more important tasks to occupants. In addition, the range and direction of forces acting on individual occupants were thought to be greater. For example, a wider variety of activities would be required of each occupant. And, because every individual in the setting was crucial for the maintenance of the setting, there would be less sensitivity to, and evaluation of, differences among people. Furthermore, since performers in the setting would be required to carry out the variety of different tasks, it was expected that there would be, on the average, a lower level of maximum performance for occupants of the setting. Since many setting occupants would have to carry out a number of different tasks, it was thought unlikely that any single occupant would achieve great proficiency at any one task. Finally, the joint influence of greater strength of forces on occupants of undermanned settings as well as a greater range of forces would result in each individual having greater functional importance within a setting, more responsibility, and a greater feeling of functional self-identity.

Experimental tests of these ideas were carried out in Barker and Gump's (1964) now well-known work on differences in the size of schools and their effect on their inhabitants. Baird (1969) was able to replicate and extend Barker and Gump's original findings in both high-school and college populations. Willems (1967, 1969) has extended the work on undermanned settings still further by examining the effects of undermanned and overmanned settings on marginal and regular students. In two field studies, Willems was able to demonstrate not only the usual effect, that small schools produced a much higher average sense of obligation among students, but also that the difference between marginal and regular students in small schools with respect to their sense of obligation was virtually nonexistent. In large schools, on the other hand, marginal students felt a much lower sense of obligation when compared with regular students. As Willems puts it, "It would appear that the small school marginal students were not experientially and behaviorally marginal while their large school counterparts were a group of relative outsiders" (Willems, 1967, pp. 1257-1258).

Wicker and his colleagues (1973) have reformulated the theory of undermanning and have examined the effect of setting size in church settings as well as in the school settings. Wicker has moved away from the measures of the absolute size of settings to more precisely defined measures involving the capacity of settings, the number of applicants to those settings, and number of persons necessary to maintain settings. He has also differentiated the roles of setting inhabitants as performers and nonperformers. This more precise specification of setting demands and characteristics promises to be of value in understanding the role and setting requirements for participation of individuals in the settings themselves.

The mental health applications of undermanning theory are several. First, the results of research in this area suggest that marginal individuals may have less opportunity to develop social skills necessary for coping and adaptation in large, overmanned settings. On the other hand, in undermanned settings the same individuals will feel a greater sense of obligation, will participate to a greater degree, and will be evaluated less negatively than they would in large settings. Thus, relatively undermanned settings may have substantially more potential for psychological growth than overmanned settings.

In addition, the undermanning literature suggests that attempts to reduce the number of participants in overmanned settings or increase the number of the settings available to applicants might provide simple but powerful preventive interventions that would have positive effects on individual growth and development.

The Taxonomic Classification of Settings

Previous efforts at classification in the field of mental health have been directed almost exclusively at the classification of psychological disorders and at the classification of individuals according to particular patterns of behavior or symptoms. Only recently have researchers concerned themselves with the systematic classification of social settings or environments (Craik 1973; Fredericksen, 1972; Indik, 1968; Moos, 1973; Price, 1974; Price and Blashfield, 1973; Sells, 1968).

There are a number of important purposes served in the development of setting taxonomies. Blashfield (1972) has suggested four such purposes for taxonomies in general: the development of a standard nomenclature; the development of a descriptive system; the prediction of behavior; and an aid in theory construction. The usefulness of a common nomenclature becomes immediately evident when one considers the various ways in which concepts such as that of "situation" or "setting" have been used in the behavioral sciences. A standard nomenclature also facilitates scientific communication among workers in the same or related fields. As Altman and Lett (1970) have noted, a good taxonomy should provide a standard meta-language to describe the concepts and variables in a given field.

One important descriptive purpose of taxonomic classification is that empirically or theoretically important differences and similarities among diverse entities in the classification system can be discovered and described. Description of the structure and relationships among the entities under consideration is also made possible by the taxonomic approach.

Taxonomies may also serve the purpose of prediction. Fredericksen (1972) has described how a taxonomy of situations may facilitate the prediction of individual behavior. He notes that, in psychology, the prediction of individual behavior has been based almost exclusively on individual differences in personality or abilities. There is no reason, however, for excluding situational variables as predictors of future individual behavior.

A final important purpose of taxonomy of settings is that of theory construction. Sells (1968), Altman (1968), Indik (1968) and others have suggested that the classification of settings may provide the basis for systems-oriented models within a particular research domain.

One such recent attempt to derive a taxonomy of settings has been conducted by Price and Blashfield (1973). Data obtained by Roger Barker on the entire population of behavior settings ($N = 455$) measured on 43 different variables in a small Midwestern town were examined. In the first of two studies, Price and Blashfield obtained factor-analytically derived dimensions or attributes along which behavior settings vary. They found that age, sex, and the role of behavior setting participants, as well as setting duration and activities within the settings (business, religious, and school), all constituted important dimensions of those settings.

Price and Blashfield's second study represented an initial attempt to classify behavior settings on the basis of their similarity in measured characteristics. A cluster analysis of the 455 settings yielded 12 distinct clusters or behavior setting types. A number of these setting types (e.g., youth performance settings, religious settings, men's and women's organizations) appeared to be of the kind that community mental health researchers would find of interest. It may be, for example, that different setting types may promote different types of coping skills and social competence.

Recently, practitioners of community psychology and community mental health have begun to emphasize even more strongly the need for information concerning the structure and dynamics of communities in which community mental health practitioners work (e.g., Golann and Eisdorfer 1972). Analyses like the one conducted by Price and Blashfield may provide useful insights into those settings particularly designed to provide specific skills and competence in specific target populations through the enactment of various roles.

The small rural town analyzed by Price and Blashfield was characterized by a relatively large number of settings associated with religious organizations and with the schools. Community mental health workers have been particularly interested in the social environments of schools (e.g., Trickett, Kelly and Todd 1972) and in religious systems (e.g., Tapp and Tapp 1972) as sources of individual support, control, and change. Taxonomic studies of the behavior settings of entire towns could prove useful in isolating systems and target individuals particularly relevant to these concerns.

The Concept of Person-Environment Fit

None of the foregoing discussion of research describing various settings either on a dimensional or typological basis should be construed to imply that all persons within a particular type of setting are affected in the same way by the characteristics of that setting. On the contrary, there is a large body of research which indicates that substantial interactions exist between the type of person inhabiting a particular kind of setting and the characteristics of the setting itself (Moos, 1969; Endler and Hunt, 1968). What is needed, then, is not only a system for describing settings, but a system which jointly describes the relationship of the characteristics of individuals to particular setting characteristics.

One promising line of attack on this problem is the work of French, Rodgers and Cobb (1972). Their conception of *person-environment fit* attempts to deal simultaneously with a number of different processes and elements. Those aspects of the environment that can be construed as "demands" are considered, as well as those that can be thought of as "resources" or "need satisfiers." In the realm of individual differences, the individual's "needs" as well as his "abilities" or "resources" are considered. Crucial to this approach is the discovery of the relationship (that is, the interaction or pairing) between environmental demands and the resources of the individual. The person-environment-fit framework considers the consequences of this relation both in terms of individual growth and psychological dysfunction.

Much of the initial empirical work using the person-environment-fit framework has been in the domain of organizational stress and studies of the effect of the work environment (Kahn 1973; Cobb 1973; French 1973). However, Pervin (1968) has discussed the issues of individual-environment fit in a somewhat broader context and has also reported work (Pervin, 1967) on the relationship between individual students' perception of the educational environment and their self-perceptions. His initial results suggest that it may be possible to predict student dropouts on this basis. Thus, the person-environment-fit concept has the advantage of simultaneously considering individual differences, environmental factors, and their interaction in the development of psychological dysfunction.

It is likely that these new research directions on man-environment relations will play an important role in the future development of efforts in the primary prevention of psychological dysfunction. As Klein notes:

The task appears to be the painstaking one of increasing our understanding of man-in-environment; that is, the interactions whereby the community shapes the development of individuals, introduces stress into their lives, and mediates ways in which the emotional hazards of living are dealt with for better or worse. One key to primary prevention in mental health, the community psychologist holds, is the community itself. As we shape the community towards meeting the needs of individuals for safety, security, and personal significance throughout the life cycle, we become truly engaged with mental *health* rather than mental *disorder*. (1971, p. *x*)

References

Altman, I., and Lett, F.E. The ecology of interpersonal relationships: A classification system and conceptual model, in J.E. McGrath (Ed.), *Social and psychological factors in stress*, pp. 177-201. New York: Holt, Rinehart & Winston, 1970.

Astin, A.W. An empirical characterization of higher educational institutions. *Journal of Educational Psychology, 53*, 224-235, 1962.

Ausubel, D.P. Personality disorder *is* disease. *American Psychologist, 16*, 69-74, 1961.

Baird, L.L. Big school, small school: A critical examination of the hypothesis. *Journal of Educational Psychology, 60,* 253-260, 1969.

Barker, R.G. *Ecological Psychology: Concepts and Methods for Studying the Environment of Human Behavior.* Stanford, Calif.: Stanford University Press, 1968.

Barker, R.G., and Gump, P.V. *Big School, Small School.* Stanford, Calif.: Stanford University Press, 1964.

Becker, H.S. *Outsiders: Studies in the Sociology of Deviance.* New York: Free Press, 1964.

Blashfield, R.K. *An Evaluation of the DSM-II Classification of Schizophrenia.* Doctoral dissertation, Indiana University, Bloomington, Ind., 1972.

Bloom, B.L. The evaluation of primary prevention programs, in L.M. Roberts, N.S. Greenfield, and M.H. Miller. *Comprehensive Mental Health: The Challenge of Evaluation.* Madison, Wis.: The University of Wisconsin Press, 1968.

Caplan, G. *Principles of Preventive Psychiatry.* New York: Basic Books, 1964.

Caplan, N., and Nelson, S.D. On being useful: The nature and consequences of psychological research on social problems. *American Psychologist, 28,* 199-211, 1973.

Cobb, S. Role responsibility: the differentiation of a concept. *Occupational Mental Health, 3,* 10-14, 1973.

Cowen, E.L. Social and community interventions. *Annual Review of Psychology,* 423-472, 1973.

Craik, K.H. Environmental psychology. *Annual Review of Psychology,* 403-422, 1973.

Denner, B., and Price, R.H. (Eds.). *Community Mental Health: Social Action and Reaction.* New York: Holt, Rinehart & Winston, 1973.

Endler, N.S., and Hunt, J. McV. S-R inventories of hostility and comparisons of the proportions of variance from persons, responses, and situations for hostility and anxiousness. *Journal of Personality and Social Psychology, 9,* 309-315, 1968.

Frederiksen, N. Toward a taxonomy of situations. *American Psychologist, 27,* 114-123, 1972.

French, J.R.P. Person role fit. *Occupational Mental Health, 3,* 15-20, 1973.

French, J.R.P., Rodgers, W., and Cobb, S. Adjustment as person-environment fit, in D. Hamburg and G. Coelho (Eds.), *Coping and Adaptation,* in press, 1973.

Goffman, E. *Behavior in Public Places: Notes on the Social Organization of Gatherings.* New York: Free Press, 1963.

Golann, Stewart E., and Eisdorfer, Carl (Eds.). *Handbook of Community Mental Health.* New York: Appleton-Century-Crofts, 1972.

Indik, B.P. The scope of the problem and some suggestions toward a solution. In B.P. Indels and F.K. Berrien (Eds.), *People, Groups, and Organizations.* Columbia University: Teachers College Press, 1968.

Kahn, R.L. Conflict, ambiguity, and overload: Three problems in job stress. *Occupational Mental Health, 3,* 2-9, 1973.

Klein, D.C. Preface, in G. Rosenblum (Ed.), *Issues in Community Psychology and Preventive Mental Health.* New York: Behavioral Publications, 1971.

Krause, M.S. Use of social situations for research purposes. *American Psychologist, 25,* 748-753, 1970.

Kuhn, T.S. *The Structure of Scientific Revolutions.* Chicago: University of Chicago Press, 1962.

Meehl, P. Schizotaxia, schizotypy, schizophrenia. *American Psychologist, 17,* 827-838, 1962.

Meehl, P. Specific genetic etiology, psychodynamics, and therapeutic nihilism. *International Journal of Mental Health, 1,* 10-27, 1972.

Moos, R. Assessment of the psychosocial environments of community-oriented psychiatric treatment programs. *Journal of Abnormal Psychology, 79,* 9-18, 1972.

Moos, R. The assessment of the social climates of correctional institutions. *Journal of Research in Crime and Delinquency, 5,* 174-188, 1968a.

Moos, R. *Evaluating Treatment Environments: A Social Ecological Approach.* New York: Wiley, 1974.

Moos, R.H. Conceptualizations of human environments. *American Psychologist, 28,* 652-665, 1973.

Moos, R.H. Situational analysis of a therapeutic community milieu. *Journal of Abnormal Psychology, 73,* 49-61, 1968b.

Moos, R.H. Sources of variance in response to questionnaires and in behavior. *Journal of Abnormal Psychology, 74,* 405-412, 1969.

Pervin, L.A. Performance and satisfaction as a function of individual-environment fit. *Psychological Bulletin, 69,* 56-68, 1968.

Pervin, L.A. A twenty-college study of student x college interaction using TAPE (Transactional Analysis of Personality and Environment): Rationale, reliability, and validity. *Journal of Educational Psychology, 58,* 290-302, 1967.

Price, R.H. *Abnormal Behavior: Perspectives in Conflict.* New York: Holt, Rinehart & Winston, 1972.

Price, R.H. The taxonomic classification of behaviors and situations and the problem of behavior-environment congruence. *Human Relations,* 1974 (in press).

Price, R.H., and Blashfield, R.K. Explorations in the taxonomy of behavior settings: Analyses of dimensions and classification of settings. Unpublished manuscript, Indiana University, 1973.

Price, R.H., and Bouffard, D.L. Behavioral appropriateness and situational constraint as dimensions of social behavior. *Journal of Personality and Social Psychology,* 1974 (in press).

Price, R.H., and Bouffard, D.L. Behavioral and situational determinants of causal attribution. Unpublished manuscript, Indiana University, 1973.

Price, R.H., and Denner, B., (Eds.). *The Making of a Mental Patient.* New York: Holt, Rinehart & Winston, 1973.

Proshansky, H.M., Ittleson, W.H., and Rivlin, L.G. *Environmental Psychology: Man and His Physical Setting.* New York: Holt, Rinehart & Winston, 1970.

Sells, S.B. General theoretical problems related to organizational taxonomy: A model solution. In B.P. Indik and F.K. Berrien, (Eds.), *People, Groups and Organizations.* Columbia University: Teachers College Press, 1968.

Sells, S.B., (Ed.). *Stimulus Determinants of Behavior.* New York: Ronald Press, 1963.

Stallones, R.A. The epidemiologist as environmentalist. *International Journal of Health Services, 3,* 29-33, 1973.

Szasz, T.S. The myth of mental illness. *American Psychologist, 15,* 113-118, 1960.

Tapp, R.B., and Tapp, J. Religious systems as sources of control and support, in S.E. Golann and C. Eisdorfer (Eds.), *Handbook of Community Mental Health.* New York: Appleton-Century-Crofts, 1972.

Trickett, E.J., Kelly, J.C., and Todd, D.M. The social environment of the high school: Guidelines for organizational change and organizational redevelopment. In S.E. Golann and C. Eisdorfer (Eds.), *Handbook of Community Mental Health.* New York: Appleton-Century-Crofts, 1972.

Wicker, A.W. Undermanning theory and research: Implications for the study of psychological and behavioral effects of excess populations. *Representative Research in Social Psychology, 4,* 185-206, 1973.

Willems, E.P. Sense of obligation to high school activities as related to school size and marginality of student. *Child Development, 38,* No. 4, 1247-1260, December 1967.

Willems, E.P., and Raush, H.L. *Naturalistic Viewpoints in Psychological Research.* New York: Holt, Rinehart & Winston, 1969.

VII

Drugs
and Social
Consequences

Commentary. The taking of drugs can be traced to the earliest recorded history of man. During the paleolithic era, for example, hallucinogenic drugs were derived from mushrooms in Siberia and the Far East to induce cheer, intoxication, and courage for tribal attacks (Brekhman and Sam, 1967). Opium and its derivatives have been used nearly 7000 years and were considered a panacea by medical practitioners of ancient times (Galen, A.D., 130-201), and even by physicians as recently as early twentieth century. One of its derivatives, morphine, became particularly popular during the Civil War, when it received wide use by wounded soldiers and those suffering from dysentery. As a consequence many Civil War veterans returned home with a condition referred to as "soldier's illness," a euphemism for morphine addiction. To treat this problem a new drug was developed that was not only less expensive as a pain reliever but which acted more rapidly to produce the desired effect. This drug, heroin, became widely prescribed in place of morphine until 1914, when the United States Congress enacted the Harrison Act, which prohibited the unauthorized sale and use of narcotic drugs (Blum, 1969).

The social consequences of this congressional act were dramatic. Almost overnight the once tolerated narcotic user became a criminal and an "addict." With the source of narcotics cut off through legal means, many turned to illegal activities in order to maintain a habit whose annual cost in the United States has been estimated to exceed eight billion dollars (Ingersoll, 1970).

According to Szasz, (1973) drug-taking has the attraction of "forbidden fruit." The more strictly it is forbidden, the greater its attraction. This view fits well with a hypothesis described in the next chapter, by Gary Fisher and Irma Strantz. They suggest that one can make predictions about behavior on the basis of man's need to explore novel experiences and participate in diverse social settings. Thus, one adaptive or coping style for a person with high exploration needs might be to seek out an environment where drug-taking is reinforced.

Apropos of this view, Jack Monroe suggests in Chapter 21 that once a person is addicted to drugs his life style becomes defined by particular environments, such as "pick-up points" where addicts obtain their illegal supply of narcotics, and environments related to "pushing" or "hustling" or illegal activities. Thus one important approach to the study of drug addiction is assessing the likelihood that an environment encourages or discourages drug taking.

Monroe distinguishes another crucial parameter defining the environment of the drug addict. He suggests that the environment relevant to the drug addict and his behavior is that which is filtered through his perceptions. This logic and approach to the study of environments has been fully developed by Moos (1974) and Moos, Shelton, and Petty (1973) who have demonstrated that outcome variables are strongly related to the way one perceives the environment.

While society no longer sanctions taking narcotics without medical approval, cigarette smoking is not only tolerated but encouraged in many environments. McArthur, Waldron, and Dickinson (1958) have suggested that the social milieu is the most important determinant in smoking behavior. In fact both current studies and historical data indicate that exposure to others who smoke, particularly if they are admired or have status, contributes significantly to the development of the smoking habit (Salber and MacMahon, 1961; Salber, MacMahon, and Harrison, 1963).

In the last chapter in this section, Bernard Mausner presents an ecological model for smoking behavior, and illustrates how the social environment encourages cigarette smoking. For example, one finds special areas set aside for smoking, with tables, matches, and ashtrays providing a framework that reinforces the tendency to smoke, as do displays of cigarettes and cigarette advertising.

Mausner suggests that the survival of cigarette smoking in contemporary society is related to the way in which cigarette smoking is perceived as an important aid to coping.

References

Brekhman, I.I., and Sam, Y.A. Psychoactive preparations used by paleoasiatic people. *Roche Report, 4*(8), 3, 1967.

Blum, R. *Society and Drugs, I.* San Francisco: Jossey-Bass, 1969.

Galen, A.D., cited in Blum, R. *Society and Drugs.* San Francisco: Jossey-Bass, 1969.

Ingersoll, J.E. Drug menace; how serious? *U.S. News and World Report*, 38-42, May 25, 1970.

McArthur, C., Waldron, E., and Dickinson, J. The psychology of smoking. *Journal of Abnormal Social Psychology, 56*:267-275, 1958.

Moos, R. *Treatment Environments: A Social Ecological Approach.* New York: John Wiley & Sons, 1974.

Moos, R., Shelton, R., and Petty, C. Perceived ward climate and treatment outcome. *Journal of Abnormal Psychology, 82*:(2)291-298, 1973.

Salber, E.J., and MacMahon, B. Cigarette smoking among high school students related to social class and parental smoking habits. *American Journal of Public Health, 51*:1780-1789, 1961.

Salber, E.J., MacMahon, B., and Harrison, S.V. Influence of siblings on student smoking patterns. *Pediatrics, 31*:(4)569-572, 1963.

Szasz, T. *The Second Sin.* New York: Doubleday, 1973.

20

An Ecosystems Approach to the Study of Dangerous Drug Use and Abuse with Special Reference to the Marijuana Issue

Gary Fisher
Cedars-Sinai Medical Center, Los Angeles
Irma Strantz
School of Public Health, University of California, Los Angeles

Introduction

This paper presents an ecosystems approach to the phenomenon of drug use and attempts to demonstrate that there exists, for any one individual, a complex of interrelated variables relative to his drug use and that it is the individual's evaluation of his drug use differential to each of these variables within his total system which determines his use or abuse of any specific drug. Some of the positions taken (e.g., Barber, 1967; Goode, 1969b; McGlothlin, 1968) have been presented before and we do not lay claim to any special new insights with respect to an ecological perspective to drug use. In spite of the foregoing, the argument set forth appears to be very much in need of being made explicit because the "drug abuse" problem continues to be relentlessly pursued in the traditional, archaic and historically dysfunctional manner, i.e., *in vacuuo.* "Abuse" is defined as "the problem" and the solution is to be rid of that problem with the measures and actions to be taken all focused on eliminating "drug abuse." Unfortunately, the situation is even less enlightened than the foregoing statement would imply as the differentiation of "use" and "abuse" is seldom made.

Some effort must be given to the examination of this use-abuse concept.

Reprinted with permission from *American Journal of Public Health*, 62:1407-1414, 1972.

Logically "use" implies the consumption of a drug which results in a constructive phenomenon for the organism (either somatic or psychological) and "abuse" implies the consumption of a drug which results in some destructive phenomenon for the organism (again, either somatic or psychological). Difficulties emerge with this definition, however, because benefits supposedly accruing in the psychological realm may have deleterious effects in the somatic realm (e.g., tranquilizers may benefit a psychic state but have physiological side-effects) and benefits accruing in the somatic realm may have deleterious effects in the psychic realm (e.g., estrogen may be helpful in treating cancer of the prostate but have disturbing psychic effects). Consequently, we may have some inconsistencies utilizing this definition. Nevertheless, the core of the matter lies in the value system of the individual and his society. To say that drug usage results in some "constructive phenomena" necessitates judgments of value as to what is constructive. For instance, the administration of a specific drug in a specific situation may prolong a life but the simple prolonging of that life does not necessarily mean that this is a constructive phenomenon for the individual experiencing that prolonging. The physician may deem the drug as having constructive results because his value is to prolong his patient's life whereas the patient, because he does not value the quality of his life that is being prolonged, may deem the drug's result to be destructive. Thus we must recognize that we cannot speak of drug use and abuse or constructive or destructive results without making explicit the value judgments within which these phenomena are being considered.

In political (and social) terms, drug "abuse" currently appears to mean drug use which is outside of medical prescription and control. Thus, by definition, illicit use, i.e., non-legal drug use, is abuse. It is illegal to have in one's possession prescription drugs without a physician's prescription for that drug. Alcohol abuse presents a different definition since the legal situation differs. Since alcohol is not a prescription (medically controlled) drug but rather a socialized drug, the definition of its abuse is in social terms. Thus, society says alcohol abuse occurs when an individual's use of that drug has destructive effects in the society, i.e., when he becomes less productive economically and his contribution to his society lessens. Medically, one can define alcohol abuse when his consumption interferes significantly with his somatic functioning, and psychologically, one could define alcohol abuse when his consumption interferes with a maximally effective state of consciousness.

That drug abuse is equated with non-medical prescription use is obviously nonsense. It we utilize the same behavioral criteria espoused for the dangers of illicit drug use, i.e., drug dependence, habituation, addiction and the consequent inability of an individual to somewhat meet life's exigencies without chemical aids, then it becomes rather clear that a great deal of prescription-drug use is in fact, drug abuse. For example, it would be rather difficult to imagine that the massive prescription writing by physicians for tranquilizers, amphetamines, anti-depressants, and barbituates have only constructive results whereas the nonprescription use of these same materials have only destructive results. Yet, in fact, this is the manner in which society deals with this phenomena through its legal system. Parenthetically, we also have the interesting economic fact that almost all of the stimulant and barbituate drugs that are sold on the black market are manufactured by the large American pharmaceutical houses.

A gross example of inconsistencies within the culture is the legal situation with respect to marijuana. Viewed either transculturally or intraculturally, marijuana and aclohol have a good deal in common in terms of their basic function of altering states of consciousness. Alcohol, in the West, is socially acceptable and legal primarily because of its psychological effects in relation to the dominant ethic of the western culture, i.e., aggressive competitiveness. Marijuana, on the other hand, is socially unacceptable and illegal because its psychological effects are in opposition to that dominant ethic. Blumer, (1967), for example, found that among ghetto youths, it was the aggressive, criminally-oriented "rowdies" who predominantly utilized alcohol and it was the non-aggressive, socially-oriented, non-violent and non-criminally-oriented youths who predominantly used marijuana. On the other hand, marijuana is socially acceptable and legal in some Eastern countries because the effects it produces are consonant with the more passive, introspective, non-action orientation of Eastern religion. Alcohol tends to produce activity, marijuana passivity. In Christian theology, good "works" (action) is the key to salvation whereas in Eastern religion, submitting to The Way is the key to enlightenment. Carstairs (1954), Fisher (1968) and McGlothlin (1968) have discussed the relation between a culture's value system and its preferred drugs.

Drug use and abuse is part of a very complex psycho-ecological system. Whether an individual will use or abuse a particular mind-altering drug will depend upon a host of facts. Nine such variables are suggested and for each variable an example is given,* suggesting how this factor may interact with other factors, resulting in greater or lesser propensity for a specific drug use: 1) the social and economic system of which he is a member, i.e., the deterrent factor in terms of being apprehended for heroin could be probably greater for a person living in a ghetto home compared with someone living in an upper-class suburbia home as the probability of police raids in the two settings is markedly different; 2) the values and belief system of his culture relevant to a drug, recognizing that that belief system is itself a result of a complex of factors (e.g., the deterrent factor in terms of harmful effects on health of marijuana use is probably greater for someone reared in the white middle class than for someone reared in a Mexican-American lower class as the white middle-class youth has been exposed to the belief system of his class and such belief system has been considerably generated by the public statements for the past thirty years of the Federal

*The examples given may not be true as they are generated from clinical experience and not research data.

Bureau of Narcotics whereas the Mexican-American youth has had considerable exposure to the actual use and effects of marijuana by relatives, friends and his culture members in general); 3) the nature of his relationship to those individuals who do, and do not, use a drug (e.g., the deterrent factor in terms of harmful personal consequences of crystal methedrine use may be greater in lower-class youth who have observed this phenomenon over a longer period of time and *in association with* a delinquent group than it would be for white middle-class youth who have had more limited experience with the drug and who have not associated its use with delinquent groups and their subsequent dysfunction); 4) the availability of the drug which, in part, is dependent upon his meeting acceptable criteria established by those who have access to the drug (e.g., the attraction factor for marijuana may be equally great in both upper-class white and lower-class ethnic groups (but not in the middle-class white group) as in both groups to be acceptable for access to the drug one must be "cool," i.e., have the right attitudes, sets of behavior, demeanor and knowledgeability about the illicit drug world); 5) the development of an attitude towards or belief in the effects of a drug consonant with his purported aim in utilizing the drug (e.g., in order to "investigate" the increased extrasensory perception qualities of LSD, one must develop a belief that such phenomena exist and that this particular drug, if utilized under particular circumstances, enhances the probabilities of exploring such phenomena); 6) a process through which he can interpret the experiences he has with the drug (e.g., in order to talk about and communicate to others about drug-induced transcendental experiences one must develop a whole set of mystic and religious concepts and structures, and a language appropriate to those concepts and in addition, must locate others who share similar concepts and language systems and through these two conditions, he can interpret, i.e., make egosyntonic, those experiences); 7) the extent to which the individual is successful in *learning* how to use the drug for his purported purpose and if his purpose changes, the extent to which he is successful in achieving these new found goals through the use of the drug (e.g., in order to obtain a marijuana "high" one must learn how to smoke, i.e., taking air with the smoke to cool it, sustaining the smoke in the lungs for a long period of time and learning to attend to cues which indicate one is getting "high"; in addition, if one begins to use marijuana in order to have greater emotional expressiveness he must "turn on" with others who share this same value so that such expressiveness will be rewarded and thereby reinforced; if he accidentally achieves a clear meditative state on occasion and finds this more rewarding he might then attempt to learn how to achieve this state again with marijuana and this might necessitate his finding a different type of person with whom to "turn on" who shares his new goals; and again, if he is not successful in achieving this new goal, he may try another drug for this purpose (such as psilocybin) and give up marijuana or he may give up his new goal and go back to a familiar setting with goals that he could achieve); 8) the interweaving of the drug experience with the individual's total life experiences and the dominance or importance of that drug experience relative to the meaning and breadth of his other life experiences, (e.g., the experience a person has with a drug in terms of its meaning to his everyday experiences will vary considerably: the less he translates what he learns from the drug experience into everyday living, the less integrated and more alien the drug experience will remain relative to his general life experiences. In general, the more egosyntonic the drug experience and the more ego-alien the rest of his daily life experiences, the greater importance will the drug experience have for him, and conversely, the more he learns to practice the insights gained from the drug experience in his everyday living, of less importance will the drug experience become and of more importance will his daily living experiences become); 9) the role of the drug experience within the total context of the person's life and the extent to which this drug use enhances or deters, his achieving his dominant goals and meeting his primary needs; (e.g., the individual will either increase, decrease or maintain his drug usage depending on the usefulness of his drug experiences in achieving his goals and meeting his needs; if he finds that the risk of being apprehended for a drug possession and the subsequent punishment is too great for the benefits he accrues from its use *relative* to the benefits he is accruing from other legitimatized activities in his life, he will lessen his use of the drug).

These nine factors at least must be considered in determining the complexity of forces operating which result in a drug's use or abuse. The simple-minded perfect correlation theory approach to drug usage, i.e., people take drugs to run away from reality or that drug usage is a breakdown of a social system, can be seen to be somewhat naive.

Consequently, in approaching a social action project aimed at the ameliorating of drug abuse it behooves the change agent (and here we include the usual policing agents and the "helping" agents, social workers, psychologists, etc.) to first investigate those psychosocial and cultural phenomena which are operating which result in drug use or abuse. He first must analyze whether use or abuse is occurring. He must first of all determine if the user, with the information available to him and on the basis of his experience, considers his drug use to be functional (usage) or dysfunctional (abusage), i.e., whether or not he sees his drug use as an integral part of his whole life style in that it enhances and enables him to meet needs and achieve goals, within his system, that he deems of value. If in fact, he evaluates his drug use as an enabling phenomenon within his total value orientation, it is highly unlikely that an external change agent is going to have much success in changing the user's *evaluation* of his drug experiences. On the other hand, if the user evaluates his drug usage as basically dysfunctional, i.e., not positively contributing to a realization of his value system, then the change agent has some entree into the user's psychological world.

It is highly relevant to cite Blumer's experience with the youthful drug users of Oakland, California. The program that he sought to establish was focused on the idea of organizing, among the youth, a core of prestigious youth leaders, who would be won over to a position of non-usage, and that these youth leaders would, by their opinion leadership position, be influential in convincing other youths to give up drug usage. The model is well-known and has been effective in Alcoholics Anonymous and amongst groups of older opiate addicts.

The results of Blumer's approach was

We found rather early that we were not having any success in developing a form of collective abstinence. It became clear that the youths were well anchored in their drug use and well fortified in their beliefs against all of the "dangers" of drug use. From their own experiences and observations they could refute the declaration that the use of harmful drugs usually led to personal or health deterioration; they viewed with contempt the use of opiates and rejected with evidence the claim that the use of harmful drugs led naturally to opiate use. They pointed out that the break-up of home life, with which many of them were very familiar, was due to other factors than the use of drugs; they were able to show that the limitation of their career opportunities came from other conditions than the use of drugs, as such. They met the fear of arrest by "developing greater skill and precautions against detection in the use of drugs." Added to these stances was a set of collective beliefs that justified their use of drugs, so that such use resulted in harmless pleasure, increased conviviality, did not lead to violence, could be regulated, did not lead to addiction, and was much less harmful than the use of alcohol, which is socially and openly sanctioned in our society. Parenthetically, we would invite any group of educators, scientists, welfare workers or police officials to try to meet effectively the well-buttressed arguments, based on personal experience and observation, that our youthful drug users present in frank, open, and uncowed discussion. In sum, we learned that youthful drug users are just not interested in abstaining from drug use. (Blumer, 1967)

If the situation is such that the user considers his usage to be functional but the change agent views such usage as dysfunctional then the only position the change agent can take is to induce a change in the *evaluation* by the user of his drug experience by changing the ecosystem of which that drug experience is but one part. The only entree the change agent has is through manipulating other variables in the ecosystem of the user. In manipulating and changing the character of the user's ecosystem lies the possibilities of changing the evaluation by the user of his drug usage. This then is the ecological approach to ameliorating drug abuse—abuse in the widest sense of dysfunction to the individual and to the wider community of which he is a part. There is, in actuality, no disparity between what is functional (or good) for an individual and what is functional for his society: a synergistic principle is posited. Experiences which are truly valid for an individual cannot be dysfunctional for his society. However, both self-deception *and* societal deception can exist. Because an individual's experience of "validity" with respect to any particular phenomenon or relationship is at odds with the culture's evaluation of the validity of that phenomenon in no way deems his experience therefore to be invalid—history, of course, is replete with such examples, e.g., Galileo and Copernicus.* Thus, for example, let us say that an individual realizes, under an experience with a psychedelic drug, that the enemy is the one "within" and not, as society deems, without, e.g., the international communist conspiracy. The individual then shifts his focus of attention and his energy may be directed towards attempts to integrating his own impulse life. This then detracts from the national anti-communist effort and the individual is experienced by his culture as being at odds with his society. If in fact, the society keeps defining the threat as without and concerts all her energy towards the development of instruments of violence and destruction in the name of self-preservation and the "enemy" defines itself in exactly the same position, then the result is a contest in "overkill" with everyone (both enemies) enjoying the benefits. Brickman (1968) has written an exciting paper wherein he attributes the hippie philosophy of non-violence as a result of his achieving, through psychedelic drug use, an ego-death, and as a consequence he has no longer to believe in and fear his own death which enables him to cease projecting his death fear, i.e., violence, onto others. The point then, that is being made, is that there is a basic harmony between an individual's growth and evolvement and his society's growth and evolvements and we must not assume, as is often done, that societal values are valid ones (valid in a pragmatic evolutionary sense) and that the individual must learn to adopt those values. Rather we must view and evaluate with as much dispassion as can be brought to bear, the utility of the value in terms of its contribution to the *evolvement* of the ecosystem of which it is a part.

   Developing conceptual ecosystems models for viewing phenomena in the behavioral sciences is not a difficult task. The difficult task is operationalizing that model into specific measurable variables which makes possible the testing of the efficiency of the model without violating the basic principles of the model. As is well acknowledged (e.g., Watt, 1966), the problem is the state of the art in measurement and this is especially true in studying a behavioral phenomenon. As a first step in approximating a translation of the ecosystem approach to drug use, an example of a research design will be given which attempts to specify the nature of some of the relationships among the interdependent variables which result in marijuana use. We recognize that the design falls short of satisfying the requirement of "totality" but nevertheless present it as a step in an attempt to evaluate more precisely the complexity of phenomena which result in drug use and abuse.

   An in-depth study of middle and upper socioeconomic class marijuana users,

---

*In modern-day psychiatry Laing (1967) for example, takes the position that Western man's belief and value system is a psychotic one and the schizophrenic psychosis is an idiosyncratic attempt to break away from this societal normative psychosis. The speculation of the relation of guru and mystics to schizophrenics is, of course, a familiar one, and the concepts that schizophrenia might be a mutant condition in the progressive evolution of man is under current popular discussion.

aged 30 years and over, residents of the Los Angeles area, is being undertaken. Patterns and purposes of marijuana usage, life style and psychological and social correlates are being examined within the ecological framework. Objectives of this research are twofold: (1) to examine the predisposing factors and effects of marijuana usage in terms of conventional adult role fulfillment and values; and (2) to contribute further to social change theory.

Kelly (1966, 1968) hypothesizes four aspects of coping behavior which are necessary for the prediction of an individual's adaptation to different systems in his environment: 1) Exploration—a preference for novel social experiences and for participation in diverse social settings; 2) Anticipation—the extent to which thought is given to future social settings; 3) Locus of Control—the extent to which reinforcements or consequences are seen as contingent upon one's own behavior or upon factors in the environment; and 4) Social Effectiveness—the extent of perceived power to change the behavior of others.

Adaptation is defined as specific to a particular environment and is dependent upon the degree of congruence between: 1) individual preferences for dealing with the environment (coping styles); 2) role requirements in the setting; 3) type and range of units for social interaction (e.g., formal, informal, and number of these social settings); and 4) structural properties of the environment (number of people, rate of population exchange, etc.).

In examining the determinants and effects of marijuana usage in an environment such as Los Angeles County, it is necessary to view these from a perspective of rapid social change. Individuals, whether high or low in terms of exploration needs, will derive both profit and loss in the process of rapid change. For example, those with strong needs to explore or try new things will be rewarded for their unique competencies which can be utilized by various sub-systems in the environment, e.g., their familiarity with alternative norms and multiple resources. Yet, unless they see themselves as personally responsible for the consequences of their behavior, personal development may suffer in other areas, such as commitment to valued norms. Those with low needs to explore may function well in a small array of settings, but opportunities for personal development may be limited. For either type of individual, marijuana usage may well represent adaptation to their personal environment. Whether this adaptation is in the service of self-actualization is a further evaluative problem.

In this study, concerned with adults and their personal environments, measurement of the independent variables of coping style has been accomplished by developing a 30-item Likert-type scale to measure three aspects of coping style (needs or preferences for Change, Order and Deference) and Locus of Control is being measured by Seeman's Index of Social and Personal Control (Neal and Seeman, 1964).

The independent variable of environment is being measured by examining the individual's total environment, that is, the full range of systems and organizations of which he is a member, i.e., work, families of origin and procreation, clubs, organizations and social groups which occupy his leisure time. His environment is given a score on a stability-fluidity continuum, based on the variables of structure, role requirements and settings. Adults in this study are residents of Los Angeles County, a highly fluid environment, which however, is composed of multiple sub-systems (families, institutions, organizations, etc.) which in themselves vary in size, longevity of association, kinds of role requirements and variety of settings. An individual could be so located in the Los Angeles environment that the systems of which he is an actual member are highly stable, with strict specialized role requirements and norms of behavior. Therefore, for an adult to smoke marijuana and still remain an adapted member of his establishment-oriented work and family sub-systems one would expect that his coping style would be characterized by both a high need for exploration and a high degree of internal control. In other words, in order for him to depart from the behavioral norms in his work and family environments, first, he must perceive himself to be in control of the consequences of his behavior and second, his high need for change must motivate him to seek new experiences in his social and recreational environment, e.g., marijuana-smoking.

The function of the systems in the individual's personal environment are measured according to two dimensions: expressiveness and instrumentality. According to Katz and Kahn (1966), when a person's intrinsic rewards are in harmony with the major productive activities of the system, his participation may be labeled as expressive. He finds the activities rewarding in themselves, with high potentials for personal growth and development. When the activities provide extrinsic rewards (e.g., pay, status or friendships), the individual's participation is instrumental in nature. A system can be highly satisfactory on both dimensions. In this research, it is postulated that the degree of discrepancy between the individual's expressive and instrumental needs and his rating of what the system actually provides in both dimensions will be an indicator of his commitment to the system in terms of adhering to its norms and role requirements, or even his remaining in it. In order to measure the discrepancy between the individual's needs and satisfactions in various aspects of his personal environment (work, family, etc.), items have been taken from the Lyman Porter questionnaire (Porter, 1961), which measures degrees of need satisfaction using a Maslow-type need hierarchy system. For example, using the self-actualization need "feeling of self-fulfillment," the smaller the discrepancy between the rating of felt need and satisfaction of this need within the system, the greater the person's commitment to the system (role requirements and norms).

Although the modified version of Kelly's ecological model is expected to be helpful in predicting which individuals will use marijuana and to what degree, certain other independent variables must be included as well. As previous marijuana studies have shown, the person who uses marijuana has a high probability of prior experiences with psychoactive drugs, expectations regarding marijuana effects consonant with personal values, and an ongoing and positive relationship with one or more marijuana users (Blum, 1969a, 1969b). In this study, we have focused on eight variables which seem to be strongly related to marijuana usage. They are *1) Law-Abidingness:* Where obedience or support of the law is intrinsic in nature (e.g., not dependent on personal agreement with the justice of a particular law) then the use of marijuana is highly unlikely. However, when the individual obeys certain laws (e.g., traffic laws, honesty in income tax and insurance claims) only because of threat of external controls, then his commitment is expedient in nature. When external controls are lax or absent or remote, then the individual will tend to break one or more of these laws without feeling intrinsic guilt. Since marijuana can be obtained easily without consorting with known criminals, and white middle- and upper-class homes and neighborhoods are far less susceptible to police raids than "hippie pads," the threat of external controls are minimal. The individual with expedient commitment to the law is highly likely to use marijuana if he is so motivated and is given the opportunity. Therefore, subjects will be questioned regarding their adherence to certain laws, their method of self-reconciliation regarding marijuana usage, their fear of discovery by police, knowledge of others who have been arrested for marijuana possession, and their attitudes to other laws which are currently being debated. *2) Prior Psychoactive Drug Use:* Adults over 40 years tend to have drug use patterns restricted to alcohol, tobacco and pain killers, and with decreasing age, the frequency of use of tranquilizers and amphetamines increases (Blum, 1969a). In this country, it has only been since World War II and the proliferation of drugs during that period, that a cultural valuation and belief system regarding drugs has arisen. It is predicted that adults must have had positive experiences with an array of psychoactive drugs in order to feel confident in experimentation with marijuana. Information will be elicited regarding family history of alcohol use, and personal use history of alcohol, tobacco, barbiturates, tranquilizers, amphetamines and hallucinogens. *3) Consonance of Marijuana Beliefs with Personal Values:* Through exposure to marijuana users, either directly or indirectly, he must see marijuana as providing results which are personally valued, e.g. relaxation, having fun (similar to effects of alcohol perhaps), sensual stimulation, enhanced social relations, new insights in self-exploration. He may also value the knowledge that with marijuana, effects are felt rapidly when smoked, dosages are controllable, content can be grossly inspected and effects dissipate rapidly. Subjects will be questioned regarding sources of information concerning marijuana effects prior to first use, kinds of information, opportunities to observe others using it and personal expectations regarding effects at time of first use and subsequent expectations. *4) Adherence to "Hang Loose" Ethic:* Several studies have shown that a growing segment of the population is rebelling against conventional Americana, i.e. property worship, disregard for humanism and personal experience in business and industry, etc. (e.g., Simmons & Winograd, 1966; Norton, 1968). Marijuana has become a symbol of the "hang loose" ethic, and the adult marijuana smoker may be overtly expressing his rejection of many aspects of the established order as well as seeking the kinds of personal experiences which marijuana smoking is supposed to engender. It is predicted that the more disaffiliated he feels, the more frequent will be his use of marijuana. Information will be elicited regarding attitudes toward social mores, religious and political systems, certain controversial laws, feelings of membership in conventional groups, participation in humanistic and mystical experiences, and subjective assessment of conventionality of own life-style. *5) Nature of Relationship with Users:* It is postulated that the middle- and upper-class adult will have been exposed to more negative attitudes toward marijuana than has the lower-class adult, particularly the Negro or Mexican-American. Whatever information had opinions he has regarding marijuana is probably based on information received through mass media, the police and the Federal Bureau of Narcotics, which since the 1930s have assiduously linked marijuana with addiction, crime, immorality and mental illness. The lower-class adult has more often based his opinion on actual use and effects of marijuana through the observation of friends, relatives and neighbors. In recent years, however, the middle- or upper-class adult may also be aware of others within his social environment (friends, family, work colleagues, youth) who use marijuana. However, unless these individuals are seen as social equals or better, and their use of marijuana has few or no demonstrable negative consequences, the likelihood of his experimentation with marijuana is decreased. Also, as has been pointed out (e.g., Becker, 1955, Goode, 1969a) if the individual who uses marijuana is part of a group, and in fact feels more like an "insider" as a result of use, then conventional conceptions of marijuana effects are regarded as uninformed and "outsider" viewpoints. Subjects will therefore be questioned regarding their relationship with the person(s) who introduced them to marijuana or provided them with the first opportunity; setting of first use; whether others persuaded them to try it; attitudes of close friends and significant others at the time regarding marijuana use; and assessment of satisfaction with friends who use marijuana in comparison with those who don't. *6) Availability of Marijuana:* Obviously, the drug must be available to the subject for him to use it with any degree of frequency. He must have a source of supply, either through friends or acquaintances. He must impress those who might supply him with marijuana with his ability to keep his "cool," and his trustworthiness. Subjects will be questioned regarding ease of obtaining marijuana, where and how usually obtained, sources when not readily available, proportion of friends and acquaintances using marijuana and typical precautions taken when using. *7) Reinforcement by Experienced Users:* During his first and subsequent exposures to marijuana, it appears that experienced users are essential in that they help him to identify changes in perception, etc. as positive in nature, and reassure him regarding negative effects such as sore throat (Becker, 1955). In order to obtain a "high" with marijuana, one must learn how to smoke it and how to recognize cues which indicate that one is getting "high."

316   Drugs and Social Consequences

It is important that whatever his aims or purposes in using marijuana, these are shared or valued by those who are teaching or assisting him. If he is interested in "introspection" or accidentally achieves a state of meditation, in company with others who disparage these effects, then his marijuana experience is likely to be frustrating and unpleasant. To achieve this state again, he will need to find a different type of person to "turn on" with, one who shares his purpose or goal. With regular marijuana use comes a new vocabulary with which to describe and interpret the drug experience. In addition, certain "props" such as incense, special music or attire may become part of the drug experience. The shared vocabulary and paraphernalia of marijuana smokers varies greatly with life-style and goals of usage. Therefore, subjects will be questioned regarding first experience with the drug (alone or with others); emotional status at the time; first effects and feelings concerning these; number of attempts before the first "high" and description of that occasion; preferences for smoking with different persons according to purpose of use; typical settings and props used; topics of discussion during use; changes in verbal repertoire; style of dress and food preferences. *8) Integration of Marijuana Usage with Daily Experiences, Needs and Ambitions:* Unless the drug experience provides the individual with certain unique and pleasurable effects which are not obtainable through other legal substances such as alcohol, his continuing usage is unlikely. Where unique and pleasurable effects are felt, the more positive its consequences in terms of his daily life, e.g., enhanced social relations, creative energies, peer group status, self-understanding, etc., the more likely his continuing use. Subjects will be questioned regarding usual drug effects, purposes of use, changes in self attributed to marijuana usage, perception of potential dangers in marijuana usage, consequences of marijuana use in other aspects of life, attempts of others to dissuade further use, plans for use in future, assessment of effects of marijuana usage on society, interest in eastern mysticism, and attitudes to strong hallucinogens.

As Figure 20-1 demonstrates, there are six dependent variables which are defined as follows: 1) *Trial only:* the subject has used marijuana from 1-3 times, with no further use; 2) *Occasional use:* the subject uses marijuana at least once a month to a maximum and including three times a month. He sees himself as a marijuana user, but does not routinely plan for its use at regular intervals; 3) *Regular use:* the subject uses marijuana at least once a week, with an average of twice a week, and sees himself as a regular user. He plans for marijuana usage whenever the situation will permit; 4) *Daily use:* the subject uses marijuana at least once a day and has integrated its usage with his daily life experiences; 5) *Previous use:* the subject has used marijuana in the past on either an occasional, regular or daily basis; 6) *No use:* the subject has never used marijuana at any time in his life. any time in his life.

In this research, there are seven hypotheses related to four categories of marijuana usage. The first six hypotheses are paired alternative ecosystem

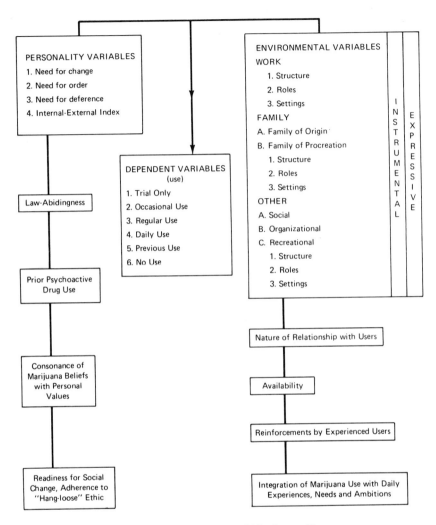

Figure 20-1. Ecosystem of Marijuana Use.

profiles which characterize three similar degrees of marijuana use. The following two hypotheses will serve as examples:

Hypothesis 1:

A middle- or upper-class adult who uses marijuana at least once, will be characterized by either of two Ecosystem Profiles:

a. He will exhibit a high need for change, a low need for deference; the locus of control will be internal; at least one aspect of his environment will be above average in fluidity; he will exhibit a low intrinsic commitment to the law; he will have a moderate to high adherence to the "hang-loose" ethic; he will have a personal history of psychoactive drug use; his expectations regarding marijuana effects will be consonant with his personal values; he will have a peer relationship (casual or close) with one or more marijuana users.

Here it is predicted that one type of middle- or upper-class adult who uses marijuana at least once will exhibit the following characteristics: (a) at least one aspect of his environment (perhaps social) is above average in fluidity, and he must have a high need for unique experiences, a low need for conformity to conventional behavior, and he must perceive himself to be in control most of the time regarding the consequences of his behavior; (b) he must believe that the marijuana laws are unjust and that middle- and upper-class adults are comparatively safe from police if marijuana is used discreetly; (c) he must have at least a moderate number of opinions which correspond to the "hang-loose" ethic, which demonstrates a readiness for social change, e.g., approves pacifism, abortion, opposes traditional sexual conventions, organized religion, etc.; (d) he must have used psychoactive substances in the past, e.g., drugs which modify the mental processes, thereby providing him with positive values regarding specific effects (e.g., feeling high) and method of use; (e) he must have acquired knowledge regarding marijuana effects (through direct or indirect exposure to marijuana users) which lead him to believe that the consequences are personally valued, i.e. relaxation, fun, sensual stimulation, self-exploration, etc.; (f) he must have a close or casual peer relationship with known marijuana users in order for him to have the opportunity to use it.

Hypothesis 2:

A middle- or upper-class adult who uses marijuana regularly will be characterized by either of two Ecosystem Profiles:

a. He will exhibit a high need for change; a low need for order; the locus of control will be internal; his total environment will be above average in fluidity; his environment will rate high on expressive, and moderate to high on instrumental dimensions; experiences with marijuana will rate high in terms of both instrumental and expressive values; reinforcements by others will be moderate to high; integration of marijuana use with daily experiences and ambitions will be high; marijuana will be available whenever needed.

Here it is predicted that one type of middle- or upper-class adult who uses marijuana regularly (at least once a week, with an average of twice a week), will exhibit the following characteristics: (a) where his total environment is fluid (work, e.g. a creative field, family, social, etc.), he must have high needs for unique experiences, low needs for planning, organizing (though work may demand this) and he must perceive himself to be in control most of the time regarding the consequences of his behavior; (b) his total environment will be highly satisfying in terms of expressive needs (worthwhile activities, etc.) and moderate to highly satisfying in terms of instrumental needs (pay, status, etc.); (c) his experiences with marijuana will be highly satisfying in terms of both instrumental values (relaxation, enhancing sensory stimuli, etc.) and expressive values (self-understanding, etc.); (d) reinforcements by others will be moderate to high in that he will tend to use marijuana mainly in company with others whose life-style and patterns and purposes of use are similar to his; (e) integration of marijuana into his life-style is high; he will tend to report that it has many positive effects on other aspects of his life, e.g. creativity, self-understanding, etc., and for these reasons, tends to plan for its use whenever the situation permits; his concern regarding apprehension by police is minimal, as is his concern regarding the critical opinions of others such as work colleagues; (f) he will report that marijuana is available whenever a new supply is needed.

Two different kinds of sampling techniques are being employed. The first, non-random in nature, is designed to elicit a comprehensive array of data pertaining to the research hypotheses as well as providing additional important information regarding marijuana use. The second technique is intended to elicit a more condensed type of data pertinent to the hypotheses by means of a mailed questionnaire to a random sample of adults. The sampling techniques are as follows: 1) Social Network Interviews: Subjects are obtained through personal referral by knowledgeable individuals (users, ex-users and non-users of marijuana), and an attempt is made to obtain further referrals to other known marijuana users in each individual's social network. These interviews are completely anonymous and no names are kept. 2) Random Sample Mailed Questionnaire; a shortened version of the interview questionnaire is being mailed to a random sample of adult residents in a middle- and upper-income area of Los Angeles. A carefully-worded letter accompanies the questionnaire, soliciting cooperation and assuring respondents of their anonymity. No respondents are excluded on the basis of non-use or of no present use.

Questionnaire and Instruments

A highly structured questionnaire has been devised which consists primarily of closed-end items pertaining to socioeconomic status; family background; non-medical drug use; first and continuing marijuana usage and related social aspects; and other variables as outlined above. For some sections of the questionnaire, two forms have been developed: 1) Interview style, highly structured for some of the sensitive or complex areas; 2) Questionnaire style, open and closed, for those same sections in the shortened mailout version. Two personality measures are also being employed: the Seeman Scale of Powerlessness and one 30-item scale constructed to measure needs or preferences for change, order and deference.

Summary

An ecosystems model for the study of drug use-abuse is presented and an attempt is made to demonstrate the operationalization of the parameters of such a model.

References

Barber, B. Drugs and Society. New York: Russell Sage, 1967.

Becker, H. Becoming a marijuana user. In D. Solomon (ed.), The Marijuana Papers, Indianapolis, Indiana; Bobbs-Merrill, 1966.

Blum, R.H. Society and Drugs. San Francisco: Jossey-Bass, 1969a. Students and Drugs. San Francisco: Jossey-Bass, 1969b.

Blumer, H. The World of Drug Abuse. ADD Center Project Final Report. Berkeley, California: University of California Press, 1967.

Brickman, H.R. The psychedelic hip scene: return of the death instinct. American Journal of Psychiatry 125:766-772, 1968.

Carstairs, G.M. Daru and Dhang: cultural factors and choice of intoxicants. Quarterly Journal of Studies in Alcoholism 15:220-237, 1954.

Fisher, G. Psychedelic drug usage: socio-political and psychological considerations. California School Health 4:40-54, 1968.

Goode, E. Marijuana and sex. Evergreen Review (May), 1969a. Marijuana and the politics of reality. Journal of Health and Social Behavior 10:83-94, 1969b. Multiple drug use among marijuana smokers. Social Problems 17:48-64, 1969c.

Katz, D. and Kahn, R.L. The Social Psychology of Organizations. New York: Wiley, 1966.

Kelly, J.G. Social adaptation to varied environments. Paper presented at the American Psychological Association, 1966. Toward an ecological conception of preventive interventions. In J.W. Carter (ed.), Research Contributions from Psychology to Community Mental Health. New York: Behavioral Publications, 1968.

Laing, R.D. The Politics of Experience. New York: Pantheon, 1967.

McGlothlin, W.H. Toward a rational view of hallucinogenic drugs. California School Health 4:1-11, 1968.

Neal, A.G. and Seeman, M. Organizations and powerlessness: a test of the mediation hypothesis. American Sociological Review 29:216-226, 1964.

Norton, W.A. The marijuana habit: some observations of a small group of users. Canadian Psychiatry Association Journal 13:163-173, 1968.

Porter, L. W. A study of perceived need satisfactions in bottom and middle management jobs. Journal of Applied Psychology 45:1-10, 1961.

Simmons, J.L. and Winograd, B. It's Happening: a Portrait of the Youth Scene Today. Santa Barbara, California: Marc-Laird, 1966.

Watt, K.E.F. The nature of systems analysis. In Systems Analysis in Ecology. New York: Academic Press, 1966.

21

An Approach to Drug Addiction Through the Assessment of Natural Environments

Jack J. Monroe
U.S. Public Health Service Hospital
Lexington, Kentucky

Traditional medical care programs provided for drug addicts by the United States Public Health Service reflect an assumption that drug abuse is a psychiatric problem. [1,2] This is not to deny other basic facts concerning this complex problem. The abuse of narcotic and other dangerous drugs by certain segments of the population can be conceptualized as a symptom of social disintegration, as can crime, suicide, or psychosis. Furthermore, illegal traffic in such drugs is so interdependent with their abuse in the United States that the total problem has become one for social control through special legislation and law enforcement.

Medical administrators at the PHS Hospitals in Lexington, Kentucky, and Fort Worth, Texas have never advocated that hospitalization should be the sole modality, or even the most crucial component, in the rehabilitation of the addict. They have stressed that the very nature of the withdrawal illness, precipitated by the abrupt cessation of opiate drug use, makes confinement in a drug-free environment an essential aspect of patient management in the early phase of treatment. As a matter of fact, the current officers in charge endorse, in principle, a proposed civil commitment law at the Federal level which would place certain addicts under the custody of the Surgeon General of the Public

Reprinted from *Rehabilitating the Narcotic Addict* (Washington, D.C., Vocational Rehabilitation Administration, Government Printing Office, 1966), 343-357.

Health Service for periods of hospitalization in an appropriate medical care facility, followed by aftercare and supervised probation in their home communities. Thus, the type of care envisioned is not restricted to the traditional medical model, but calls for an imaginative social psychiatry. The internal environment of the hospital would constitute only a part of a larger therapeutic community, including the addict's own neighborhood, which could be many miles removed from the hospital. If the Federal Commitment Law for addicts is passed, PHS administrators may be asked for specific recommendations concerning the location and staffing of aftercare facilities. Their mental health staffs could reasonably be expected to provide leadership in implementing the new addiction programs. Should this occur, PHS clinicians, who for the most part are psychodynamically oriented, would need to assume a social psychiatric orientation to include an adequate conception of the addict's natural environment, and the role it plays in his illness.

The term "natural environment" as used in the title of this paper can mean any one of various arrangements of people interacting in a defined social setting. The definition would include the internal environments of institutions, such as hospitals, prisons, and schools, which have an organismic character, as well as political or administrative subdivisions of people, such as census tracts, districts or neighborhoods. Thus, one might substitute the words "natural groups," as opposed to "experimental or control subjects," without altering the basic sense the above term is meant to convey.

Search for an Adequate Conceptual Model

The search is for an adequate conceptual model for properly integrating variables concerning (a) the addict, (b) his hospital treatment, and (c) his home community or neighborhood. The traditional ecological approach to behavior disorders [3] exemplifies a kind of environmental analysis, but, as an evaluative model for social psychiatry, it leaves much to be desired. [4,5,6] Quoting from Kennedy, [6] "This is because such approaches make zones and/or external zonal conditions the independent variables and fail to consider the part played by culture in the creation of behavior." He pointed out that indices of the ecological sort have not provided an understanding of how culture "reflects into pathology."

Shevky and his associates [7,8,9,10] have developed a method of social area analysis by combining census tract information into three dimensions which they call "social rank," "urbanization" and "segregation." While these dimensions have the advantage of a high degree of generality, not only across census tracts within cities, but across cities as well, [11] reliance upon them to explain variation in human behavior is open to the same kind of criticism as that directed toward the earlier ecological studies.

Clausen and Kohn [4] and Mintz and Schwartz [5] stressed the difficulties in inferring etiology of mental disorders from sociocultural variables, as usually defined in ecological studies. At best, such studies relate to a social definition of mental disorder, rather than to a psychogenesis of behavior. From a psychological viewpoint, it would seem not enough to specify the level of social rank, degree of urbanization and segregation, or even the amount of "general stress," e.g., social disintegration, existing in a given environment in order to predict behavioral outcomes accurately. One must not only estimate the adaptive modes of community members, particularly of those members who exhibit the behavior under study, but also of the residual population. Finally, one needs to look for interaction between sources of environmental stress and the variable modes of adaptation as they relate to behavior of individuals. Not all who live in a given environment are subjected to the same sociocultural experiences. Furthermore, some individuals may develop psychological immunity or special vulnerability to stress.

Thus, the classical ecological approach ignores crucial interactional variables which bridge environmental conditions and human behavior. The basic structure of a more appropriate model will rest ultimately in an "ecological psychology." While no such school of psychology has yet developed, a strong ecologic emphasis can be seen in recent statements of Sells [12] and others. [13]

Assessment of Institutional Environments
and Behavioral Change

There have been no adequately controlled studies of institutional care of drug addicts. Clinicians who treat addicts have lacked the conceptual tools for integrating personality, behavioral change, and social environmental dimensions in a single evaluative model. While several psychometric scales have been developed for describing addict types, [14,15,16,17,18,19] there are no standardized techniques available for adequately measuring patient care or assessing the natural habitats of drug addicts.

Studies of the internal environment of the mental hospital [20,21] and of the prison community [22,23] represent a suitable research model for investigating therapist-patient and staff-inmate relationships. The therapeutic impact of any medical care or correctional facility on its members could conceivably be expressed by indexing patients or inmates at the time of discharge for the kinds and degrees of role relationships developed with custodial and treatment staff, as well as with other patients or inmates, during the course of institutional residence.

Role behaviors of patients and staff could be studied in two ways: (1) in terms of perceptions or expectations of one's own behavior and the behavior of others; and (2) in terms of actual transactions or encounters between patient and staff, the purpose of such encounters being defined by each, and the extent to which these purposes were served. The latter measurements could be based, in fact, upon recorded events in the daily work schedules of the staff, but it should include information of informal or unscheduled contacts of patients with staff, and with other patients as well.

Emerging interest among social psychologists in Skinner's notion of "verbal community" [24] is currently producing concepts and methods which have considerable promise in delineating functional subsystems of a language universe. Ultimately, it may be possible to manipulate such verbal systems in a desired direction, thus providing a technological basis for behavioral change.

Verbal behaviors of patients and staff represent natural response systems which convey role orientations. The addict argot, on the one hand, and mental health terminology, on the other, are dramatic examples of different verbal systems. The words one uses can be thought of as instruments which conceptualize and, thus, structure his social environment. Patients and staff can be differentiated on the basis of their ideologies. Among the staff there are multiple ideologies concerning patient care. The doctors have one ideology, reflected in their verbal responses or terminologies, while the correctional officers have another. Production-oriented industrial supervisors may exhibit still a third ideology distinguishable in their specialized language used to define the hospital mission. Moreover, all patients do not share the addict argot. The above natural systems lend themselves to experimental and statistical analysis, and can be modified. Ultimately, by selectively reinforcing the more adaptive responses of patients, it may be possible to provide them with more socially acceptable role definitions. While they may retain the older definitions as well, they will at least have available to them alternative modes of response, which if differentially reinforced in aftercare facilities, or when under supervision in their home communities, could lead to lasting behavioral changes.

Recent work in the assessment of student productivity in colleges and universities [25,26,27] has produced a body of concepts which are highly relevant to problems anticipated in classifying drug addiction communities. Linton [28] pointed out that the major portion of community forces is transmitted through people. Astin and Holland [27] adopted a similar rationale in constructing The Environmental Assessment Technique, a method designed to assess college environments. They assumed that the salient features of a social environment are dependent upon the typical personal orientations of its members. It seemed to follow that if the characteristics of the people in a given group were known, one could specify the social climate produced by the group. The above method grew out of Holland's theoretical formulation of vocational choice. [29] Later, Astin [30] developed the Inventory of College Activities, an instrument for assessing college environments through observable events ("stimuli"). Earlier, Pace and Stern [25] and Thistlethwaite [26] had presented methods for measuring psychological "climates" of colleges by asking the student to rate his environment on a set of items similar to those used in personality inventories. Astin referred to their methods as an "image" approach. In his Inventory, Astin utilized three types of information in assessing college communities: (1) observable events (stimulus approach), (2) the college "image," and (3) the personal orientations of students. He found that the stimulus approach yielded different environmental patterns than did the "image" approach, but both of these were somewhat dependent upon the personal orientations (i.e., the personalities) of the students enrolled in the institutions.

Astin's approach to the college environment would appear to be applicable to the analysis of urban neighborhoods, where the social environments to be studied can be limited geographically to census zone populations.

Previous Studies in Drug Addiction

No truly comprehensive study of drug addiction has ever been attempted in a social psychiatric setting. This is not to say that no relevant research has been done on important psychological and sociological aspects of the problem.

The most significant psychological research in drug addiction was initiated more than a decade ago by Wikler, Hill and their associates at the Addiction Research Center in Lexington, Kentucky. Essentially, their contribution was the formulation of specific drug actions and the roles they play in human motivation. [31,32,33]

Extensive studies of gross patterns of addiction in the United States are currently being made by O'Donnell, Ball and their associates in the Social Science Section of the Addiction Research Center. From admission data provided by the two Federal hospitals, they have retrieved identifying information, demographic data, and type of drug used, on all addicts admitted for treatment since the first hospital opened in 1935. They have published several significant papers describing changing patterns and regional variation in drug abuse. [34,35,36,37,38]

Thus, most studies in addiction have concentrated on either the addict himself or upon gross community factors as they relate to drug use. Seldom have both approaches been combined in the same study. The work of Chein and his associates [39] is a possible exception. Chein's studies of addicts and controls in New York City exemplifies a multidisciplinary approach to the problem which combined social and psychological dimensions in an attempt to explain variation in addiction rates across census zones. His most important contribution was not so much his psychology of addiction as his painstaking ecological correlations between zonal conditions and drug use. However, Bates [40] had meager success in reproducing Chein's findings when he used the Lexington and Fort Worth hospital admission rates to reflect relative prevalence of drug addiction in the major cities of the United States.

Addiction research at Lexington, and Chein's work in New York City, do not exhaust the fund of scientific knowledge in the drug addiction field. Over the years several significant studies have been reported from the Clinical Services at the Fort Worth PHS Hospital. [41,42,43,44]

Numerous writers, some of whom are former Public Health Service officers who once served in one of the Federal hospitals for drug addicts, have formulated ideas about drug addiction, including their personal philosophies of how the problem should be handled. [45,46,47,48,49,50]

Several follow-up studies have reported abstinence rates which vary from less than 10 percent to over 90 percent of posthospitalized drug addicts. [51,52,53,54,55,56] It is quite impossible to explain such differences in outcome, since none of the studies adequately specified the types of addicts, nature of treatment, or kinds of posthospital environments investigated.

A Proposed Program for the Lexington PHS Hospital

The general objective of a proposed program would be to develop *environmental assessment profiles* to classify census zone populations on dimensions which are presumably related to drug abuse. Addict neighborhoods, defined in terms of census tracts or zones (i.e., several tracts) could be indexed on the basis of information from three sources: *(1)* personal orientations, i.e., modes of adaptation of addicts drawn from designated census areas, *(2)* the addicts' impressions or perceptions of their social environments, including their verbal reports of observable events which occur in their neighborhoods, and *(3)* reported facts from census measurements of zonal populations. Verbal reports of hospitalized addicts would be supplemented by reports from addicts residing in the census tracts who have never been treated at Lexington, as well as from the residual populations of the same communities.

Additional objectives of the program would be: (1) to collect community adjustment criteria including patterns of drug use and abstinence on posthospitalized addicts in two or more census zones, and (2) to analyze such criteria as a function of (a) the addicts' characteristic mode of adaptation, (b) predominant role relationships developed in the hospital, (c) addicts' perceptions of their "home" environments, and (d) ecological conditions which differentiate such environments.

The work would be carried out in three phases: (1) hospital studies to isolate the natural habitats of addicts treated at Lexington, (2) hospital and field studies to construct environmental assessment profiles for classifying such habitats, and (3) additional hospital and field studies to demonstrate the usefulness of the profiles in predicting drug use and abstinence patterns, and to measure the impact of role relationships developed in the hospital upon those patterns.

Specific Projects

Delineation of the Natural Habitats
of Drug Addicts

Home addresses given by urban addicts upon admission to the Lexington hospital provide an inadequate basis for delineating ecologically-defined areas which may be highly relevant for drug addiction. Addresses given for official records often specify dwellings of primary group members, i.e., parents, spouses, or other relatives. The heads of such households, except when the addict himself is so designated, are usually not addicted. These dwelling units and their immediate surroundings constitute only one of several habitats which presumably contribute to drug addiction or sustain periods of abstinence. Furthermore, especially when actively addicted, a family member who uses drugs probably spends less time at the given address than he spends in his drug procurement habitat, which may be a considerable distance from his home. Also, during periods of abstinence, the postaddict may inhabit still a third environment which may be different, ecologically, from the two habitats specified above. Such would likely be the case if the postaddict were under the supervision of a probation officer, were receiving outpatient psychiatric care, or were engaged in a lawful occupation.

The purpose of this study would be to delineate the multiple habitats of urban drug addicts.

By studying the natural histories of hospitalized addicts from large urban communities, it is hypothesized that at least two ecologically different environments could be specified. One of these might be called the drug procurement habitat, i.e., the "pick-up point," where addicts obtain their illegal supply of narcotic drugs. The same geographically defined area would be associated in addicts' life histories with their initial introduction to drugs, and with relapse following periods of abstinence. A second habitat, which would differ from the first on ecological dimensions, would be related to periods of abstinence and lawful employment. A third addict environment might be associated with "hustling." It may be shown that addicts practice illegal rackets to obtain money in different environments than those in which they live, work, or procure drugs.

The factor analytic structure of ecological dimensions which define the various environments inhabited by addicts may disprove the hypothesis of multiple habitats. Perhaps initial drug use and relapse, on the one hand, and abstinence or lawful employment, on the other, are bipolar manifestations of a single factor. The home habitat, i.e., the environment inhabited by the addict's primary group, may constitute a separate factor, or it may load on one of the poles of the single factor.

Outcomes of this study would be directly relevant to the development of environmental assessment profiles for estimating the degree of drug "risk" in urban neighborhoods. Such profiles, in turn, would provide a method of matching the prospective social environments of "treated" and "control" groups of hospitalized addicts, thus facilitating the planning and execution of controlled studies to evaluate the hospital program.

*Subcommunites in the Internal Environment
of the Lexington Hospital*

A concept of "prisonization" has been advanced by sociologists [23] to define the "taking on, in greater or lesser degree, the folkways, mores, customs, and general culture of the penitentiary." Wheeler [22] provided methods for studying the above phenomena in the prison community. Essentially, Wheeler used a questionnaire to elicit verbal reports from prisoners concerning (1) their approval (or disapproval) of inmate behavior in hypothetical prison situations, (2) their opinions of how other inmates would view such behavior, (3) their approval (or disapproval) of staff behavior in prison situations, (4) their opinions of other inmates' expectations of staff in those situations, (5) the degree of contact of inmates with each other and their participation in staff sponsored activities, and (6) verbal reports of the inmates concerning their personal backgrounds and their self-concepts.

Portions of the above questionnaire were also rated by the custodial and treatment staffs of the prison. Verbal responses of staff to hypothetical situations were accepted as representative of societal expectations of inmate behavior. Only those items which produced a consensus in staff expectations were retained in the questionnaire.

Wheeler found that the inmate value system, i.e., the "prisonization syndrome," conflicted more with staff expectations among inmates who were in the middle of their terms of incarceration. Apparently, during the first half of his prison sentence the inmate's values became more and more like those of the prison population. As the time approached for him to return to the outside community, however, he tended to abandon the prison code and adopt the mores of society.

It is perhaps significant that an attempt to demonstrate the above phenomenon in prisoner addicts at the Lexington Hospital failed to replicate Wheeler's findings. [57].

It is submitted that the development of the prisonization syndrome depends upon a compatibility between the addict's value system which he brings to the hospital and the predominant value system which he encounters in the institution. It is further submitted that such values are transmitted through verbal behavior. [58] It is hypothesized that the internal environment of the Lexington Hospital is comprised of multiple verbal communities. For example, the Northern urban minority group member who uses heroin as a drug of choice would belong to a different verbal community than would the rural, white morphine user from the South. There may be many verbal communities within the addict population which correspond to separate and different sociocultural environments outside the hospital.

Thus, by collecting verbal responses shared by functional subgroups of patients and staff in the hospital, it should be possible to delineate multiple value systems. By estimating the number of encounters between members of such groups, and the degree of satisfaction gained from such encounters, it should be possible to predict changes in the value systems of individuals.

It is hypothesized that two or more verbal communities can be identified within the hospital staff. It is further hypothesized that certain staff subgroups may share the value systems of certain patient subgroups, and that relationships between patients and patient and staff, patients and patients, and staff and staff can be predicted on the basis of shared verbal responses to stimulus situation.

Finally, it is submitted that the development of the prisonization syndrome among incarcerated addicts can be predicted from membership in designated verbal communities, and from role identifications and relationships which develop in such communities.

It is hypothesized that membership in certain verbal communities will be related to significant behavioral outcomes both in the hospital and after discharge. Members of certain subgroups will be found more acceptable for psychotherapy than others, and will seek such treatment both in the hospital and in aftercare facilities. In general, posthospitalized addicts will seek subgroups in the community with whom they share verbal responses. Some of these groups would tend to contribute to a member's relapse to drugs; and others would sustain him in periods of abstinence.

The significance of the above study is that verbal communities subgoups, and that relationships between patients can be modified. Individuals in one subgroup can be taught the verbal responses of another, thus opening up to them alternative modes of adaptation.

Addict's Perceptions of their
Sociocultural Environments

To say that abuse of narcotic drugs is a sociological problem conveys too little or too much about addiction. There are sociologists who assume that everything known about addicts and their patterns of drug use, abstinence, and relapse can be explained by their social environments. To the psychodynamically-oriented clinician such a position is untenable. The traditional medical model and the ecological school of sociology appear at first glance to be at opposite poles in their basic assumptions concerning mental disorder. In actual fact, however, the clinician's understanding of environment may be quite similar to that held by the orthodox human ecologist, namely, that it is something "out there," represented by the natural world which surrounds the human organism. Hollingshead [59] raised a number of searching questions concerning ecological explanations. "What aspects of the human community as conceived by the ecologist are attributable to noncultural and what ones to cultural factors?" Pirey, [60] in discussing Hollingshead's question, said: "There can be no environment apart from that which is defined into being by social and cultural processes . . . cultural factors intervene at every point between noncultural factors and the human community." In the words of George H. Mead, the environment is never appropriately designated as something that is "just there." "The community as such creates its environment by being sensitive to it." [61]

From a psychological viewpoint, it is submitted that the environment which is relevant to the drug addict and his drug behavior is that which is screened through his perceptions. Stated in another way, "it may not be so much the environment but the way the addict perceives it that makes a difference."

Admittedly, the above distinction may simply reflect a methodological dilemma. Not all members who inhabit a given natural environment are subjected to the same sociocultural factors. Unless there is some evidence that a given factor has been experienced, there is little justification for asking whether or not it made a difference. Thus, it may be feasible to think in terms of the potential environment and the active environment of the addict. For purposes of this study, the potential environment will be defined by census measures of zonal populations, using methods of social area analysis described by Shevky and Bell. [9] The active environment of addicts will be defined in terms of their perceptions of sociocultural aspects of the urban neighborhoods in which they live. Addict's verbal reports of environmental characteristics, including their recollection of human events that have occurred in their neighborhoods, will be elicited by using work association methods, self-rating questionnaires, sentence completion blanks, and responses to photographs of natural structures taken in their neighborhoods.

It is hypothesized that the addict's perceptions of their neighborhoods will yield different environmental patterns than those gained from Shevky's methods of social area analysis. Furthermore, the perceptual approach will isolate sociocultural dimensions which will predict more effectively admission rates to the Lexington Hospital than will the orthodox ecological approach.

Assessment of Drug Risk in Selected
Census Tracts

By "drug risk" is meant the sociocultural attributes of the addicts' neighborhood which are conducive to drug use or which sustain abstinence. Thus, drug risk which has a plural connotation can be either high or low (plus or minus). High drug risk (plus) would be conducive to initial drug use and relapse, while low drug risk (minus) would sustain abstinence and lawful employment.

It is proposed to study two or more census tracts in each of five cities: New York, Chicago, Washington, D.C., Atlanta, and Birmingham. For a tract to be selected for study it must have contributed at least 20 addicts to the Lexington Hospital in the past five years. In each city, two or more tracts will be studied which can be differentiated on the census measures which Chein and his associates [39] found to be related to prevalence of drug use. Presumably, such tracts would differ on drug risk as defined above.

Community surveys will be conducted for three purposes: (1) to collect information on drug relapse and abstinence patterns among addicts, treated at Lexington during the preceding five years, who are currently living in the census tracts studied; (2) to sample the residual populations of the same census areas for their factual information, opinions, and attitudes concerning (a) community programs in education, health, welfare, and economic opportunity; (b) addiction and crime in relation to medical care and law enforcement; and (3) the Lexington Hospital's impact, either directly or indirectly, upon the lives of individuals in the communities.

The significance of this study is that it will provide follow-up data on addicts treated at Lexington, and will presumably permit observations on other addicts who have never been treated at Lexington, as well as nonaddicts from the same communities. Prevailing social attitudes held by addicts and nonaddicts from tracts with different addiction rates can be compared.

Significance of the Proposed
Research Program

The proper execution of the proposed studies will provide information of both practical and theoretical significance. The psychological and sociocultural dimensions, formulated and measured as proposed above, will provide a social psychiatric model within which to assess specific experimental treatments of hospitalized addicts conducted by the Clinical Services at Lexington. The studies will also permit observations on addicts and nonaddicts, alike, in their natural habitats.

Correlations between antecedent and outcome variables in the natural histories of drug addicts, derived from these studies, will lend themselves to etiological inferences, and may lead ultimately to a more adequate theory of drug addiction.

References

1. Lowry; J.: Hospital treatment of the narcotic addict, Fed. Prob. 20: 42-51, 1956.
2. Rasor, R.: Narcotic Addicts: Personality Characteristics and Hospital Treatment, in Hoch, P., and Zubin, J. (Eds.): Problems of Addiction Habituation, New York, Grune & Stratton, 1959.
3. Faris, R., and Dunham, W.: Mental Disorders in Urban Areas, Chicago, University of Chicago Press, 1960.
4. Clausen, J., and Kohn, M.: The ecological approach in social psychology, Am. J. Sociol. 60: 140-151, 1954.
5. Mintz, N., and Schwartz, D.: Urban ecology and psychosis: community factors in the incidence of schizophrenia and manic-depression among Italians in Greater Boston, Internat. J. Social Psychiat. 10: 101-118, 1964.
6. Kennedy, M.: Is there an ecology of mental illness? Internat. J. Social Psychiat. 10: 119-133, 1964.
7. Shevky, E., and Williams, M.: The Social Areas of Los Angeles: Analysis and Typology, Berkeley, University of California Press, 1949.
8. Shevky, E., and Bell, W.: Social Area Analysis: Theory, Illustrative Application and Computational Procedures, Stanford, Stanford University Press, 1955.
9. Shevky, E., and Bell, W.: Social Area Analysis, in Theodorson, G. (Ed.): Studies in Human Ecology, New York, Harper & Row, 1961.
10. Bell, W.: Economic, family, and ethnic status: an empirical test, Am. Sociol. Rev. 20: 45-52, 1955.
11. Van Arsdol, M., Camelleri, S., and Schmid, C.: The Generality of Urban Social Area Indexes, in Theodorson, G. (Ed.): Studies in Human Ecology, New York, Harper & Row, 1961.
12. Sells, S.B.: Ecology and the Science of Psychology, Multivar. Behav. Res., 1: 131-144 (April) 1966.
13. Barker, R.: Exploration in ecological psychology, Am. Psychol. 20: 1-14, 1965.
14. McLean, A., Monroe, J., Yolles, S., Hill, H., and Storrow, J.: Acceptability for psychotherapy of institutionalized narcotic addicts, Arch. Neurol. & Psychiat. 74: 356-362, 1955.
15. Monroe, J., and Hill, H.: Hill-Monroe Inventory for predicting acceptability for psychotherapy in the institutionalized narcotic addict, J. Clin. Psychol. 14: 31-36, 1958.
16. Hill, H., Haertzen, C., and Glaser, R.: Personality characteristics of narcotic addicts, J. Gen. Psychol. 62: 127-139, 1960.
17. Monroe, J., and Astin, A.: Identification processes in hospitalized narcotic drug addicts, J. Abnorm. & Social Psychol. 63: 215-218, 1961.
18. Monroe, J., Miller, J., and Lyle, W.: Description of Psychologic, Demo-

graphic, Addiction History, and Treatment Related Variables Employed in the Screening of Addict Patients. Experimental Test Manual, Lexington, Kentucky, USPHS Hospital, 1963.

19. Monroe, J., Miller, J., and Lyle, W.: The extension of psychopathic deviancy scales for the screening of addict patients, J. Educ. & Psychol. Measur. 22: 47-56, 1964.

20. Jones, M.: The Therapeutic Community, New York, Basic Books, Inc., 1953.

21. Stanton, A., and Schwartz, M.: The Mental Hospital, New York, Basic Books, Inc., 1954.

22. Wheeler, S.: Social Organization in a Correctional Community, Doctoral dissertation, Seattle, University of Washington, 1958.

23. Clemmer, D.: The Prison Community, New York, Rinehart & Co., 1959.

24. Skinner, B.: Verbal Behavior, New York, Appleton-Century-Croft, Inc., 1957.

25. Pace, C., and Stern, G.: An approach to the measurement of psychological characteristics of college environments, J. Educ. Psychol. 49: 269-277, 1958.

26. Thistlethwaite, D.: College press and student achievement, J. Educ. Psychol. 50: 183-191, 1959.

27. Astin, A., and Holland, J.: The environmental assessment technique: a way to measure college environments, J. Psychol. 52: 308-316, 1961.

28. Linton, R.: The Cultural Background of Personality, New York, Century, 1945.

29. Holland, J.: Some Explorations of a Theory of Vocational Choice, Evanston, Illinois, National Merit Scholarship Corporation, 1961.

30. Astin, A.: The inventory of college activities (ICA): assessing the college environment through observable events, Paper presented at the annual meeting of the American Psychological Association, Chicago, 1965.

31. Hill, H., Kornetsky, C., Flanary, H., and Wikler, A.: Effects of anxiety and morphine on discrimination of intensities of painful stimuli, J. Clin. Invest. 31: 473-480, 1952.

32. Hill, H.: The social deviant and initial addiction to narcotics and alcohol, Quart. J. Stud. Alcohol, 23: 562-582, 1962.

33. Wikler, A.: Conditioning Factors in Opiate Addiction and Relapse, in Wilner, D., and Kassebaum, G. (Eds.): Narcotics, New York, McGraw-Hill Book Co., Inc., 1965.

34. O'Donnell, J.: A follow-up of narcotic addicts: mortality, relapse and abstinence, Am. J. Orthopsychiat. 34: 948-954, 1963.

35. Ball, J.: Two patterns of narcotic drug addiction in the United States, J. Criminal Law, Criminol. & Police Sci. 56: 203-211, 1965.

36. Ball, J., and Cottrell, E.: Admissions of narcotic drug addicts to Public Health Service Hospitals, 1935-63, Pub. Health Rep. 80: 471-475, 1965.

37. Ball, J., and Pabon, D.: Locating and interviewing narcotic addicts in Puerto Rico, Sociol. & Social Res. 49: 401-411, 1965.

38. Ball, J., and Bates, W.: Migration and residential mobility of narcotic addicts, Social Problems, 14: 56-69, 1966.
39. Chein, I., Gerard, D., Lee, R., and Rosenfeld, E.: The Road to H, New York, Basic Books, Inc., 1964.
40. Bates, W.: Personal communication, 1965.
41. Lewis, J., and Osberg, J.: Observation of institutionalized treatment of character disorders, Am. J. Orthopsychiat. 28: 730-749, 1958.
42. Blachly, P., Pepper, B., Scott, W., and Baganz, P.: Group therapy and hospitalization of narcotic addicts, Arch. Gen. Psychiat. 5: 393-396, 1961.
43. Berliner, A.: The helping process in a hospital for narcotic addicts, Fed. Prob. 26: 57-62, 1962.
44. Baganz, P., and Maddux, J.: Employment status of narcotic addicts one year after hospital discharge, Pub. Health Rep. 80: 615-622, 1965.
45. Lindesmith, A.: Opiate Addiction, Bloomington, Indiana, Principia Press, 1947.
46. Nyswander, M.: The Drug Addict as a Patient, New York, Grune-Stratton, 1956.
47. Ausubel, D.: Controversial issues in the management of drug addiction: legalization, ambulatory treatment, and the British system, Ment. Hyg. 44: 535-544, 1960.
48. Winick, C.: Maturing Out of Narcotic Addiction, Bull. Narcot. 14: 1-7, 1962.
49. Kolb, L.: Drug addiction, Springfield, Illinois, Charles C. Thomas, 1962.
50. Schur, E.: Narcotic Addiction in Britain and America: the Impact of Public Policy, Bloomington, Indiana, Indiana University Press, 1962.
51. Quinn, W.: Narcotic addiction-medical and legal problems with physicians, California Med. 94: 214-217, 1961.
52. Hunt, G., and Odoroff, M.: Follow-up study of narcotic drug addicts after hospitalization, Pub. Health Rep. 77: 41-54, 1962.
53. O'Donnell, J.: A post-hospital study of Kentucky addicts—a preliminary report. J. Kentucky St. M.A. 61: 573-577, 1963.
54. Diskind, M., and Klonsky, G.: A second look at the New York State parole drug experiments, Fed. Prob. 28:34-41, 1965.
55. Vaillant, G.: A 12-year follow-up of New York City addicts: I. Relation of treatment to outcome, Am. J. Psychiat. 122: 727-737, 1966.
56. O'Donnell, J.: The Relapse Rate in Narcotic Addiction: a Critique of Follow-up Studies, in Wilner, D., and Kassebaum, G. (Eds.): Narcotics, New York, McGraw-Hill Book Co., 1965.
57. Harris, H., Holston, J., Jackson, E., Reece, V., and Smith, M.: Socialization in a Correctional Community vs. Socialization in an Addict Prison Community, Joint Master's Thesis in Social Work, University of Louisville, Louisville, Kentucky, 1965.
58. Cressey, D.: Social psychological foundations for using criminals in the rehabilitation of criminals, J. Res. Crime & Delinq., 2: 49-59, 1965.

59. Hollingshead, A.: Community Research: Development and Present Condition, in Theodorson, G. (Ed.): Studies in Human Ecology, New York, Harper & Row, 1961.
60. Pirey, W.: In discussion of Hollingshead, A.: Community Research: Development and Present Condition, in Theodorson, G. (Ed.): Studies in Human Ecology, New York, Harper & Row, 1961.
61. Meade, G.: Mind, Self and Society, Chicago, University of Chicago Press, 1934.

22 An Ecological View of Cigarette Smoking

Bernard Mausner
Beaver College

The purpose of this article is to explore the implications of an ecological model of smoking behavior. The model derives from the thinking of epidemiologists about the nature of the causes of disease and from the kind of theorizing about behavior which has been common in social psychology in the last generation. Figure 22-1, drawn from the volume on smoking behavior which has reported most of our preliminary work (Mausner & Platt, 1971), shows the basic character of this model.

There are three components: input (i.e., environment), mediating systems, and output (i.e., behavior). The input is specified in terms of three aspects of the environment: biological, social, and physical. Although these three may be distinguished conceptually, their interrelations sometimes make the distinction hard to apply in the real world. In the brackets are found theoretical constructs. And last, to the right under outputs, are a variety of measurable behaviors. The implications of this model for two areas related to smoking behavior are explored in this article. The first is the study of change in smoking among individual smokers. The second is an analysis of society's reactions to the problems of smoking. The rationale for our entire discussion is the assumption, first, that an understanding of an individual's smoking is impossible without a clear picture of the role that smoking behavior plays in his entire life pattern.

Reprinted with permission from *Journal of Abnormal Psychology*, 81:115-126, 1973.

Second is the assumption that we cannot understand the smoking behavior of individuals without considering the individual within his sociocultural framework.

A Model for Smoking Behavior

Figure 22-2 shows the model applied to an analysis of smoking behavior. Among inputs is the cigarette itself as a biological entity. Cigarettes yield a complex "soup" with a variety of pharmacological effects; nicotine, tar, and carbon monoxide are only the best known of its components. The social environment not only includes the smoking behavior of others and the reactions of others to smokers but also encompasses the many ways in which society legitimates cigarette smoking. These are evidenced in physical aspects of the environment—special areas set aside for smoking, physical arrangements such as tables with matches and ashtrays, which provide a framework reinforcing the tendency to smoke, and, of course, the displays of cigarettes and cigarette advertising.

The constructs within the brackets in Figure 22-2 include the many physiological mechanisms which are affected by the intake of tobacco smoke and the signals which stimulate sensory systems sensitive to various aspects of the cigarette. However, in the current article, the primary emphasis is on "events in the head."

Given the well-known hazards of smoking, it might be generally accepted that cigarette smokers perceive themselves as taking a fairly considerable risk. It has become increasingly common in recent years to approach the analysis of risky

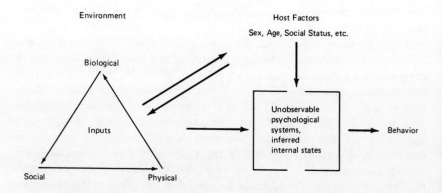

Figure 22-1. An Ecological Model for the Determinants of Behavior. (Reprinted with Permission from Smoking: A Behavioral Analysis by B. Mausner and E.S. Platt. Copyrighted 1971 by Pergamon Press, Inc.).

behaviors through a subjective expected utility model. A recent survey of the literature by Mitchell and Biglan (1971) detailed a wide variety of areas in which subjective expected utility is a useful framework for an understanding of decision and choice. A specific example of this approach is found in the work of Vinokur and his colleagues (Burnstein, Miller, Vinokur, Katz, & Crowley, 1971; Vinokur, 1971), who applied a subjective expected utility model to an analysis of the so-called risky shift phenomenon. In addition to the current writer, several others (Janis & Mann, 1968; Straits, 1965) have attempted to use utility models for an understanding of smoking behavior. The current paper focuses on the use of subjective expected utility as a unifying construct.

In Figure 22-2 at the right, listed under outputs, are smoking a, b, c, . . . n. A large body of research has accumulated in recent years which demonstrates that cigarette smoking is not in itself a unitary phenomenon. The implications of this notion are discussed in detail in the following section, Patterns of Smoking.

The final aspect of the model is a loop which leads from smoking behavior to inputs. The smoking of a cigarette has many different kinds of consequences. Some of these are listed on the diagram. Smoking a cigarette yields information-rich stimulation, an impact on social interaction, a variety of pharmacological effects, and a heightened sense of self. Thus the smoking of each cigarette either weakens or strengthens the subjective expected utility of further smoking by providing inputs which affect the smoker, even if only to a minute degree.

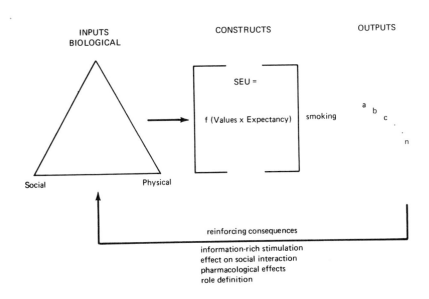

Figure 22-2. Model for Smoking Behavior.

Patterns of Smoking

The concept that cigarette smoking represents a variety of different sources of reward and is embedded in a large variety of different behaviors is by now quite familiar. Theoretical discussions by Tomkins (1966b) and both conceptualizations and data presented by Horn and Waingrow (1966), McKennell (1968), and Mausner and Platt (1971) have provided a basis for a picture of cigarette smoking as fulfilling many different functions. In terms of our ecological model the smoking of each cigarette is a function of an interaction between the inputs in that situation and the consequences of the smoking. In Figure 22-2, subscripts a, b, c, . . . n under output represent different complex behavior patterns, each revolving about the smoking of a cigarette but each including a variety of other behaviors. The other behaviors might include drinking coffee, typing, driving, talking with friends at a cocktail party, putting a client or interviewee at ease, or running a complex high-speed machine. Thus each behavioral complex, although it is labeled "smoking a cigarette," really consists of an integrated net of inputs, events in the head, and associated collateral behaviors. One could consider the actual smoking a final common path for a wide variety of these behavioral complexes.

Although I have presented my notions about patterns of smoking elsewhere (Mausner & Platt, 1971), it may be appropriate at this point to summarize them briefly. The data support the concept that smoking may represent three kinds of functions. The first derives from the stimulus properties of the cigarette. Thus the taste and smell of a cigarette may provide simple pleasure. It may give the smoker a pickup when he is tired. It can provide reduction of tension and for those smokers described as "psychologically addicted" a relief from the discomfort produced by craving. These functions of the cigarette may be due to a number of different components of the cigarette as stimulus. Included are the pharmacological effect of the substances in the smoke, the physical stimulation produced by the hot air and by the irritating particles, and the sensory impact of the manipulation of the hands and mouth. The second dimension revolves around the social aspects of cigarette smoking. Cigarettes can provide a cement which increases the cohesiveness of social groups. When one person begins to smoke, this may trigger smoking by others with whom he or she is interacting. There is no question that a great deal of smoking, although far from all, is part of a complex social ritual. The last dimension is the most difficult to specify in behavioral terms. But there seems to be some evidence that the use of cigarettes is a form of expressive behavior which functions for many smokers as a part of the definition of self-concept. There is a widespread acceptance of the notion that much smoking among adolescents plays this function, although some writers are skeptical of the continued importance of this function of smoking among adults.

I would like to cite a specific example which may help to clarify the concept of smoking as a final common path. One of the organizers of this conference, Joseph D. Matarazzo, informed me (personal communication, 1972) that a number of his clients in marriage counseling say that they have difficulty in adjusting sexually and that they often smoke cigarettes almost compulsively after they have engaged in intercourse because of the tensions aroused between themselves and their partners. This pattern of postcoital smoking certainly fits in with the notion that cigarettes may be used to reduce tension. However, I expect we have all seen the classical bedroom scene in contemporary Swedish movies in which, after climax, one of the lovers lights a cigarette for the other as well as for himself or herself. The two then smoke together in peaceful relaxation, staring into the distance. The smoking obviously reinforces the sense of communion and peace which derives from the scene. What a very versatile act is smoking!

Implications of the Ecological Model
for an Understanding of Change in
Smoking among Individuals

We know all too little about the forces which lead people to stop smoking. As a number of writers have pointed out, there is a puzzling discrepancy between the extreme difficulty psychologists find in inducing change in smoking and the fact that a very large number of people, estimated to be some twenty-nine million, have succeeded in giving it up, probably most of them without the benefit of formal assistance. It would seem simple to find out what leads to cessation of smoking merely by asking ex-smokers. However, this has not turned out to be very fruitful since they give a wide variety of answers, none of which seem to add up to anything which can be applied to the induction of change in others. One of the major problems, of course, is that retrospective accounts of a phenomenon as complex as giving up smoking are necessarily very weak.

Many writers (e.g., Horn, 1971) discuss change in terms of two processes. The first is decision, the second implementation. Decision is inferred, usually from verbal behavior. Implementation should be demonstrated through observed change in smoking levels, although the data are usually derived from self-reports.

As was pointed out above, if the process of decision is basic to change, then a subjective expected utility model is an ideal approach to the study of the first steps in cessation. Unhappily, the decisional pattern for smoking is probably more like a messy bush, to use Raiffa's (1970) picturesque phrase, than a neatly shaped tree. Even after smokers have officially "stopped smoking," they may have to replay many of the anxious moments which preceded that "decision" each time they are faced by the temptation to smoke. And it would be hard to describe the branches which led up to a presumed moment of decision. You get a neat tree only when you ask people to generalize about their reasons for smoking or stopping or to discuss their anticipations of the future course of their smoking. The difference between the actualities of transitions and the character of these generalizations may account for the unilluminating quality of retrospective data about the transition from smoking to nonsmoking status.

However, we should not underestimate the frequency of moments of crisis in which a quantal change in subjective expected utility leads to an event in the head which we may label a "decision to stop smoking." It is an important subject for research to try to determine what factors lead to such moments and the character of the changes in subjective expected utility which are followed by actual changes in smoking behavior.

After the smoker has "decided to stop" comes the struggle to keep from backsliding. Whether or not temporary cessation of smoking is maintained is probably dependent on a great many factors in the life of the smoker. Here again, the ecological model may enable us to identify the determinants of implementation.

Some Data on the Determinants of Decision

At this point, I should like to introduce some evidence from a recent study of smoking behavior in a group of adults. The study will be reported in detail elsewhere,* but a brief summary may be useful here. The major purpose of the study was to discover some of the factors which determine the effectiveness of role playing as a procedure for inducing change in smoking. The population was a group of parents belonging to the Parent-Teachers Association (PTA) of three schools in a suburban school district near Philadelphia. These had been recruited by telephoning all of the members of the PTA, asking all smokers as well as a random sample of nonsmokers and ex-smokers to attend pretest sessions at the school, and then asking subjects who completed the pretest to participate in the experiment.

In the role playing, one group of subjects played the role of a physician describing the work of a diagnostic clinic devoted to uncovering the ill effects of smoking and then urging an individual patient to stop smoking on the basis of laboratory tests showing damage to his heart and lungs. Other subjects played the role of a writer learning about the work of the clinic or a writer who himself becomes a patient in such a clinic. There were two control groups. One was exposed to semiprogrammed written materials to learn the information that was presented in the role playing. The other carried out irrelevant role playing devoted to driver safety.

Merely taking a test of subjective expected utilities led to enough change among the control groups so that the experiment was not "a success," although approximately one third of the subjects playing the "doctor's" role did reduce

*B. Mausner. A study of cigarette smoking in adults. Manuscript in preparation, 1972.

their smoking levels substantially, a change roughly equivalent to that found in previous experiences in role playing (Mausner & Platt, 1971; Platt, Krassen, & Mausner, 1969).

The primary predictors of short-range change in smoking were scores on a test of subjective expected utility. The form of the test is shown in Figure 22-3.

During the pretest, subjects have been asked to indicate the value they placed on a wide variety of outcomes of continuing to smoke or not smoking and then to give an estimate of their expectation that these outcomes would occur if they continued to smoke or if they stopped. Subjective expected utility scores are calculated by multiplying the value by the expectancy separately for continuing and for stopping, as well as for the difference in expectation between continuing and stopping.

Subjects who cut down or stopped after the experiment had a significantly

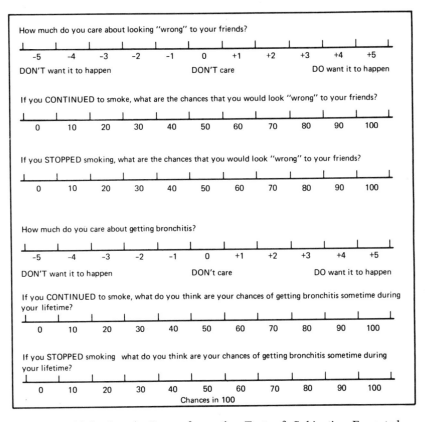

Figure 22-3. Sample Items from the Test of Subjective Expected Utility.

higher pretest subjective expected utility for stopping than those whose smoking was relatively little affected (see Table 22-1). In contrast, there was no difference between the two groups in subjective expected utility for continuing to smoke (see Table 22-2).

These results are almost exactly equivalent to those obtained from a population of male college students (Mausner & Platt, 1971). Reinforcing the distinction between the impact of utilities for continuing and utilities for stopping are the data comparing ex-smokers, nonsmokers, and smokers. Again, we find that ex-smokers and nonsmokers have markedly higher subjective

Table 22-1

Comparison of the Subjective Expected Utility for Stopping Smoking among Subjects Who Reduced Smoking Levels by One-Half Pack or More (Changers) with Those Who Did Not (Nonchangers) after Role-Playing or Control Procedures

Variance	SS	df	MS	F	p
Between	10952	1	10952	5.39	<.05
Within	209120	103	2030		
Total	220073	104			

Statistic	Changers	Nonchangers
$\bar{X}$: Value × Stopping	101.9	74.2
SD	41.3	45.7
N	17	88

Table 22-2

Comparison of the Subjective Expected Utility for Continuing to Smoke among Subjects Who Reduced Smoking Levels by One-Half Pack or More (Changers) with Those Who Did Not (Nonchangers) after Role-Playing or Control Procedures

Variance	SS	df	MS	F	p
Between	1044	1	1044	.44	ns
Within	244363	103	2372		
Total	245407	104			

Statistic	Changers	Nonchangers
$\bar{X}$: Value × Continuing	54.1	45.5
SD	54.8	47.5
N	17	88

expected utility for stopping than current smokers, but that subjective expected utility for continuing is essentially the same among all three.

The Determinants of Decision

What these data say is that people make the decision to stop smoking, not because they have a heightened fear of the consequences of continuing to smoke but because they have an increased expectation of benefits from stopping. Almost everybody is agreed that continuing to smoke is a bad thing. What seems to differentiate those people who stop smoking from those who continue is that the people who continue find not smoking more aversive than continuing to smoke, whereas those who stop are able to convince themselves that not smoking might be worthwhile after all.

A factor analysis of the subjective expected utility test (see Table 22-3) indicated that several specific areas of content in the test clearly differentiate changers from nonchangers, ex-smokers from smokers. One of the most powerful predictors of change was the factor which described the utility of health; subjects who cut down had developed an increased subjective expected utility for improvement in health should they stop smoking. In contrast, a factor which consisted of items describing the use of smoking for tension release also predicted change. Smokers who expected difficulty in handling tension were likely not to reduce their levels of smoking after the experiment; those who expected to be able to handle tension without cigarettes did cut down.

Is is probable that the failure of most aversive conditioning techniques to affect smoking behavior significantly is due to the balance of utilities I have just described. Unfortunately, it is not possible to make *not* smoking more attractive by making *some* smoking aversive. As Premack (1970) pointed out so wittily in his paper in the previous conference in this series, it is only too easy for a person subjected to aversive conditioning to smoke under conditions in which the smoking is not aversive.

Premack's solution, like Homme's (1965), is to make a negative reaction to cigarettes hard to evade by putting the aversion inside the head of the smoker through the use of so-called "coverants." That is, the smoker has to learn to associate feelings of shame or guilt over smoking with events having a high probability of occurrence. Unhappily, as Premack himself pointed out, the degree to which fresh feelings of shame can continue to be aroused is also very limited. And thus it is likely that aversive coverants will have little permanent effect on many smokers.

How, then, can we stimulate increased utility for not smoking? An interesting tack is suggested by the work of Cautela (1971), a clinical psychologist who trains his patients to engage in mediating responses which are intended to reinforce, positively or negatively, desirable or undesirable behaviors. Actually,

Table 22-3

Summary of Factor Analysis of Expectancy for Various Outcomes of Continuing or Ceasing to Smoke

Factor	Loading	% of Variance
1. Self-Concept		8.8
Feeling proud of yourself	−.68	
Other smokers envious of you	−.62	
Nonsmokers respecting you	−.51	
Saving money	−.65	
2. Tension Reduction		9.1
Being nervous	−.70	
Enjoying your coffee	−.57	
Feeling depressed or blue	−.62	
Being energetic	+.45	
Irritable with people	−.45	
Concentrating well	+.59	
Feeling really good when you first get up in the morning	+.45	
Working well	+.45	
Feeling like "yourself"	+.62	
Becoming upset easily	−.59	
3. Health		8.2
Becoming short of breath	+.42	
Getting lung cancer	+.58	
Getting heart disease	+.70	
Having your teeth and fingers stained	+.74	
Getting bronchitis	+.71	
Coughing a lot in the mornings	+.71	
4. Hedonic-Esthetic		6.8
Enjoying your meals	+.76	
Your home having a pleasant odor	+.55	
Having a good appetite	+.75	
Feeling really good when you first get up in the morning	+.43	
Gaining a noticeable amount of weight	+.53	
5. Stimulation		5.4
Having something to perk you up	+.67	
Something to relieve short periods of boredom	+.73	
6. Social Stimulation (other)		4.1
New friends you make would be nonsmokers	+.71	
Looking "wrong" to your friends	−.77	

Note: N = 164 adults, pretest. Plus sign indicates positive, a minus sign, negative loadings for the scale on the individual factor.

Cautela discussed smoking briefly, but like most clinicians he interpreted the problem as one of need for aversive conditioning. His solution, and he has apparently actually tried this, is to use a kind of "interior aversion" reminiscent of Homme's or Premack's coverants.

I would be more hopeful if someone could teach smokers to fantasize success in not smoking. It is possible that an application of McClelland's (1969) techniques for teaching people how to develop high achievement needs might help cigarette smokers create a resolve to stop smoking. We have made some attempts to develop a "future diary" for smokers in which they try to describe in very detailed and circumstantial manner the events which would take place if they successfully coped with cigarette smoking. So far these attempts have not been evaluated experimentally, but I have found that people can write such an account or role play the fantasy of success, and they seem to enjoy doing it. One of the possible limitations of this approach is that by now a great many smokers have a history of unsuccessful attempts at stopping. It may be, therefore, that imagining success will not be very convincing. However, it is certainly worth a try.

Implementation

It is widely accepted among those engaged in the control of smoking that a person's pattern of smoking is a critical factor in determining whether or not he can succeed in stopping and that people whose patterns differ should use different approaches in their attempts to stop. Several workers (American Cancer Society, 1969; Frederickson, 1969; Horn, 1967) have proposed that smokers could be helped if they knew which patterns were most important in their smoking and had some rational way of reworking their lives to find substitute sources of satisfaction. To return to our discussion of postcoital smoking, this formulation would require teaching the first couple how to handle their tension in some other way than smoking. It might even suggest the desirability of using aversive coverants for the second couple, although it would be a shame to mar the lovely scene. It would obviously be pointless to assist the second couple in finding alternate sources of tension reduction, since their smoking has nothing to do with tension. Similarly, it might be fruitless to try to assist the first couple to stop smoking by finding alternate ways of feeling warm and close, since obviously their smoking is a result of conflict rather than affiliation.

The thesis that one must analyze patterns of smoking and base a prescription for change on these analyses sounds very reasonable. But there are some data which make it a bit suspect. In our study the subjects who maintained reduced smoking levels 6 months after role playing had much higher scores on the scale of Psychological Addiction than subjects who had reverted to their original levels of smoking (see Table 22-4). This might lead to the fatalistic notion that people who use smoking to reduce tension or who crave cigarettes are extremely unlikely to give them up. However, the analysis of differences between changers and nonchangers hides the fact that many of those who have succeeded in stopping were originally smokers for whom a response to craving was an important aspect of smoking. This is not only borne out by our prospective study of the effects of role playing on smoking but also by an analysis of the differences between ex-smokers and current smokers in the same population. We did a factor analysis of the patterns test for our ex-smokers and discovered that the usual array of factors did not emerge. Instead, we found a strong first factor accounting for almost a quarter of the variance in the test. This factor included a conglomerate of items relating to tension reduction, craving, stimulation, and social induction. Almost as many ex-smokers as current smokers are above the midpoint of the scale (300) on this factor. In fact, the mean score for both ex-smokers and current smokers was about 300. Many of our ex-smokers have vivid recollections of the importance of smoking in fulfilling a variety of needs. Nevertheless, they were able to stop. And their abstention seemed to be stable, since virtually none of the ex-smokers we identified at the initial pretest had resumed smoking on our 6-month follow-up. It is my understanding that Horn has similarly failed to find clear-cut relations between patterns of smoking and long-range change. His conclusions are, of course, more solidly based than ours since they are derived from national samples rather than a small local population.

Thus we seem to have a contradiction. Subjects who reported that they use cigarettes to reduce tension or to assuage a craving did not change their smoking patterns after role playing. And when they did cut down temporarily, as happened to some of the boys in the group of college students reported in Mausner and Platt (1971), they were almost always among those who returned

Table 22-4
Comparison of Patterns of Support Scores of Changers and Nonchangers (Criterion: Regressed Smoking Scores at 6-Month Follow-Up)

Variance	SS	df	MS	F	p
Between	69565	1	69565	8.69	<.01
Within	1176525	147	8003		
Total	1246090	148			

Statistic	Changers	Nonchangers
X for psychological addiction	263.3	306.9
SD	78.7	96.6
N	64	85

to previous levels of smoking during the succeeding 6 months. Yet the ex-smokers in our population have mean scores on several factors in the test of patterns of support *higher* than the current smokers. On the use of smoking for the reduction of tension, there were as many ex-smokers whose recollections placed them above the midpoint of the scale as there were current smokers in that range.

There are several possible explanations for the contradiction. The same person might report higher levels of need for smoking as an ex-smoker than he would if tested while he were still smoking, either as a result of nostalgia for the benefits of cigarettes or as a way of justifying the effort needed to quit or as a way of inflating his accomplishment. These explanations assume that in fact the differences in patterns of support found on comparisons of retrospective accounts by ex-smokers and reports by current smokers are specious. There is no direct evidence to support this.

Another kind of mechanism seems to me more likely. The "changers" in our role-playing experiments are primarily people who reduced their levels of smoking, some by sizable amounts; very few actually stopped completely. Our subjects, after all, were not volunteers for a smoking clinic. They were people who were participating in a study not because they wanted to stop smoking but because they wanted to earn money either for themselves (the college students) or for an organization (our PTA groups). The number of people who stopped completely was, therefore, actually below the spontaneous levels found by Horn in the population at large. This may have happened because people who are about to change may refuse to participate in experiments whose purpose seems redundant to them.

It is possible that dependence on cigarettes for reduction of tension or satisfaction of craving makes it difficult to maintain a reduced schedule of smoking but has no effect on the success of attempts to stop entirely. This makes a certain amount of sense in terms of some elementary notions from the experimental study of learning. Reduced levels of smoking imply that there will be times when the smoker aborts learned tendencies to smoke; this has some similarity to a kind of aperiodic reinforcement schedule which is almost guaranteed to make the extinction of a response extremely unlikely. Presumably, for smokers who quit entirely the response can be extinguished in the same way that any other response is extinguished at a zero level of reinforcement. If this analysis is correct, it lends support to Tomkins' assertion that "addicted" smokers, that is those who report a craving for cigarettes, cannot cut down gradually but must stop cold. It adds to the group who should quit cold those smokers for whom tension release is an important aspect of smoking and perhaps, all of McKennell's "dissonant smokers" for whom smoking fulfills important needs of any kind.

A further point must be made about the use of information concerning patterns of support for smoking. Many of the systems of recommendations for smokers revolve around the notion that each pattern may be treated as a unitary process. Thus, we have recommendations for people whose smoking is primarily a response to the need for tension reduction, or primarily social. However, very few smokers show one and only one pattern. We have 400 or 500 profiles of patterns of support from smokers in our various experimental samples; virtually none could be interpreted easily as evidence that the subject was a "positive affect" or "negative affect" smoker. In fact, there is some indication that the affective patterns form a kind of cumulative scale, leading from simple pleasure through tension reduction to "psychological addiction" or craving. In addition, each smoker reported greater or lesser use of smoking for social or role-defining purposes.

Furthermore, we know very little about the relation between the generalizations people give (i.e., answers to questions on the test of patterns of support) and the actual role played by individual cigarettes in the flow of behavior. Our one small diary study revealed discrepancies between diary material and the results of interviews and tests; subjects who rated themselves as highly dependent on cigarettes for the release of tension actually reported only a few instances of smoking in response to externally caused tension. Hunt and Matarazzo (1970), in their paper in the previous symposium in this series, interpreted this to mean that most smoking is "purely habitual," that is, affect free. That is possible, but I do not feel that this smoking is really independent of the fulfillment of needs. We have never found an independent factor for habitual smoking; in our analysis of protocols on the test of patterns of support, "habit" has always been tied to items concerning self-image. The original Horn-Waingrow test did not include items relating to the role-defining properties of smoking and therefore did yield a factor consisting solely of "habit" items. The point is not trivial. Each instance of smoking, no matter how apparently automatic its origin, seems to reinforce the smoker's concept of himself or herself as a "smoker." And each cigarette probably adds its tiny bit to the reinforcement of smoking behavior as it furnishes pleasure, stimulation, or a feeling of social closeness in varying proportions depending on the smoker's style of life and on the setting in which the particular act of smoking is taking place.

The trouble is that we know all too little. We desperately need studies of the natural history of change in smoking. Retrospective accounts are hard to interpret. The discrepancy between our data from diaries and those from interviews or paper-and-pencil tests, referred to above, illustrates this difficulty of interpretation. I am also reminded of Horn's observation that there was a considerable increase in the number of people who stopped smoking after the first surgeon general's report, but that the reasons they gave for stopping were identical with those given by the smaller number of people who stopped *before* the report.

Should we take a leaf from Barker's (1968) book and follow smokers about, observing them in the act of trying to change? It would certainly be useful to be able to specify the "behavior settings," as Barker calls them, in which smoking takes place. Should we ask people engaged in trying to stop smoking to keep detailed diaries? Should we use the techniques of the marketing analysts and assemble panels who meet with us regularly to discuss their problems? In some ways, the smoking clinics could represent a valuable source of such information. Their participants have already been gathered together and many clinics do include discussion groups in which people report their experiences as they are trying to stop smoking. However, I do not know of any systematic attempt to take advantage of this potential gold mine of information.

I am not sure what the implications of this discussion are for programs to help smokers stop. The moral *seems* to be that a systematic analysis of life patterns, the chipping away at individual ecological determinants of behavior and their relationship to ideas, the slow reworking of life patterns is essential to stopping smoking. Actually, I know of no evidence from an analysis of the experiences of ex-smokers which would demonstrate that this is so. I also know of no evidence to the contrary. Clearly, people who stop smoking *must* rearrange their lives to a considerable degree. Does that necessarily mean that the only way of stopping smoking is to engage in a conscious attempt to rearrange one's life? Or is it possible that for reasons which we do not fully understand some people manage to stop and that the rearrangements of their lives are a consequence rather than a cause of the stopping?

Implications of the Ecological Model
for an Analysis of Societal Reactions
to Cigarette Smoking

To the observer, the reaction of most of the world to the dangers of smoking has been weak and sluggish. There *has* been a drop in smoking among adult men, but over 4 in 10 are still smoking regularly. The amount of smoking among adult women has dropped only slightly, and the use of cigarettes seems to be increasing among adolescents (Horn, 1971). While many factors other than actual consumption may affect cigarette production, it is hardly cheering news that the number of cigarettes manufactured in each month in the first half of 1971 was slightly *higher* than during the equivalent period of 1970 (U.S. Treasury Department, 1971). Even if the portrayal of these trends is not entirely accurate, the data hardly argue that smoking is a vanishing phenomenon.

We have used the utility model to study individual smokers. Can we apply a similar model to society? As many observers have noted (e.g., Trilling, 1971), high Western society places great value on achieving, on doing, and places very little or in fact, a negative value on experiencing, withdrawing, subsisting. I think that we can make a case for the notion that cigarettes are used in our society as a major source for the fulfillment of these values. The factors in the various tests

352   Drugs and Social Consequences

of patterns of smoking describe cigarettes as leading to an enhanced ability to
achieve, to better social functioning, to self-definition. The data in the first
portion of our volume on smoking (Mausner & Platt, 1971), in which we
described the natural history of smoking, make it evident that many people use
cigarettes as an important aid to coping. The descriptions smokers give of the
functions of smoking clearly illustrate this. Cigarettes make it possible to get up
and face the world, to calm down when tension becomes too great to bear. They
take the edge off boring, repetitive tasks like driving, typing, tending machines.
Even the social role of smoking aids in coping as the `smoker is helped in his
search for ways of escaping isolation. The fact that smoking is expressive
behavior and thus helps define self-concept also makes the cigarette a useful
prop in the daily struggle to play out one's role. Of course, cigarettes also furnish
sensual gratification. But the point I am making is that the sensual gratification,
which our society might normally view with some suspicion (perhaps by defining
tobacco as a *drug*), is legitimized by the ego-enhancing character of smoking.

The fact that contemporary Western society perceives cigarettes as an
important aid to coping is probably central to the continued survival of cigarette
smoking. As long as it is seen that way, the use of cigarettes will continue to be
accepted by most of the population despite the resultant high cost in illness and
premature death. The benefits of smoking are too consonant with the dominant
values of this society to permit its being relinquished.

But if this is so, how can we hope for change? I have already suggested that
the key to the decision to stop smoking is an expectation of a better life without
cigarettes. The goal is clear; drastic action will occur when cigarette smoking is
no longer seen as a way of helping people cope but instead when *not* smoking is
seen as a way of living well. How to accomplish such a change is not so clear, but
it may be that the single most important task of the psychologist who wants to
have an impact on smoking is not a search for ways to help individual smokers
conquer their dependency but the development of ways to create a change in
society's perception of the utility of smoking.

Summary

The results of an ecological analysis of the smoking behavior of individuals show
that a primary factor in the decision to stop is an increase in the subjective
expected utility of not smoking. As I have noted above, virtually everybody,
smokers, ex-smokers, and non-smokers alike, agrees that smoking is not a good
thing (cf. the national surveys cited by Horn, 1971). People who still smoke,
though, have no confidence that not smoking is any better. We now have some
understanding of the change in utilities which either accompanies or precedes
decision. However, we have not achieved any clear understanding of *why* the
change in utilities occurs in some people and not in others. The results of our

experimentation are paradoxical. Some people change their utilities after minimal exposure to information which is apparently relatively irrelevant. For example, in one study on physician's influence we found that a fair number of people in our control group changed their smoking behavior after merely being asked how much they smoked by a nurse in a doctor's office. Others fail to stop smoking even after massive exposure to new information (Mausner & Platt, 1966) or a terrifying experience of pretending to have lung cancer and facing the necessity for an operation (Platt et al., 1969). Thus the focus of research for the future should be on a search for ways of predicting the circumstances under which the utility of not smoking may be increased to the point at which people make the decision to try to stop.

If we have fair enlightenment on the reasons people continue to smoke or decide to try to stop, I think we have had relatively little success in understanding the process by which these decisions are implemented. We have a good theoretical model in the ecological approach which ought to be able to generate fairly precise and clean-cut experimentation with procedures for reshaping the lift patterns of smokers in order to make implementation of the decision to stop easier. As I have indicated, I am not sure that this model will turn out to be useful. There is too little evidence about the sequence of events relating changes in the ex-smoker's way of life to his success at refraining from cigarettes. An ecological approach to further research on smoking might provide some of the answers.

The data from the test of patterns of support describe the roots of smoking behavior; those from the test of subjective expected utility define attitudes towards smoking. Both sets of data reinforce the notion that cigarette smoking, for many people, is an important source of ego strength. It not only yields a variety of pleasurable sensations but, more important, helps the smoker cope with the demands of life, eases and promotes his or her social interactions, and is a valuable aid to the establishment of a sense of identity. As such, the activity of smoking is congruent with the dominant problem-solving, achievement-oriented values of high Western society. There is little wonder that people find it so hard to give it up or that social response to the dangers of smoking has been so weak. The search for effective means of changing social values associated with smoking may be the main order of business in the years ahead for those who seek to accomplish any large-scale change in smoking behavior.

References

American Cancer Society. *If you want to give up cigarettes*. New York: Author, 1969.

Barker, R.G. Ecological psychology. *Concepts and methods for studying the environment of human behavior*. Stanford, Calif.: Stanford University Press, 1968.

Burnstein, E., Miller, H., Vinokur, A., Katz, S., & Crowley, J. Risky shift is eminently rational. *Journal of Personality and Social Psychology*, 1971, *20*, 462-471.

Cautela, J.R. Covert conditioning. In A. Jacobs & L.B. Sachs (Eds.), *The psychology of private events*. New York: Academic Press, 1971.

Chein, I., Gerard, D.L., Lee, R.S., & Rosenfeld, E. (With collaboration of D.M. Wilner). *The road to H.: Narcotics, delinquency, and social policy*. New York: Basic Books, 1964.

Frederickson, D.T. How to help your patient stop smoking. *National Tuberculosis and Respiratory Disease Association Bulletin*, 1969, *55*, 6-11.

Homme, L.E. Perspectives in psychology: XXIV. Control of coverants, the operants of the mind. *Psychological Record*, 1965, *15*, 501-511.

Horn, D. How to stop smoking: Counsel for physician and patient. Paper presented at the Scientific Program, Clinical Applications of Advances in Cancer Research, Georgetown University, March 11, 1967.

Horn, D. The smoking problem in 1971. Paper presented at the meeting of the American Cancer Society's 13th Annual Science Writers' Seminar, Phoenix, Arizona, April 6, 1971.

Horn, D., & Waingrow, S. Some dimensions of a model for smoking behavior change. In, From Epidemiology to Ecology—A panel discussion; smoking and health in transition. *American Journal of Public Health and the Nation's Health*, 1966, *56* 21-26. (Supplement)

Hunt, W.A. (Ed.) *Learning mechanisms in smoking*. Chicago, Aldine, 1970.

Janis, I.L., & Mann, L. A conflict-theory approach to attitude change and decision making. In A.G. Greenwald, T.C. Brock, & T.M. Ostrom (Eds.), *Psychological foundation of attitudes*. New York: Academic Press, 1968.

Mausner, B., & Platt, E.S. Knowledge, attitudes and behavior: Studies in smoking. (Final report to U.S. Public Health Service) Washington, D.C.: National Institute of Mental Health, September 1966.

Mausner, B., & Platt, E.S. *Smoking: A behavioral analysis*. New York: Pergamon Press, 1971.

McClelland, D.C. *Motivating economic achievement*. New York: Free Press, 1969.

McClelland, D.C., Davis, W.N., Kalin, R., & Wanner, E. *The drinking man*. New York: Free Press, 1972.

McKennell, A.C. British research into smoking behavior. In E.F. Borgatta & R.R. Evans (Eds.), *Smoking, health and behavior*. Chicago: Aldine, 1968.

Mitchell, T.R., & Biglan, A. Instrumentality theories: Current uses in psychology. *Psychological Bulletin*, 1971, *76*, 432-454.

Platt, E.S., Krassen, E. & Mausner, B. Individual variation in behavioral change following role playing. *Psychological Reports*, 1969, *24*, 155-170.

Premack, D. Mechanisms of self-control. In W.A. Hunt (Ed.), *Learning mechanisms in smoking*. Chicago: Aldine, 1970.

Raiffa, H. *Decision analysis. Introductory lectures on choices under uncertainty.* Reading, Mass.: Addison-Wesley, 1970.

Straits, B.C. Sociological and psychological correlates of adoption and discontinuation of cigarette smoking. (Report to the Council for Tobacco Research, U.S.A., Grant 354) Unpublished progress report, University of Chicago, 1965.

Tomkins, S. Psychological model for smoking behavior. *American Journal of Public Health*, 1966, **56**, 17-20. (a)

Tomkins, S. Theoretical implications and guidelines to future research. In B. Mausner & E. Platt, Behavioral aspects of smoking: A conference report. *Health Education Monographs*, 1966, Supplement No. 2, 35-48. (b)

Trilling, L. Aggression and utopia: A note on William Morris's *News from nowhere.* Paper presented at the meeting of the American Association for the Advancement of Science, Philadelphia, December 1971.

U.S. Treasury Department, Internal Revenue Service. *Statistical release—Cigarettes and cigars: January-August, 1971.* (Report Symbol NO-CP: AT-69) Washington, D.C.: Author, 1971.

Vinokur, A. Cognitive and affective processes influencing risk taking in groups: An expected utility approach. *Journal of Personality and Social Psychology*, 1971, **20**, 472-486.

VIII

Urban Stress and Contemporary Life

Commentary. The movement into large urban centers has been particularly accelerated in the last century. In the United States, for example, about 6 percent of the population lived in urban areas in 1800, 15 percent in 1850, 40 percent in 1900, and today nearly 75 percent live in cities or their suburbs (Keyfitz and Flieger, 1971). Today urban life extends well beyond the city, and only the remotest communities are able to maintain a barrier to the stresses inflicted on the modern city dweller.

There are many forms of urban stress, such as crowding, noise, automobile congestion, and other problems less intensified in the countryside. René Dubos points out in the first chapter in this section that urban man has learned to tolerate intense stimulation and high levels of noise and air pollution. Not only does he tolerate these, but he is practically unaware of the subtle changes these "insults" register upon his body. Dubos feels that the increase in chronic and degenerative disease can be attributed in large part to the environmental and behavioral changes that have come from industrialization and urbanization. He suggests that many health problems reflect an inadequate adaptive response to environmental influences which differ significantly from the conditions under which man evolved.

Stanley Milgram (1970) formulates the problem from a different perspective. He links the individual's experience to circumstances of urban life via the concept of "input overload." Input overload refers to a person's inability to process inputs from the environment because there are too many to cope with. Thus, input B cannot be processed until input A is taken care of. Urban life, then, may be viewed as a continuous set of chance meetings with overload.

Milgram suggests that "overload characteristically deforms daily life on several levels, impinging on role performance, the evolution of social norms, cognitive functioning, and the use of facilities." Consequently in the presence of overload adaptations must occur. Milgram describes six adaptive responses to overload: allotting less time to each input; disregarding low-priority inputs; shifting the burden to the other party in the transaction; blocking the input before it enters the system; weakening the intensity of inputs by filtering devices; and creating specialized institutions to absorb inputs that would otherwise overwhelm the individual.

One of the most visible qualities of urban life is the high noise level that pervades almost any city. The issue has been brought into sharp focus recently with evidence suggesting that many teenagers have suffered permanent hearing loss following long exposures to amplified rock music, and by public concern about high-intensity noise caused by supersonic transport should it be put into commercial service (Ehrlich & Ehrlich, 1972). If we consider that heavy traffic can produce noise levels of over 100 decibels, and that noise of 90 decibels may cause irreversible changes to the nervous system and possible permanent hearing loss, a higher incidence of hearing problems in urban areas is not surprising (National Center for Health Statistics, 1972).

Aside from hearing problems, noise has been shown to have other health effects. In Chapter 24 Joseph Anticaglia and Alexander Cohen review the literature on potentially harmful extra-auditory effects, and present evidence illustrating how noise acting as a nonspecific physiologic stress can alter endocrine, cardiovascular, and neurologic functions, and also cause biochemical changes to workers in noisy industries. They indicate, for example, that noise, particularly of sudden onset, can cause a decrease in salivary and gastric secretions and a general slowing of digestive functions. According to the authors these changes appear to be part of a generalized stress reaction to noise.

As suggested earlier, urban centers have annexed the countryside and given birth to microcosms of urban life "far from the madding crowd." As a result of urban sprawl the "commuter" has emerged to take the sting out of living at high densities by traveling to the city and back to a quasi-rural life after work. While one can thus enjoy the benefits of city life and also escape some of its disadvantages, the commuting process itself has stressful consequences.

In the last chapter in this section, P.J. Taylor and S.J. Pocock examine the common feeling that long and uncomfortable journeys impose a strain on the commuter that has serious effects on his health. Their study of the relationship between the pattern of commuter travel to work and absence due to illness of office workers in Central London has turned up some interesting data. They suggest that the most important factor related to both certified and uncertified illness absence is associated with the complexity of the journey, or specifically the number of stages involved in the journey from home to work. This is an important finding and complements the theory of the effects of "input overload." The more decisions and alternatives the commuter is required to face the more adaptive responses must occur to cope with the continuous deluge of environmental stimuli.

References

Ehrlich, P., and Ehrlich, A. *Population, Resources, Environment*. San Francisco: W.H. Freeman, 1972.

Keyfitz, N., and Flieger, W. *Population, Facts and Methods of Demography*. San Francisco: W.H. Freeman, 1971.

Milgram, S. The experience of living in cities. *Science, 167:*1461-1468, 1970.

National Center for Health Statistics, Health Services and Mental Health Administration, DHEW, No. (HSM)72-1024, 1972.

23 The Crisis of Man in His Environment

René Dubos
Rockefeller University

The general worry about the environment has resulted in a distortion of the meaning conveyed by the phrase 'human ecology'. At present, this phrase is exclusively identified with the social and biological dangers that man faces in the modern world. But there is more to human ecology than this one-sided view of man's relation to his environment. In the long run, the most important aspect of human ecology is that all environmental factors exert a direct effect on the development of human characteristics, in health as well as in disease. In fact, it can be said that the body and the mind are *shaped* by the adaptive responses that man makes to the physico-chemical, social, behavioural, and even historical stimuli that impinge on him from the time of conception to the time of death. Genetically and phenotypically, man is being constantly transformed by the environment in which he lives.

Human ecology therefore involves both the pathological and the formative effects of the total environment. I shall first illustrate by a few examples these two aspects of the problem, then attempt to formulate a general approach to the study of the interplay between man and environmental forces.

The general state of public health has greatly improved during the past century, but therapeutic procedures have played a relatively small role in this achievement. Advances in health and in the expectancy of life have come chiefly

Reprinted with permission from *Ekistics* 27(160):151-154, 1969.

from higher standards of living, and from the application of natural sciences to the *prevention* of infectious and nutritional diseases.

Although the early sanitarians did not use the phrase 'human ecology', their slogan 'pure air, pure water, pure food' implied sound ecological concepts. Their awareness of the effects that environmental factors exert on biological health was furthermore supplemented by a shrewd understanding of man's emotional needs. For example, they advocated that urban areas be ornamented with trees and flowers and that city dwellers be given ready access to country lanes.

Thanks to their efforts, we have gone far towards solving the problems of infectious and nutritional disease generated by the first Industrial Revolution. Unfortunately, the new revolution in the ways of life and in the environment that is now occurring in technological societies is bringing about profound changes in the pattern of diseases, causing in particular alarming increases in various types of chronic and degenerative disorders.

Whereas the nineteenth century was concerned with malnutrition, overwork, filth, and microbial contamination, the diseases most characteristic of our times result in large part from economic affluence, chemical pollution, and high population densities. The medical problems are still largely environmental in origin, but they have different ecologic determinants.

The average expectancy of life has increased all over the world and especially in prosperous countries as a result of the prevention of early deaths that used to be caused by acute infections and malnutrition. But, contrary to general belief, life expectancy past the age of forty-five has not increased significantly anywhere in the world, not even in the social groups that can afford the most elaborate medical care. It is no longer permissible to take comfort in the belief that various types of vascular diseases, of cancers, of chronic ailments of the respiratory tract, have become more prevalent simply because people live longer in affluent societies. The increase in chronic and degenerative diseases is due in part at least, and probably in a very large part, to the environmental and behavioural changes that have resulted from industrialization and urbanization.

The so-called diseases of civilization are certainly the results of man's failure to respond successfully to the stresses of the modern environment. But there is as yet no convincing knowledge of the mechanisms relating the environment and the ways of life to the increased incidence of chronic and degenerative diseases among adults. Granted the deficiencies in etiological understanding, it is obvious nevertheless that man feels threatened and is threatened by the constant and unavoidable exposure to the stimuli of urban and industrial civilization; by the varied aspects of environmental pollution; by the physiological disturbances associated with sudden changes in the ways of life; by his estrangement from the conditions and natural cycles under which human evolution took place; by the emotional trauma and the paradoxical solitude in congested cities; by the monotony, the boredom, indeed the compulsory leisure ensuing from automated work. These are the very influences which are now at the origin of most medical problems in affluent societies. They affect all human beings, irrespective of genetic constitution. They are not inherent in man's nature but the products of the interplay between his genetic environment and the new world created by social and technological innovations. To a very large extent the disorders of the body and mind are but the expression of inadequate adaptive responses to environmental influences which differ drastically from the conditions under which man evolved.

As already mentioned, hardly anything is known concerning the natural history of the diseases characteristic of modern civilization—let alone concerning methods for their treatment. It is urgent, therefore, to develop a new science of human ecology focused on the conditions prevailing in the technological environment.

One can take it for granted that medical science will continue to develop useful techniques for treating cancers, vascular diseases, and other degenerative disorders; methods for organ transplants and for the use of artificial prostheses will certainly be improved during the forthcoming decades. But most of the conditions that will thus be treated need not have occurred in the first place. Greater knowledge of the environmental determinants of disease would certainly constitute the most important factor in helping biomedical sciences to improve human health. Prevention is always better than cure, and also much less expensive.

As presently managed, the technological urban civilization subjects all human beings to endless and dangerous stresses. Yet men of all ethnic groups elect to live in huge megalopolises, and indeed manage to function effectively in this traumatic environment. Most of them seem to develop tolerance to environmental pollutants, intense stimuli, and high population density, just as they develop herd immunity to microbial pathogens that are ubiquitous.

The acquisition of tolerance, however, is not an unmixed blessing. Air pollution provides tragic evidence of the fact that many of the physiological, mental, and social processes which make it possible to live in a hostile environment commonly express themselves at a later date in overt disease and in economic loss. During the past two centuries, for instance, the inhabitants of the industrial areas of Northern Europe have been exposed to large concentrations of many types of air pollutants produced by incomplete combustion of coal, and released in the fumes from chemical plants. Such exposure is rendered even more objectionable by the inclemency of the Atlantic climate. However, long experience with pollution and with bad weather results in the development of physiological reactions and living habits that obviously have adaptive value, since Northern Europeans seem to accept almost cheerfully conditions which appear unbearable to a non-experienced person.

Unfortunately, adaptation to the stresses of the present often has to be paid in the form of physiological misery at some future date. Even among persons who seem to be unaware of the smogs surrounding them, the respiratory tract registers the insult of the various air pollutants. Eventually, the cumulative effects of irritation result in chronic bronchitis and other forms of irreversible pulmonary disease. Generally, however, this does not happen until several years later.

Chronic pulmonary disease now constitutes the greatest single medical problem in Northern Europe, as well as the most costly. It is increasing in prevalence at an alarming rate also in North America and it will undoubtedly spread to all areas undergoing industrialization. There is good evidence, furthermore, that air pollution contributes to the incidence of various cancers—not only pulmonary carcinoma. It also increases the number of fatalities among persons suffering from vascular disorders. The delayed effects of air pollutants thus constitute a model for the kind of medical problems likely to arise in the future from the various forms of environmental pollution.

Noise levels that are accepted almost as a matter of course bring about a progressive impairment of hearing; pathogens that do not cause destructive epidemics because they are ubiquitous and have therefore elicited herd immunity can generate endogenous infections when resistance to them is decreased by physiological or mental stress; crowding, regimentation, or intense stimuli that become acceptable through habituation indirectly elicit physiological or behavioural disorders. In brief, most adaptive adjustments to deleterious influences are achieved at the price of bodily or mental disturbances later in life. Some at least of these disturbances contribute to the diseases of civilization.

From the point of view of the general biologist, an environment is suitable if it enables the species to reproduce itself and increase its population; but this concept is not applicable to man. An environment allowing man to produce a family and to be economically effective during his adult years should be regarded an unacceptable one if it generates disease later in life. This, of course, is the case for many modern technological and urban environments, which rarely destroy human life but frequently spoil its later years.

Human ecology thus differs from orthodox biomedical sciences in the much greater emphasis that it should put on the indirect and delayed effects of environmental forces, even when these do not appear to cause significant damage at the time of exposure.

Man's responses to the environmental forces that impinge on him determine to a very large extent how his genetic potentialities are converted into existential, phenotypic reality.

Contrary to what is commonly assumed, genes do not determine the traits by which we know a person; they only govern the responses he makes to environmental stimuli. Such responses become incorporated, usually in an irreversible manner, in the person's whole being and thus mould his individuality. This is true not only for emotional characteristics, but also for most other physical, physiological, and mental characteristics. Man makes himself in the very act of responding to his environment through an uninterrupted series of feedback processes. Since each person continues to respond to environmental stimuli throughout his life and to be lastingly modified by such responses, individuality can be defined as the continuously evolving phenotype.

Many of the most striking differences in size, shape, attitudes, and mental abilities between ethnic groups are not innate; they are expressions of environmental influences. In other words, men are as much the products of their environment as of their genetic endowment. This is what Winston Churchill had in mind when he asserted: 'We shape our buildings, and afterwards our buildings shape us.'

The influences experienced very early in life during the formative phases of development deserve emphasis, because they exert profound and lasting effects on the anatomical, physiological, and behavioural characteristics of the adult. Experimentation in animals and observations in man have revealed that the foetus and the newborn can be so profoundly affected by environmental conditions acting indirectly through the mother, or directly after birth, that the adult reflects throughout his life the consequences of this early experience. Early influences are of particular importance because man's body and brain are incompletely developed at the time of birth. Hence, the need for precise observations and searching experimental studies concerning the conditions of prenatal and early postnatal life.

Biological and social deprivation are well known to have deleterious effects on development. For example, there is now overwhelming evidence that various types of deprivation early in life exert irreversible damage on learning ability—a fact of obvious importance in all underprivileged populations. On the other hand, it is also possible that some of the conditions prevailing in affluent societies have undesirable consequences.

It is known that injection into newborn mice of particulate materials separated from urban air greatly increases the frequency of various types of tumours during the adult life of these animals. If this observation can be extrapolated to human beings, the worst effects of environmental pollution are yet to come, since it is only during the past decade that large numbers of babies have been exposed to high levels of pollutants in urban areas.

It is known also that animals offered a rich and abundant regimen early in life thereby become conditioned to large nutritional demands as adults and tend to become obese. This may explain why the bigger baby does not necessarily become a healthy adult.

By acting on the child during his formative stages, the environment thus shapes him physically and mentally, thereby influencing what he will become and how he will function as an adult. For this reason, environmental planning plays a key role in enabling human beings to actualize their potentialities.

Children who are denied the opportunity to experience early in life the kind of stimuli required for mental development do not acquire the mental resources that would be necessary for the full utilization of their free will. It is not right to say that lack of culture is responsible for the behaviour of slum children or for their failure to be successful in our society. The more painful truth is that these children acquire early in life a slum culture from which escape is almost impossible. Their early surroundings and ways of life at a critical period of their development limit the range of manifestations of their innate endowment and thus destroy much of their potential freedom.

It would be unethical and in any case futile to try creating one particular type of environment optimum for all of mankind. Such a course would impose a common pattern of development on all human beings and thus would be tantamount to suppressing their freedom. Society should instead provide as wide a range of environmental conditions as practically and safely possible so that each human being can select the experiences most suitable to the development of his attributes and to the prosecution of his goals.

Human potentialities, whether physical or mental, can be realized only to the extent that circumstances are favourable to their existential manifestation. For this reason, diversity within a given society is an essential component of true functionalism; the latent potentialities of human beings have a better chance to emerge when the social environment is sufficiently diversified to provide a variety of stimulating experiences, especially for the young. As more and more persons find it possible to express their biologic endowments under a variety of conditions, society becomes richer and civilizations continue to unfold. In contrast, if the surroundings and ways of life are highly stereotyped, the only components of man's nature that flourish are those adapted to the narrow range of prevailing conditions.

Thus, one of the most important problems of human ecology is to study the effects of environmental forces not only in the here and now, but also with regard to their future consequences.

24 Extra-Auditory Effects of Noise as a Health Hazard

Joseph R. Anticaglia
Alexander Cohen
U.S. Department of Health, Education and Welfare, Public Health Service

Introduction

That noise can adversely affect man is well documented. It can cause permanent hearing impairment,[1] interfere with speech communication,[2] hinder job performance, at least on certain tasks, and act as a source of annoyance.[3] There is much conjecture, however, as to whether excessive noise can also cause health effects of an extra-auditory nature. The prevailing view of many noise experts in the United States is that man's tolerance to noise is quite high and that he can adapt to the noise conditions encountered in present-day environments without harmful effects.[4] While there is evidence to support adaptation to noise, even of high level, there are also indications that prolonged exposure to undue noise may lead to health problems.[5,6]

This paper reviews current knowledge about the extra-auditory effects of noise on man with particular reference to occupational noise conditions and exposures. Its intent is to create active interest in and concern about this subject in those specialists having medical, hygiene, and safety responsibilities in industry. Increasing levels of noise due to growing mechanization in industry as well as expanding use of equipment producing strong acoustic energy in the

Reprinted with permission from *American Industrial Hygiene Association Journal*, May-June, 1970 (pp. 277-281).

infra- and ultrasonic regions warrant constant vigil about the consequences of such exposures to the total health state of the worker.

This review classifies noise according to its effects on different body functions reflecting neurosensory, endocrine, biochemical, cardiovascular, and other processes.

Effects of Noise on Neurosensory Processes

The auditory pathways of the nervous system are organized into two distinct systems (Figure 24-1). One is a specific projection system whose primary function is to transmit neural impulses underlying sound or noise stimuli from the ear receptors to the higher brain centers for perception and interpretation. The other is a nonspecific projection system which branches off the main auditory pathway into an activating-regulating center, called the reticular formation, and then spreads diffusely into different functional areas of the brain as well as affecting the peripheral autonomic system.[7] This nonspecific projection system is concerned with the arousal and regulation of different sensory, motor, and autonomic activities and is believed to be responsible for many of the observed extra-aural effects of noise or sound stimulation.

Bombarding the reticular formations with high-level noise or, for that matter, with any other source of physical stimuli can create conditions of overarousal and cause individuals to show signs of undue excitability and nervousness. As such, overstimulation of the reticular formation might be the basis for the hyperactive state of reflexes and the desynchronization patterns found in electroencephalographic responses of weavers exposed to intense loom noise.[8]

Noise may produce a number of reflex-like reactions, the most common of which is the startle response usually caused by the occurrence of loud, unexpected sound.[9,10] The components of this startle response are flexion of the arm, arching of the torso, widening of the mouth, and eyeblink. These reactions in themselves have no health significance. However, in many industrial situations a noise may startle a person into injuring himself or others. The physiologic changes accompanying the startle reaction (for example, rise in blood pressure, increase in sweating, changes in breathing) do show adaptations with repeated noise presentations, but the behavioral components noted above seem surprisingly resistant to extinction. A group of experienced marksmen, for example, still show the eyeblink response in firing their weapons.[10]

Steady-state noise of fairly high level, 110 to 120 dB,* has certain effects on nonauditory sensory functions which deserve mention in connection with health and safety problems. For example, Stevens[11] found that high-level noise reduces the speed by which the eye moves through certain angles to focus clearly on

*All such notations noted herein refer to decibels in sound pressure level re 0.0002 microbar measure on C-scale.

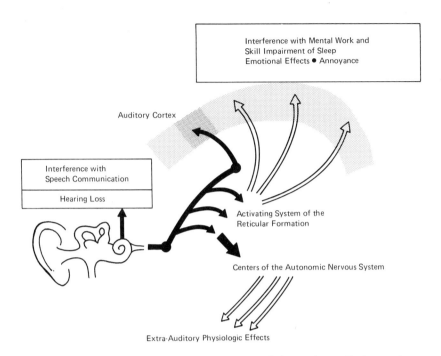

Figure 24-1. The Physiologic Organization of the Auditory Pathways in the Brain, and Their Relation to the Effects of Noise on Man (modified from Grandjean[7]).

objects. This result was believed to be due to noise affecting the ciliary muscles which control the curvature of the lens of the eye. In another experiment, Benko[12] examined workers exposed to 110 to 124 dB of noise and reported a narrowing of their visual field as well as some modification of the perception of color with a trend toward protanomalia (partial deficiency for perceiving red). Although the laboratory effects were temporary in nature,[13,14] the effect of concentric narrowing of the visual field found in individuals exposed to intense noise for many years in their work situations was permanent.[15]

Complaints of nystagmus and vertigo have been reported under noise conditions in the laboratory as well as in field situations. The levels needed to cause such effects are quite high, typically 130 dB or more.[16] Less intense noise conditions (about 120 dB), however, can upset one's balance, particularly if the noise stimulation is unequal at the two ears. This was most clearly shown in a laboratory study in which subjects were required to balance themselves on rails of different widths.[17] All these effects are believed to be due to noise directly stimulating the vestibular organ whose receptors are part of the inner ear structure.[18]

Noise-induced changes in equilibrium and visual functions are sometimes dismissed as of little practical importance because generally high noise levels are needed to produce these changes and their overall magnitudes are quite small. One must hasten to point out, however, that noise levels in military and industrial environments have sharply risen with the introduction of more powerful tools and power sources such that they are comparable to, if not higher than, the levels found in laboratory conditions where such effects have been displayed.[3] Furthermore, the many hazards inherent in certain industrial operations may make these effects, while small, tragically significant from the standpoint of potential accidents and injury.

Noise and Endocrine-Biochemical Effects

The best evidence that noise may act as a physiological stress comes from direct analysis of changes in the adrenal cortex and evidence of the secretion of corticosteroids in the blood and urine.[4,19] It appears that noise activates corticotropin secretion via a hypothalmic-hypophyseal mechanism which influences the release of adrenocortical as well as gonadal and thyrotropic hormones.[20-22] The adrenocortical response induces a variety of biochemical changes which depict the organism's attempt to cope with environmental stress. Given protracted periods of exposure to intense noise, particularly of high frequency, animals show marked depletion of adrenal constituents, which indicates that their physiological tolerance or ability to adapt to the stressful situation has been exceeded.[4] Under these conditions, there may be signs of gastroduodenal ulcers and other pathologic changes in the liver and kidney. It is plausible to expect similar findings in man, but neither the levels nor the exposure conditions needed to exceed human physiologic tolerance to noise are known. Related to noise effects on the adrenals are associated electrolytic imbalances (potassium, sodium, calcium, magnesium) and changes in the blood glucose level.[20,23,24]

Reactions provoked by noise on glands influencing sexual and reproductive functions are as yet unclear.[22,25] Noise-induced inhibition and stimulation of gonadotropin and ovarian hormones have been observed. Hence, nothing conclusive or definite can be said to support the claim that exposure to high-level industrial noise can affect sexual functions. Similarly, the action of noise on thyroid activity is quite variable and inconclusive.[20]

Noise and the Cardiovascular System

As regards the cardiovascular system, noise has been reported to cause vasoconstriction,[6,26,27] fluctuations in arterial blood pressure, and even alterations of some functional properties of cardiac muscle.[28,29] Plethysmography, oscillography, electrocardiology, ballistic cardiography, and the usual blood pressure recordings have been utilized in evaluating these various cardiovascular changes.

Vasoconstriction of the small arterioles of the extremities occurs with noise exposures of moderate level (about 70 dB) and can become progressively stronger with increasing noise intensity.[6,26,27] Coupled with this vasoconstriction appear to be changes in arterial blood pressure. These changes may reflect compensating heart action to overcome the vasoconstrictive effects of noise. Along these lines, there have been reports of a decrease in the systolic and an increase in the diastolic blood pressure in workers exposed to industrial noise during the course of their working day.[30,31]

There is also some laboratory evidence to show that high-level noise exposure can alter the functional properties of cardiac muscles. Changes in the electrocardiogram, ECG suggestive of ischemia and bradycardia (decrease in the cardiac rate) have been noted.[28,32] This has been reported mainly in the foreign scientific literature, which, also cite data linking intense occupational noise exposure with increased incidence of cardiovascular irregularities in workers. A German study, for example, has shown a high incidence of abnormal heart rhythms in steel workers exposed to intense noise levels in their workplaces.[7] A Russian study reported workers in noisy ball-bearing and steel plants to show evidence of retardation of intraventricular activity.[33] Others have noted that some workers exposed to severe industrial noise were found to suffer from impaired circulation in the peripheral vascular areas and to voice complaints of precordial distress and discomfort from an apparent increase in heart action and breathlessness.[33,34]

The effects of noise on the cardiovascular system noted above are by no means definitive enough to support the conclusion that noise causes cardiovascular disorders. They do suggest and should invite much more study and effort aimed at clarifying their health significance. It is truly surprising to find that very little if any work has been done in the United States in this problem area.

Other Nonaural Effects of Noise

Noise, particularly of sudden onset, can cause reductions in salivary and gastric secretions and a general slowing of digestive functions. These changes together with other effects on respiratory dynamics seem to be part of a generalized stress reaction to noise.[7,35]

The potential health problems associated with high-level exposures to sources of extremely low or extremely high frequency must also receive greater interest. To date, observations concerning infrasonic noises—that is, noise having energy below 20 cycles per second—have been restricted to short-term, high-level exposures such as those encountered in launching rocket boosters or in certain phases of space vehicle acceleration.[5,36] The levels of 140 dB or more encountered in these instances mechanically drive the chest inward, causing complaints of substernal pressure and coughing and gagging sensations. These reactions are further accentuated if there are also present strong audible sounds of low frequency which can excite the mechanical resonances of the chest. No conclusive information is available in the literature regarding long-term exposure problems and/or possible adaptation. Also, possible problems of physical fatigue following infrasound exposure have been mentioned but not seriously investigated.

Workers using ultrasonic cleaners and drills complain of subjective effects, including fatigue, headaches, nausea, and malaise.[37-39] The occurrence of such effects depends more on sound energy in the upper end of the audible frequency range than on that in the ultrasonic region per se—that is, above 20,000 cycles. Energy around 16,000 Hz seems particularly critical in this regard, showing covariation with the undue symptoms noted above. The physiologic basis for these reactions is still not evident. Incidentally, workers having hearing loss for these high-frequency sounds do not seem to display the same ill effects as those who have normal hearing.[38,39] No information is available as regards the effects of long-term exposure and possible adaptation to these high-frequency sounds.

Comments and Summary

There is no question that noise or sound can cause physiologic changes. At issue is whether long-term repetitive exposures to noise can induce physical changes that are eventually degrading to the health of the individual. The position of United States experts that noise has no ill effects is difficult to defend at this time in view of the absence of systematic study and objective data in this area. For example, epidemiological surveys concerned with the incidence of acute and chronic ailments in different work groups have never been undertaken in this country and are greatly needed. Such information could corroborate or refute findings from the European literature which, as already noted, suggest apparent associations between noise and adverse health effects. Whatever correlations can be found between the noise and health problems in a field situation would obviously have to stand more definitive, controlled tests in the laboratory to demonstrate true cause-effect relationships.

As a final comment, it is important to state that the overall assessment of noise effects in this paper has not taken account of special groups that may enter into a noisy work situation with pre-existing disorders. Presently, we know very little about the stress tolerance of individuals with chronic neurologic, cardiovascular, and gastrointestinal problems. The impact of noise on such individuals would seemingly be greater than that on workers who are in a normal, healthy condition.

References

1. Rudmose, W.: Hearing Loss Resulting from Noise Exposure. In *Handbook of Noise Control* (C.M. Harris, Ed.). Chapter 9, McGraw-Hill Book Co., New York (1957).
2. Hawley, M.E., and K.D. Kryter: Effects of Noise on Speech. In *Handbook of Noise Control* (C.M. Harris, Ed.), Chapter 9, McGraw-Hill Book Co., New York (1957).
3. Cohen, A.: *Noise and Psychological State*. Proceedings of National Conference on Noise as a Public Health Hazard, American Speech and Hearing Association, Rept. No. 4, pp. 74-88, Washington, D.C. (February, 1969).
4. Anthony, A., and E. Ackerman: *Stress Effects of Noise in Vertebrate Animals*. WADC Tech. Rept. 58-622, Wright Patterson AFB, Ohio (1959).
5. Von Gierke, H.E.: On Noise and Vibration Criteria. *Arch. Environ. Health 11:* 327-339 (1965).
6. Jansen, G.: *Effects of Noise on the Physiological State*. Proceedings of National Conference on Noise as a Public Health Hazard, American Speech and Hearing Association, Rept. No. 4, pp. 89-98, Washington, D.C. (February, 1969).
7. Grandjean, E.: *Biological Effects of Noise*. Department of Hygiene and Work Physiology, Swiss Federal Institute of Technology, Zurich (undated).
8. Granati, A., F. Angeleri, and R. Lenzi: L'Influenza dei Rumori sul Sistema Nervoso. *Folia Med. (Naples) 42:* 1313-1325 (1959).
9. Booker, H.E., F.M. Forster, and H. Klove: Extinction Factors in Startle (Acoustico-Motor) Seizures. *Neurology 15:* 1095-1103 (1965).
10. Landis, C., and W.A. Hunt: *The Startle Pattern*, Farrar Book Co., New York, p. 184 (1939).
11. Stevens, S.S.: *The Effects of Noise and Vibration on Psychomotor Efficiency*. Preliminary Report. Psychoacoustics Laboratory, Harvard University (1941).
12. Benko, E.: Objek-und Farbengesichtsfeldeinengung bei Chromschen Larmschaden. *Ophthalmologica 138:* 449-456 (1959).
13. Grognot, P., and G. Perdriel: Influence of Noise on Certain Visual Functions. *Med. Aeronaut. 14(1):* 25-30 (1959).
14. Ogielska, E., and K. Brodziak: L'Influence du Bruit sur le Champ Visuel. *Ann. Occulist. (Paris) 198(2):* 115-122 (1965).
15. Benko, E.: Further Information about the Narrowing of the Visual Fields Caused by Noise Damage. *Ophthalmologica 140(1):* 76-80 (1962).
16. Ades, H.W., A. Graybiel, S.N. Morrill, G.C. Tolhurst, and J.I. Niven: *Nystagmus Elicited by High Intensity Sound.* Research Project NM 13 01 99 Subtask 2, Report 6, U.S. Navy Research Laboratory, Pensacola, Florida (1957).

17. Nixon, C.W., C. Harris, and H. F. von Gierke: *Rail Test To Evaluate Equilibrium in Low Level Wide Band Noise.* AMRL-TR-66-85. Wright Patterson Air Force Base, Ohio (1966).

18. McCabe, B.F., and M. Lawrence: Effects of Intense Sound on Non-Auditory Labyrinth. *Acta Oto-Laryngol. 49:* 147-157 (1958).

19. Miline, R., and O. Koghak: L'Influence du Bruit et des Vibrations sur les Glands Surrenales. *Compt. Rend. Assoc. Anatomistes 38:* 692-703 (1952).

20. Bugard, P.: Rumori e Sistema Endocrino. *Folia Med. (Naples)* Anno XLVII No. 8, 717-729 (1964).

21. Biro, J., V. Szokolai, and A.G. Kovach: Some Effects of Sound Stimuli on the Pituitary Adrenocortical System. *Acta Endocrinol. 31:* 541-552 (1959).

22. Sackler, A.M., A. Weltman, M. Bradshaw, and P. Justshuk: Endocrine Changes due to Auditory Stress. *Acta Endocrinol. 31:* 405-418 (1959).

23. Sera, G.: Risposte Neuroumorali alla Stimolasione Acustica Intermittente. *Acta Neurol. (Naples) 19:* 1018-1035 (1964).

24. Grognot, P.: L'Influence de l'Exposition aux Bruits sur le Taux du Potassium Plasmatique. *Presse Thermale Climat. 98:* 201-203 (1961).

25. Zondek, B., and I. Tamari: Effect of Audiogenic Stimulation on Genital Function and Reproduction. *Amer J. Obstet. Gynecol. 80(6):* 1041-1048 (1960).

26. Lehmann, G., and J. Tamm: Changes of Circulatory Dynamics of Resting Men under the Influence of Noise. *Intern. Z. Angew. Physiol. 16(3):* 217-227 (1956).

27. Straneo, G., and P. Seghizzi: L'Azione del Rumori sul Sistema Vascolare Periferico. *Folia Med. (Naples) 25:* 572-577 (1962).

28. Taggola, A., G. Straneo, and G. Bobbio: Modificazione della Dinamica Cardiaca Indotte dal Rumore. *Lavoro Umano 15(12):* 571-579 (1963).

29. Strakhov, A.B.: Influence of Intense Noise on Certain Functions of the Organism. *Hyg. Sanit. 29(4):* 34-44 (1964).

30. Floss, E.F.: Changes in the Physiologic Functions of Children Exposed to Noise. *Z. Ges. Hyg. 10(2):* 81-96 (1964).

31. Ponomarenko, I.: The Effect of Constant High Frequency Industiral Noise on Certain Physiologic Functions in Adolescents. *Gigiena i Sanit. 31(2):* 188-193 (1966).

32. Fusco, M., C. D'Amato, and R. Fimiani: Axione dei Rumori sul Reograma Cerebrale e Periferico e sull Electroencefalogramma. *Folia Med. (Naples) 48:* 88-98 (1965).

33. Shatalov, N.N., A. Saitanov, M. Bradshaw, and K. Glotova: On the Problem of the State of the Cardiovascular System During the Action of Continuous Noise. *Labor Hyg. Occup. Disease 6(7):* 10-14 (1962).

34. Corporale, R., and M. DePalma: Effect of High Intensity Noise on the Human Body. *Riv. Med. Aeronaut. Spaz. 26(2):* 273-290 (1963).

35. Maugeri, S.: Respiratory Effects of Industrial Noise. *Lavoro Umano. 17(7):* 331-338 (1965).

36. Mohr, G.C., J. Cole, E. Guild, and H.E. von Gierke: Effects of Low Frequency and Infra-Sonic Noise on Man. *Aerospace Med. 36:* 817-824 (1965).
37. Skillern, C.P.: Human Response to Measured Sound Pressure Levels from Ultrasonic Devices. *Amer. Ind. Hyg. Assoc. J. 26(2):* 132-136 (1965).
38. Acton, W.I., and M.B. Carson: Auditory and Subjective Effects of Airborne Noise from Industrial Ultrasonic Sources. *Brit. J. Ind. Med. 24:* 297-304 (1967).
39. Acton, W.I.: A Criterion for the Production of Auditory and Subjective Effects due to Airborne Noise from Ultrasonic Sources. *Ann. Occup. Hyg. 11:* 227-234 (1968).

25 Commuter Travel and Sickness Absence of London, Office Workers

P.J. Taylor
S.J. Pocock
London School of Hygiene and Tropical Medicine

Daily travel to and from work is a characteristic feature of life in all industrialized countries, and with the tendency for more people to live outside the centres of towns and cities the length of the commuter's journey has increased. Nowhere in Britain is this problem more marked than in London where public transport is stretched to the limits of its capacity.

It is a common belief that long and uncomfortable journeys impose a strain upon the commuter which produces fatigue and impairs health. Liepmann (1944) cites many statements in support of this view but noted that objective evidence was scanty and sometimes inconsistent. In a review of the health of London's travelling public, Norman (1959) stated that there was no evidence that those who commuted for two or three hours every day were any less fit than those who 'lived over the shop'. He quoted the study of Williams and Hirch (1950) in support of his statement that travel in buses and underground trains did not increase the spread of infectious disease, but his own studies on sickness rates among bus drivers and conductors could provide only indirect evidence on passengers.

Absence from work due to certified (or uncertified) incapacity is not synonymous with morbidity since many factors, of which ill health is only one,

Reprinted with permission from *British Journal of Preventive & Social Medicine*, 26:165-172, 1972.

combine to decide whether or not a worker will 'go off sick' (Froggatt, 1970). A recent review of absenteeism states that it increases with the length of the journey (Jones, 1971) but provides no evidence in support. Vernon, Bedford, and Warner (1931) studied miners in six collieries in Scotland, finding some evidence that men with longer journeys had more sickness absence, but there was a closer relationship with voluntary absenteeism. A more elaborate study of 26 coal mines by Buzzard and Liddell (1963) showed only a slight positive association, and when each mine was considered separately the patterns were inconsistent. Liepmann's (1944) studies in the London area failed to show any conclusive association, and Wyatt, Marriott, and Hughes (1943) found higher rates of absence in women only when journeys exceeded one hour in duration. Refinery employees, whose journeys were all less than one hour, showed no evidence of an association (Taylor, 1966).

All these studies, however, measured the journey only in terms of distance or duration, and most used lost time as the only measure of absence. The present investigation was designed to obtain more detailed information about the journeys of office workers in Central London, and to study several factors in relation to both frequency and severity of certified and uncertified sickness absence.

Methods

Selection of Sample Population

To reduce the number of complicating factors we sought a reasonably homogeneous sample of employees in one organization. Several large organizations, unconnected with public transport, were approached. Only two kept comprehensive sickness absence records and one agreed to help when the support of the Unions had been obtained.

The employees worked in three large office blocks, two in the City of London and one nearby in Holborn. All were employed on a five-day week and most started work between 08.30 and 09.00 hours. We defined our sample as office workers under the age of 70 who had been continuously employed in the same building between April 1969 and June 1970. The sample totalled 2,045 persons.

Travel Questionnaire

A self-administered questionnaire was distributed to all persons in our sample; anonymity was preserved by a 'tear-off' attachment which was removed before the completed forms were returned to us. A serial number on both parts of the form enabled subsequent queries to be raised with the personnel department.

A brief introduction explained that the survey was to study problems of commuter journeys and that records of absence due to ill health would also be used. The questionnaire asked for details of the journey to work used most often in the previous 12 months. To facilitate the description, the employee was asked to divide the journey into 'stages', giving times and details of each. A stage was defined as that part of the journey in which neither the method of transport nor the vehicle was changed. Any walk taking more than five minutes was to be included as a separate stage.

For each stage we asked for: the starting time, the type of transport (British Rail train, London Transport train, bus, driver of car, passenger in car, walk, or other means of transport), and the individual's opinion of the stage on a four-point scale (very crowded/congested, crowded/congested, comfortable, fairly empty). For train stages the names of both stations were required, for other stages the two districts.

The employee was asked for the usual total duration of his journey and also to record which of five alternatives most nearly described his opinion of the whole journey: very comfortable, fairly comfortable, neither particularly comfortable nor uncomfortable, fairly uncomfortable, and very uncomfortable.

Objective Assessment of Crowding

British Rail (BR) and London Transport (LT) agreed to provide us with their own assessments of crowding for as many of the train journeys described in the questionnaire as possible. This was done by their staff without reference to the respondent's own assessment.

For BR journeys we were given the 'loading factors' calculated from the results of a routine survey in October 1969. This factor is defined as the ratio of the number of persons on the train to the number of seats on the train expressed as a percentage. Thus a loading factor of 100% would mean that the number of passengers was the same as the number of seats. If the loading factor was higher at a station shortly before the terminal this figure was adopted instead of the terminal loading. We obtained such factors for all but 13 of the 1,315 BR journeys.

For LT trains the loading factor was calculated on a somewhat different basis, being the ratio of the average number of passengers to the 'tolerable load' expressed as a percentage, the tolerable load being 2.8 times the seating capacity. The reason for this difference is that about half the floor space of LT underground carriages is designed for standing passengers. These loading factors were assessed at 15 minute intervals and did not refer to specific trains as a frequent service operates at peak hours. We obtained loading factors for all but 87 of the 1,009 LT train journeys; the others ended at stations for which this information was not available. Unfortunately it was impracticable to obtain loading factors for bus journeys.

Personal Details and Sickness Absence

On the reverse side of the form we were provided with facts from company records including sex, marital status, grade of job (management, executive, and clerical), and the number of spells and calendar days of sickness absence in the 12 months ending 31 March 1970. Absence was divided into three categories: uncertified, certified due to influenza, and certified due to all other causes.

Date Processing and Analysis

All the information was coded and transferred to punched cards. Subsequent analysis was carried out first using the computer of BR and later that of the University of London.

Results

Response Rate

We received 1,994 completed questionnaires, giving a response rate of 97.5%. Fifty-one persons failed to respond after a second questionnaire, all but one were male, and their ages and job grades were similar to those of the respondents. Their sickness absence experience was neither unduly high nor unduly low.

Personal Details

In our sample of 1,994 persons, 1,677 (84%) were male and 317 were female, of whom 185 (58%) were married. In job grade, 266 were management, 1,217 were executive, and 511 were clercial. Most of the women (80%) were in the clerical grade. We divided our sample into three age groups by their years of birth; 427 (21%) were born between 1900 and 1919, 918 (46%) between 1920 and 1939, and 649 (33%) since 1940. These we describe as older, middle aged, and younger employees respectively.

Duration of Over-all Journey

There was a wide range from 12 minutes to 2½ hours, with a median duration of one hour. The distribution of travelling time in five-minute intervals is shown in

Figure 25-1. The marked peak at one hour is attributable to many giving this time in preference to one within five minutes on either side. Women had somewhat shorter journeys than men, 55% having journeys of 50 minutes or less whereas this applied to only 32% of the men. The duration of the journey was not related to age.

Number of Stages. The average number of stages was 2.84, and the distributions of total stages and those involving public transport (Table 25-1) show that the majority of our sample had between two and four stages, with one or two by public transport. Women had slightly fewer stages than men. Although there was a positive association between the over-all duration of the journey and the number of stages, the correlation coefficient of 0.45 indicates that this was not very close.

Types of Transport. One thousand eight hundred and ninety (94.8%) of our respondents used some form of public transport for at least one stage of their journey. The largest number of people (66.0%) used BR train, 50.7% used LT train, and 22.8% travelled by bus. Many people (40.9%) used more than one type of public transport in the course of their journey (Table 25-2).

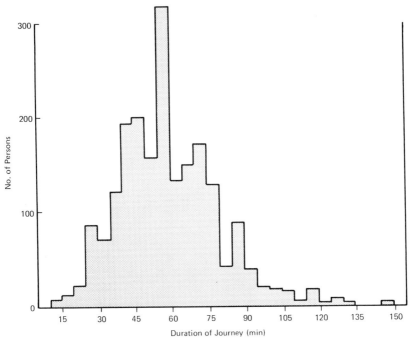

Figure 25-1. Distribution of Travelling Time in 5-minute Intervals (no. of persons = 1,994).

Table 25-1
Distributions of Total and Public Transport Stages

Total No. of Stages	No. of Persons	(%)	No. of Public Stages	No. of Persons	(%)
1	183	(9.2)	0	104	(5.2)
2	421	(21.1)	1	846	(42.4)
3	973	(48.8)	2	795	(39.9)
4	364	(18.2)	3	223	(11.2)
5 or more	53	(2.7)	4 or more	26	(1.3)
Total	1,994	(100.0)	Total	1,994	(100.0)

A car was used by 412 persons (20.6%), and for 88 of these this was the only vehicle. Since 256 also used a BR train and 183 an LT train but only 29 caught a bus, it seems that although the use of a car involved less use of public transport, this is only marked in the case of bus journeys. Moreover, since most used cars only for the first stage the average number of stages at 2.75 was not much less than that for all respondents. On the other hand, car users tended to have longer journeys than the rest. The use of a car decreased with age among the men and only 15% of women used a car; 80% of car users drove themselves.

Walking for at least one stage (i.e., for more than 5 minutes) was reported by 1,410 of the respondents and just over a quarter of these had more than one walk as part of their journey to work. However, only 16 people walked all the way to work.

Table 25-2
Numbers Using Types of Public Transport

Type of Public Transport	No. of Persons
None	104
BR train only	596
LT train only	408
Bus only	70
BR train and LT train	432
BR train and bus	214
LT train and bus	96
BR train, LT train and bus	74
Total	1,994

Opinions on Comfort

The distribution of opinions on the overall comfort of the journey, recorded on the five-point scale, showed that less than one-third considered it as fairly or very uncomfortable (Table 25-3). There was no significant difference between men and women in this, but the proportion of men who considered the journey fairly or very uncomfortable fell with increasing age from 37.5% in younger men to 30.3% in the middle-aged and 23.3% in the older men. Opinion, however, did not relate to the number of stages nor to the total duration of the journey; scoring opinion from one to five, the correlation coefficients were only 0.10 and 0.09 respectively.

Opinions on separate stages allowed us to relate these to the type of transport. LT trains were described as very crowded or crowded by 78% of those who used them, buses by 54%, and BR trains by 52%. For stages both by car and on foot over 80% described conditions as comfortable or fairly empty.

Objective Assessment of Train Loading

For BR journeys the median loading factor was in the range 80-89%, and just over one-third of the trains were rated at 100% or more. For LT trains, using their load factor based on 2.8 persons per seat, the median was in the range of 60-69%, which is approximately equivalent to 1.7 persons per seat.

We compared the individual's assessment of his train journey with the loading factor. For BR trains the median load factors for opinions very crowded, crowded, and comfortable were in the ranges 100-109, 90-99, and 70-79% respectively. For LT trains the corresponding ranges were 60-69, 50-59, and

Table 25-3
Distribution of Opinion of Overall Comfort

Opinion	No. of Persons	(%)
Very comfortable	67	(3.4)
Fairly comfortable	604	(30.3)
Neither particularly comfortable nor uncomfortable	709	(35.6)
Fairly uncomfortable	487	(24.3)
Very uncomfortable	127	(6.4)
Total	1,994	(100.0)

40-49%. These trends indicate some degree of association but there was considerable scatter showing substantial variation in opinion. A further reason for this scatter may be the difference between the overall crowding on the train from start to finish of the journey and the situation at the end.

Sickness Absence Rates

The experience of our sample was fairly typical for office workers. Men had lower rates than women, married women had more than single (Table 25-4). The total calendar days lost by the sample in the year was 8.5 per person at risk. The usual relationship of absence with age was also found with the frequency of uncertified spells in men falling sharply with increasing age, whereas certified spells for influenza and other causes did not change to any great extent.

Within age groups, the job grade also had a very marked effect on absence rates. The rates among men in the middle-aged group (Table 25-5) show that for all types of absence the rates were highest in the clerical group and lowest among management. Similar differences were observed in other age groups.

The Journey and Sickness Absence

Personal factors, such as sex, age, and occupational status, must always be taken into account before any attempt can be made to study another factor in relation to sickness absence. Without this, spurious associations can be observed.

In this study we allocated employees into 12 strata determined by their sex,

Table 25-4
Frequency and Severity of Sickness Absence by Sex and Marital Status in Year Beginning April 1969

		Male	Unmarried Female	Married Female	Total
	No. of persons	1,677	132	185	1,994
Uncertified	Spells/person	1.12	1.89	1.90	1.24
	Days/person	1.65	2.62	2.71	1.82
Certified 'flu	Spells/person	0.19	0.26	0.28	0.20
	Days/person	1.36	1.56	3.41	1.56
Other certified	Spells/person	0.37	0.69	1.03	0.46
	Days/person	4.02	7.11	13.38	5.10
All types	Spells/person	1.68	2.84	3.21	1.90
	Days/person	7.03	11.29	16.50	8.48

Table 25-5
Frequency and Severity of Sickness Absence in Middle-Aged Men by Job Grade

		Management	Executive	Clerical
	No. of persons	153	600	74
Uncertified	Spells/man	0.69	1.07	1.69
	Days/man	1.27	1.61	2.18
Certified 'flu	Spells/man	0.16	0.21	0.30
	Days/man	1.08	1.52	2.57
Certified other	Spells/man	0.28	0.35	0.87
	Days/man	2.60	4.21	7.15
All types	Spells/man	1.13	1.63	2.86
	Days/man	4.95	7.34	11.90

age group, marital status (for women), and job grade. We used the technique of indirect standardization which enabled us to allow for these factors when comparing groups of employees classified according to their journeys. Although all previously mentioned aspects of the journey were studied to see whether any association could be found with any of the forms of sickness absence, only those results suggesting a possible relationship are presented.

Uncertified Absence and the Journey

Since both frequency (spells) and severity (days) are highly skewed in their distribution, it is difficult to apply formal tests of significance. For this reason we also used the percentage of persons with two or more spells as a third measure of uncertified absence.

In Table 25-6 we present absence rates (standardized for age, sex, and status) for the sample divided into users of private transport, the number of stages, duration of the journey, and overall opinion of the journey.

Car users had an estimated 20% more days and 17% more spells of this form of absence than persons who did not use private transport. The 6% difference in the number of persons having two or more spells is significant ($P < 0.05$). This applied to both those persons using a car and public transport in different stages and those who used a car for the whole journey, but the increase was most marked in the younger men who had 38% more days off than younger men who did not use cars. Those who used other methods of private transport (cycle, moped, motor-bike, etc.) had the lowest rates of uncertified absence but this is based on a small number.

People having only one or two stages had less uncertified absence than those

Table 25-6
Uncertified Absence and the Journey to Work (Annual Frequency, Severity and
Percentage of Persons with Two or More Spells Standardized for Age, Sex and
Job Grade)

	No. of Persons	Days Rate	Spells Rate	% with 2+ Spells
Private transport				
None	1,524	1.76	1.21	33.0*
Car	412	2.12	1.41	39.2*
Other	58	1.21	0.84	23.5
No. of stages				
1 or 2	604	1.69	1.14	29.9**
3	973	1.87	1.29	35.9 ⎫
4 or more	417	1.90	1.28	36.0 ⎭ 35.9**
Duration				
−70 min	1,453	1.77	1.21	33.1 ⎫
71-90 min	418	1.91	1.28	34.7 ⎭ 33.5*
over 90 min	123	2.11	1.50	43.2*
Overall opinion				
Comfortable	671	1.72	1.16	31.7
Neither	709	1.86	1.28	34.9
Uncomfortable	614	1.87	1.28	35.5
All persons	1,994	1.82	1.24	34.0

Difference significant at 5% (*) and 1% (**) levels (Cochran's test).

with more. The 6% difference in the numbers with two or more spells was highly
significant ($P < 0.01$). However, any further increase in the number of stages
beyond three did not seem to affect this. For stages of public transport only, the
249 persons having three or more such stages had more absence than the rest
with a 10% increase in days lost.

The duration of the journey showed an effect only among those who took
more than an hour and a half. Such persons had 17% more days and 22% more
spells than the rest.

Overall opinion of the journey showed a slight association, but the differences
were not significant. No relationships could be shown with other journey factors
including loading assessments.

To assess the association of these factors after allowing for inter-association
with other journey factors an analysis of variance was carried out with days of
uncertified absence as the dependent variable (using a square root transformation to eliminate skewness). This showed that the use of a car remained as a

highly significant factor; the number of stages and overall opinion were of borderline significance, but the duration of journey was not significant when the other three factors had been allowed for.

Certified Influenza and the Journey

The large outbreak of A_2 (Hong Kong) influenza in the course of the year enabled us to assess whether travel in crowded conditions could be shown to influence the spread of the disease.

For this analysis we used the percentage of persons with certified absence due to influenza standardized for age, sex, and employment status. In Table 25-7 this rate is shown for the sample divided according to the use of public transport, the overall opinion of the journey, and also for the loading factors for BR and LT train journeys.

As LT trains provide the most crowded form of public transport we looked at

Table 25-7
Certified Influenza and the Journey to Work (Annual Percentage of Persons Certified, Standardized for Age, Sex, and Job Grade)

	No. of Persons	% with 'Flu
Public transport		
Use of LT trains	1,010	16.5
Other public transport only	880	19.3
No public transport	104	19.0
Overall opinion		
Comfortable	671	16.4
Neither	709	18.6
Uncomfortable	614	18.8
Crowding in LT trains		
Load factor 0−	136	15.5 ⎫ 17.0*
50−	109	20.9 ⎭
70−	54	30.9*
Crowding in BR trains		
Load factor 0−	101	22.4 ⎫ 21.7*
70−	176	21.3 ⎭
100	185	13.3*
All persons	1,994	17.9

*Difference significant at 5% level (Cochran's test).

the experience of their passengers in our sample and found that they had a slightly lower rate of influenza than those who used only other public transport. Moreover, those who used no public transport at all had just as much influenza as the rest. Among the 299 persons using LT trains as their only form of transport, for those whose journey was most crowded (LT loading factor of 70% or more) the spells rate of influenza was 31% compared with 18% among those whose loading factor was less; however, there were only 54 people in the former group. A similar comparison among those using only BR trains, however, produced the paradoxical result of the higher rate of influenza among those whose loading factor was under 100%.

None of the other journey factors showed any association with influenza although there was a slightly higher rate among those whose overall opinion of the journey was poor.

Other Certified Absence and the Journey

As with uncertified absence we used three measures for this analysis, spells, days, and the percentage of persons with one or more spells. In Table 25-8 these absence rates are shown in relation to the number of stages, the duration of the journey, and the use of a car, there being no evidence of association with other journey factors.

Table 25-8
Other Certified Absence and the Journey to Work (Frequency, Severity, and Percentage of Persons with Any Spells, Standardized for Age, Sex, and Job Grade)

	No. of Persons	Days Rate	Spells Rate	% Persons with any Spells
No. or stages				
1-3	1,577	4.74	0.46	31.0
4 or more	417	6.60	0.46	30.2
Duration				
Up to 90 min	1,871	5.06	0.45	30.6
Over 90 min	123	5.92	0.59	35.7
Private transport				
Car	412	4.57	0.39	31.1
No private transport	1,524	5.24	0.47	30.7
All persons	1,994	5.11	0.46	30.8

The most important of these was the number of stages as persons with four or more had 39% more days away than the rest. As the spells rate was not higher this means that those with four or more stages took longer absences. This tendency was confined to men and is best illustrated by the fact that 5.6% of men with four or more stages but only 3.0% of other men had 28 days or more of such absence ($P < 0.05$).

The duration of the journey was of less importance, and although those with longer journeys had more spells their average length was slightly less. The use of a car was associated with slightly fewer spells of about the same length.

Analysis of variance was not done for this form of absence as the extreme skewness of its distribution, coupled with the fact that the majority of people had none, makes the use of this technique unreliable.

Discussion

This investigation had two main objectives—to assess the daily journey to work as experienced by a sample of commuters, and to assess whether their sickness absence could be related to any aspect of these journeys. It was subject to a number of limitations of method which should be considered before attempting to interpret the results.

The large number of variables known to influence rates of sickness absence made it necessary for us to select a reasonably homogeneous population, and one for which comprehensive and reliable records of all sickness absence were routinely kept. Our sample formed part of the workforce of a large organization with centres in many parts of the country. A full sick pay scheme with payment of normal wages from the first day has been in operation for a number of years, and as we considered only the office workers, these cannot be considered as representative of all workers in Central London.

The use of a self-administered questionnaire without further independent verification was necessary to preserve the anonymity of individuals. We considered that as journeys to work usually follow a set pattern, the scope for error seems small. We checked each completed form and were able to clarify the few clerical errors and inconsistencies at second hand with the individual by means of the code number. We were encouraged by the response rate and believe that the respondents took the investigation seriously. Our questions were restricted to the journey to work because we considered it would have more immediate bearing on a decision to go to work or stay at home and we were reluctant to double the size of the questionnaire and risk a greater number of refusals. It is of interest, however, that some added comments on the form that their homeward journey was more unpleasant.

The reliability of the sickness absence records should also be considered, but as the organization has an elaborate system of reporting all absence there seemed little chance of an appreciable error of under-reporting. Allowing employees to take a few days off work on the grounds of ill health without having to produce a medical certificate probably results in some occasions when ill health may not have been the main reason. It is relevant in this context that absence for other reasons is uncommon in this organization.

Previous studies have usually measured only the distance or time of the journey. For commuter journeys to Central London the distance itself can be of less importance as fast main line services may result in some living 30 miles away having a quicker journey than others living only 5 or 10 miles away from the office across London. A measure of the complexity of the journey was also required and for this we chose the number of stages. It could be argued that a long main line journey to a terminal near the office, which might take the same time as a more complicated journey involving bus, train, underground, and a walk, might be less likely to encourage an employee to stay at home. The association between duration and the number of stages was positive but not particularly close, and it seems that these are very different measures of a journey.

The interpretation of an individual's opinion about the comfort of the journey as a whole is difficult. Some are more likely to complain than others, and we found this in younger employees. Furthermore, people who complain may well be those more likely to go sick. It is of some interest that more assessed their journey as comfortable than as uncomfortable, although some of the latter felt so strongly that they chose to add explanatory notes on their forms. The lack of any strong association between subjective and objective assessments of crowding on train journeys may be because the loading factors were measured at or near the station at which the passenger left the train.

The relationships we were able to show between some factors of the journey and sickness absence raise a number of important points. Uncertified absence accounted for 21% of all sickness days recorded. This high proportion reflects the liberal policy of the organization, and it was this type of absence that showed most of the positive associations with journey factors. The bulk of sickness absence, however, was covered by a medical certificate. The fact that the number of stages was related to both certified and uncertified absence suggests that this is the most important factor. Combining all types of absence and allowing for age, sex, marital status, and job grade by indirect standardization, those whose journeys involved up to three stages had 8.17 calendar days per person in the year. Those with four or more stages had 9.75 days, a 19% increase. The fact that the latter group contained a higher proportion of men with four weeks or more of certified absence (excluding influenza) is perhaps an indication that those who are off sick with more serious conditions may extend their absence if they face a more complicated journey.

The total duration of the journey showed some association with absence but this was less important than the number of stages. It was only significant with uncertified absence and when the time exceeded one and a half hours.

The situation for people using a car for part or all of the journey is curious. They had significantly more uncertified absence, but their certified sickness was slightly below average in both frequency and severity. This makes it unlikely that they included a disproportionate number with chronic conditions, particularly as the use of a car was more common in younger men. While some people may use a car because it is the only means of getting from home to the station, others may use it to make their journey more comfortable than it would be by public transport. While it is possible that such people are more sensitive to minor ailments causing the odd day off, it could also be a convenient excuse for an absence when the car breaks down. The importance of behavioural aspects of sickness absence is now well recognized (Office of Health Economics, 1971), but the arrangements for this investigation did not enable us to include measures of job satisfaction.

Our failure to demonstrate any association between the use of public transport and sickness absence carries some important implications, particularly in regard to influenza. Respiratory conditions including bronchitis are always the commonest single cause of certified sickness absence in Britain (Department of Health and Social Security, 1971). It is generally accepted that transmission of the infectious group of such conditions is by droplet. The attack rate of certified influenza among our sample was comparable with that for the whole country (Miller, Pereira, and Clarke, 1971). Our failure to demonstrate higher rates among those who used public transport came as a surprise. One might have supposed that the close proximity of passengers in crowded LT underground or BR surface trains would facilitate such transmission. Perhaps the period of time for which our respondents were exposed each day was too short, perhaps the propaganda such as ... 'Coughs and sneezes spread diseases, trap the germs in your handerkchief' has had a lasting effect; perhaps the habitual silence of the commuter reduces transmission, or perhaps there are other factors not allowed for in this investigation which would account for our findings.

In conclusion, this study has demonstrated the problems that arise when associations are sought between two complex phenomena. While there appears to be no dramatic association between the journey to work and sickness absence in our selected sample, the complexity of the journey proved to be the most important of the factors we studied. It may be that those whose health or morale was affected by a difficult journey had already taken steps to obviate this by changing their job or by moving house.

Summary

The relationship between the pattern of commuter travel to work and sickness absence has been studied in a population of 1,994 office workers in Central London.

The median time for the whole journey was one hour and the average journey had 2.8 stages. One-third of the sample considered their journey to be uncomfortable. The number of stages of the journey was the most important factor to relate to both certified and uncertified sickness absence. The use of a car or a journey lasting over one and a half hours was associated with higher uncertified rates of absence. The incidence of certified influenza did not relate to any aspect of the journey including the use of public transport.

We are extremely grateful to all our respondents and to those members of the organization's personnel department who assisted us in the collection of the information. We are also most grateful to British Rail and the Department of the Environment for supporting this investigation and to BR and LT staff who assisted us by providing loading factors.
Copies of the questionnaire will be provided on request.

References

Buzzard, R.B., and Liddell, F.D.K. (1963). Coalminers attendance at work. Medical Research Memorandum 3. National Coal Board Medical Service.

Department of Health and Social Security (1971). Annual Report 1970. Cmnd. 4714. H.M.S.O., London.

Froggatt, P. (1970). Short-term absence from industry. *Brit J. industr. Med.*, 27, 199.

Jones, R.M. (1971). Absenteeism. Department of Employment, Manpower Papers No. 4. H.M.S.O., London.

Liepmann, Kate K. (1944). *The Journey to Work, its Significance for Industrial and Community Life.* Kegan Paul, Trench, Trubner and Co., London.

Miller, D.L., Pereira, M.S., and Clarke, M. (1971). Epidemiology of the Hong Kong/68 variant of influenza A_2 in Britain. *Brit. med. J.*, 1, 475.

Norman, L.G. (1959). The health of London's travelling public. *Roy. Soc. Hlth J.*, 79, 229.

Office of Health Economics (1971). Off Sick, O.H.E. Publications, No. 36.

Taylor, P.J. (1966). M.D. thesis, pp. 70 and 88, University of London.

Vernon, H.M., Bedford, T., and Warner, C.G. (1931). Two Studies of Absenteeism in Coal Mines, *Rep. Industr. Hlth Res. Bd (Lond.),* No. 62, H.M.S.O., London.

Williams, R.E.O., and Hirch, Ann (1950). Bacterial contamination of air in underground trains. *Lancet,* 1, 128.

Wyatt, S., Marriott, R., and Hughes, D.E.R. (1943). A Study of Absenteeism among Women. *Rep. industr. Hlth Res. Bd (Lond.),* Emergency Report No. 4. H.M.S.O., London.

IX

Theory and
Research

Commentary. Kelly (1966) has suggested that mental health research should have an ecological framework. His point of view is equally applicable to physical health research. He feels that pathology should be redefined in terms of an "outcome of reciprocal interactions between specific social situations and the individual, and that the research task is to clarify the precise relationship between individual behavior and social structure that differentially affect various forms of adaptive behavior."

From a research point of view a social environment approach to the study of health and disease is a rather recent phenomenon. This late development can be attributed to many things, but among the most important are the collaboration between behavioral and medical investigators and the development of innovative methods capable of defining and measuring such an unwieldy variable as the social environment. While neither of these developments has completely resolved all problems related to environmental health research, the last decade has seen attempts to produce meaningful empirical studies.

The Midtown Manhattan study is one example of a collaborative approach to research involving psychiatrists, psychologists, sociologists, anthropologists, psychiatric social workers, and biostatisticians (Srole, Langner, Michael, Opler and Rennie, 1962). The Midtown investigation, which was large in focus, goals, strategy, and operational scope, studied mental health and its relationship to environmental and demographic variables in a densely populated section of Manhattan.

The investigators reported fewer than one-fifth of the sample to be free from significant symptoms of psychiatric disorders. The mild and moderate levels of symptom formation comprised nearly 60 percent of the sample and the marked, severe, and incapacitated grades represented approximately 20 percent. The authors indicate that these results are similar to those in other eastern cities. Parental socioeconomic status (SES) was related to the mental health of the offspring: the best mental health occurred in subjects whose parents were in the higher SES groups and poorer mental health occurred in subjects whose parents were in low SES groups.

Among the important empirical research on social environments it is worth noting studies carried out by Pace and Stern (1958), Astin and Holland (1961), Barker (1968), Moos and Houts (1968), and Moos (1974).

In Chapter 26, Z.J. Lipowski emphasizes the importance of an "ecological perspective" in psychosomatic medicine. He suggests that psychosomatic medicine should be concerned with social, psychological, and biological variables as interacting forces. By integrating trends in experimental and clinical research, and their relationship to the social environment and health and disease, Lipowski attempts to provide a theoretical framework for psychosomatic medicine. He argues that this integrationist approach provides a basis for a unified theory of man in a changing social environment which has practical application for the clinician in his medical practice.

In Chapter 27 Barbara Dohrenwend reviews the literature on the effects of stressful life events and their relationship to organic illness, psychological distress, and severe psychological disorders. Studies of life events indicate two conceptions of stressfulness: undesirability of life events and life change. Undesirable life events are defined as an event or change that others would generally view as undesirable. Life change may also be undesirable or desirable. It is usually associated with some adaptive or coping behavior on the part of the person involved. The author attempts to unravel methodological problems arising from the variety of measures of stressful life events derived from different conceptions. She raises two questions: What is the strength of the relationship between the two conceptions of stressful life events and the expected consequences of stressful life events? and How are the various measures related to each other? Measures of life change correlate more highly with symptoms of illness than do undesirable life events. Thus Dohrenwend concludes that it is life *change* that is stressful, rather than simply undesirable life events. For example, marriage, which is usually thought of as a positive life event, may be just as stressful as divorce, usually viewed as a negative life event.

References

Astin, A.W., and Holland, J.L. The environmental assessment technique: A way to measure college environments. *Journal of Educational Psychology, 52*: 308-316, 1961.

Barker, R. *Ecological Psychology*. Stanford: Stanford University Press, 1968.

Kelly, J.G. Ecological constraints on mental health services. *American Psychologist, 21*:535-539, 1966.

Moos, R.H. *Evaluating Treatment Environments: A Social Ecological Approach*. New York: John Wiley & Sons, 1974.

Moos, R.H., and Houts, P. The assessment of the social atmospheres of psychiatric wards. *Journal of Abnormal Psychology, 73*:595-604, 1968.

Pace, C.R., and Stern, G.G. An approach to the measurement of psychological characteristics of college environments. *Journal of Educational Psychology, 49*:269-277, 1958.

Srole, L., Langner, T.S., Michael, S.T., Opler, M.K., and Rennie, T. *Mental Health in the Metropolis: The Midtown Manhattan Study, I*. New York: McGraw-Hill, 1962.

26 Life Events as Stressors: A Methodological Inquiry

Z.J. Lipowski
Dartmouth Medical School

The scope of psychosomatic medicine has broadened to a point where people begin to wonder what the limits of its boundaries are. A puzzled observer asks: "Has psychosomatic medicine any limits? If so, what and why? If not, has the term outlived its usefulness, being neither definable nor even describable?"[1] These are valid questions. There is justification in talking about the *second phase* of development of our discipline,[2] one whose growing diversity makes attempts at integration difficult but necessary if we are to maintain its identity and sense of direction. This writer has formulated a comprehensive definition of psychosomatic medicine reflecting both its scientific and clinical aspects.[2] It expresses a conception of our field as one whose main goal is twofold: to strive for a unified theory of mind-body-environment interrelations; and to apply what knowledge we gain to improve the care of the sick, to help prevent some illness, and ultimately to enhance the quality of human existence. We do not need to be too concerned with sharp delimitation of the boundaries of our field. To do so might lead to premature closure on many promising lines of unorthodox thought. It would mean missing an opportunity and the intellectual challenge of constructing a unified theory from elements supplied by disparate methods of observation and explanatory systems. To meet this challenge, however, an *ecological perspective* must be added to the traditional focus of our discipline.

Reprinted with permission of *Comprehensive Psychiatry,* 14(3):203-215, 1973.

As Dubos[3] expressed it, "Psychosomatic medicine, concerned primarily with the causation of organic disease by mental disturbances, was an outgrowth of the enlargement of thought brought about by the Freudian revolution." He goes on to say that the observation that what happens in the mind affects the body and vice versa makes it "misleading to single out certain diseases as having psychosomatic origin . . . The understanding and control of disease requires that the body-mind complex be studied in its relations to external environment." This is also the thesis of the present article. It does not call for rejection of what was achieved in the first phase of psychosomatic medicine, but stresses a broadening of the whole conception of the latter, to include environmental variables into our theoretical framework and research projects to a much greater extent than before.[4]

Psychosomatic Medicine and the Social Environment

It is often asserted that factors inherent in the social environment are no less relevant to the well-being of individuals, to issues of health and disease, than the biological and physicochemical characteristics of the physical environment. The validity of this assumption is being tested by research relating specific social factors to psychophysiological processes of individuals and morbidity of various social groups. This calls for both individual-oriented and epidemiological studies. Psychosomatic medicine has often ignored social variables. In many psychosomatic studies the main emphasis has been on psychodynamic explanatory concepts, such as intrapsychic conflicts of the approach-avoidance type and the related emotions; attitudes; ego defenses; and attempts at regressive, nonverbal communication utilizing autonomic nervous pathways instead of language and gesture. These psychological concepts have then been causally related to particular modes of physiological dysfunction and disease. When the social environment was considered by psychosomatic investigators, it was often in a general sense as a source of deprivation, temptation, loss, or danger, which elicits specific emotional responses and their physiological concomitants. Further, psychosomatic research seldom ventured beyond the family environment.

Relevant explanatory hypotheses have revolved around inhibited expression of dependent needs and consequent intensification of intrapsychic conflicts over impulses to express disavowed desires and emotions, especially aggression. This methodological approach has yielded important observations but it needs to be supplemented by inclusion into our inquiry and theoretical formulations of the influence of a whole range of social variables on psychophysiological processes.

We cannot view currently prevalent psychodynamic conceptions as immutable laws of human behavior. Intrapsychic conflicts, for example, which played such a prominent role in psychosomatic hypotheses of Alexander and his followers, may well undergo significant changes under the influence of changing values and their impact on psychological development of children. Certain impulses, sexual, dependent, or aggressive, may be losing their pejorative connotation and the consequent need for their repression and other defenses against their intrusion into consciousness, if not their outward expression. Thus the most often postulated unconscious approach-avoidance conflicts may gradually cease being unconscious, and the expression of relevant impulses may lead to conscious, interpersonal conflicts, or even no conflicts at all. And yet physiological dysfunctions and specific diseases purportedly dependent on the existence of such unresolved conflicts continue to develop with no perceptible change in their incidence. Further, other psychosocial variables, such as approach—approach, choice and decision conflicts,[5] value conflicts, status incongruity,[6,7] increased rate of social change, dissonance between expectations and gratification, and a host of other currently prevailing factors may well supersede the previously mentioned psychodynamic variables as potential sources of psychic distress, physiological dysfunction and disease. Their influence may be expressed by non-specific general susceptibility to any physio- and psychopathological processes. It is psychosomatic research in all its aspects—experimental and clinical, human and animal, epidemiological as well as that focused on unique subjective responses of individuals—which should throw light on these questions. The foundations for this broad approach were laid in the milestones of psychosomatic literature.[8-12]

The Ecological Dimension of Psychosomatics

Human ecology has been defined as the study of the relations between man and his environment, both as it affects him and as he affects it.[13] To be methodologically useful, however, the ecological dimension of psychosomatics needs to be defined in more specific terms. Both physical and social environment is relevant to psychosomatic relationships in four overlapping ways: (1) as a source of stimulus and information input; (2) as an instigator of goal-directed thought and action; (3) as a source of stimuli which give rise to somatic perceptions; (4) as a source of factors which alter cerebral function and structure and thus impair adaptive capacities of the individual. Each of these four aspects may influence psychophysiological functioning of man and lead to behaviors which in turn modify the environment. There is thus a dynamic interplay in the man-environment system whose detailed study is the aim of psychosomatic research. Each of these aspects of the environment needs further elaboration for the sake of clarity.

First, environment concerns us as a source of information input in a broad sense. As Hinkle[4] states: "A meaningful hypothesis about the relation of a man to his social and interpersonal environment, and the effect of this upon his health, must take into account the *information* that he receives from this environment, and the way that he *evaluates* it" (italics mine). Thus, the key intervening variable here is a cognitive one, namely subjective *meaning*. This writer has proposed that we may distinguish four major categories of subjective meaning of perceived events, situations, and objects. They are: *threat, loss, gain* (or its promise), and *insignificance.*[14] These categories are not necessarily mutually exclusive. The evaluation and meaning are both conscious and unconscious, and the two may be at variance with each other. It is especially in uncovering the unconscious meaning of information for the individual that psychoanalytic method and theory continues to play an indispensable role in psychosomatics. Threat, loss and gain are classes of meaning of key importance for psychosomatic research and theory. They are so by virtue of their power to evoke emotional, behavioral, and physiological responses. They are also central to the concept of psychological stress and its consequences, whether desirable or pathogenic. Gain is linked conceptually with appetitive drives, hopeful anticipation, striving, pleasure and satiety.

There are other features of information input relevant to psychosomatics. They include *quantity, novelty, clarity, consistency,* and *attractiveness* of information as experienced by its recipients. These characteristics have attracted increasing scientific interest only recently. What concerns a psychosomatic investigator is the psychophysiological effects of these variables. We are especially interested in such effects when there is personally experienced information underload or overload, when information is novel, discrepant or ambiguous, or when it elicits appetitive drives beyond the individual's capacity for consummation. All these situations are potential sources of information-derived stress with its varied psychological and somatic components.

Second, social environment instigates activity at both cognitive and motor levels. This is the domain of interpersonal relationships, of prevalent values and norms of behavior, of competitive striving and its goals, of feedback in the form of rewards and punishments. There is a growing number of studies attempting to relate these social variables to psychophysiological responses.[15-17]

Third, environment is a source of somatic perceptions. The latter constitute an internal, somatic information input which may be endowed with personal meaning. From then on the four categories of meaning mentioned earlier come into play.

Fourth and last, environmental factors may cause changes in the biological substrate of psychic processes and thereby alter a person's habitual modes of perceiving, thinking and feeling. This is a class of environmental factors which may influence psychosomatic relationships *without* the interposition of symbolic stimuli.

Application of this schema to a concrete example of an important contemporary problem may help to clarify it further. Let us consider pollution of the physical environment. It may affect individuals and be relevant to psychosomatics in the following ways: First, it gives rise to social communications which alert individuals to the noxious aspects of pollution and may make them view the environment as personally threatening. The alerted subject may then notice and interpret certain sensory cues, such as color of the water or smell of the air, as subjectively meaningful danger signals. These in turn may make him view his physical environment as alien and potentially lethal. It should be feasible to design research to determine how this type of information affects individuals psychologically and physiologically. Second, information about pollution leads to the formulation of values, norms and problem-solving actions related to the quality of the environment as well as to relevant social interactions, cooperative or hostile. Third, noxious biological, chemical, or physical pollutants may cause tissue changes. These in turn may give rise to somatic perceptions, e.g., of impaired breathing or diarrhoea, which become endowed with symbolic meaning in terms of the categories described above. Such a meaning may be both conscious and unconscious and evoke emotional responses with their physiological concomitants, thus giving rise to more somatic perceptions which in turn may be interpreted as threatening. This is an example of positive feedback which magnifies the emotional response to the original somatic perception. Fourth, some pollutants may bring about changes in the physico-chemical milieu of the brain and alter its function.

It is clear that each of these aspects of pollution may affect a person's psychophysiological functioning and the study of the effects of pollution on humans would be incomplete if any of these aspects was ignored. This may serve as a paradigm of the psychosomatic approach to certain aspects of the physical environment, or of the ecological dimension of psychosomatics.

Some Relevant Social Variables

Information Inputs

It is difficult to demarcate sharply the social and nonhuman environment since the latter is increasingly modified and shaped by human activity. As the above example of environmental pollution illustrates, man-made influence on the environment results in symbolic and physical stimuli both of which, though by means of different pathways, may result in psychological and physiological changes. Our primary concern in this section is with the *symbolic stimuli,* or *information inputs* emanating from the social environment.

One aspect of information relevant to psychosomatics is *quantity* of information or stimulus input. Of more particular interest are conditions of information underload and overload because of their potentially detrimental psychophysiological effects. A great deal has been learned about such effects of information underload, usually referred to as sensory deprivation. Knowledge about its effects has been admirably summarized in a volume edited by Zubek.[18] One of the major theoretical formulations attempting to account for the phenomena of sensory underload and overload is Zuckerman's theory of *optimal level of stimulation*.[19] The key postulate of this theory asserts that every individual has characteristic optimal levels of stimulation and arousal for cognitive and motor activity and positive affective tone. It follows that deviations from the optimal level for the given individual at the given point in his life cycle are likely to result in subjectively unpleasant experience and some pattern of psychophysiological derangement. These experiential, behavioral, and physiological responses may be subsumed under the term *stress*.

For some reason studies of *information overload* have lagged behind those of sensory deprivation, despite their obvious relevance to the contemporary environment in technological societies. Miller,[20] a pioneer in this field, describes mechanisms of adjustment to information input overload and suggests that it may have psychopathological consequences. He postulates, for example, that certain conditions, such as infection or trauma, may exacerbate schizophrenic symptoms as a result of lowering of channel capacity for the inflow of information, a capacity perhaps abnormally low in schizophrenics to start with. Spitz[21] proposed that surfeit of emotional stimuli in infancy might have psychopathogenic effects in later life. Ludwig[22,23] reports preliminary results of the first major research project on the effects of sensory overload on human subjects. He describes altered state of consciousness ("psychedelic" effects) in 40% of normal volunteers subjected to two and one-half hours of overload with two types of sensory input: light and sound. These findings seem to support Lindsey's earlier assumption of common factors in sensory deprivation, distortion and overload.[24] What is still missing, is the study of selected physiological variables, along with the behavioral and experiential ones, in states of sensory overload. Experiments in which rats were exposed to intense sound, light, and motion stimuli ("stressors") consistently produced significant increases in systolic blood pressure, hypertrophy of the left ventricle and evidence of hyperfunction of the adrenal cortex.[25] Relevance of these findings for humans is unknown.

A most recent contribution to this field is a study of Gottschalk et al.[26] It differs in details of design and psychological indices used from Ludwig's study, but it also purports to investigate the effects of visual and auditory stimulus overload on humans. The significant findings include increase in social alienation—personal disorganization scores and cognitive impairment after exposure to overstimulation. The cognitive impairment correlated with preexposure field dependence scores suggesting greater susceptibility of field-dependent subjects to cognitive disorganization under sensory overload.

Both Ludwig and Gottschalk et al., refer to their respective experiments as involving "sensory overload." This term raises the question of the difference, if any, between concepts of stimulus and information overload, respectively. The former concept implies quantity, the latter, meaning. It is questionable, however, if any type, intensity, or patterning of sensory stimuli is anything but variation of information input. Even apparently "meaningless" stimuli, such as white noise or colored lights, may and apparently do evoke associative thoughts and images in the subject and are, in this sense, personally meaningful information, however idiosyncratic the latter may be. This view made the writer include this experimental work under the heading "information overload." The terms "information" and "stimulation" have been used interchangeably here.

The potential importance of this budding field of inquiry lies in its relevance to environmental psychology, especially problems of urban environment. The latter has been stated to constitute "a continuous set of encounters with overload, and of resultant adaptations."[27] There are other situations where at least some individuals will experience overload. They include overcrowding,[28] driving conditions,[28] certain occupations,[28] exposure to various communication media, etc. Experimental animal research on the effects of crowding led Welch[29] to propose a theoretical principle related conceptually to that derived from work on sensory deprivation: that every environment exerts its own characteristic *mean level of stimulation* which is largely determined by social interaction and emotional involvement. The mean level is reflected in reticular activation and endocrine secretions, and influences the animal's resistance to disease.[29]

Cassel,[30] reviewing epidemiological studies of human populations, suggests that increased population density enhances the importance of the social environment as a source of stimuli which evoke physiological responses influencing general susceptibility to disease. Quality of social interactions and position within the group seem to be important, in addition to the sheer quantity and novelty of stimuli.

We thus have converging lines of evidence which may be tentatively summed up in the following hypotheses:

(1) Each individual is characterized by an *optimum level* of stimulus or information input which he can tolerate and process. This level may fluctuate over time and a person's life-cycle.

(2) Each individual has for him a characteristic and enduring stimulus or information *need*. This need acts as motivational factor in seeking or avoiding (or oscillation between both) a stimulus level which is consonant with pleasure. There is some evidence that this need is greater in extraverts than introverts.[30a]

(3) Each social environment is characterized by the *mean level* of stimulation which will affect different individuals according to their individual stimulus tolerance and need.

(4) Extreme deviations of stimulus input result in excessive autonomic and cortical arousal leading to cognitive disorganization, unpleasant feelings, and objective decrement in cognitive and/or motor performance. This state is a form of *psychological stress*, one elicited by excess or deficiency of symbolic stimuli.

(5) Contemporary technological society provides numerous opportunities for arousal of stimulus need, its satisfaction, as well as for information overload.

(6) Such repeated or sustained arousal may lead to physiological changes as well as behaviors enhancing the subject's general *susceptibility to illness*. The specific form and severity of the latter will be co-determined by intra-individual specific somatic vulnerability as well as current environmental noxae.

These hypotheses await testing through multidisciplinary research. The question of their validation has obvious social and clinical relevance. One notes, however, that investigators often cultivate their respective gardens while ignoring what goes on outside their territorial fence. There is a host of studies pertaining to the tolerance of and need for stimulation from early infancy to old age which await meaningful conceptual integration.

Korner[31] summarizes observations on neonates which reveal individual differences in the responsiveness to and synthesis of sensory stimuli. Thus some infants readily become overwhelmed by overstimulation unless a mothering person provides a "stimulus barrier." Others, by contrast, display high sensory thresholds to all sensory stimuli and need a great deal of stimulation for optimal development. Korner postulates that the most enduring characteristics of an individual derive from his capacity to cope with sensory stimuli and his individual stimulus needs. She proposes that there are two basic regulatory strategies for dealing with overstimulation: one aimed at diminishing the sensory input; the other employing motor or affective discharge and experiencing strong excitation as ego-syntonic. These two basic coping strategies are linked to specific ego defenses and cognitive styles which may be regarded as their enduring characterological derivatives. These basic stimulus needs and coping styles may be reflected in later life in behavioral dispositions referred to as stimulus-seeking,[32] reducing or augmenting sensory inputs,[32] impulsiveness or reflectiveness, field dependence or independence, as well as optimal level of stimulation. These individual differences may also co-determine the modes in which different subjects *cope* with stimulus or information overloads.[33,34] What remains to be investigated is the physiological responses which accompany these different modes of coping with overstimulation and their relevance, if any, to general or specific disease susceptibility. This may well emerge as a major task of psychosomatic research in the coming years.

It may be argued that the concept of quantity of information is more cogent for engineering than psychology. When applied to humans, quantity of information can hardly be teased away from its other attributes, especially the *meaning* of information for the recipient as well as its novelty, consistency, etc. Thus when we talk of informational underload and overload we must consider the effects of these latter characteristics in addition to sheer quantity. They will be discussed briefly.

Novel stimuli induce the orienting reaction. According to Sokolov[35] this reaction includes numerous autonomic arousal responses, such as dilated pupils, increased blood supply to the head, respiratory irregularity, etc. One may postulate that there is an optimal level for such arousal and that its excess is stressful. Inconsistency or ambiguity of information may reflect social change or, more specifically, the spread of discrepant values and guidelines for choice and action. There is some experimental evidence that inconsistent or conflicting information may have a high physiologically arousing potential.[16] Prevalent values influence people's expectations, goals and striving. They influence the quality of interpersonal relationships and have a decisive effect on which social events and situations will mean threat, loss, or gain, achievement or failure, for the individual, and thus partly determine the psychophysiological response to information received or action undertaken. Toffler[36] gives an outspoken account of the current value crisis in technological societies and the related choice and decision conflicts. The latter are closely related to this writer's theory of *attractive stimulus overload*.[5] The concept of "attractiveness" in this context refers to the capacity of information to arouse an appetitive state and approach tendencies in the recipient. It is postulated that attractive information overload is a hallmark of affluent societies with pervasive social, psychological and one may predict, physiological consequences. On the one hand there is an over-abundance of information and stimuli arousing desire for consummation, at both material and symbolic levels. This surfeit coupled with a wide range of available options for choice as well as discrepant value systems results in approach–approach and decision conflicts. Several behavioral coping strategies with this predicament have been described.[33] They are aimed at avoidance or reduction of stimulation, or are ceaseless, repeated attempts at approach and consummation. The poor exposed to this form of overload are aroused and expectant but unable to approach the proffered attractive goals for economic reasons and are frustrated. Those endowed with the economic means are often hampered by psychological and temporal limitations for approach behavior and consummation. For them, the decision and choice conflicts are a potential source of frustration and discontent. These hypothetical formulations await experimental validation through psychosomatic research. The only relevant study to date is Masserman's experiment.[37] He subjected normal monkeys to increasingly difficult choices between nearly equally desirable food. After ten days in the difficult-choice situation, the animals developed neurotic disturbances, such as tics, agitation, distractibility, and destructiveness. These effects were similar to those induced by aversive conflicts.

Social Change and Health

Dubos[3] asserts that social change may be a cause of disease and that prevalent chronic neoplastic and degenerative diseases are "diseases of civilization," in some way related to affluence. This is a vague generalization whose validity may only be tested by identifying and studying those social factors which can be related to social change in specific areas of living and linked causally to affluence. Hypotheses presented above are an attempt at just such identification of some relevant social variables. Three major research approaches attempting to relate social factors to morbidity have employed *epidemiological, psychodynamic* (individual), and *experimental animal* approaches, respectively. These approaches are complementary rather than mutually exclusive.

Representative examples of these studies are provided by the work of Hinkle, Holmes, Rahe, and others on the relation between life change and general susceptibility to disease,[38,39] the work by Engel, Schmale and their collaborators on the giving-up—given-up complex as a common setting for the onset of any illness,[40] and the studies by Henry et al., of effects of social stimulation on hormonal and cardiovascular functions in mice.[41] One may argue that the former two types of study reflect the impact of the social environment on the individual's value system and his consequent evaluation of life events which are, in part at least, an expression of his interaction with, subjective evaluation of and his coping with his social environment. The informational feedback from the social environment has a crucial influence on man's setting of his goals, definition of his social role and status, his actual behavior, and his evaluation of himself and his actions. These factors are closely related to subjective meaning of social events, to what constitutes social stress,[42] to status integration,[6] and other social variables whose causal relationship to affective response, physiological dysfunction and disease has been postulated. Reviews of the role of these factors in two prevalent causes of morbidity and mortality, i.e., essential hypertension,[43] and coronary heart disease[7] illustrate this. One may postulate, for example, that particular personality dispositions leading to a behavior pattern characterized by upward social mobility and ceaseless striving in a competitive environment offering an overabundance of options and incentives for striving, may represent a constellation of psychosocial factors conducive to the development of coronary artery disease.

The Role of Mediating Physiological Mechanisms

How do social stimuli and the psychological responses to them disturb homeostatic mechanisms of the human organism? What are the physiological pathways which intervene between symbolic stimuli and changes in body cells, tissues and organs? In other words, by what mechanisms does the information input from the environment bring about somatic changes which may contribute to the development of disease?

These questions are the subject of research cutting across many biological disciplines. Until the above questions are answered, psychosomatic hypotheses will remain only plausible guesses. Yet progress is evident in this difficult area, one which has come to occupy the center of the stage in current psychosomatic research. It would be beyond the scope of this article to summarize the vast number of relevant studies. Only the most prominent and promising lines of investigation will be referred to.

The most intensive research activity has centered on neuroendocrine mechanisms, especially the role of the hypothalamus, reticular activating system, the limbic system, and the pituitary-adrenal axis. The reader is referred to relevant comprehensive reviews.[44-53] Solomon has pursued promising research on the influence of psychological stress on immune reactions.[51] A relationship between social class and achievement and striving for it on the one hand and serum urate levels on the other, has been proposed.[52]

The majority of the studies in question have focussed on physiological correlates of stress and emotion. Both these constructs are not free of ambiguity, although Lazarus must be credited with bringing some order into semantic chaos surrounding them.[53] Of particular interest to our thesis that symbolic stimuli may affect physiological functions is the finding that those stimuli which are subjectively stressful can be discriminated on the basis of EEG tracings.[54]

An Attempt at Integration

An appropriately sceptical and cautious viewpoint widely held among psychosomatic researchers is that to attempt integration of psychosomatic relationships at this stage is both premature and doomed to failure. There is yet a cogent argument that such attempts, however inadequate and tentative they may be, are of value as they point to meaningful relationships not noticed before and pinpoint gaps in our knowledge which stimulate further research. Without theorizing, our field could hardly advance and would likely disintegrate into a mass of unrelated observations and hypotheses. Thus, its potential for developing a unified theory of human behavior as well as its clinical applicability would be impeded. The following attempt at an integrative summary of the preceding discussion may serve as a conceptual framework, tentative and incomplete, bringing together the psychosomatic and ecological dimensions of human psychobiology.

Man's social environment is a source of symbolic stimuli, that is, events and situations which impinge on individuals as information. The latter is processed at the psychological level of organization and endowed with subjective meaning, conscious and unconscious. The nature of the meaning is determined by the person's individual characteristics, innate and learned, enduring and current. Depending on the way in which information is evaluated by the subject, it sets off affective and psychomotor responses as well as physiological changes which provide feedback modifying the cognitive processes whereby information is evaluated. These activities are studied by psychological observation methods and expressed in statements, descriptive and theoretical, couched in the language of psychology, the person language. All these processes are subserved by the activity of the central nervous system. External stimuli undergo screening at the level of the reticular activating system which serves an arousing function for cerebral cortex and prepares it for reception of specific stimulus input and its processing. Some of the incoming stimuli may set off impulses transmitted from the cell assemblies in the reticular activating system to the limbic system and the hypothalamus, and by activating these structures bring about emotional and autonomic arousal. The latter results in affective tone as well as neuroendocrine activities which lead to a homeostatic change whose pattern is partly determined by individual and partly by stimulus-bound response specificity. Affective and autonomic arousal appears to be achieved by both cortical and subcortical activity which function as an integrated whole. A symbolic stimulus may thus lead to affective and physiological changes both through evaluative, cognitive processes of the cerebral cortex, and by the direct outflow of impulses from the reticular activating system to neural structures controlling all bodily processes. The pattern of physiological changes induced by the central nervous system's integrative activity may give rise to somesthetic perceptions, that is feedback which in turn augments or inhibits the activity of cortical and subcortical neural structures. The result at the psychological level of abstraction involves modification of the information processing, planning of action and readiness for and direction of the manifest behavior. The somesthetic perceptions elicited by the motor and secretory activity provide somatic information input which may be endowed with any of the subjective meanings mentioned before. Both external and somatic information inputs are evaluated in the light of individual's accrued learning, his values, goals and motives. These contribute the third information input in the form of memories, imagery, fantasies, and directed thoughts. The outcome of the processing of these information inputs, their respective subjective meanings and related affective concomitants, is a pattern of physiological arousal mediated by neuroendocrine regulating mechanisms. If such an arousal exceeds, by virtue of its intensity and/or duration, the person's adaptive capacity, then a state of general susceptibility to illness may ensue. This state may be viewed as the final common path for psychological stress. Whether an illness follows and what form it takes, will then depend on additional factors, inherent in the person and his environment. These factors include specific individual predisposition, innate or acquired, to respond with dysfunction of a given organ or tissue as well as on the presence of physical, chemical or biological noxae within the organism or impinging on it from outside. An additional set of determinants includes the effectiveness of the subject's psychobiological defense mechanisms and the degree of support he receives from his social milieu. If biological, psychological, and social defenses and supports fail, or the individual engages in behavior increasing his illness susceptibility, an organismic state called disease follows. The latter implies failure of adaptive capacity at some level of organization from the molecular to the symbolic. Once disease develops, a new set of psychosocial and physiological processes is set into motion which influence the course and outcome of every disease. It is at this point that a comprehensive diagnosis and management which take cognizance of the patient's psychological, social and biological liabilities, strains and strengths may be applied in the service of optimal recovery and rehabilitation.

The task of psychosomatic medicine is threefold: First, to break down the enormous complexity of the above processes into conceptually tractable and researchable interrelationships among selected social, psychological and biological variables. This is an analytic approach. Second, to integrate the diverse elements of empirical knowledge to formulate higher order generalizations about environment-mind-body transactions. This is a synthetic approach. And third, to translate the knowledge so gained into guidelines for clinical action: preventive, therapeutic, and rehabilitative. This is the applied, practical approach of direct relevance to medicine. Neither of these three approaches can be dispensed with if psychosomatic medicine is to remain a viable and practically useful field of knowledge.

Conclusions

This article continues the series of papers in which the writer has attempted to delineate salient issues in contemporary psychosomatic medicine: investigative, clinical and theoretical.[2,14,55-57] The focus of the present paper is on a relatively neglected aspect of the field, one which may be called its *ecological dimension*. More specifically, a set of postulates is put forth to underscore the various aspects of information or stimulus overload as a class of variables linking conceptually man's social environment with his psychophysiological functioning. Information is seen as a heuristically useful concept for psychosomatic formulations and research on the impact of social events and change on psychological and physiological processes codetermining health and illness. It is a tentative attempt to add a new perspective to psychosomatic theory and integrate it into the main body of its hypotheses relating the psychological and biological factors whose interplay determines human behavior and functions at all levels of organization, from the molecular to the symbolic. No claim is made that information is the only relevant variable. The author does assert, however, that it helps to identify specific aspects of our social environment and lends itself to formulation of testable hypotheses. Their ultimate result is hoped to lead to guidelines for practical action aimed at prevention of some potentially pathogenic aspects of a technological society which exert their effects on the individuals through the medium of symbolic, man-made stimuli.

Summary

This article formulates the ecological dimension of psychosomatic medicine and stresses its indispensability for a comprehensive conception and further development of the latter. Special emphasis is laid on various aspects of information input overload as a paradigm of current social change relevant to psychophysiological functioning of individuals in technological societies and to issues of health and disease. An attempt is also made to outline a comprehensive theoretical framework integrating growing diversity of trends in research, experimental and clinical, pertinent to the central concern of psychosomatics: the interrelationships of psychological, biological and social variables as they influence health and disease. It is argued that this integrationist approach enhances the dual social role of psychosomatics: to strive for a unified theory of man in a changing social environment, and to work out practical guidelines for preventive and remedial action applicable to medical practice.

References

1. Spaulding WB: Psychosocial Aspects of Physical Illness in Lipowski ZJ (ed.): Advances in Psychosomatic Medicine, Vol VIII. Basel, Karger, 1972

2. Lipowski, ZJ: New perspectives in psychosomatic medicine. Can Psychiat Assoc J 15:515, 1970

3. Dubos R: Man, Medicine, and Environment. New York, Praeger, 1968

4. Hinkle LE: Ecological observations of the relation of physical illness, mental illness, and the social environment. Psychosom Med 23:298, 1961

5. Lipowski ZJ: The conflict of Buridan's ass or some dilemmas of affluence: The theory of attractive stimulus overload. Am J Psychiatry 127:273, 1970

6. Dodge DL, Martin WT: Social Stress and Chronic Illness. Notre Dame, Ind., Univ of Notre Dame Pr, 1970

7. Jenkins DC: Psychologic and social precursors of coronary disease. New Eng J Med 284:244, 1971

8. Alexander F: Psychosomatic Medicine. New York, Norton, 1950

9. Grinker RR: Psychosomatic Research. New York, Norton, 1953

10. Wolff HG: Stress and Disease. Springfield, Ill, Thomas, 1953

11. Engel GL: Selection of clinical material in psychosomatic medicine. Psychosom Med 16:368, 1954

12. Mirsky AI: The psychosomatic approach to the etiology of clinical disorders. Psychosom Med 19:424, 1957

13. Rogers ES: Human Ecology and Health. New York, Macmillan, 1960

14. Lipowski ZJ: Psychosocial aspects of disease. Ann Intern Med 71:1197, 1969

15. Leiderman HP, Shapiro D (eds): Psychobiological Approaches to Social Behavior. Stanford, Calif, Stanford Univ 1964

16. Shapiro D, Crider A: Psychophysiological approaches in social psychology, in Lindzey G, Aronson E. The Handbook of Social Psychology, 2nd ed. Reading, Mass, Addison-Wesley, 1969

17. Shapiro D, Schwartz GE: Psychophysiological contributions to social psychology. Ann Rev Psychol 21:87, 1970

18. Zubek JP, Ed: Sensory Deprivation. New York, Appleton-Century-Crofts, 1969

19. Zuckerman M: Theoretical formulations, in Zubek JP (ed): Sensory Deprivation. New York, Appleton-Century-Crofts, 1969, pp 407-432

20. Miller JG: Information input overload and psychopathology. Am J Psychiatry 116:695, 1960

21. Spitz RA: The derailment of dialogue: Stimulus overload, action cycles, and the completion gradient. J Am Psychoanal Assoc 12:752, 1964

22. Ludwig AM: "Psychedelic" effects produced by sensory overload. Read at the 124th annual meeting of the American Psychiatric Association, Washington, DC, 1971

23. Ludwig AM: Self-regulation of the sensory environment. Arch Gen Psychiatry 25:413, 1971

24. Lindsey DB: Common factors in sensory deprivation, sensory distortion and sensory overload. Sensory Deprivation, Edited by P Solomon, et al. Cambridge, Mass, Harvard Univ Pr, 1965

25. Smookler HH, Buckley JP: Effect of drugs on animals exposed to chronic environmental stress. Federation Proc 29:1980, 1970

26. Gottschalk LA, Haer JL, Bates DE: Changes in social alienation, personal disorganization and cognitive-intellectual impairment produced by sensory overload. Arch Gen Psychiatry 27:451, 1972

27. Milgram S: The experience of living in cities. Science 167:1461, 1970

28. Carson DH, Driver BL: An environmental approach to human stress and well-being: With implications for planning. Mental Health Research Institute, The University of Michigan, July, 1970

29. Welch BL: Psychophysiological response to the mean level of environmental stimulation: A theory of environmental integration. Symposium on Medical Aspects of Stress in the Military Climate. Washington, DC, Walter Reed Army Institute of Research, 1964

30. Cassel J: Health consequences of population density and crowding. in press

30a. Elliott CD: Noise tolerance and extraversion in children, BR J Psychol 62:375, 1971

31. Korner AF: Individual differences at birth: Implications for early experience and later development. Am J Orthopsychiatry 41:608, 1971

32. Sales SM: Need for stimulation as a factor in social behavior. J Personal Soc Psychol 19:124, 1971

33. Lipowski ZJ: Surfeit of attractive information inputs: A hallmark of our environment. Behav Sci 16:467, 1971

34. Miller JG: Psychological aspects of communication overloads, in Waggoner RM, Carek DJ (eds) International Psychiatry Clinics: Communication in Clinical Practice. Boston, Little, Brown, 1964

35. Sokolov YN: Perception and the Conditioned Reflex. New York, Macmillan, 1963

36. Toffler A: Future Shock. New York, Random House, 1970

37. Masserman J: The effect of positive-choice conflicts on normal and neurotic monkeys. Am J Psychiat 115:481, 1963

38. Rahe RH: Subjects' recent life changes and their near-future illness susceptibility, in Lipowski ZJ (ed): Psychosocial Aspects of Physical Illness, Advances in Psychosomatic Medicine, Vol VIII. Basel, Karger, in press

39. Wyler AR, Masuda M, Holmes TH: Magnitude of life events and seriousness of illness. Psychosom Med 33:115, 1971

40. Schmale AH: Giving up as a final common pathway to changes in health, in Lipowski ZJ (ed): Psychosocial Aspects of Physical Illness, Advances in Psychosomatic Medicine, Vol VIII. Basel, Karger, 1972

41. Henry JP, Meehan JP, Stephens PM: The use of psychosocial stimuli to induce prolonged systolic hypertension in mice. Psychosom Med 29:408, 1967

42. Levine S, Scotch NA (eds): Social Stress. Chicago, Aldine, 1970

43. Henry JP, Cassel JC: Psychosocial factors in essential hypertension. Am J Epidem 90:171, 1969

44. Black P (ed): Physiological Correlates of Emotion. New York, Academic Press, 1970

45. Levi L (ed): Society, Stress and Disease. London, Oxford University Press, 1971

46. Mason JW: A review of psychoendocrine research on the pituitary-adrenal cortical system. Psychosom Med 30:576, 1968

47. Mason JW: A review of psychoendocrine research on the sympathetic-adrenal medullary system. Psychosom Med 30:631, 1968

48. Mason JW: "Over-all" hormonal balance as a key to endocrine organization. Psychosom Med 30:791, 1968

49. Teichner WH: Interaction of behavioral and physiological stress reactions. Psychol Rev 75:271, 1968

50. Wolf S: Emotions and the autonomic nervous system. Arch Intern Med 126:1024, 1970

51. Solomon GF: Stress and immune resistance to disease. In press.

52. Mueller EF, et al.: Psychosocial correlates of serum urate levels. Psychol Bull 73:238, 1970

53. Lazarus RS: Psychological Stress and the Coping Process. New York, McGraw-Hill, 1966

54. Berkhout J, Walter DO, Adey RW: Alterations of the human electro-encephalogram induced by stressful verbal activity. Electroenceph clin Neurophysiol 27:457, 1969

55. Lipowski ZJ: Review of consultation psychiatry and psychosomatic medicine, I. General principles. Psychosom Med 29:153, 1967

56. Lipowski ZJ: Review of consultation psychiatry and psychosomatic medicine, II. Clinical aspects. Psychosom Med 29:201, 1967

57. Lipowski ZJ: Review of consultation psychiatry and psychosomatic medicine, III. Theoretical issues. Psychosom Med 30:395, 1968

27 Psychosomatic Medicine in a Changing Society: Some Current Trends in Theory and Research

Barbara Snell Dohrenwend
*The City College of the City University
of New York*

In 1907 a physician who had observed the effects of a severe earthquake on the population of Messina described a clinical syndrome that he labeled "earthquake neurosis." He noted that it " . . . was produced immediately, that in general its duration was brief, as in acute illnesses, and that the symptoms disappeared without leaving any trace" (quoted without reference by Murri, 1912:537). It now appears that the syndrome is not specific to earthquakes, since observers have reported similar responses to a variety of public disasters. One of the most widely known of these reports is Lindemann's account (1944:146-147) of the reactions of survivors and others who lost a friend or relative in a Boston night club fire. In this account he emphasized the importance of the situation and the irrelevance of personal factors as determinants of extreme grief reactions.

The power of the situation to induce symptoms of psychological distress regardless of personal predisposition was demonstrated again in two studies of general populations exposed to disasters, both of which revealed incidence rates of post-disaster symptomatology approaching 100 per cent. In the first of these investigations, a systematic sample of the population of a rural section of Arkansas was interviewed shortly after the area had been hit by a severe tornado. Ninety per cent of those interviewed reported " . . . some form of acute emotional, physiological or psychosomatic after-effect" (Fritz & Marks,

Reprinted with permission of *Journal of Health & Social Behavior*, 14:167-175, June, 1973.

413

1954:34). The most common of these symptoms were "nervousness, excitability, hypersensitivity," reported by 49 per cent, and "Sleeplessness or poor sleep," reported by 46 per cent.

In the most ambitious study to date of popular reactions to disaster, Sheatsley and Feldman (1964) conducted interviews with a systematic sample of the population of the United States about one week after the assassination of President Kennedy. Among the questions in their structured interview were fifteen symptom items of the type that have been used to assess mental health in general populations (Gurin et al., 1960; Langner, 1962). Eighty-nine per cent of Sheatsley and Feldman's sample reported having one or more of these symptoms during the first four days following the assassination. By the time of the interviews, almost all of which were conducted on the seventh and eighth days after the assassination, only 50 per cent of respondents reported that they still had one or more symptoms.

By no means all of the untoward events experienced by members of a community are public disasters such as an earthquake or a presidential assassination. Probably, in a nation at peace with itself and with the rest of the world, almost all of the crises that most people experience in their lifetimes are private events such as the death of a relative or friend, illness, or an economic setback. Two recent studies have shown that such stressful life events, like stressful public events, induce transient symptoms of psychological disturbance (Dohrenwend and Dohrenwend, 1969:126-130; Myers et al., 1972). These events have also been shown to have more serious effects on health; specifically, they have been related to the onset of serious psychological disorders (Brown and Birley, 1968; 1970) and to varied and, in some cases, serious organic illnesses (Antonovsky and Kats, 1967; Rahe, 1968; Theorell and Rahe, 1970). At the same time, stressful life events, unlike stressful public events, are necessarily part of everyone's experience. This pervasiveness, together with the recent demonstrations of their varied relations to illness, has drawn increasing attention to stressful life events as an important subject of study in public health research.

Definition of Stressful Life Events

Investigators studying the effects of an earthquake, a tornado, or a presidential assassination have not found it necessary to argue that these events are stressful. In contrast, most investigators concerned with life events have deemed it necessary to explain their choice of the events they studied in terms of an explicit definition of stressful events. These definitions have revealed, however, not one but two distinct conceptions of the characteristic that makes an event stressful.

The first conception is exemplified by the work of Brown and Birley in which they demonstrated associations between antecedent stressful events and episodes of schizophrenia (1968) or severe depression (1970). In these studies they used "... a list of events which on common sense grounds are likely to produce emotional disturbance in many people" (1968:204). In defining stressful life events as negative or undesirable in quality Brown and Birley remained close to the conception of stressfulness most obviously implied by studies of public crises and disasters.

The second, less obvious conception of stressful life events focuses on change as the critical factor (e.g. Fröberg et al., 1971:291-292). This conception has been the basis for two measures of amount of exposure to such events. The first, relatively simple measure was used, for example, in a review of the literature on class and race differences in exposure to stress. For this purpose stressful events were defined as "objective events that disrupt or threaten to disrupt the individual's usual activities" (Dohrenwend and Dohrenwend, 1970:115), with the proviso that the events might be either undesirable or desirable in character. The measure of amount of exposure to stressful events in a given period of time was simply the number of such events experienced.

The second, more elaborate and sophisticated measure based on the conception of life change as stressful was developed by Holmes, Rahe, and their colleagues. After collecting a list of "... life events empirically observed to cluster at the time of disease onset," Holmes and Rahe (1967:215-217), observed that "... only some of the events are negative or 'stressful' in the conventional sense, i.e. are socially undesirable." Instead, they noted, "There was identified ... one theme common to all these life events. The occurrence of each usually evoked or was associated with some adaptive or coping behavior on the part of the involved individual." To measure total exposure to stressfulness, these investigators did not simply count the number of events experienced, however, but introduced a major refinement by collecting judgments of the amount of readjustment required by each event on the list. Total exposure to stressful events was then calculated by summing the readjustment scores of all events experienced by an individual in a given period of time. Using this measure, Rahe (1968) showed that individuals who had experienced events that yielded higher total readjustment scores were more likely than individuals with lower total readjustment scores to become ill during a subsequent observation period, and that, among those who became ill, the ones with higher total scores suffered a larger number of illnesses. In further work, Theorell and Rahe (1970) demonstrated that increases in readjustment scores were associated with episodes of coronary heart disease.

These different conceptions and the variety of measures of stressful life events derived from them pose two methodological questions: How are the various measures related to each other? How do they compare with each other in terms of their relations to expected consequences of stressful life events? The present investigation is designed to provide empirical evidence on these questions.

Procedure

Data Collection

We will draw on interviews conducted in a cross sectional survey of 124 heads of families. These respondents are a systematic subsample of a cross sectional sample of 257 that was interviewed as part of a larger methodological study (Dohrenwend et al., 1970). The 257 respondents were divided into approximately equal subsamples to whom different interview schedules were administered. One of these schedules provides the data for the present investigation.

The sample consists of both men and women, married and single, including special groups of single female household heads, sampled on a probability basis from the general population of Washington Heights, Manhattan. The aim in selecting the sample was to give equal representation to white Protestants of American ancestry, Jews, Irish, Blacks, and Puerto Ricans. Moreover, the attempt was made to draw the sample in such a way as to balance educational levels within each ethnic group, with partial success. The completed sample is short on poorly educated respondents among white Protestants and to a lesser extent, among Jews. We are also somewhat short of college graduates among Puerto Ricans and among women who head households in which no husband is present. The 257 interviews obtained in the total cross sectional sample represent a completion rate of 66 per cent of the respondents designated for interview. The distribution of respondents in the subsample of 124 according to four demographic variables to be utilized in the analysis, age, sex, ethnicity, and family income, is shown in Table 27-1.

At the end of the interview, the respondent was asked, "What was the last major event that, for better or for worse, changed or interrupted your usual activities?" This question was followed by probes concerning the date and other particulars of the event. Following these probes, all respondents were presented with a checklist of events, shown in Table 27-2, which was introduced as follows: "Some things happen to most people at one time or another; other things happen to only a few people. Which of these events have you experienced during the last 12 months?"

Life Event Measures

To build an index of the undesirability of events experienced, all events reported by the respondents were classified as culturally defined losses or gains or as ambiguous in this respect according to the following definitions.

Loss: An event or change that other people would generally think undesirable.

Table 27-1
Selected Characteristics of 124 Survey Respondents

Age	%
Less than 30	7.3
30-39	29.8
40-49	24.2
50-59	24.2
60 or more	14.5
Sex	
Male	37.9
Female	62.1
Ethnicity	
White Protestant	31.5
Jewish	18.5
Irish	14.5
Black	25.0
Puerto Rican	10.5
Family Income	
Less than $3000	13.7
$3000-$4999	22.6
$5000-$7499	20.2
$7500-$9999	17.7
$10,000 or more	25.8

Gain: An event or change that other people would generally think desirable.
Ambiguous: An event or change whose desirability is ambiguous because
people probably disagree about its desirability (or for lack of information
about the event).

The coding of events was highly reliable; two coders working independently
agreed on the classification into these three categories of 87 per cent of the
events reported.

In this classification system, as in similar systems used by other investigators
(e.g. Myers et al., 1971), the undesirability of an event is defined in public terms
rather than in terms of the respondent's assessment of his experience. Thus, for
example, although a number of respondents characterized a divorce as a change
for the better this event was classified as a loss rather than a gain. This type of
definition, by providing a uniform, objective measure of the undesirability of life

Table 27-2
Check List of Life Events Used on Survey

Started to school, training program
Graduated from school, training program
Failed school, training program
Moved to better neighborhood
Moved to worse neighborhood
Engaged
Married
Widowed
Divorced
Separated
Other broken love relationship
  Explain:
Birth of first child
Birth of child other than first
Serious physical illness to self
Serious injury to self
Serious injury to loved one
  Who?
Serious physical illness to loved one
  Who?
Death of a loved one
  Who?
Started to work on a job for the first time
Expanded business
Promoted or moved to more responsible job
Changed to more secure job
Business failed
Demoted or changed to less responsible job
Laid off
Fired
Other (Explain:)

events, avoids one possible source of confounding between the measure of stressful life events and measures of their possible effects on the individual.

In order to compute a total score to describe each individual's experience in terms of undesirability, each loss was assigned a score of plus one, each ambiguous event a score of zero, and each gain a score of minus one. The individual's score was the algebraic sum of all the events he reported.

Two measures were developed to indicate the amount of change involved in the reported life events. The first was simply the number of events reported by a respondent as occurring during the designated time period. The second was based on the "social readjustment ratings" collected by Holmes and Rahe (1967) for 43 events empirically found to be associated with illness onset. They obtained these ratings by asking judges to " . . . rate a series of life events as to their relative degrees of necessary readjustment." Further instructions were: "The mechanics of rating are these: Event 1, Marriage, has been given an arbitrary value of 500. As you complete each of the remaining events think to yourself, 'Is this event indicative of more or less readjustment than marriage?' 'Would the readjustment take longer or shorter to accomplish?' If you decide the readjustment is more intense and protracted, then choose a *proportionately larger* number . . . If you decide the event represents less and shorter readjustment than marriage then indicate how much less by placing a *proportionately smaller* number in the opposite blank" (Holmes and Rahe 1967:213). For the present analysis the scores used are geometric means of ratings obtained from a "sample of convenience" of 394 American subjects that was heterogeneous with respect to social class, sex, age, race, religion, and marital status (Masuda and Holmes, 1967). Within this sample, the ratings given by different status groups, such as male versus female and single versus married, generally yielded rank correlations above .90 (Holmes and Rahe, 1967).

To utilize these social readjustment ratings, two coders independently judged which of the events reported by our respondents corresponded to those on the rated list. They agreed for 87.8 per cent of the events reported on our survey. Most disagreements were resolved cautiously in favor of deciding on no correspondence. Among events on which it was agreed that a correspondence existed, the two independent coders agreed about the particular correspondence for 94.1 per cent of the instances.

A measure of life change was constructed from these readjustment ratings, following the procedures used by Holmes and Rahe (1967), by summing the readjustment ratings for all events a respondent had reported in the last year to which these ratings could be assigned. Although all obviously major events such as marriages, divorces, births, deaths, illness, job changes, etc., as well as common minor events such as vacations were included, this measure necessarily omitted events reported by our respondents that were not on Holmes and Rahe's list. Insofar as omitted events had an impact on the respondents who reported them, their omission would tend to attenuate relations between this life change measure and the measure of effects of events. However, insofar as this attenuation occurred it does not account for the results obtained. On the contrary, in its absence the observed differences between correlations might have been larger.

The social readjustment ratings of events were also used to construct a second undesirability measure. For this purpose, each loss was assigned the appropriate rating with a positive sign and each gain the appropriate rating with a negative sign. Thus we allowed for the possibility of major losses having a greater tendency than minor losses to increase symptoms of distress and major gains having a greater tendency than minor gains to reduce symptoms. The total score for each respondent consisted of the algebraic sum of the positive and negative readjustment ratings of events reported for the last year.

In summary, four life events measures were constructed, two to indicate the undesirability of a respondent's life events and two to indicate the amount of life change they involved. For one measure of each type each event was given a weight of one, except that ambiguous events were weighted zero in the undesirability measure. For the other measure of each type, events were weighted according to the social readjustment ratings provided by Holmes and Rahe (1967) and by Masuda and Holmes (1967). These four life event measures are described in Table 27-3.

Measures of Effect on Stressful Life Events

Two measures representing different conceptions of the psychological effect of stressful life events were constructed from Langner's (1962) 22-item symptom scale. The first is a dichotomous measure dividing respondents into those who were more likely and those who were less likely to be psychologically impaired, using the cutting point of four or more symptoms on the basis of Langner's finding that scores above this cutting point "identified only 1 per cent of the psychiatrically evaluated Wells, but ... almost three quarters of the entire Impaired group" (1962:275). This score can be used to test the hypothesis that relatively stressful life events are associated with impaired rather than healthy psychological functioning.

The second effect measure was a continuous symptom score obtained by

Table 27-3
Measures of a Respondent's Stressful Life Events

Weight Assigned to Each Event	Conception of Property That Makes Events Stressful	
	Undesirability	Amount of Change Entailed
One	# losses minus # gains	# events
Social readjustment rating*	Sum of readjustment ratings for losses minus sum of readjustment ratings for gains	Sum of readjustment ratings for all events

*From Holmes and Rahe, 1967; Masuda and Holmes, 1967.

adding all responses coded as symptomatic by Langner. This score can be used to test the hypothesis that the relation between level of stressful life events and psychological symptoms is a continuous one: The greater the life stress the greater the psychological distress.

Results

Relations Among Measures of Stressful Life Events

It is obvious that the measures for which each event was given a weight of one and the measures in which each event was weighted according to its social readjustment rating are not independent, since respondents with a greater number of events will tend to have higher scores on both measures. There is, however, no *a priori* reason to assume that undesirability measures and life change measures will be correlated. Nor does the evidence indicate that they were when each event was given a weight of one. The majority of respondents reported one loss or one gain, with the average being 1.5 losses and 1.2 gains.

In contrast, the measures of undesirability and of life change that were weighted according to social readjustment ratings of life events were not independent. Comparison of the readjustment ratings of life events classified as losses as against those classified as gains revealed that the mean rating for losses was 413 as against 225 for gains. Ambiguous events fell between with a mean of 327.

As a test of the relationship between the two measures based on social readjustment ratings, we divided the respondents into three approximately equal groups having low, medium, and high life change scores and cross classified each respondent as having only gains, mixed gains and losses, or only losses. The relationship was in the direction to be expected from the means for different categories of events; the majority of respondents with low life change scores reported only gains while the majority with high life change scores reported only losses. The overall relationship was highly significant (X^2 = 40.15 df = 4, $p < .001$).

Given this relationship between undesirability of events and amount of life change, it is not surprising that measures of undesirability and measures of life change have yielded similar results in studies of effects of stressful life events. The question is whether one shows a stronger relation to measures of expected effects when they are compared directly.

Relation of Life Event Measures to Psychological Symptom Measures

Table 27-4 gives the correlations between the four life event measures and the two psychological symptom measures. These correlations are based on measures all of which yielded skewed data. However, since this characteristic, which tends to reduce the size of product moment correlations, affected all of the correlations, their comparisons should not be influenced by it. Moreover, an analysis using contingency tables and partitioned Chi-square yielded results consistent with those reported here.

We note first that comparisons between correlations involving undesirability measures as against those involving change measures appear to yield inconsistent results. When each event was given a weight of one, the undesirability measure yielded the higher correlations; whereas when each event was weighted according to its social readjustment rating, the change measure yielded the higher correlations. This apparent inconsistency is resolved, however, when we consider these results in the light of the relationship between the undesirability of events and their social readjustment ratings.

The change measure for which each event was given a weight of one yielded the lowest correlations. This measure implies that each event should have equal impact regardless of its undesirability and regardless of the readjustment it might require. The assumption that gains and losses have opposite effects, implied by scoring the former minus one and the latter plus one, increased the correlations. This difference between the correlations suggests that undesirable life events are more likely than desirable ones to be associated with elevated psychological symptom scores. However, this interpretation is open to question because, in adding information to the life event measure about the undesirability of life events, we also added, in attenuated form, information about their social readjustment ratings. This contamination occurred because gains, with the lowest average social readjustment rating, were scored minus one, ambiguous

Table 27-4
Correlations between Measures of Stressful Life Events and Measures of Psychological Symptoms

Symptom Measure	Measure of Stressful Life Events			
	Each Event Weighted one[a]		Each Event Weighted According to Social Readjustment Rating	
	Desirability Measure	Change Measure	Desirability Measure	Change Measure
Dichotomous: 0-3 vs. 4 or more symptoms	.28[b]	.18[c]	.35[b]	.40[b]
Continuous	.29[b]	.24[b]	.29[b]	.35[b]

[a]For desirability measure ambiguous events were weighted zero.
[b]$p < .01$.
[c]$p < .05$.

events, with an intermediate average readjustment rating, were scored zero, and losses, with the highest average social readjustment rating, were scored plus one. Therefore, we cannot infer that the higher correlations for the undesirability as against the change measure in the first comparison necessarily indicate that undesirability of life events is more strongly associated with level of psychological symptom scores than amount of life change.

This dilemma is resolved by the results of the comparison of the undesirability and the change measures for which events were weighted according to their social readjustment ratings. Consider the change measure first. Because of the relation between the undesirability of events and their social readjustment ratings, respondents with low life change scores were more likely to have experienced gains than respondents with high life change scores and, conversely, those with high life change scores were more likely to have experienced losses. Thus, the relatively high correlations between this measure of life change and psychological symptom scores could be due primarily to either aspect, undesirability or life change, of respondents' life events.

To the extent that the correlations with the change measure were due to the undesirability of life events, they should be improved by assigning negative readjustment ratings to gains and positive readjustment ratings to losses, thus distinguishing a change for the better from a change for the worse. The correlations in Table 27-4 show, however, that the undesirability measure based on directed social readjustment ratings yielded lower correlations with the psychological symptom measures than the change measure in which the readjustment ratings of all events were summed without regard to the undesirability of the events. Moreover, the scatter plots for these correlations indicate that the negative life change scores obtained by assigning negative readjustment ratings to gains were unrelated to symptom levels. Thus, the evidence from the correlations in Table 27-4 is consistent with the conclusion that life change is a more useful conception than undesirability of the characteristic that makes life events stressful.

This interpretation of the correlational results rests on the assumption, however, that the relations between stressful life events and psychological symptom scores are not simply a reflection of underlying associations of each with social status variables. There is, for example, evidence of an inverse relation between social class and stressful life events (Dohrenwend, 1970) as well as evidence that both sex and social class are strongly associated, the latter inversely, with symptom scores based on Langner's inventory (Dohrenwend and Dohrenwend, 1969:65; Phillips and Segal, 1969). However, the partial correlations between the life change measure based on social readjustment ratings and psychological symptom scores, with social class, sex, age, or ethnicity controlled, are all significantly different from zero at the .01 level of probability. This finding that status variables do not explain the relationship between stressful life events and psychological symptom measures is consistent with results reported by other investigators (Myers et al., 1971; Myers et al., 1972).

In Table 27-4, we presented the correlation of each life event measure with two symptom measures based on different conceptions of the psychological effect of stressful life events. The question is whether the measures of stressful life events do better at predicting the entire range of symptom scores or at predicting the dichotomous score designed to indicate health versus impaired psychological functioning.

Only the least sensitive life events measure, the one designed to indicate change by simply counting the number of events reported, was clearly more highly correlated with the continuous than with the dichotomous system measure. In contrast, the change measure based on social readjustment ratings of events, which was the life event measure most closely associated with symptom measures, was more highly correlated with the dichotomous than with the continuous symptom measure. The scatter plot of the relation between this life change measure and continuous symptom scores indicates that there was little relationship between these two variables among respondents with symptom scores in the high range, particularly those with six or more symptoms. These results suggest that the most sensitive measure of stressful life events, life change scores based on social readjustment ratings of events, contributes little to the explanation of differences in symptom levels within the range that may indicate psychological impairment.

Discussion

In studies of effects of stressful life events the question of whether undesirability or change is the characteristic that makes events stressful has not been directly posed heretofore. The analog to this issue has been investigated, however, in recent research on physiological responses to psychosocial stressors. This work was based on the ideas of Selye, who posited a specific stress response to any environmental changes requiring adaptation and noted, for example, "Normal activities—a game of tennis or even a passionate kiss—can produce considerable stress . . . " (Selye, 1956:53).

To determine whether, as Selye suggested, pleasant and unpleasant stimuli produce similar physiological effects, Levi recorded affective and physiological responses to a series of films selected to contrast in the amount and kinds of emotions they would be expected to arouse. From this research he concluded, "Enhancement [of physiological response] occurs not only in response to stimuli which most subjects rate as predominantly 'unpleasant' but also when the self-ratings indicate predominantly 'pleasant' emotional reactions in most of the subjects, as in the case of viewing the comedy 'Charley's Aunt' " (Levi, 1972:146).

This physiological evidence strengthens the inference drawn from the present study that change rather than undesirability is the characteristic of life events that should be measured for the more accurate assessment of their stressfulness. Further research is needed, however, to determine whether this inference concerning life events holds for effects such as serious psychological and organic illnesses as well as for relatively mild psychological symptoms. The cumulative gain in knowledge from the considerable effort now going into research on varied effects of stressful life events will be accelerated by resolution of this methodological issue.

References

Antonovsky, A., and R. Kats.
  1967 "The life crisis history as a tool in epidemiological research," Journal of Health and Social Behavior 8 (March):15-21.
Brown, G.W., and J.L.T. Birley.
  1968 "Crises and life changes and the onset of schizophrenia." Journal of Health and Social Behavior 9 (June):203-214.
  1970 "Social precipitants of severe psychiatric disorders." Pp. 321-325 in E.H. Hare and J.K. Wing (eds.), Psychiatric Epidemiology: Proceedings of the International Symposium held at Aberdeen University 22-5 July 1969. New York: Oxford University Press.
Dohrenwend, B.P., E.T. Chin-Song, G. Egri, F.R. Mendelsohn and J. Stokes.
  1970 "Measures of psychiatric disorder in contrasting class and ethnic groups." Pp. 159-202 in E.H. Hare and J.K. Wing (eds.), Psychiatric Epidemiology: Proceedings of the International Symposium held at Aberdeen University 22-5 July 1969. New York: Oxford University Press.
Dohrenwend, B.P., and B.S. Dohrenwend.
  1969 Social Status and Psychological Disorder: A Causal Inquiry. New York: John Wiley.
Dohrenwend, B.S.
  1970 "Social class and stressful events." Pp. 313-319 in E.H. Hare and J.K. Wing (eds.), Psychiatric Epidemiology: Proceedings of the International Symposium held at Aberdeen University 22-5 July 1969. New York: Oxford University Press.
Dohrenwend, B.S., and B.P. Dohrenwend.
  1970 "Class and race as status related sources of stress." Pp. 111-140 in S. Levine and N.A. Scotch (eds.), Social Stress, Chicago: Aldine.
Fritz, C.E., and E.S. Marks.
  1954 "The NORC studies of human behavior in disaster." Journal of Social Issues 10(3):26-41.
Fröberg, J., C.-G. Karlsson, L. Levi and L. Lidberg.
  1971 "Physiological and biochemical stress reactions induced by psycho-social stimuli." Pp. 280-295 in L. Levi (ed.), Society, Stress and

Disease: The Psychosocial Environment and Psychosomatic Diseases. New York: Oxford University Press.

Gurin, G.J. Veroff and S. Feld
1960 Americans View Their Mental Health. New York: Basic Books.

Holmes, T.H., and R.H. Rahe.
1967 "The social readjustment rating scale." Journal of Psychosomatic Research 11 (2):213-218.

Langner, T.S.
1962 "A twenty-two item screening score of psychiatric symptoms indicating impairment." Journal of Health and Human Behavior 3 (Winter):269-276.

Levi, L.
1972 "General discussion." Pp. 143-149 in L. Levi (ed.), Stress and Distress in Response to Psychosocial Stimuli. Stockholm: Almqvist & Wiksell.

Lindemann, E.
1944 "Symptomatology and management of acute grief." American Journal of Psychiatry 101 (September):141-148.

Masuda, M., and T.H. Holmes.
1967 "The social readjustment rating scale." Journal of Psychosomatic Research 11 (2):219-225.

Murri, A.
1912 "Delle neurosi da trauma." La Riforma Medica 28 (11 May):533-540.

Myers, J.K., J.J. Lindenthal, and M.P. Pepper
1971 "Life events and psychiatric impairment." Journal of Nervous and Mental Disease 152 (March):149-157.

Myers, J.K., J.J. Lindenthal, M.P. Pepper and D.R. Ostrander.
1972 "Life events and mental status: A longitudinal study." Journal of Health and Social Behavior 13 (December):398-406.

Phillips, D.L., and B.F. Segal.
1969 "Sexual status and psychiatric symptoms." American Sociological Review 34 (February):58-72.

Rahe, R.H.
1968 "Life-change measurement as a predictor of illness." Proceedings of the Royal Society of Medicine 61 (November):44-46.

Selye, H.
1956 The Stress of Life. New York: McGraw-Hill.

Sheatsley, P.B., and J. Feldman.
1964 "The assassination of President Kennedy: public reaction." Public Opinion Quarterly 28 (Summer):189-215.

Theorell, T., and R.H. Rahe.
1970 "Life changes in relation to the onset of myocardial infarction." Pp. III-1-III-20 in Psychosocial Factors in Relation to the Onset of Myocardial Infarction and to Some Metabolic Variables—A Pilot Study by T. Theorell. Stockholm: Department of Medicine, Seraphimer Hospital, Karolinska Institutet.

X

**Toward
A Healthy
Environment**

428

Commentary. During the past decade the gross national product in the United States has nearly doubled, while the quality of life has been deteriorating. Air and water have become more polluted; the incidence of robbery and murder has increased; chances of dying from emphysema, bronchitis, asthma, cancer, and heart disease have increased; a person must travel further, on crowded highways or inadequate public transportation systems, to reach solitude. Contrary to appearances no conspiracy exists to destroy the environment; rather, efforts of groups and committees to change a course of impending disaster have been ineffectual. Individuals seem to have an even greater impact with respect to change. For example, despite the opposition of powerful economic interests Rachel Carson in 1962 warned the public in *Silent Spring* of the danger of poisoning the environment with chemicals. This resulted in legislation outlawing the use of DDT and requiring more careful study of chemicals before allowing their widespread use.

The social and physical environment of man are inextricably tied to each other. In order to maintain a healthy environment we must have some measure of the nature of this interaction. Stuart Udall, then Secretary of the Interior, suggested in 1968:

We have had no environmental index, no census statistic to measure whether the country is more or less habitable from year to year. A tranquility index or a cleanliness index might have told us something about the condition of man, but a fast-growing country preoccupied with making and acquiring material things has had no time for the amenities that are the very heart and substance of daily life.

Is there any compromise between the acquisition of material goods and maintaining a healthy environment? Lewis Mumford, in the first chapter in this section, suggests that socialization was the price of better health in the early industrialized city. A pure water supply, a collective disposal of garbage, waste, and sewage, could not be left to the profit-minded private conscience. And as Mumford points out, when socialization became more widespread toward the middle of the nineteenth century, the general death rate and the infant mortality rate declined rapidly.

In Chapter 29 René Dubos proposes that a healthy environment must be viewed in terms of adaptation. He suggests that disease is part of the environment. With each new era and civilization man will be burdened by diseases created by the unavoidable failures of adaption to the new environment. From Dubos's point of view, one of our contemporary diseases—boredom—is a disease that has replaced a disease of yesterday—fatigue. Physical exhaustion was common in the past. Today's automation and labor-saving devices may serve to complicate the future by creating mental disorders related to boredom. Dubos feels that man must deal with social, physical, and biological variables as interacting forces that are unpredictable and forever changing. Dubos suggests that health is an elusive concept that can be interpreted differently depending on the environment. For example, social aggressiveness is unacceptable and regarded as a form of disease by the Pueblo Indians, whereas in our Western culture it is viewed as a desirable attribute because it facilitates the achievement of power and the acquisition of wealth.

Dubos argues that in order to move toward a healthier environment it is necessary to create a social climate in which the study of long-range health consequences is considered an essential part of technological research.

In the closing chapter Hugh Iltis, Orie Loucks, and Peter Andrews consider the possibility that the optimum environment for man is related to his evolutionary development. The authors argue that man's response to his environment is based on years of selection and adaptation. Our houses are attempts to imitate not only the climate but our evolutionary past. For example, we keep pets, furnish with indoor plants, build greenhouses and swimming pools, and vacation in natural settings such as the mountains or the seashore. Such environmental stimuli as brick and asphalt, suggest the authors, may be inimical to our health. We may be healthier in an environment that includes diversity and natural beauty, especially the color green and the motions and sounds of other animals.

It seems ironic that during the same era that man took his first step into outer space a growing awareness has developed throughout the world of how unique and precious is the environment in which we live.

Reference

Udall, S.L. *1976: Agenda for Tomorrow.* New York: Harcourt, Brace & World, 1968.

28

The Counter-Attack

Lewis Mumford

Perhaps the greatest contribution made by the industrial town was the reaction it produced against its own greatest misdemeanors; and, to begin with, the art of sanitation or public hygiene. The original models for these evils were the pest-ridden prisons and hospitals of the eighteenth century: their improvement made them pilot plants, as it were, in the reform of the industrial town. Nineteenth-century achievements in molding large glazed drains and casting iron pipes, made possible the tapping of distant supplies of relatively pure water and the disposal, at least as far as a neighboring stream, of sewage; while the repeated outbreaks of malaria, cholera, typhoid, and distemper served as a stimulus to these innovations, since a succession of public health officers had no difficulty in establishing the relation of dirt and congestion, of befouled water and tainted food, to these conditions.

On the essential matter of urban deterioration, John Ruskin had spoken to the point. "Providing lodgements for [working people] means," he said, "a great deal of vigorous legislation and cutting down of vested interests that stand in the way; and after that, or before that, so far as we can get it, through sanitary and remedial action in the houses that we have, and then the building of more, strongly, beautifully, and in groups of limited extent, kept in proportion to their

From *The City in History*, © 1961 by Lewis Mumford. Reprinted by permission of Harcourt Brace Jovanovich, Inc.

streams, and walled round, so that there may be no festering and wretched suburb anywhere, but clean and busy streets within, and the open country without, with a belt of beautiful garden and orchard round the walls, so that from any part of the city perfectly fresh air and grass and the sight of the far horizon may be reachable in a few minutes walk." That happy vision beckoned even the manufacturers who, here and there, in Port Sunlight and Bournville, began to build industrial villages that rivalled in comeliness the best of the later suburbs.

To bring back fresh air, pure water, green open space, and sunlight to the city became the first object of sound planning: the need was so pressing that despite his passion for urban beauty, Camillo Sitte insisted upon the *hygienic* function of the urban park, as a *sanitary green*, to use his own expression: the 'lungs' of the city, whose function became newly appreciated through their absence.

The cult of cleanliness had its origins before the paleotechnic era: it owes much to the Dutch cities of the seventeenth century, with their plentiful water supplies, their large house windows showing up every particle of dust inside, their tiled floors; so that the scrubbing and scouring of the Dutch housewife became proverbial. Cleanliness got new scientific reinforcements after 1870. As long as the body was dualistically separated from the mind, its systematic care might be slighted, as almost an indication of more spiritual preoccupations. But the new conception of the organism that grew up in the nineteenth century, with Johannes Müller and Claude Bernard, reunited the physiological and the psychological processes: thus the care of the body became once more a moral and esthetic discipline. By his researches in bacteriology Pasteur altered the conception of both the external and the internal environment of organisms: virulent microscopic organisms flourished in dirt and ordure, and largely disappeared before soap-and-water and sunlight. As a result, the farmer milking a cow today takes sanitary precautions that a mid-Victorian London surgeon did not trouble to take before performing a major operation, till Lister taught him better. The new standards for light, air, and cleanliness which Florence Nightingale established for hospitals, she even carried into the white-walled living room of her own home—a true prelude to Le Corbusier's admirably hygienic 'Esprit Nouveau' in modern architecture.

At last, the industrial town's indifference to darkness and dirt was exposed for what it was, a monstrous barbarism. Further advances in the biological sciences threw into relief the misdemeanors of the new environment with its smoke and fog and fumes. As our experimental knowledge of medicine increases, this list of evils lengthens: it now includes the two hundred-odd cancer-producing substances still usually found in the air of most industrial cities, to say nothing of the metallic and stone dusts and poisonous gases that raise the incidence and increase the fatality of diseases of the respiratory tract.

Though the pressure of scientific knowledge worked slowly to improve conditions in the city as a whole, it had a quicker effect on the educated and comfortable classes: they soon took the hint and fled from the city to an environment that was not so inimical to health. One of the reasons for this tardy application of modern hygiene to city design was the fact that individual improvements in the hygienic equipment of dwellings made a radical alteration in costs; and these costs were reflected in heavier municipal investments in collective utilities, and in heavier municipal taxes to keep them up.

Just as early industrialism had squeezed its profits not merely out of the economies of the machine, but out of the pauperism of the workers, so the crude factory town had maintained its low wages and taxes by depleting and pauperizing the environment. Hygiene demanded space and municipal equipment and natural resources that had hitherto been lacking. In time, this demand enforced municipal socialization, as a normal accompaniment to improved service. Neither a pure water supply, nor the collective disposal of garbage, waste, and sewage, could be left to the private conscience or attended to only if they could be provided for at a profit.

In smaller centers, private companies might be left with the privilege of maintaining one or more of these services, until some notorious outbreak of disease dictated public control; but in the bigger cities socialization was the price of safety; and so, despite the theoretic claims of laissez faire, the nineteenth century became, as Beatrice and Sidney Webb correctly pointed out, the century of municipal socialism. Each individual improvement within the building demanded its collectively owned and operated utility: watermains, water reservoirs, and aqueducts, pumping stations: sewage mains, sewage reduction plants, sewage farms. Only the public ownership of land for town extension, town protection, or town colonization was lacking. That step forward was one of the significant contributions of Ebenezer Howard's garden city.

Through this effective and widespread socialization, the general death rate and the infant mortality rate tended to fall after the eighteen-seventies; and so manifest were these improvements that the social investment of municipal capital in these utilities rose. But the main emphasis remained a negative one: the new quarters of the city did not express, in any positive way, the understanding of the interplay between the organism as a whole and the environment that the biological sciences brought in. Even today one would hardly gather from the fashionable pseudo-modern use of large sealed glass windows, that Downes and Blunt had established as early as 1877 the bactericidal properties of direct sunlight. That irrationality betrays how superficial the respect for science still is in many presumably educated people, even technicians.

For the first time, the sanitary improvements made originally in the Sumerian and Cretan palaces, and extended to the patrician families of Rome at a later date, were now made available to the entire population of the city. This was a triumph of democratic principles that even dictatorial regimes could not inhibit: indeed, one of the greatest public benefits conferred by the overthrower of the

Second French Republic, was in the redoubtable cleaning up of Paris under Baron Haussmann, a service far more essential, indeed far more original, than any of his more famous acts of town planning proper.

New York was the first big city to achieve an ample supply of pure water, through the building of the Croton system of reservoirs and aqueducts, opened in 1842; but in time every big city was forced to follow this example. Sewage disposal remained a difficult matter, and except in cities small enough to have sewage farms capable of transforming all such waste, the problem has not yet been adequately solved. Nevertheless, the standard of one private, sanitary toilet per family—a water closet connected to public mains in closely built communities—was established by the end of the nineteenth century. As for garbage, the usual dumping or burning of this valuable agricultural compost remains one of the persistent sins of unscientific municipal housekeeping.

The cleaning of streets remained a more difficult problem, until Belgian blocks and asphalt became universal, the horse was eliminated, and the public water supply became plentiful; yet in the end it proved easier to handle than the cleansing of the air. Even today, the screening out of the ultraviolet rays, through excess of dust and smoke, remains one of the vitality-lowering attributes of the more congested urban centers, which the showy but technically antiquated motor car has increased rather than lessened, even adding the invisible poison of carbon monoxide. As a partial offset, the introduction of running water and baths into the dwelling house—and the intermediate stage of re-establishing public baths, abandoned after the Middle Ages—must have helped in reducing both disease generally and infant mortality in particular.

All in all, the work of the sanitary reformers and hygienists, a Chadwick, a Florence Nightingale, a Louis Pasteur, a Baron Haussmann, robbed urban life at its lower levels of some of its worst terrors and physical debasements. If the creative aspects of city life were diminished by industrialism, the evil effects of its waste-products and excrement were also in time reduced. Even the bodies of the dead contributed to the improvement: they formed a green ring of mortuary suburbs and parks around the growing city; and here, again, Haussmann's bold and masterly treatment of this problem must earn a respectful salute.

The new industrial environment was so glaringly lacking in the attributes of health, that it is hardly any wonder that the counter-movement of hygiene provided the most positive contributions to town planning during the nineteenth century. The new ideals were provisionally embodied in a Utopia, called 'Hygeia, or the City of Health,' brought forth by Dr. Benjamin Ward Richardson in 1875. Here one discovers unconscious holdovers that reject the accepted degree of overcrowding; for whereas, less than a generation later, Ebenezer Howard provided 6,000 acres to hold and encircle 32,000 people, Richardson proposed to put 100,000 people on 4,000 acres. In the new city, the railroads were to be underground, despite the coal-burning locomotives then current; but no cellars of any kind were to be permitted in houses, a prohibition that was given statutory backing in England. But the construction was to be of brick, inside and outside, capable of being hosed down—a recurrent masculine dream—and the chimneys were to be connected to central shafts, to convey the unburned carbon to a gas furnace where it would be consumed.

Archaic as some of these proposals now are, in many ways, Dr. Richardson was not merely ahead of his own times: he was equally ahead of our own day. He proposed to abandon "the old idea of warehousing diseases on the largest possible scale," and advocated a small hospital for every 5,000 people. By the same token, the helpless, the aged, and the mentally infirm were to be housed in modest-sized buildings. Richardson's physical conceptions of the city are now dated: but his contributions to collective medical care are still, I submit, worth pondering. With ample rational justification he proposed to go back to the high medical and human standards of the medieval town.

The Underground City

Mainly, it was by the reactions that it produced, by the exodus that it prompted, that the paleotechnic regime had an effect upon future urban forms. These counter-attacks were abetted, from the eighteen-eighties on, by a transformation with industry itself, furthered by the applications of science directly to invention; for the new regime was based on electric energy and the lighter metals, like aluminum, magnesium, and copper, and on new synthetic materials, like rubber, bakelite, and the plastics. The inner improvement of the industrial town proceeded partly from these innovations, which we associate with the spread of the private bathroom, the telephone, the motor car, and radio communication; but the even deeper reaction to the classic pattern of Coketown was that embodied in the emerging concept of the Welfare State. There is no better witness to the impoverished or positively evil conditions brought in by the industrial town than the mass of legislation that has accumulated, in the last century, aimed at their correction: sanitary regulations, health services, free public schools, job security, minimum wage provisions, workers' housing, slum clearance, along with public parks and playgrounds, public libraries and museums. These improvements have yet to find their full expression in a new form of the city.

But the archetypal industrial town nevertheless left deep wounds in the environment; and some of its worst features have remained in existence, only superficially improved by neotechnic means. Thus the automobile has been polluting the air for more than half a century without its engineers making any serious effort to remove the highly toxic carbon monoxide gas from its exhaust, though a few breaths of it in pure form are fatal; nor have they eliminated the unburned hydrocarbons which help produce the smog and blankets such a motor-ridden conurbation as Los Angeles. So, too, the transportation and highway engineers who have recklessly driven their multiple-laned expressways into the heart of the city and have provided for mass parking lots and garages to store cars, have masterfully repeated and enlarged the worst errors of the railroad engineers. Indeed, at the very moment the elevated railroad for public transportation was being eliminated as a grave nuisance, these forgetful engineers re-installed the same kind of obsolete structure for the convenience of the private motor car. Thus much of what appears brightly contemporary merely restores the archetypal form of Coketown under a chrome plating.

But there is one aspect of the modern city where the hold of Coketown grips even tighter, and the final effects are even more inimical to life. This is in the knitting together of necessary underground utilities to produce a wholly gratuitous result: the underground city, conceived as an ideal. As one should expect of a regime whose key inventions came out of the mine, the tunnel and the subway were its unique contributions to urban form; and not uncharacteristically, both these utilities were direct derivatives of war, first in the ancient city, and later in the elaborate sapping and mining necessary to reduce the baroque fortification. Though the surface forms of Coketown's transportation and shelter have been widely replaced, its underground network has prospered and proliferated. The water main and the sewer, the gas main and the electric main, were all valuable contributions to the upper level city; and under certain limited conditions, the underground railroad, the motor car tunnel, and the underground lavatory could be justified. But these utilities have now been augmented by underground shops and stores, finally by the underground air raid shelter, as if the kind of environment that served the physical mechanisms and utilities of the city brought any real advantages to its inhabitants. Unfortunately, the underground city demands the constant attendance of living men, also kept underground; and that imposition is hardly less than a premature burial, or at least preparation for the encapsulated existence that alone will remain open to those who accept mechanical improvement as the chief justification of the human adventure.

The underground city is a new kind of environment: an extension and normalization of that forced upon the miner—severed from natural conditions, under mechanical control at every point, made possible by artificial light, artifical ventilation, and the artificial limitations of human responses to those that its organizers deem profitable or serviceable. This new environment coalesced gradually out of a series of empirical inventions: hence even in the most ambitious metropolises, only rarely have the streets or the underground utilities (like the great sewers of Paris) been designed with a view to their economic repair and connection with neighboring buildings, though it is plain that in the more crowded quarters of a city, a single tunnel, accessible at intervals, should serve as a collective artery, and would in the long run effect great economies.

In analyzing the costs of housing a generation ago, Henry Wright discovered that the cost of a whole room was buried in the street, in the various mechanical utilities necessary for the house's functioning. Since then, the relative cost of these underground pipes and wires and conduits has increased; while with every extension of the city, as with every increase of internal congestion, the cost of the whole system disproportionately increases, too.

Given the pressure to sink capital more extensively into the underground city, less money becomes available for space and architectural beauty above ground: indeed, the next step in the city's development, already taken in many American cities, is to extend the principle of the underground city even to the design of buildings that are visibly above ground, and so defeat art at every point. With air conditioning and all-day fluorescent lighting, the internal spaces in the new American skyscraper are little different from what they would be a hundred feet below the surface. No extravagance in mechanical equipment is too great to produce this uniform internal environment: though the technical ingenuity spent on fabricating sealed-in buildings cannot create the equivalent of an organic background for human functions and activities.

All this is merely by way of preparation. For the successor of the paleotechnic town has created instruments and conditions potentially far more lethal than those which wiped out so many lives in the town of Donora, Pennsylvania, through a concentration of toxic gases, or that which in December 1952 killed in one week an estimated five thousand extra of London's inhabitants. The exploitation of uranium to produce fissionable materials threatens, if continued, to poison the lithosphere, the atmosphere, the biosphere—to say nothing of the drinking water—in a fashion that will outdo the worst offenses of the early industrial town; for the pre-nuclear industrial processes could be halted, and the waste products be absorbed or covered over, without permanent light.

Once fission takes place, however, the radioactivity released will remain throughout the life of the products, sometimes a life measured in many centuries or even millennia: it cannot be altered or disposed of without contaminating, ultimately, the area where it is dumped, be it the stratosphere or the bottom of the ocean. Meanwhile, the manufacture of these lethal materials goes on, without abatement, in preparation for collective military assaults aimed at exterminating whole populations. To make such criminally insane preparations tolerable, public authorities have sedulously conditioned their citizens to march meekly into cellars and subways for 'protection.' Only the staggering cost of creating a whole network of underground cities sufficient to house the entire population as yet prevents this perverse misuse of human energy.

The Victorian industrialist, exposing his fellow citizens to soot and smog, to vile sanitation and environmentally promoted disease, still nourished the belief that his work was contributing, ultimately, to 'peace and plenty.' But his heirs in the underground city have no such illusions—they are the prey of compulsive fears and corrupt fantasies whose ultimate outcome may be universal annihilation and extermination; and the more they devote themselves to adapting their urban environment to this possibility, the more surely they will bring on the unrestricted collective genocide many of them have justified in their minds as the necessary price of preserving 'freedom' and 'civilization.' The masters of the underground citadel are committed to a 'war' they cannot bring to an end, with weapons whose ultimate effects they cannot control, for purposes that they cannot accomplish. The underground city threatens in consequence to become the ultimate burial crypt of our incinerated civilization. Modern man's only alternative is to emerge once more into the light and have the courage, not to escape to the moon, but to return to his own human center—and to master the bellicose compulsions and irrationalities he shares with his rulers and mentors. He must not only unlearn the art of war, but acquire and master, as never before, the arts of life.

29

The Mirage of Health

René Dubos
Rockefeller University

The concept of perfect and positive health is a utopian creation of the human mind. It cannot become reality because man will never be so perfectly adapted to his environment that his life will not involve struggles, failures, and sufferings. Nevertheless, the utopia of positive health constitutes a creative force because, like other ideals, it sets goals and helps medical science to chart its course toward them. The hope that disease can be completely eradicated becomes a dangerous image only when its unattainable character is forgotten. It can then be compared to a will-o'-the-wisp luring its followers into the swamps of unreality. In particular, it encourages the illusion that man can control his responses to stimuli and can make adjustments to new ways of life without having to pay for these adaptive changes. The less pleasant reality is that in an ever-changing world each period and each type of civilization will continue to have its burden of diseases created by the unavoidable failures of adaptation to the new environment.

Nothing illustrates better the collective loss of objectivity created by the mirage of health than the constant reiteration that recent advances have brought about a spectacular increase in the expectancy of life. It is true, of course, that the expectancy of life *at birth* has been increasing steadily during the past few

From *Man Adapting* (New Haven, Conn.: Yale University Press, 1965), pp. 346-361. Copyright ©1965 by Yale University.

decades, this increase is due almost exclusively to the virtual elimination of deaths during infancy, childhood, and early adulthood. In contrast, the life expectancy of adults is not very different now from what it was a few generations ago, nor is it greater in areas where medical services are highly developed than in less prosperous countries. True longevity has increased very little, if at all.

The present clamor for better medical care and more hospital facilities makes it clear that today as in the past we live in a disease-ridden society. Needless to say, the increase in medical needs does not necessarily imply a parallel increase in the prevalence of disease. To a certain extent, it comes from the fact that we are more exacting than our ancestors in matters of health, and especially are we less willing to accept the infirmities, pains, and blemishes, the catarrhs, coughs, and nauseas that used to be regarded as inevitable accompaniments of life. But granted that health criteria are constantly rising and that we are less and less willing to accept passively physical and physiological imperfections, it is also true that the modern ways of life are creating problems of disease that either did not exist a few decades ago or are now more common than in the past.

A few examples contrasting the medical problems of recent history with those characteristic of the present times will suffice to show how the pattern of diseases rapidly changes with the conditions of life.

Whereas microbiological pollution of water used to be responsible for much disease among our ancestors, chemical air pollution is now taking the limelight. Chemical fumes from factories and exhausts from motor cars are causing a variety of pathological disorders that bid fair to continue increasing in frequency and gravity and may become serious health handicaps in the near future. There is reason to fear also that various types of radiation will soon add their long-range and unpredictable effects to this pathology of the future.

During recent decades, we have gone far toward controlling microbial spoilage of food, but some of the new synthetic products that have become part and parcel of modern life are responsible for an endless variety of allergic and other toxic effects.

Nutritional deficiencies have now become rare in wealthy countries; but a new kind of malnutrition is arising from the fact that the nutritional regimens formulated for physically active human beings are no longer suited to automobile-borne and air-conditioned life in the twentieth century.

In the past many human beings suffered from physical exhaustion; now labor-saving devices and especially automated operations threaten to generate a type of psychiatric disturbances that will greatly complicate the medicine of tomorrow; boredom is replacing fatigue.

Who could have dreamed a generation ago that hypervitaminoses would become a common form of nutritional disease in the Western world; that the cigarette industry, air pollutants, and ionizing radiations would be held responsible for the increase in certain types of cancer; that the introduction of detergents and various synthetics would increase the incidence of allergies; that advances in chemotherapy and other therapeutic procedures would create a new staphylococcus pathology; that patients with various forms of iatrogenic disease would occupy such a large number of beds in the modern hospital; that some maladies of our times could be referred to by an eminent British epidemiologist as "pathology of inactivity" and "occupational hazards of sedentary and light work"?

There is reason to believe that the changes in ways of life and in technology are responsible in part for the degenerative diseases characteristic of our civilization. But while this state of affairs demands serious attention, it need not create panic. The increased prevalence of certain diseases is not a new phenomenon. Disease presents itself in different forms today simply because the world is changing and demands new adaptive responses from human beings.

Health as Ability to Function

The complex nature of man's response to his environment accounts for many of the difficulties experienced in developing methods for the prevention of disease. It is also responsible for the fact that the precise meanings of the words health and disease differ from one social group to another or even from person to person. Furthermore, the meanings change with time as well as with the environment and ways of life.

The definitions of health and disease that are commonly given by encyclopedias and academies remind one of Diafoirus' statement in Molière's play *Le Médecin malgré lui* that "opium induces sleep by virtue of the fact that it possesses a sleep producing property." In words that bring to mind this empty definition by which Molière poured ridicule on the ignorant and pretentious physicians of his time, modern dictionaries define disease as any departure from the state of health and health as a state of normalcy free from disease or pain. In 1946 the medical experts of the World Health Organization tried to sharpen and to enlarge the meaning of the word health by affirming that it implies not merely the absence of disease but rather a *positive* attribute, like a kind of primeval euphoria that would enable men to take advantage of all their potentialities for vigor and happiness. The introductory paragraph of the Constitution of the World Health Organization states: "Health is a state of complete physical, mental, and social well-being and is not merely the absence of disease or infirmity."

Health will be considered in the following pages from a more prosaic point of view. Instead of assuming that an ideal state of positive health can be achieved by eradicating all diseases from a utopian world, I shall take the view that the man of flesh, bone, and illusions will always experience unexpected difficulties as he tries to adapt to the real world, which is often hostile to him. In this light, positive health is not even a concept of the ideal to be striven for hopefully. Rather it is only a mirage, because man in the real world must face the physical, biological, and social forces of his environment, which are forever changing, usually in an unpredictable manner, and frequently with dangerous consequences for him as a person and for the human species in general. In the picturesque words of an English public health officer, "Man and his species are in perpetual struggle—with microbes, with incompatible mothers-in-law, with drunken car-drivers, and with cosmic rays from Outer Space. . . . The 'positiveness' of health does not lie in the state, but in the struggle—the effort to reach a goal which in its perfection is unattainable" (Gordon, 1958).

The evaluation of health and disease varies from person to person because it is conditioned by highly individual requirements and subjective reactions. In consequence, the words health and disease cannot be defined universally or statically. A Wall Street executive, a lumberjack in the Canadian Rockies, a newspaper boy at a crowded street corner, a steeple chase jockey, a cloistered monk rising during the night to pray and chant, and the pilot of a supersonic combat plane have very different physical and mental needs. The various imperfections and limitations of the flesh and the mind do not have equal importance for them. As pointed out by Ruth Benedict in *Patterns of Culture*, social aggressiveness is socially unacceptable and regarded as a form of disease by the Pueblo Indians, whereas this attribute is desirable in the countries of Western civilization because it facilitates the achievement of power and the acquisition of wealth.

Health is an even more elusive concept in the case of women. A farmer's wife with several children and a New York fashion model of the same age have very different physical requirements and therefore have different concepts of health. Furthermore, it is apparent from the history of fashions and from contemporary tastes that ideals of the feminine figure and complexion have undergone a wide gamut of changes in the course of time, and still differ at present from one country to the other. The fleshiness of the Paleolithic Venuses or of Reuben's goddesses reflects an attitude toward womanhood oddly different from the tastes that generated the slenderness of the English pre-Raphaelite models or of the American flapper in the 1920s. Entertainingly enough, sexual selection of hyperthyroidism occurred in much of Southern Europe during the sixteenth and seventeenth centuries, because this disease was then considered to enhance the attractiveness of young women. Lest this should appear nonsensical to us, we should remember that the dictates of publicity certainly affect our own concepts of health and physical attractiveness.

It must be acknowledged that history records many situations in which human beings seem to have achieved a state of physical development that can be regarded as healthy according to any criterion. In the account of his travels, for example, Christopher Columbus expressed admiration for the beautiful physical state of the natives he had found in the West Indies. Captain Cook, Bougainville, and the other navigators who discovered the Pacific islands also marvelled at the vigor of the Polynesians at that time; and similar reports came from the European explorers who first saw the American Indians in the Great Plains and in the Rio Grande valley. Even in modern times, people like the Xavantes Indians or the Mebans of East Africa generally remain vigorous as long as they live in isolated communities and retain their ancestral ways of life.

In practically all cases, however, primitive people have undergone physical decadence within one generation after having had extensive contacts with the white man. It would seem therefore that the health of primitive people, like that of animals in the wild state, depends upon their ability to reach and maintain some sort of equilibrium with their environment. In contrast, all of them are likely to fall prey to disease when their ancestral conditions of existence suddenly break down. For them, and certainly for us also, health can be regarded as an expression of fitness to the environment, as a state of adaptedness.

The societies of Polynesians, American Indians, Eskimos and other people who appeared so vigorous when first seen by European explorers provide examples of what Arnold Toynbee has called "arrested civilizations." They represent societies that lived for long periods of time under fairly stable physical and social conditions and had little if any contact with the outside world. New diseases appeared among them as soon as their *status quo* was disturbed, because changed conditions made new adaptive demands for which they were not prepared.

The examples mentioned above, among countless others which could have been selected, illustrate that it is not possible to define health in the abstract. Its criteria differ with the environmental conditions and with the norms and history of the social group. The criteria of health are conditioned even more by the aspirations and the values that govern individual lives. For this reason, the words health and disease are meaningful only when defined in terms of a given person functioning in a given physical and social environment. The nearest approach to health is a physical and mental state fairly free of discomfort and pain, which permits the person concerned to function as effectively and as long as possible in the environment where chance or choice has placed him. "Work is more important than life," Katherine Mansfield confided to the last pages of her journal. Searching for a definition of health as she was dying of tuberculosis, she could only conclude: "By health I mean the power to live a full, adult, living, breathing life in close contact with what I love—the earth and the wonders thereof. . . . I want to be all that I am capable of becoming."

Hygeia: A City of Health

During the late eighteenth and early nineteenth centuries, there was a strong revival of the Hippocratic doctrine which taught that man had a good chance of escaping disease if he lived reasonably. This doctrine encouraged for a while the illusion that civilized man could recapture physical well-being and primeval vigor simply by returning to the ways of nature. Despite its romantic appeal, however, the literature based on the naive belief in the virtues and perfect health of the noble savage had little influence in modifying behavior. It did not transform civilized Europeans into children of nature. But the new attitude was important nevertheless, because it created an intellectual climate favorable for the Sanitary Revolution. In this atmosphere, the philosophers of the Enlightenment and the practical sanitarians who followed them found it possible to raise the environmental concept of health from the individual to the social level. The social reforms that provided a partial solution to the health problems created by the Industrial Revolution emerged from this new medical philosophy.

Around the middle of the nineteenth century, laymen as well as physicians became increasingly concerned with the fact that disease and physical frailty were most common among the poor classes. In *Conditions of the Working Man in England* Engels wrote of the "pale, lank, narrow chested, hollow-eyed ghosts," riddled with scrofula and rickets, who haunted the streets of Manchester and other manufacturing towns. If ever men lived under conditions completely removed from the state of nature dreamed of by Rousseau and his followers, it was the English proletariat of the 1830s. Public-minded citizens came to believe that, since disease always accompanied want, dirt, and pollution, health could be restored only by bringing back to the multitudes pure air, pure water, pure food, and pleasant surroundings.

The sanitary ideal developed at first without any support from laboratory science. As mentioned earlier, it emerged from the conviction that the high rates of disease and death were largely preventable because they were due to filth, dirt, crowding, and other social factors that could be corrected. Simple as this concept was, however, it would not have become a creative force in medicine and public health if it had not been publicized and instrumented by intensely dedicated social reformers.

In Germany the most picturesque and influential of the pioneers in sanitation was the chemist Max von Pettenkofer, who regarded hygiene more as an all-embracing philosophy of life than as a laboratory science. In Munich he persuaded the city fathers to bring clear water in abundance from the mountains, to clean streets and houses, to cart away refuse and garbage, to dilute the sewage downstream in the Isar, and even to plant trees and flowers, which he regarded as essential to the mental well-being of the population because they satisfy esthetic longings. Following these measures, the typhoid mortality in Munich fell from 72 per million in 1880 to 14 in 1898. The city soon became one of the healthiest in Europe, thanks to the efforts of this imaginative and enterprising hygienist who was not a physician and did not believe in the germ theory of disease. Max von Pettenkofer's lectures *The Health of a City* conveyed to the general public the view that collective cleanliness was the surest approach to health.

In England the frontal assault on filth with the goal to create a healthier world became a national commitment involving all social groups. The campaign was carried out by members of the aristocracy like Lord Ashley, statisticians like William Farr, clergymen like Charles Kingsley and Frederick D. Maurice, physicians like Southwood Smith and John Simon, bureaucrats like Edwin Chadwick, and by thousands of anonymous zealots who belonged to the Health and Towns Association, a movement that constitutes the prototype of the present-day voluntary health associations throughout the world.

The aim of the Health and Town Association was to

substitute health for disease, cleanliness for filth, order for disorder . . . prevention for palliation . . . enlightened self-interest for ignorant selfishness and bring home to the poorest . . . in purity and abundance, the simple blessings which ignorance and negligence have long combined to limit or to spoil: *Air, Water, Light.*

The association undertook a program of education in all phases of welfare and recommended steps for improving the attractiveness of habitations and surrounding areas. It even encouraged the development of gardens and the maintenance of lanes about large cities for the enjoyment of the public. Faith in the healing power of pure air, with much contempt for the germ theory of disease, was also the basis of Florence Nightingale's reforms of hospital sanitation during the Crimean War. "There are no specific diseases," she wrote. "There are specific disease conditions." According to her beliefs, these conditions could be removed by improving the environment. John Simon was the standard-bearer of this philosophy of public health in the field of governmental administration. The official outcome of the Sanitary Movement in England was the Public Health Act of 1875.

In the fall of the same year, the physician and sanitarian Benjamin Ward Richardson outlined before the Health Section of the Social Science Association a utopian picture of *Hygeia: A City of Health.* His purpose was "to show a working community in which death . . . is kept as nearly as possible in its proper or natural place in the scheme of life." Richardson's Hygeia is noteworthy among the long list of utopias for being devoted almost exclusively to health problems and for stressing that preventive measures are of greater social importance than curative treatments. His emphasis on the need for social control of the environment was the more remarkable because it was in such obvious conflict with the political philosophy of extreme individualism advocated by Herbert Spencer and so widely accepted during the Victorian era.

Richardson's description of Hygeia was received with much enthusiasm and reported at length in British, American, and Continental newspapers. Hygeian city planning, Hygeian residences, and Hygeian household products achieved wide popularity on both sides of the Atlantic Ocean and became the symbols of a new kind of social idealism. The following quotation from a recent analysis of

Richardson's original text gives some idea of the scope of his vision and the extent to which it has influenced modern life and is still influencing social planning.

Richardson limited his city to 100,000 persons. He provided, moreover, a limit of 25 persons per acre and houses which should not exceed four stories in height. For maximum ventilation and sunlight, every house had its own ample garden in back. Even public buildings were invariably surrounded by lawn and garden space.

The paved streets, of course, were spaciously wide and were kept spotlessly clean. They were washed daily, and debris was carried away beneath the surface. To eliminate noise and accidents, surface streetcars were eliminated in favor of an underground railway system.

Individual houses in Hygeia were built uniformly on brick arches in order to ensure good drainage and ventilation. For the same reason, wall bricks were perforated in order to allow constant circulation of air at all times and in winter to help in heating. Interior wall bricks, which came in various colors, were glazed for ease of washing and so that unsanitary wall papers with their poisonous pastes could be avoided.

There were no dank cellars or evil basement habitations about which the Dickens of the City of Health could moralize. All rooms were above ground. Reversing normal practice, Richardson placed the kitchens on the upper floors. There they were lighter and cleaner, and odors disappeared more quickly than when they were on the bottom floor. Bedrooms were large, airy, well lighted, and kept free of all unnecessary furniture. Similarly, unsanitary, dirt-catching carpets were never laid on living room floors. Bedrooms as well as bathrooms were provided with hot and cold water taps, while a continuous water supply and carefully designed plumbing eliminated the danger from the sewer gases which Victorians feared so much. It went almost without mention in 1875 that all houses were serviced by underground water, gas, and sewerage pipes.

The means of ensuring clean soil, clean water, and clean air for the citizens of Hygeia were far in advance of Victorian realities. The filtered water supply of the city was tested twice every day, while a large generator passed ozone into the drinking water whenever an excess of organic impurities existed. Scavengers came around every day to remove garbage and refuse in closed vans. Sewage was disposed of on sewage farms far out of town. Similarly, noisy factories, laundries, slaughter houses, and other offensive trades had to be located outside of the city. The conduct of such establishments, of course, as well as the raising of animals for meat, was carefully supervised.

In various respects Hygeia would have been a Methodist's delight. By ways which Richardson left unexplained, the use of tobacco had totally disappeared. Similarly, the citizens miraculously seemed to have lost their thirst for alcoholic beverages. This presumably had eliminated alcoholism, while it had also caused a great decline in the number of the insane.

If Richardson accomplished these results in Hygeia largely by wishful thinking or by unspecified administrative fiat, he was much less vague about the actual presence of sickness and how to prevent or deal with it. Drawing from the experience of the sanitary revolution, he could picture the "principal sanitary officer" of Hygeia at the head of an entire hierarchy of medical officers, registrars, sanitary inspectors, chemists, and scavenging personnel. This body of men enforced all of the meticulous sanitary rules of the city, which began with providing for the basic cleansing needs and went on to cover such things as the use of public buildings, the conduct of funerals and burials, and working conditions in various trades. Textile workers, for one example, were not allowed to take any of their work to their homes, so that diseases in their families would not spread to the purchasers.

To inhibit the high infant mortality which was the plague of the nineteenth century, Richardson suggested a large number of public homes where trained nurses would care for infants and small children. For the rest of the populace of Hygeia there was a system of model hospitals, unique in some respects, but reminiscent of the plans of More, Mercier, and Cabet [Cassedy, 1962].

Von Pettenkofer's *The Health of a City* and Richardson's *Hygeia: A City of Health* are predicated on the nineteenth-century creed that "Pure Air, Pure Water, and Pure Food" constitute the necessary ingredients of a healthy life. On the other hand, these two books also mark the end of the first phase of the sanitary era because, as they are being published, laboratory science had begun to take the limelight on the health scene. The new laboratory knowledge was rapidly rendering obsolete the Victorian philosophy of health and was taking its place in medical schools and departments of sanitation. The general cleansing of the environment was almost forgotten as disinfection, vaccination, vitamins, drugs, and diagnostic laboratories became the new themes of the health slogans. Charles V. Chapin, the dynamic Health Commissioner of Providence, Rhode Island, went as far as to state that it mattered little hygienically whether the city's streets were cleaned or not, provided microbes were kept under control and people were protected against infection by the proper vaccines.

Environmental Health

Experience has now proved that it is not sufficient to clean up the environment, control pathogens, and provide abundant nutrition to bring the City of Health into being. Everywhere in the countries of Western civilization, the chronic diseases of degenerative, metabolic, or neoplastic nature have come to take the place of infectious and nutritional diseases. There is as yet no solution in sight for these new plagues of civilized life, and the disturbing fact is that the climate of opinion in the lay and scientific public discourages any vigorous social effort to develop preventive measures against them.

Under the alluring title "Progress in Cures," a popular magazine quoted an "American scientist" in 1962 as stating: "The five most-wanted cures are . . . a drug to cure cancer; a drug to maintain emotional equilibrium; a penny-a-day birth-control pill; a 'virus killer' to kill viruses as antibiotics kill bacteria; a 'youth pill' to delay man's aging process and prevent such degenerative diseases as arthritis" (*Ladies Home Journal*, October 1962). This statement might be dismissed as merely a trivial example of shallow and irresponsible journalism, but in fact it symbolizes an attitude that is unfortunately very common not only among laymen but also among scientists, and dangerous for the future.

As we have seen, the disease problems created by the Industrial Revolution stimulated in the Western world a crusading spirit that engendered great social reforms and a healthier environment. In contrast, as the magazine article mentioned above illustrates, the solution to the medical problems of our times is sought not in environmental or social reforms, but in pills. A few weeks after publication of the Surgeon General's Report on cigarette smoking, a survey among high school students in Westchester County, New York, revealed that awareness of the danger had not affected their cigarette consumption. The reason was plain from the answer made by a White Plains high school senior who was a heavy smoker: "When I reach the age to develop lung cancer, *they* will have discovered a drug to cure it" (italics mine).

This answer is significant on two accounts. First, it expresses an attitude that tends to substitute for personal responsibility a hope that somebody else—symbolized by the anonymous *they*—will find a painless and effortless solution for all problems. Secondly, it illustrates how the approach to health through reform of the ways of life has been replaced by a formula that requires no greater effort than a telephone call to the drug store. Yet it is certain that now as in the past the only real solution to any disease problem is prevention rather than cure, and that prevention demands both concerted social effort and personal discipline.

Like the lay public, the scientific community has paid little heed to the fact that the diseases characteristic of our times are to a large extent the consequence of changes in the ways of life and in the environment. The search for the environmental determinants of disease is not a fashionable topic and carries little scientific prestige. As a result, so little effort has been devoted to the subject that the relevant information available is at best only suggestive and usually not sufficient to provide a basis for social action. The lack of interest in the role of the environment in the causation of disease came to light, for example, at the hearings held before the Subcommittee of the Committee on Appropriations, House of Representatives, Eighty-Sixth Congress, Second Session on "Environmental Health Problems." In answer to a plea for enlarged Federal support to the program, Congressman John E. Fogarty, chairman of the Subcommittee, pointed out to Surgeon General Leroy Burney that "environmental health doesn't seem to ring a bell with people.... To the average person, if you start talking environmental health, they are just not interested."

It is of course extremely difficult to determine the precise origin of any environmental insult and to attribute the guilt to any particular person or groups of persons. For example, every member of the community has a share of guilt in air and water pollution. Collectively we discharge into the environment the immense amount of chemical and organic refuse of our industrial and urban society, as if we hoped that somehow or other the collective garbage would get lost and disappear without trace. But in fact it lingers with us, polluting the air we breathe, the water we drink, and the food we eat. A few decades ago, pollution meant a dead animal, putrefying garbage, or ill-smelling water, which could readily be detected and therefore stimulated public protest. In contrast, we cannot smell the ionizing radiations, the nitrogen oxides in the air, the chemicals in the water, or the penicillin in the milk. Yet none of us can escape exposure to the pollutants that are the products of our collective life. It is estimated that by 1970, 75 percent of the people of the United States will be huddled on 10 percent of the land area, where all the environmental pollutants will also be concentrated.

Fifty years ago, when the horse was the chief source of energy for transportation, there were stables on every block and countless flies. The automobile has done away with this breeding ground for flies and has generated many forms of social advance. The price, however, is chemical pollution of the air with the unknown consequences that it may entail, in addition to the more than 40,000 deaths and the millions of persons maimed every year on the highways. Bumper crops and the countless conveniences of daily life go hand in hand with the yearly introduction of some 500 new chemicals, many of which survive the destructive forces of nature and therefore accumulate in our environment and our bodies. These paradoxes of modern life point to a kind of social problem that had not been anticipated either by the sanitarians or by the laboratory scientists who so earnestly believed they knew how to build the City of Health. The flaws in their plans arise from inconsistencies and conflicts in our value systems. Crudely stated, the question is to decide whether health or economic growth should have priority in determining the type of environment in which we live.

It is important to acknowledge that conflicts exist between commercial profits and prevention of disease, because awareness of this fact leads in many cases to technical solutions that are compatible with both kinds of values. In 1906, for example, three-quarters of the dairy herds of the New York City milkshed contained tuberculous cows; living tubercle bacilli could be recovered from more than 10 percent of the milk samples examined. The public health demand for pasteurized milk was at first opposed with the arguments that heating would destroy the value of milk and that the capital and maintenance costs needed for pasteurization plants would price milk off the market. When the dairy industry was compelled to meet the challenge, however, it developed efficient and inexpensive techniques even while it was fighting the very principle of pasteurization. Similarly, there is reason to believe that if the public were really concerned, it could compel the various industries to eliminate many types of environmental pollutants, and to investigate more thoroughly than is done at present the potential health dangers of technological innovations.*

---

*There is as yet no evidence that the general public is much concerned with the dangers to health posed by modern technologies. On the other hand, several isolated groups of scientists have taken it as their social responsibility to discuss in public the health and social

Making studies of the health aspects of technological innovations a part of development research would naturally increase costs, and might even retard economic growth in some cases, but the overall results would be of benefit to the community in the long run. A kind of crusade similar to that conducted by the nineteenth-century sanitarians is needed to create the social atmosphere in which the study of long-range health consequences is considered an essential part of technological research. In fact, a precedent and a model for this attitude is provided by the large-scale efforts that have been made during the past few decades to determine the biological effects of ionizing radiations long before they were used in industrial practice.

Granted that the threats to health posed by the present-day technologies are often exaggerated, there are many facts that justify, nevertheless, anxiety for the future. One of the alarming aspects of environmental pollution is that despite all the new powers of science, or rather because of them, man is rapidly losing control over his environment. He introduces new forces at such a rapid rate, and on such a wide scale, that the effects are upon him before he has a chance to evaluate their consequences. A few examples will suffice to illustrate how technological developments can have dangerous effects that are recognized only after the biological damage has been done.

The photochemical conversion of hydrocarbons and nitrous oxides into the toxic products responsible for the Los Angeles type of smog was recognized only after the California economy had become dependent on an excessive concentration of industries and automobiles. The absorption of radioisotopes in the human body became known only several years after the beginning of large-scale nuclear testing. The resistance of synthetic detergents to bacterial decomposition became evident only after their universal use as household items had led to their accumulation in water supplies. Many drugs have been used indiscriminately before their potential toxic effects could be recognized. In this regard, the thalidomide tragedy served to highlight a situation of far more general significance; for example, more than 10 years of widespread use of the tetracyclines elapsed before it was noticed that these drugs accumulate in certain tissues and can interfere with bone growth.

In brief, the techniques available for developing new means of action are far more powerful than those available for recognizing the long-range biological effects of new technological innovations. Even when thorough studies are carried out in advance, and elaborate precautions are taken, some new technologies are bound to result in accidents, and in manifestations of chronic toxicity that cannot be foreseen. This is the price of change and of industrial growth. To require a certificate of absolute safety as a condition for the acceptance of a new product, or technological procedure, would be to paralyze progress, indeed would be incompatible with social growth.

---

implications of science. The Greater St. Louis Citizens' Committee for Nuclear Information has been a pioneer in this movement. Its journal *Nuclear Information* has recently been renamed *Scientist and Citizen* to reflect the broadening of its field of interest, especially with regard to environmental pollution. The activities of the various local groups concerned with informing the general public on the implications of science are now coordinated through a national Scientists Institute for Public Information (SIPI).

30 Criteria for an Optimum Human Environment

Hugh H. Iltis
Orie L. Loucks
Peter Andrews
University of Wisconsin, Madison

... To answer "what does man now need?" we must ask "where has he come from?" and "what evidence is there of continuing genetic ties to surroundings similar to those of his past?"

Theodosius Dobzhansky and others have stressed that man is indeed unique, but we cannot overlook the fact that the uniqueness does not separate him from animals. Man is the product of over a hundred million years of evolution among mammals, over 45 million years among primates, and over 15 million years among apes. While his morpholgy has been essentially human for about two million years, the most refined neurological and physical attributes are perhaps but a few hundred thousand years old.

G.G. Simpson notes that those among our primate ancestors with faulty senses, who misjudged distances when jumping for a tree branch or who didn't hear the approach of predators, died. Only those with the agility and alertness that permitted survival in ruthless nature lived to contribute to our present-day gene pool. Such selection pressure continued with little modification until the rise of effective medical treatment and social reforms during the last five generations. In the modern artificial environment it is easy to forget the

Reprinted by permission of Science and Affairs, from *Bulletin of the Atomic Scientists*, January, 1970, (pp. 3-5). Copyright © 1970 by the Educational Foundation for Nuclear Science.

451

implications of selection and adaptation. George Schaller points out in "The Year of the Gorilla" that the gorilla behaves in the zoo as a dangerous and erratic brute. But in his natural environment in the tropical forests of Africa, he is shy, mild, alert and well-coordinated. Neither gorilla nor man can be fully investigated without considering the environments to which he is adapted.

Unique as we may think we are, it seems likely that we are genetically programmed to a natural habitat of clean air and a varied green landscape, like any other mammal. To be relaxed and feel healthy usually means simply allowing our bodies to react as evolution has equipped them to do for 100 million years. Physically and genetically we appear best adapted to a tropical savanna, but as a civilized animal we adapt culturally to cities and towns. For scores of centuries in the temperate zones we have tried to imitate in our houses not only the climate, but the setting of our evolutionary past: warm humid air, green plants, and even animal companions. Today those of us who can afford it may even build a greenhouse or swimming pool next to our living room, buy a place in the country, or at least take our children vacationing at the seashore. The specific physiological reactions to natural beauty and diversity, to the shapes and color of nature, especially to green, to the motions and sounds of other animals, we do not comprehend and are reluctant to include in studies of environmental quality. Yet it is evident that nature in our daily lives must be thought of, not as a luxury to be made available if possible, but as part of our inherent indispensable biological need. It must be included in studies of resource policies for man.

Studies in anthropology, psychology, ethology and environmental design have obvious implications for our attempts to structure a biologically sound human environment. Unfortunately, these results frequently are masked by the specifics of the studies themselves. Except for some pioneer work by Konrad Lorenz followed up at several symposia in Europe, nothing has been done to systematize these studies or extend their implications to modern social and economic planning. For example, Robert Ardrey's popular work, "The Territorial Imperative," explores territoriality as a basic animal attribute, and tries to extend it to man. But his evidence is somewhat limited, and we have no clear conception of what the thwarting of this instinct does to decrease human happiness. The more extensive studies on the nature of aggression explore the genetic roots of animal conflicts, roots that were slowly developed by natural selection over millions of generations. These studies suggest that the sources of drive, achievement, and even of conflict within the family and war among men are likely to be related to primitive animal responses as well as to culture.

Evidence exists that man is genetically adapted to a nomadic hunting life, living in small family groups and having only rare contact with larger groups. As such he led a precarious day-to-day existence, with strong selective removal due to competition with other animals, including other groups of humans. Such was the population structure to which man was ecologically restricted and adapted until as recently as 500 generations ago. Unless there has since been a shift in the major causes of human mortality before the breeding age (and except for resistance to specific diseases there is no such evidence), this period is far too short for any significant changes to have occurred in man's genetic makeup.

Studies of neuro-physiological responses to many characteristics of the environment are also an essential part of investigating genetic dependence on natural as opposed to artificial environment. The rapidly expanding work on electroencephalography in relation to stimuli is providing evidence of a need for frequent change in the environment for at least short periods, or, more specifically, for qualities of diversity in it. There is reason to believe that the electrical rhythms in the brain are highly responsive to changes in surroundings when these take the full attention of the subject. The rise of mechanisms for maintaining constant attention to the surroundings can be seen clearly as a product of long-term selection pressures in a "hunter and hunted" environment. Conversely, a monotonous environment produces wave patterns contributing to fatigue. One wonders what the stimuli of brick and asphalt jungles, or the monotony of corn fields, do to the nervous system. Biotic as well as cultural diversity, from the neurological point of view, may well be fundamental to the general health that figures prominently in the discussions of environmental quality.

The interesting results of Maxwell Weismann in taking chronically hospitalized mental patients camping are also worth noting. Hiking through the woods was the most cherished activity. Some 35 of the 90 patients were returned to their communities within three months after the two-week camping experience. Other studies have shown similar results. Many considerations are involved, but it seems possible that in a person whose cultural load has twisted normal functioning into bizarre reactions, his innate genetic drives still continue to function. Responses attuned to natural adaptations would require no conscious effort. An equally plausible interpretation of Weismann's results is that the direct stimuli of the out-of-doors, of nature alone, produces a response toward the more normal. A definitive investigation of the bases for these responses is needed as guidance to urban planners and public health specialists.

These examples are concerned with the negative effects which many see as resulting from the unnatural qualities of man's present, mostly urban, environment. Aldous Huxley ventures a further opinion as he considers the abnormal adaptation of those hopeless victims of mental illness who appear most normal: "These millions of abnormally normal people, living without fuss in a society to which, if they were fully human beings, they ought not to be adjusted, still cherish 'the illusion of individuality,' but in fact they have been to a great extent deindividualized. Their conformity is developing into something like uniformity. But uniformity and freedom are incompatible. Uniformity and mental health are incompatible as well. . . . Man is not made to be an automaton, and if he becomes one, the basis for mental health is lost."

Clearly, a program of research could tell us more about man's subtle genetic dependence on the environment of his evolution. But of one thing we can be sure: only from study of human behavior in its evolutionary context can we investigate the influence of the environment on the life and fate of modern man. Even now we can see the bases by which to judge quality in our environment, if we are to maintain some semblance of one which is biologically optimum for humans.

We do not plead for a return to nature, but for re-examination of how to use science and technology to create environments for human living. While sociological betterment of the environment can do much to relieve poverty and misery, the argument that an expanding economy and increased material wealth alone would produce a Utopia is now substantially discounted. Instead, a natural concern for the quality of life in our affluent society is evident. But few economists or scientists have tried to identify the major elements of the quality we seek, and no one at all has attempted to use evolutionary principles in the search for quality. Solutions to the problems raised by attempts to evaluate quality will not be found before there is tentative agreement on the bases for judging an optimum human environment. A large body of evidence from studies in evolution, medicine, psychology, sociology, and anthropology suggests clearly that *such an environment will be a compromise between one in which humans have maximum contact with the properties of the environment to which they are innately adapted, and a more urban environment in which learned adaptations and social conventions are relied upon to overcome primitive needs.*

Our option to choose a balance between these two extremes runs out very soon. . . .

Index

Index

About the Editors

Paul M. Insel is Associate Director of the Social Ecology Laboratory at Stanford University; and Research Associate and Clinical Instructor in the Department of Psychiatry at Stanford University School of Medicine. He has published in diverse fields such as behavior genetics, social attitudes, group processes and social ecology, and is the co-editor of *Issues in Social Ecology: Human Milieus.*

Rudolf H. Moos is Director of the Social Ecology Laboratory at Stanford University and Professor in the Department of Psychiatry at Stanford University School of Medicine. He has published widely in psychology, psychiatry, and other behavioral science journals and has pioneered much of the research in social ecology and the human environment. He is the author of *Evaluating Treatment Environments: A Social Ecological Approach* and co-editor of *Issues in Social Ecology: Human Milieus.*